Lecture Notes in Computer Science 7192

Commenced Publication in 1973
Founding and Former Series Editors:
Gerhard Goos, Juris Hartmanis, and Jan van Leeuwen

W0235104

Nina Taft   Fabio Ricciato (Eds.)

Passive and Active Measurement

13th International Conference, PAM 2012
Vienna, Austria, March 12-14, 2012
Proceedings

 Springer

Volume Editors

Nina Taft
Technicolor
735 Emerson Street
Palo Alto, CA 94301, USA
E-mail: nina.taft@technicolor.com

Fabio Ricciato
FTW Forschungszentrum
Telekommunikation Wien GmbH
Donau-City-Straße 1
1220 Wien, Österreich
E-mail: fabio.ricciato@ftw.at

ISSN 0302-9743   e-ISSN 1611-3349
ISBN 978-3-642-28536-3   ISBN 978-3-642-28537-0 (eBook)
DOI 10.1007/978-3-642-28537-0
Springer Heidelberg Dordrecht London New York

Library of Congress Control Number: 2012931773

CR Subject Classification (1998): C.2, H.4, K.6.5, D.2, D.4.6, E.1

LNCS Sublibrary: SL 5 – Computer Communication Networks and Telecommunications

Typesetting: Camera-ready by author, data conversion by Scientific Publishing Services, Chennai, India

Printed on acid-free paper

Springer is part of Springer Science+Business Media (www.springer.com)

Preface

The 2012 edition of the Passive and Active Measurement Conference (PAM) was the thirteenth of a series of successful events. Since 2000, PAM has provided a forum for presenting and discussing innovative and early work in the area of Internet measurement. This event focuses on research as well as practical applications of network measurement and analysis techniques. This year PAM expanded its scope and encouraged submissions in a broad set of topics that reflect the widening uses of network measurement and analysis methods. The aim was to facilitate understanding of the expanding role that measurement techniques play as they become building blocks for a variety of networking environments, application profiling, and for cross-layer analysis. The conference's goal is to provide a forum for current work in its early stages. This year's conference was held at Tech Gate in Vienna, Austria, co-located with the fourth edition of the Traffic Monitoring and Analysis Workshop (TMA) organized by the TMA Cost Action IC0703.

PAM 2012 attracted 83 submissions. Each paper was carefully reviewed by at least three members of the Technical Program Committee. The reviewing process led to the acceptance of 25 papers. The papers and demos were arranged in eight sessions covering the following areas: traffic evolution and analysis, large-scale monitoring, evaluation methodology, malicious behavior, new measurement initiatives, reassessing tools and methods, perspectives on Internet structure and services, and application protocols.

We would like to thank all members of the Technical Program Committee for their timely and thorough reviews. Special thanks to Paul Barford for handling all papers with PC-Chair conflict. We would also like to thank Antonio Pescapè, Christina Philippi and Philipp Svoboda for their efforts in the organization of the event.

Last but not least, we are extremely grateful to the sponsors whose financial and organizational support allowed us to keep registration costs low.

March 2012

Fabio Ricciato
Nina Taft

Organization

Organizing Committee

General Chair

Fabio Ricciato   University of Salento, Italy and FTW, Austria

Program Chair

Nina Taft   Technicolor Research Palo Alto, USA

Publicity Chair

Antonio Pescapè   University of Naples, Federico II, Italy

Local Arrangements Chairs

Christina Philippi   FTW, Austria
Philipp Svodoba   Technical University of Vienna, Austria

Program Committee

Virgilio Almedia   Universidade Federal de Minas Gerais, Brazil
Paul Barford   University of Wisconsin Madison, USA
Nevil Brownlee   University of Auckland, New Zealand
Matthew Caesar   University of Illinois Urbana-Champaign, USA
Martin Casado   Nicira, USA
Rocky K.C. Chang   Hong Kong Polytechnic University
David Choffnes   University of Washington, USA
Christophe Diot   Technicolor, France
Richard Gass   Telefonica, Spain
Saikat Guha   Microsoft Research India
John Heidemann   USC/Information Sciences Institute, USA
Thomas Karagiannis   Microsoft Research Cambridge, UK
Kirill Levchenko   University of California San Diego, USA
Olaf Maennel   Loughborough University, UK
Anirban Mahanti   NICTA, Australia
Gregor Maier   ISCI, USA
Priya Mahadevan   PARC, USA

Richard Mortier   University of Nottingham, UK
Hung Nguyen   University of Adelaide, Australia
Saverio Niccolini   NEC Laboratories Europe
Jeff Pang   AT&T Research, USA
Fabian Schneider   Université Pierre et Marie Curie, LIP6, France
Vyas Sekar   Intel Labs, USA
Subhabrata Sen   AT&T Research, USA
Yuval Shavitt   Tel Aviv University, Israel
Kurt Tutschku   University of Vienna, Austria
Udi Weinsberg   Technicolor Research Palo Alto, USA
Minlan Yu   UC Berkeley / USC, USA

Steering Committee

Nevil Brownlee   University of Auckland, New Zealand
Ian Graham   Endace, New Zealand
Arvind Krishnamurthy   University of Washington, USA
Bernhard Plattner   ETH Zurich, Switzerland
Fabio Ricciato   University of Salento, Italy and FTW, Austria
George Riley   Georgia Institute of Technology, USA
Neil Spring   University of Maryland, USA
Nina Taft   Technicolor, USA

Sponsoring Institutions

Kapsch CarrierCom
Technicolor
FTW

Table of Contents

Malicious Behavior

New Measurement Initiatives

Reassessing Tools and Methods

Perspectives on Internet Structure and Services

Application Protocols

Unmasking the Growing UDP Traffic
in a Campus Network

Changhyun Lee, DK Lee, and Sue Moon

Department of Computer Science, KAIST, South Korea

Abstract. Transmission control protocol (TCP) has been the dominating protocol for Internet traffic for the past decades. Most network research based on traffic
analysis (e.g., router buffer sizing and traffic classification) has been conducted
assuming the dominance of TCP over other protocols. However, a few recent
traffic statistics are showing a sign of significant UDP traffic growth at various
points of Internet links [21]. In this paper we show that the UDP traffic has grown
significantly in recent years on our campus network; we have observed a 46-
fold increase in volume (from 0.47% to 22.0% of total bytes) in the past four
years. The trace collected in 2011 shows that the grown volume is not from a
small number of UDP hosts nor port numbers. In addition, the recent UDP flows
are not sent at constant bit rate (CBR) for most cases, and the aggregated traffic
shows burstiness close to TCP traffic.

1 Introduction

Transmission control protocol (TCP) has been the main protocol of Internet traffic for
the past decades; the widely accepted notion is that TCP accounts for more than 90%
of the total traffic. User datagram protocol (UDP), on the other hand, has consumed
only a small share of Internet traffic as it has been mainly used for limited purpose
such as online gaming and multimedia streaming. Hence network engineering research
has been based on the dominance of TCP traffic [5–7]. Traffic classification has also
concentrated on identifying TCP applications, and only a few popular UDP applications
such as PPLive and SopCast have been studied [8, 9]. In addition, network experiments
with synthetic traffic have mostly focused on generating realistic TCP traffic while they
often model UDP traffic as simple packet bunches sent at constant bit rate [19].

Recently, a few traffic statistics are showing the sign of UDP traffic growth at various
points of Internet links [21]. The reported trend has not been studied thoroughly yet, and
the cause and the impact of growing UDP traffic to the Internet are to be discovered. Although most traffic measurement studies have been about TCP, some previous research
papers have looked at the characteristics of UDP traffic in terms of size, arrival, port
usage of flows [14, 16, 18, 20]. However, the traffic traces used in those papers do not
reflect the most recent trend as they are all collected before 2009 when only a small
portion of UDP traffic around 5% or even less is reported.

In this work we report on the excessive growth in UDP traffic by continuous monitoring of the same network link for four years. We show the contribution of UDP to the
overall traffic is no longer negligible according to the measurements from our campus
network; we have witnessed a 46-fold increase in volume (from 0.47% to 22.0% of total

N. Taft and F. Ricciato (Eds.): PAM 2012, LNCS 7192, pp. 1–10, 2012.

bytes) for the past four years. With the UDP trace collected in 2011, we characterize the UDP volume growth in terms of flow size, communication pattern, and sending rate. Here we refer to the total number of bytes as volume. Our results show that the growth in volume is mainly from the increase in the flow size rather than in the number of flows, and most UDP flows are not sent at constant bit rate (CBR). We have also found that the growth is not attributed to a small number of UDP servers nor port numbers. UDP is used by peer-to-peer file transfers today. Finally, we show the recent UDP traffic has comparable burstiness to that of TCP traffic.

The rest of this paper is organized as follows. Section 2 provides the data sets used in this work and evidences of recent growth in UDP traffic in terms of absolute volume, flow size, and packet size. In Section 3, we observe the sign of peer-to-peer applications on UDP by analyzing port usage and communication patterns between hosts. We then study the rate variation of UDP flows and burstiness of UDP traffic in Section 4, Last, Section 5 concludes with the implications and lessons from our findings.

2   Growth Trend of UDP Traffic

2.1   Data Sets

We have collected the packet-level traces from 2008 to 2011 and captured the growth trend of UDP traffic on our campus network link. KAIST has a population of about 10,000, faculty, staff, and students all included and it owns 2 /16 prefixes and 80 /24 prefixes. A nearby college of about 1,100 got merged with KAIST in 2009 and KAIST acquired 1 of the 2 /16 prefixes and another 1 Gbps link to the outside. The campus network was reorganized in September 2009 that all traffic from the dormitories was routed via the new link and the rest of the configuration has remained almost the same. From 2008 to 2011, the overall population of KAIST grew from 7,000 to 10,000, mostly from the merger and the increase in the incoming student body size. Even with the increase in the overall population and network capacity, KAIST has not changed the traffic filtering policy: ICMP packets are dropped at the gateway but no traffic suspected to be peer-to-peer downloads.

We use GPS-synchronized servers with DAG 4.3GE cards [1] and collect header-only traces from the 1 Gbps link that connects classrooms, labs, and offices to a commercial ISP; we were not able to collect payload information due to the privacy concern in our campus.

Table 1 shows the summary of collected traces used in this paper. The traces from 2008 to 2011 are all collected on weekdays and captured at the same time of the day to

Table 1. Collected packet traces from 2008 to 2011

Trace name	Time of collection	Duration	Data rate
k-2008	2008/03/19 Wed 14:00	60min	937.2Mbps
k-2009	2009/04/27 Mon 14:00	60min	927.8Mbps
k-2010	2010/08/31 Tue 14:00	60min	868.5Mbps
k-2011	2011/01/07 Fri 14:00	60min	855.8Mbps

minimize errors from the diurnal effect in Internet usage. Traces *k-2008* and *k-2009* are before the merger and network reconfiguration and include traffic from the dormitories. The slight decrease in the overall data rates in 2010 and 2011 is attributed to the extra network capacity, but the link is still quite heavily utilized. In the spring of 2011 KAIST added another 1 Gbps link to the Internet.

In the rest of this paper we use the incoming traffic from the Internet core to KAIST to represent end-users' Internet usage.

2.2   Growth in UDP Traffic Volume

In Figure 1(a), we have found that UDP traffic has increased up to 22% over the past four years; the minimum among the traces is 0.47% in 2008. Surprisingly, the absolute volume of UDP traffic has grown significantly from 3.90 Mbps to 179.39 Mbps (46-fold growth in four years) in Figure 1(b). We see no sign of letting up in the UDP traffic growth. The growth trend is in compliance with a previous report [21], and we also find the similar trend from a trans-Pacific link of Japanese backbone networks [2] and CAIDA's two monitors in Chicago [4]. The UDP data rate of the Japanese traces from 2006 to 2011 has been growing, and the largest portion observed is around 30%. CAIDA's Chicago monitors report $15 \sim 18\%$ in the average UDP data rate in August of 2011, which is about 5% higher than the recent two year's average on the same links. Although we show a single one-hour trace in 2011 in this paper for representation, the other traces collected in 2011 have similar shares of UDP around 20%, which is much larger than the share in 2008.

The number of UDP flows within an hour has also grown from 2.6 million in 2008 to 5.2 million in 2011, but not as much as in volume; we identify a UDP flow as a set of packets that have the same source and destination IP addresses and port numbers. The increase in the number of flows from 2008 to 2011 is only 2-fold. The more critical cause of the recent UDP traffic growth is the change in the size of each flow than in the total number of flows; the average flow size is 0.71 KB in 2008 and 16.32 KB in 2011. Previous work on TCP traffic trend has shown that the TCP flow size distribution has remained similar from 2001 to 2009 [17], and our result on UDP here is in contrast to their finding. We give more details on the flow size evolution of recent UDP traffic in the next section.

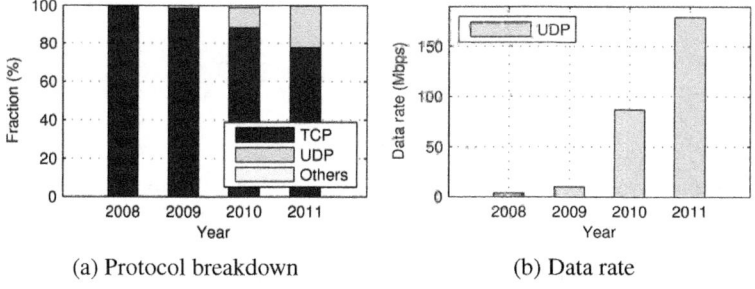

(a) Protocol breakdown   (b) Data rate

Fig. 1. UDP traffic growth from 2008 to 2011

2.3   Growth in UDP Flow Size

The common perception about UDP flows is that they are small and short, and it is supported by previous studies on the flow size of TCP and UDP [16,21,22]. We seek to verify whether it still holds for the recent UDP traffic. Figure 2 shows the cumulative volume by the flow size for the UDP traffic in trace *k-2011*. The figure also includes the distribution for UDP traffic in trace *k-2008* and TCP traffic in *k-2011* for comparison. We find that, in *k-2011*, flows larger than 100 KB take up 97.5% of the total volume. The same analysis on TCP traffic has shown 91.2%. Large flows dominate in UDP traffic as much as in TCP traffic or even more in some traces.

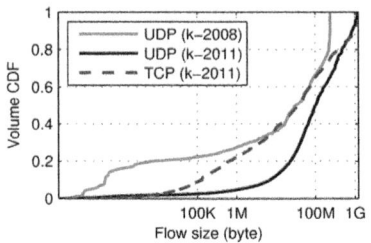

Fig. 2. Cumulative volume vs. flow size

The packet size of UDP traffic has also grown dramatically from 2008 to 2011. Figure 3 shows the cumulative distribution of packet size over four years. The portion of UDP packets larger than 1,400 bytes is 43.2% in *k-2011*, while only 0.34% in *k-2008*. We have found an interesting trend that the packet size distribution of UDP from 2008 to 2011 has become bimodal like that of TCP; in *k-2011*, packets either smaller than 100 bytes or larger than 1,400 bytes contribute 89.2% of the total packets for UDP and 91.5% for TCP.

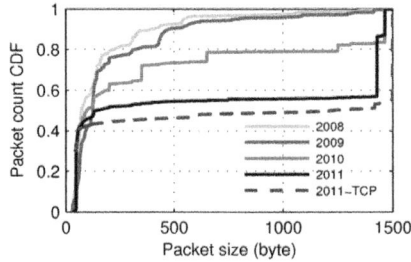

Fig. 3. Evolution in UDP packet size from 2008 to 2011 (top to bottom)

Last we look at the duration of UDP flows. A flow's duration is calculated as the time between the first and the last packet within a flow. We find that 76.4% of flows have zero duration because they consist of only one packet. The lifetime of the flows with more than two packets spans up to one hour, an upper limit imposed by our data collection. In summary, there are a number of very short UDP flows of one packet, but a small number of large flows take up most of the volume.

3   UDP for P2P

In this section we take a close look at the UDP traffic from the most recent trace *k-2011*. We analyze port number usage and communication patterns between hosts, and investigate the types of traffic contributing to the recent growth in UDP. From the result, we provide evidences that UDP is now used for peer-to-peer applications.

3.1   Port Usage in UDP Traffic

Port number usage is one of the key measures to understand the type of traffic and often used for identifying applications such as web surfing, online gaming, and peer-to-peer transfer with fixed port numbers [11, 13, 14, 18, 21]. Figure 4 plots the cumulative UDP traffic volume against the source and destination ports in *k-2011*. First, the source port numbers used by UDP flows are distributed all over the port allocation range. The largest volume on a single port number is 2.15% at the port 47,391. The volume 2.15% is not so high compared to TCP traffic as it carries much volume on port 80 (HTTP), and traces from various network links report up to 62.9% of the total volume from HTTP [10, 13, 15]. We define a popular port as the port having more than 0.0015% out of the total volume; the threshold 0.0015% is set to the expected volume per port if traffic is distributed evenly over the port numbers. For the source port case, there are 2, 496 popular ports, and they account for 95.97% of the total traffic volume. Other than the well-known port 53 is used by queries to the DNS servers in KAIST, we are not able to map the popular port numbers to known applications only with the packet headers.

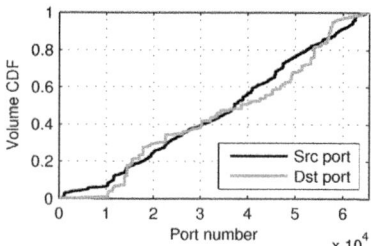

Fig. 4. Cumulative volume by the port number in *k-2011*

We apply the same analysis on destination ports. There are 594 popular ports and they are responsible for 99.23% of total traffic. The port 53,952 carries the largest per-flow volume of 5.42%. Compared to the source port case, only a quarter of destination ports carry more traffic. Out of 594 ports 546 has 99% of volume coming from single nodes. Each of these nodes has a large number of flows up to thousands with the same destination port number but with different source port numbers. That is, a single destination port use used for multiple downloads of heavy volume on a single node. We investigate further the traffic distribution by the host in the next section.

3.2   Communication Patterns between Hosts

Our next interest is the communication pattern between hosts of UDP flows. Analyzing the communication patterns, we try to determine if the recent UDP traffic comes from peer-to-peer type (many-to-many) transfers or server-to-client type (one-to-many) transfers. We take a similar methodology used in Karagiannis *et al.*'s work [12]. From the flow records, we first count the number of unique campus IP addresses per off-campus IP address. In the rest of this section we count only those flows larger more than 100 KB in the analysis. The threshold of 100 KB is arbitrary, but insensitive enough to exclude DNS and scanning traffic and to capture bulk transfers. As shown in Figure 5(a), most off-campus hosts (82.5% of the total) have only one corresponding host on campus, and the maximum number of corresponding hosts on campus is six. It means that no popular UDP source host exists outside for hosts on campus, and the growth in UDP traffic is not attributed to a single or several numbers of UDP off-campus servers. On the other hand, the same analysis on TCP traffic shows that the most popular server has sent traffic to 203 on-campus IPs within an hour in the same trace.

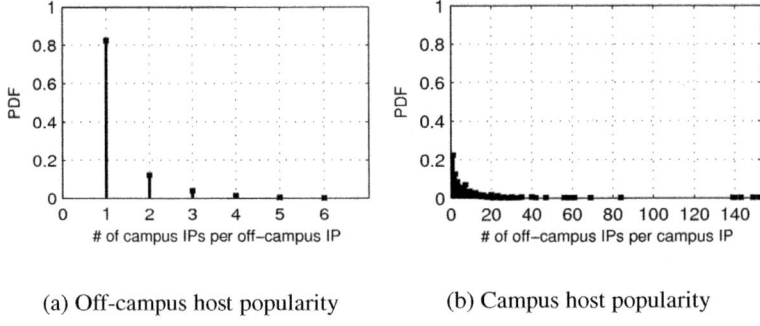

(a) Off-campus host popularity   (b) Campus host popularity

Fig. 5. Communication pattern of UDP flows

   Figure 5(b) shows the number of unique off-campus IP addresses per campus IP address in the flow records, and the number goes up to more than hundred. Remember that all flows are larger than 100 KB here. That is, hosts on campus download UDP traffic from a large number of hosts outside. From the communications patterns by the host and the port in Section 3.1 we conclude that most UDP traffic is from peer-to-peer transfers than server-to-client transfers.

4   Burstiness of UDP Traffic

UDP traffic has increased to take up almost 20% of the total link capacity on our very congested link. If it is constant bit rate, not adaptive or responding to the network congestion, it would be equal to decreasing the available bandwidth and have an unfair share of bandwidth over TCP flows. When UDP is relatively a negligible portion of the overall traffic, this unfair advantage is not very important. Now it is an issue.

   We use the standard deviation in flow throughput to first see if UDP flows are CBR or not. We count the number of bytes delivered in a time unit of one second and calculate its standard deviation per flow. We compute the same for TCP flows to compare with. Figure 6 shows the cumulative distributions of the standard deviation. As in the previous section all flows accounted for in this section are larger than 100 KB. In *k-2008* most UDP flows have zero standard deviation. However, as time progresses to 2011, UDP traffic shows an increasing tendency of variability in throughput. By *k-2011* about top 18% of both UDP and TCP flows have the standard deviation greater than 1.6 Mbps. The portion of UDP flows with almost zero variability drops to less than 30%.

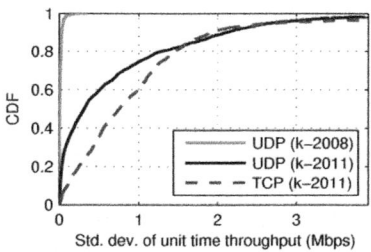

Fig. 6. Standard deviation of unit time throughput

Here we have looked at the throughput variability only in the time unit of a second and on a per-flow basis. One second is rather a long time for a router queue to buffer packets in today's Internet where most backbone links are 1 Gbps or higher: that is, too coarse a time scale. How variable or bursty is the aggregate UDP traffic in finer time scales? In Figure 7 we examine the burstiness of aggregate UDP traffic in time units of 0.01 s, 0.1 s and 1 s. At the time scale of 0.01 s the traffic looks more bursty than in the other two scales, but the other two look similar.

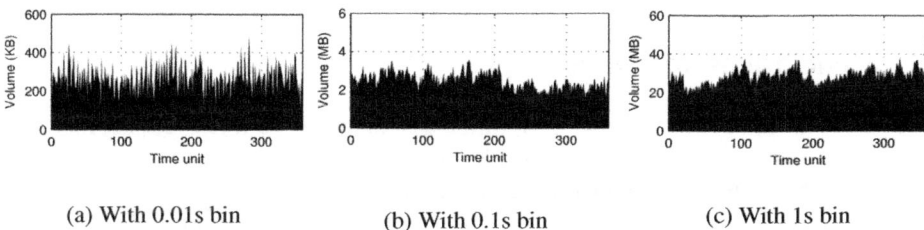

(a) With 0.01s bin   (b) With 0.1s bin   (c) With 1s bin

Fig. 7. Burstiness in aggregate UDP traffic from *k-2011*

Burstiness in traffic has a great impact on router queue and end-host buffer size provisioning. Self-similarity in Internet traffic has long been reported and its causes have been studied [23] A common technique to analyze the scaling behavior in traffic is the wavelet analysis and its energy plot [24]. The energy plot in Figure 8 shows the variance of the wavelet coefficients that reflects the variance of traffic counting process X_j at a time scale T_j. If the traffic is self-similar, the plot should be a straight line, of which slope is the scaling exponent. If the traffic is Poisson, the plot should be a horizontal line.

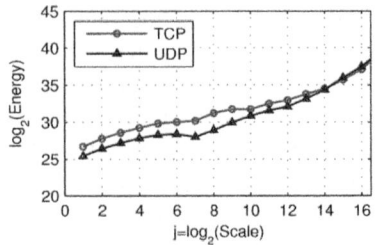

Fig. 8. Wavelet energy plot for TCP and UDP traffic from *k-2011*

TCP traffic from *k-2011* in Figure 8 shows almost a straight line, signifying that it is close to self-similar. UDP traffic on the other hand has a slight tip near $j = 7$ or the time scale of 256 ms, where $j = 1$ is in 2 ms. The scaling exponent (or the Hurst parameter) for TCP is 0.865 and for UDP 0.831. Multi-scaling behaviors on high-speed links and similar dips in the time scale of hundreds of milliseconds have been reported [25]. We have no basis to imply that two dips have a common cause and leave it for future work.

Burstiness in UDP traffic does not instantly translate to use of congestion control by the applications. MPEG-coded video can by itself be bursty. However, the communication patterns of UDP hosts imply peer-to-peer transfers and the latest version of μtorrent, a popular client of BitTorrent, has announced the use of a proprietary congest control mechanism [3]. Our experiment of a μtp transfer on a controlled node shows that most data packets has a signature size of 1,466 bytes, and we have identified 26.8% of total UDP traffic volume in *k-2011* to have the packet size. This is an upper bound as we may have false positives in our classification. The large volume of UDP flows with a proprietary congestion control contributes to the new kind of burstiness in today's Internet traffic.

5   Conclusions and Discussion

In this work we have shown that UDP traffic has increased 46-fold over past four years on our campus network. Using packet header traces, we give a first characterization report on the growth. From the trace collected in 2011, we have found that large flows have become dominant in UDP just as in TCP. They are mostly from P2P applications, and the aggregate UDP traffic exhibits burstiness similar to TCP.

Our findings provide several guidelines to classifying UDP traffic. First, port-number based classification can hardly work on recent UDP traffic. Port numbers seem to be randomly assigned to flows. This is an opposite result to the previous work on TCP traffic [13]. However, a destination port, once assigned, is used for multiple downloads from different hosts and ports, just as in TCP-based peer-to-peer applications. Thus the communication patterns can be a clue as in [11, 12]. In addition, we have found that certain UDP packet sizes, e.g., 1,466 bytes in *k-2011*, is observed more frequently than others. Packet sizes of UDP packets can be a good signature in identifying UDP applications. This is hardly the case for TCP since applications all work under TCP's policy.

Our observation on UDP traffic growth has implications to network simulation and experiments. In previous network experiments with synthetic traffic, UDP flows have been generated in a simple manner of constant bit rate and often ignored for their minor volume. While this has been valid for traditional UDP traffic, our measurements show that the packet sending behavior is much more bursty than simple CBR. Our measurement analysis underlines the rising need to account for "lower-than best effort" traffic in realistic network simulation.

Acknowledgements. This research was supported by the KCC (Korea Communications Commission), Korea, under the R&D program supervised by the KCA (Korea Communications Agency) (KCA-2011-08913-05002).

References

1. Endace, http://www.endace.com
2. Samplepoint-F Traces from MAWI Working Group Traffic archive (2006-2011), http://mawi.wide.ad.jp/mawi
3. What is μTorrent's μtp?, http://www.utorrent.com/help/documentation/utp
4. CAIDA's Passive Network Monitor Statistics, http://www.caida.org/data/realtime/passive/
5. Appenzeller, G., Keslassy, I., McKeown, N.: Sizing Router Buffers. In: Proc. ACM SIG-COMM (2004)
6. Beheshti, N., Ganjali, Y., Ghobadi, M., McKeown, N., Salmon, G.: Experimental Study of Router Buffer Sizing. In: Proc. ACM SIGCOMM IMC (2008)
7. Dhamdhere, A., Jiang, H., Dovrolis, C.: Buffer Sizing for Congested Internet Links. In: Proc. IEEE INFOCOM (2005)
8. Finamore, A., Mellia, M., Meo, M., Rossi, D.: KISS: Stochastic Packet Inspection Classifier for UDP Traffic. IEEE/ACM Trans. Netw. 18, 1505–1515 (2010)
9. Fu, T.Z.J., Hu, Y., Shi, X., Chiu, D.M., Lui, J.C.S.: PBS: Periodic Behavioral Spectrum of P2P Applications. In: Moon, S.B., Teixeira, R., Uhlig, S. (eds.) PAM 2009. LNCS, vol. 5448, pp. 155–164. Springer, Heidelberg (2009)
10. Henderson, T., Kotz, D., Abyzov, I.: The Changing Usage of a Mature Campus-wide Wireless Network. In: Proc. ACM Mobicom (2004)
11. Karagiannis, T., Broido, A., Faloutsos, M., Claffy, K.: Transport Layer Identification of P2P Traffic. In: Proc. ACM SIGCOMM IMC (2004)
12. Karagiannis, T., Papagiannaki, K., Faloutsos, M.: BLINC: Multilevel Traffic Classification in thee Dark. In: Proc. ACM SIGCOMM (2005)
13. Kim, H., Claffy, K., Fomenkov, M., Barman, D., Faloutsos, M., Lee, K.: Internet Traffic Classification Demystified: Myths, Caveats, and the Best Practices. In: Proc. ACM CoNEXT (2008)
14. Lee, D., Carpenter, B., Brownlee, N.: Observations of UDP to TCP Ratio and Port Numbers. In: Proc. IEEE ICIMP (2010)
15. Maier, G., Feldmann, A., Paxson, V., Allman, M.: On Dominant Characteristics of Residential Broadband Internet Traffic. In: Proc. ACM SIGCOMM IMC (2009)
16. Olivier, P., Benameur, N.: Flow Level IP Traffic Characterization. In: Proc. ITC (2001)
17. Qian, F., Gerber, A., Mao, Z., Sen, S., Spatscheck, O., Willinger, W.: TCP Revisited: A Fresh Look at TCP in the Wild. In: Proc. ACM SIGCOMM IMC (2009)

18. Rodrigues, L., Guardieiro, P.: A Spatial and Temporal Analysis of Internet Aggregate Traffic at the Flow Level. In: Proc. IEEE GLOBECOM (2004)
19. Sommers, J., Barford, P., Greenberg, A., Willinger, W.: An SLA Perspective on the Router Buffer Sizing Problem. ACM SIGMETRICS Perform. Eval. Rev. 35, 40–51 (2008)
20. Thopmson, K., Miller, G., Wilder, R.: Wide-area Internet Traffic Patterns and Characteristics. IEEE Network 11, 10–23 (1997)
21. Zhang, M., Dusi, M., John, W., Chen, C.: Analysis of UDP Traffic Usage on Internet Backbone Links. In: Proc. IEEE/IPSJ SAINT (2009)
22. Kim, M., Won, Y., Hong, J.: Characteristic Analysis of Internet Traffic from the Perspective of Flows. Elsevier Computer Communications 29, 1639–1652 (2005)
23. Park, K., Willinger, W.: Self-Similar Network Traffic and Performance Evaluation. John Wiley & Sons, Inc., New York (2002)
24. Abry, P., Veitch, D.: Wavelet Analysis of Long-Range-Dependent Traffic. IEEE Trans. on Information Theory 44, 2–15 (1998)
25. Zhang, Z., Ribeiro, V., Moon, S., Diot, C.: Small-Time Scaling Behaviors of Internet Backbone Traffic: An Empirical Study. In: Proc. IEEE INFOCOM (2003)

Investigating IPv6 Traffic
What Happened at the World IPv6 Day?

Nadi Sarrar[1], Gregor Maier[2], Bernhard Ager[1], Robin Sommer[2,3], and Steve Uhlig[4]

[1] TU Berlin / Telekom Innovation Laboratories, Berlin, Germany
[2] International Computer Science Institute, Berkeley, CA, USA
[3] Lawrence Berkeley National Laboratory, Berkeley, CA, USA
[4] Queen Mary, University of London, London, UK

Abstract. While the IETF standardized IPv6 more than fifteen years ago, IPv4 is still the prevalent Internet protocol today. On June 8th, 2011, several large content and service providers coordinated a large-scale IPv6 test-run, by enabling support for IPv6 simultaneously: the World IPv6 Day. In this paper, we compare IPv6 activity before, during, and after the event. We examine traffic traces recorded at a large European Internet Exchange Point (IXP) and on the campus of a major US university; analyzing volume, application mix, and the use of tunneling protocols for transporting IPv6 packets.

For the exchange point we find that native IPv6 traffic almost doubled during the World IPv6 Day while changes in tunneled traffic were limited. At the university, IPv6 traffic increased from 3–6 GB/day to over 130 GB/day during the World IPv6 Day, accompanied by a significant shift in the application and HTTP destination mix. Our results also show that a significant number of participants at the World IPv6 Day kept their IPv6 support online even after the test period ended, suggesting that they did not encounter any significant problems.

1 Introduction

The fourth incarnation of the Internet Protocol (IPv4) successfully supported the phenomenal growth of the Internet since its introduction in 1981. Yet, due to this unexpected success, the pressure from the IPv4 address space exhaustion is being felt more and more. This led to the standardization of IPv6 more than 15 years ago, which provides a significantly larger address space. Since then, the transition from IPv4 to IPv6 is happening at a lethargic pace. One of the reasons for the hesitant adoption of IPv6 by end-users is the limited amount of content available through IPv6. A reason for network operators is the fear of breaking critical services. Indeed, the current best practices for deploying IPv6, such as white-listing of well-known network regions, are very conservative. Furthermore, such approaches prevent us from gaining insights into the challenges involved with a global transition to IPv6.

To fill the gap, several operators coordinated a joint experiment on June 8th, 2011: the World IPv6 Day. For the duration of that day, the participants agreed to enable IPv6 support in parts of their networks. Participants included Comcast, Google, Facebook, Microsoft, and many others. Their observations have been reported at the IETF 81 meeting. They found that besides a significant and sustained increase of IPv6 traffic on and

N. Taft and F. Ricciato (Eds.): PAM 2012, LNCS 7192, pp. 11–20, 2012.
© Springer-Verlag Berlin Heidelberg 2012

Table 1. Overview of data sets. All data sets are from 2011.

Name	Type	Location	Start date	Duration	Name	Type	Location	Start date	Duration
JUN1	Packet	Campus	Thu, Jun 2	9 d	IXP1	sFlow	IXP	Wed, Jun 1	22 d
JUN2	Packet	Campus	Fri, Jun 17	4 d	IXP2	sFlow	IXP	Mon, Aug 8	7 d
JUN3	Packet	Campus	Fri, Jun 24	7 d					

after the World IPv6 Day, the awareness of IPv6 increased dramatically, and the experience obtained through real IPv6 deployments and measurements were invaluable. The presented results were focused mainly on operational questions, e. g., bandwidth, number of clients, and "IPv6 brokenness".

In this paper, we complement these observations by investigating IPv6 traffic characteristics from two vantage points in the Internet. We examine the use of tunneled IPv6, the presence of applications in IPv6 traffic, and highlight the major IPv6 traffic contributors in the Internet. Our study is based on two traces of production Internet traffic. The first was collected at a large European Internet Exchange Point (IXP) interconnecting hundreds of networks. The second has been gathered at a major US university, a fundamentally different vantage point compared to the IXP, both in scale and level of traffic aggregation. Combined, the two data sets enable us to take a broad look at the impact of the World IPv6 Day.

To the best of our knowledge, this paper is the first systematic study of what has happened around the World IPv6 Day. Our contributions include characterizations of:

Traffic volume: In both traces, we observe a steep and sustained increase of IPv6 traffic. Native IPv6 traffic doubled at the IXP and increased more than 20-fold at the campus.

Tunneling mechanisms: Encapsulated packets contribute a large fraction of IPv6 traffic at the IXP. Teredo tunnels are widespread but mostly idle.

Application mix: Since the World IPv6 Day, the application mix of native and 6in4 IPv6 traffic changed fundamentally and now exhibits similarities to IPv4.

Traffic contributors: Since the World IPv6 Day, YouTube is the main contributor at the campus vantage point. A large content provider is the main contributor at the IXP.

The remainder of this paper is organized as follows. In Section 2, we provide details about our two data sets. We investigate overall IPv6 traffic volume and tunnel encapsulations in Section 3 and the application mix in Section 4. In Section 5 we identify the content providers that contribute most traffic before, during, and after the World IPv6 Day. We present related work in Section 6 and summarize our results in Section 7.

2   Data Sets

We base our analysis on network traffic gathered at the Internet uplink of a major US university and at a large European Internet Exchange Point (IXP). Table 1 gives an overview of our data sets.

In addition to analyzing native IPv6 traffic, we also investigate commonly used tunnel encapsulation methods to transfer IPv6 datagrams over IPv4. In particular, we analyze *Teredo* (RFC 4380), *6in4* (RFC 4212), and *AYIYA*[1] encapsulations. We note that 6in4 encapsulation also covers *6to4* (RFC 3068) and *6rd* (RFC 5969). Some tunneled traffic can be detected by filtering on a specific UDP port; Teredo uses UDP port 3544, and AYIYA commonly runs on port 5072. In contrast, 6in4 has its own IP protocol number, 41, which can be used for filtering. In all of our analyses, we further verified that the tunnel payload actually contains an IPv6 packet to mitigate against false positives.

Internet Exchange Point: The IXP data sets consist of anonymized sampled sFlow records from the whole traffic exchanged at the IXP. More than 400 networks currently exchange traffic at this IXP. sFlow does not employ flow record aggregation like Net-Flow. Instead, sFlow samples one out of n packets and exports the initial portion of it as a sFlow record. The sFlow probes at the IXP use a sampling ratio of $1:2^{14}$. We use a customized version of `sflowtool` [14] to extract relevant portions from the sFlow data. As a sFlow record corresponds to the initial portion of a packet, it is possible to examine the protocol and tunneling stack.

US university: We base our analysis of IPv6 traffic at the US university campus on packet level traces collected at the university's central uplink to the Internet. We limited the trace collection to native IPv6 traffic, 6in4 encapsulated traffic and IPv4 traffic on Teredo's well-known UDP port. We then analyze these traces using a customized version of the Bro IDS [13] capable of analyzing tunneled IPv6 traffic.

3   Traffic Volume and Tunneling

We start by investigating the overall volume of IPv6 traffic before, during, and post the World IPv6 Day. This enables us to calibrate our expectations for subsequent analyses when we dig deeper into used protocols, applications, and traffic contributors.

In Figure 1 and Figure 2 we plot the total bandwidth of IPv6 traffic (native and tunneled) over time at the IXP and the US university, respectively. The World IPv6 Day is highlighted by a gray bar. We observe that before the official start of the World IPv6 Day (at midnight UTC), IPv6 traffic begins to ramp up as content providers enable IPv6 on their systems. During the World IPv6 Day, we observe a 30 % increase of IPv6 traffic at the IXP and an increase from 3–6 GB/day to over 130 GB at the university. We also find that the IPv6 traffic volume remains high after the World IPv6 Day officially ended, indicating that a significant number of participants kept their IPv6 support enabled, and suggesting that they did not encounter significant problems. This is consistent with other reports [1, 9, 15] that observed similar behavior during and after the World IPv6 Day.

Analyzing IPv6 traffic in 1 hour bins shows a clear time-of-day pattern (plot not shown). During and after the World IPv6 Day, the traffic volume during the busy-hour has increased significantly while the traffic dips during off-hours has remained unchanged, indicating that only peak usage has changed but not baseline activity.

We next turn to the question of how much IPv6 traffic is tunneled versus native IPv6 traffic. At the university campus we find hardly any tunneled traffic. At the IXP tunneled traffic is more common. In Figure 3, we plot the IPv6 volume by tunnel encapsulation type for the IXP data sets. During and after the World IPv6 Day, we observe a significant

---
[1] http://www.sixxs.net/tools/ayiya/

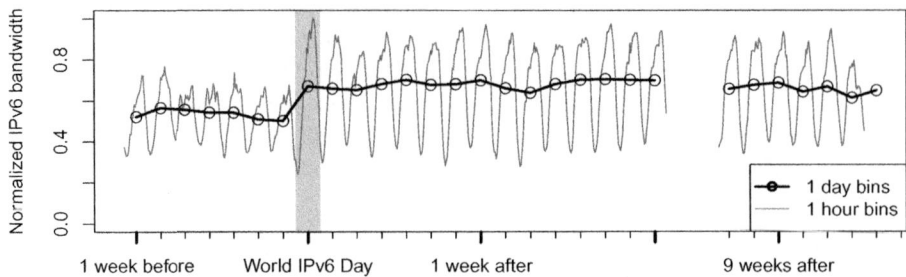

Fig. 1. Total IPv6 traffic volume (IXP). The tick marks are at noon UTC.

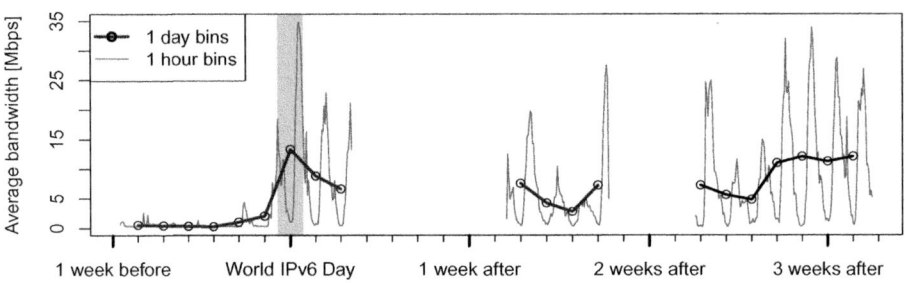

Fig. 2. Total IPv6 traffic volume (campus). The tick marks are at noon UTC.

increase in native IPv6 traffic, while tunneled traffic remains essentially unchanged. The fraction of tunneled traffic decreases accordingly from 69 % to 58 % on average.

We next compare the packet size distributions of IPv4 and IPv6 traffic during the World IPv6 Day and plot the results in Figure 4. We remove the tunnel headers and plot the size of the innermost IPv4 or IPv6 packet. IPv4 shows the usual distribution with peaks at small packet sizes (32 %) and large packet sizes $\geq 1,492$ bytes (25 %). The packet size distribution for IPv6 at the US university resembles the one of IPv4. However, since an IPv6 header is larger than an IPv4 header without options, we find that the "small" packets for IPv6 are slightly larger. We also observe an additional mode at 1,280 bytes for IPv6. This represents the minimum MTU for IPv6 (RFC 2460), and the recommended MTU for tunneling mechanisms in order to mitigate problems with fragmentation (RFC 4380, RFC 4212).

We observe a different packet size distribution for IPv6 at the IXP that shows a significantly larger fraction of small packets. More than 82 % of all IPv6 packets are at most 72 bytes in size. Moreover, we notice two modes in the distribution of larger packets, one at the full MTU, and another one at 1,280 bytes. The latter is more pronounced than in the campus data set.

To understand what causes this disparity, we take a closer look at the IPv6 packet size distribution at the IXP by breaking it down according to the type of packet encapsulation. Figure 5 compares the IPv6 packet size distributions for native, 6in4, Teredo, and AYIYA packets. We find strong differences between different encapsulation techniques. Native IPv6 traffic is the only significant source of full-sized 1,500 byte packets,

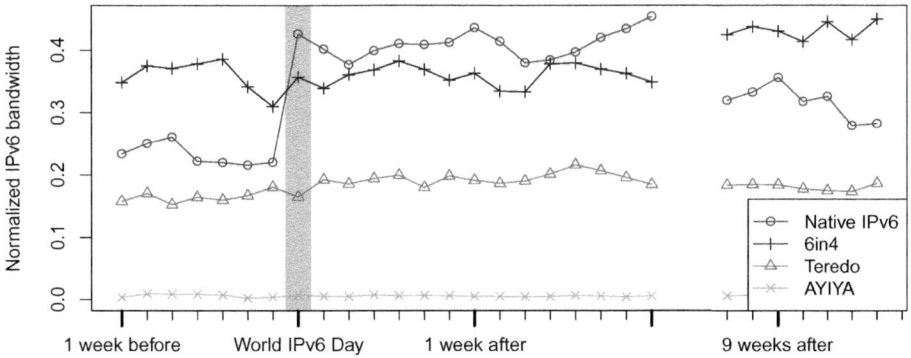

Fig. 3. IPv6 traffic volume by tunnel encapsulation (IXP)

since tunneled traffic needs room for additional encapsulation headers. In contrast to the native IPv6 traffic in the campus data set, we still observe larger fractions of small packets and a stronger mode at 1,280 bytes. While the packet size distributions for native, 6in4, and AYIYA traffic show some similarities to IPv4, we find that 98 % of Teredo packets are small. A closer examination reveals that at our vantage point, Teredo is mostly composed of control traffic: 76 % of all observed Teredo packets are keep-alive messages (IPv6 headers without payload), and 23 % are ICMP messages. Since Teredo contributes 62 % of IPv6 packets during the IPv6 day, we conclude that Teredo skews the overall packet size distribution dramatically.

4   Application Mix

We now turn to the application layer protocol mix of IPv6 traffic. We utilize Bro's dynamic protocol detection framework [4] to classify application layer protocols in the university data sets. As the IXP data set only provided sampled packet headers, we rely on well-known port numbers to identify applications. We use a selection of 86 well-known ports which have been shown to work reasonably well [11]. We report the top protocols and aggregate other traffic on well-known ports into the category *well-known*. If the port numbers do not allow to infer the application layer protocol, we attribute the traffic to the *unknown* category.

Figure 6 shows the daily application mix for native IPv6 traffic at the IXP for IXP1 and IXP2. The World IPv6 Day is highlighted by a red rectangle and IXP1 and IXP2 are separated by a red vertical line. Prior to the World IPv6 Day, NNTP was the strongest contributor with about 40 % of the volume, a protocol now frequently used for file-sharing [7]. While we cannot reliably identify P2P traffic in the IXP dataset, its share must be less than 30 % (sum of "well-known" and "unknown" categories). In contrast, Labovitz [8] reports P2P as the main contributor in IPv6 traffic before the World IPv6 Day, with 61 % of the total volume. ICMPv6 contributes 10 % to 13 % of the overall traffic volume. During the World IPv6 Day, the application mix has changed substantially. HTTP is dominating with more than 60 % of the traffic volume, NNTP dropped

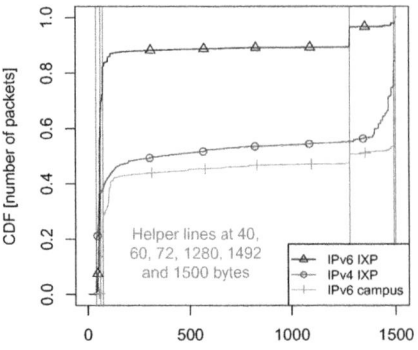

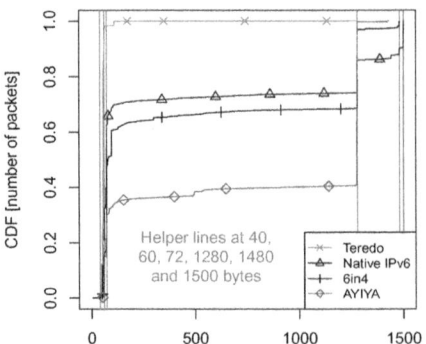

Fig. 4. Packet size distributions of IPv4 and IPv6 traffic (IXP and campus)

Fig. 5. Packet size distributions per encapsulation type (IXP)

to 7 % and ICMP to 6 %. In addition, "unknown", and "well-known" now account for less than 15 %. After the World IPv6 Day, the application mix stays roughly similar to the one during the World IPv6 Day, with HTTP loosing about 7 to 10 % of its popularity and ICMPv6 slowly rising up to 9 %.

In Figure 7, we plot the application mix for the campus data sets. We again highlight the World IPv6 Day with a red rectangle and separate different traces with a vertical line. Similar to the IXP we notice a strong shift in the application mix during and after the World IPv6 Day. Before the World IPv6 Day, DNS traffic is in general the main contributor. During the ramp-up to the World IPv6 Day, at and post the World IPv6 Day, we see that HTTP is dominating with a share of up to 97 %. The DNS traffic volume remains unchanged (1–2 GB/day), indicating that it is caused by server-to-server DNS communication and not client requests.

Inside 6in4 tunnels: Since we separately observe multiple different IPv6 tunneling mechanisms at the IXP, we next analyze a breakdown of the application mix according to the tunneling protocol. However, we discuss only 6in4 tunnels since Teredo is almost entirely control traffic and AYIYA lacks volume to provide meaningful results. In 6in4 traffic, which is responsible for more than 32 % of the volume, the most prevalent packets are IPv6 fragments. Further examination of these fragments reveals that half of them have a size of 1,280 bytes (at offset 0), while the other half has 96 bytes. Almost all of the fragments use UDP as transport protocol. We investigated the fragments with offset 0 to get the UDP port numbers, which appear to be random. Assuming these fragments belong together, the size of the original IPv6 packet before fragmentation would have been 1,320 bytes, which is the minimum IPv6 MTU of 1,280 plus the size of an IPv6 header. We speculate that a broken client software tried to send packets with minimum MTU to prevent fragmentation but forgot to account for the IPv6 header. Before the World IPv6 Day, HTTP was typically at 1–5 % of the traffic volume. During and after the World IPv6 Day, the HTTP fraction increases to 10–16 %. Unknown traffic is at 45 % before and at 52 % during and after the World IPv6 Day.

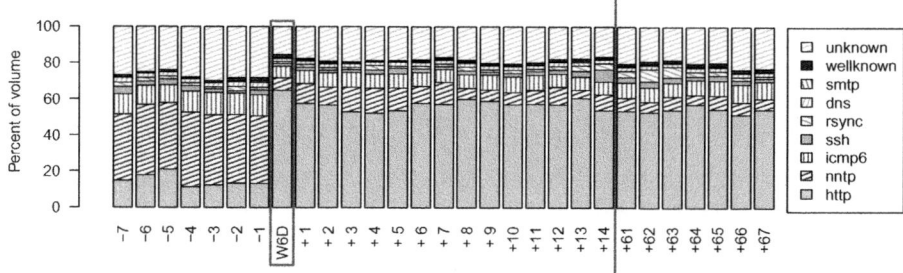

Fig. 6. Application mix per day for *native* IPv6 traffic (IXP)

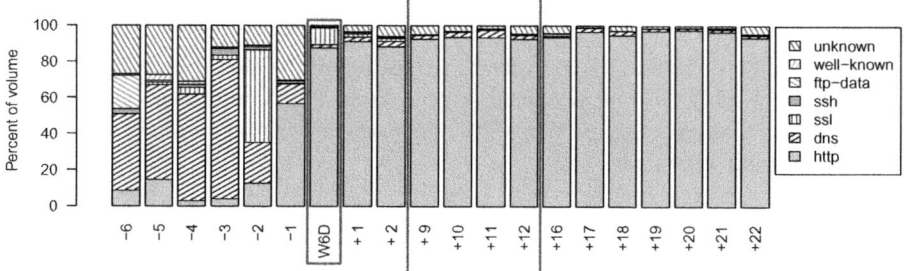

Fig. 7. Application mix per day for *all* IPv6 traffic (campus)

5   Traffic Sources

Since HTTP dominates in the campus environment (up to 97 % of total volume), we analyze HTTP in more detail. We utilize Bro's HTTP analyzer and extract the HTTP server name from the Host header field. We use this information to group HTTP requests by their destination (e.g., YouTube) and plot the result in Figure 8. The "open source" category consists of HTTP-enabled open source software sites, including freebsd.org, mozilla.com, and ubuntu.com. The "gov" and "edu" categories contain all sites under their respective top level domains.

We find that the mix of popular HTTP sites varies from day to day before the World IPv6 Day. Open source and edu sites have significant shares and a large fraction of the traffic is generated by "other" sites. During and after the World IPv6 Day, we observe a significant change with YouTube and Google being responsible for most IPv6 HTTP traffic. According to our data, Google enabled IPv6 just before the official start of the World IPv6 Day and disabled IPv6 again after the World IPv6 Day. In contrast, we observe that YouTube kept IPv6 enabled after the World IPv6 Day. Considering that HTTP dominates the application mix and YouTube dominates the HTTP mix after the World IPv6 Day, we conclude that a large volume of IPv6 traffic after the World IPv6 Day is contributed by YouTube.

At the IXP we see more than 3,500 unique IPv6 prefixes. We investigate the largest prefixes in terms of IPv6 traffic volume. Figure 9 shows three out of the top 10 prefixes from the World IPv6 Day. With the help of the IXP we were able to identify prefix A as belonging to a large content provider, and prefixes B and C as large IPv6 enabled

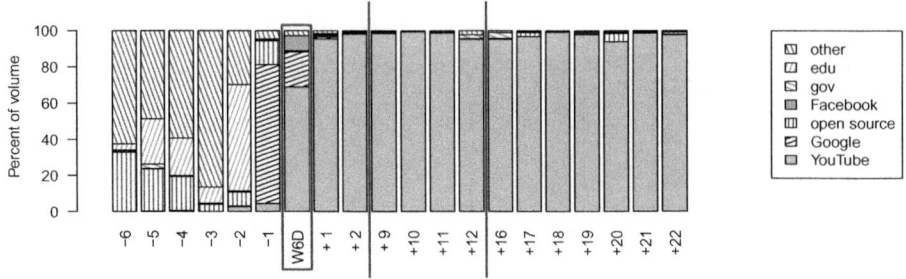

Fig. 8. Daily HTTP mix (campus)

stub networks. Only prefix A is actively participating on the World IPv6 Day. Yet, all of them see a roughly ten-fold sustained increase in traffic volume since the IPv6 day. This highlights that passively participating networks can exhibit as much of a change as actively participating ones.

6 Related Work

To the best of our knowledge this paper is the first to perform a systematic study of the IPv6 traffic around the World IPv6 Day. However, there are a number of reports about IPv6 and the World IPv6 Day in the proceedings of the IETF 81 meeting in Canada, July 2011, contributed by the Operations and Management working group.

Palmer and Thaler from Microsoft provide an experience report [12] about the IPv6 activation of several Microsoft's domains. They report having only few connectivity issues. Windows Vista and Windows 7 dominate the observed system types. 91 % of the connections were native IPv6, and less than 1 % were using Teredo. This is consistent with our results about the idleness of Teredo tunnels, and also surprising since Microsoft has enabled Teredo tunneling as a default service since Windows Vista.

Bob Hinden from Check Point reports in [6] about their experience of enabling IPv6 for their company website by using load balancers to handle IPv6. They encountered less difficulties than expected and kept IPv6 active after the World IPv6 Day.

Comcast provides a summary of their IPv6 experiences in [1]. Comcast deployed SMTP over IPv6 by duplicating their infrastructure. Consistent with our results, they report a significant sustained increase of IPv6 traffic at the World IPv6 Day.

In contrast to this study, the above reports were limited to either a few web sites of a single operator, or in case of Comcast to a set of test customers. Still, the reported IPv6 traffic trends and conclusions are consistent with our results.

Hurricane Electric is an early IPv6 adopter—they enabled IPv6 in 2001. Similar to other reports, they observed [9] an IPv6 traffic increase during and after the World IPv6 Day. They also report on path MTU problems and ICMPv6 blocking caused by too aggressive filtering. In addition, they find that 11 % of ASes are present in the IPv6 routing table in August 2011, up from 3.6 % three years earlier.

Wijnen et al. [15] present results from active measurements including DNS, ping6, traceroute6, and HTTP probes. The data was gathered from 40 different vantage points

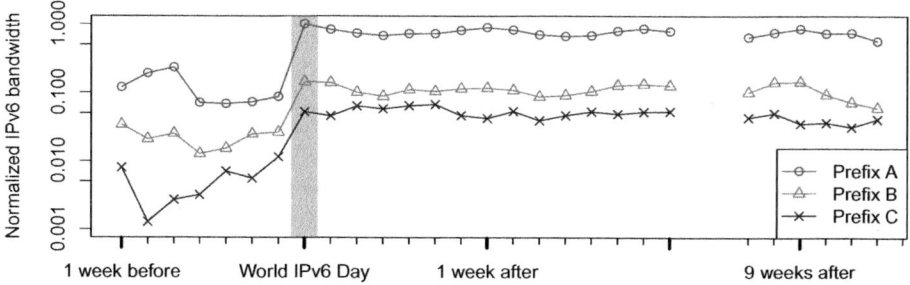

Fig. 9. Normalized bandwidth of *all* IPv6 traffic per prefix before, at, and post the World IPv6 Day (IXP). The plot shows three examples out of the top ten high-volume IPv6 prefixes. Note the log-scale y-axis.

from June 1st through June 11th, 2011. For example, they performed DNS AAAA queries to participating websites and found that nearly all World IPv6 Day participant web sites could be resolved successfully from all of their vantage points. Interestingly, the results also indicate effects due to negative caching of DNS records, as a number of vantage points were not able to resolve AAAA records of some participant, while other vantage points were. Furthermore, they show that after the World IPv6 Day, a number of web sites disabled IPv6 connectivity immediately, while DNS servers continued to return AAAA records for as long as half a day.

Claffy [3] provides an extensive survey of available data that enables tracking of IPv6 deployments, performs comparisons with IPv6 at the topology and the DNS level, and calls out to researchers and industry to provide more data. With our paper, we can contribute to some of the areas identified by Claffy, in particular utilization at access and interconnection links, application mix, and IPv6 tunneling.

Labovitz [8] performs a pre World IPv6 Day study of IPv6 traffic across several providers and presents an application mix including tunneled traffic in which P2P traffic dominates. In addition, our paper characterizes how different tunneling protocols are being used.

Cho et al. [2] performed a very early study of IPv6 path problems and latencies compared to IPv4. Limoncelli et al. [10] compare rollout strategies for IPv6. Guérin et al. [5] model incentives in IPv6 deployment.

7   Summary

In this paper, we conduct the first systematic analysis of IPv6 traffic around the World IPv6 Day. We rely on data collected at two vantage points: a large European Internet Exchange Point and the campus of a major US university. We analyze the traffic volume, application mix, and the use of tunneling protocols for transporting IPv6 packets.

We find that native IPv6 traffic almost doubled during the World IPv6 Day, while changes in tunneled traffic were limited. Teredo tunnels contribute a significant fraction to IPv6 traffic, yet only carry control traffic. We observe significant changes in the application mix during the World IPv6 Day, with the IPv6 application mix becoming similar to the IPv4 one. We find a large amount of fragmented IPv6 packets inside 6in4 tunnels for which broken software is a likely cause. Our results also show that a significant number of participants at the World IPv6 Day kept their IPv6 support online even after the test period ended, suggesting that they did not encounter any significant problems.

Acknowledgements. This work was supported in part by a fellowship within the post-doctoral program of the German Academic Exchange Service (DAAD) and by NSF Awards CNS-0855125 and OCI-1032889. Any opinions, findings, and conclusions or recommendations expressed in this material are those of the authors or originators and do not necessarily reflect the views of DAAD or the National Science Foundation.

References

1. Brzozowski, J., Griffiths, C.: Comcast IPv6 Trial/Deployment Experiences, Internet-Draft: draft-jjmb-v6ops-comcast-ipv6-experiences-01 (July 2011)
2. Cho, K., Luckie, M., Huffaker, B.: Identifying ipv6 network problems in the dual-stack world. In: Proceedings of the ACM SIGCOMM Workshop on Network Troubleshooting: Research, Theory and Operations Practice Meet Malfunctioning Reality, NetT 2004, pp. 283–288. ACM, New York (2004)
3. Claffy, k.: Tracking ipv6 evolution: data we have and data we need. SIGCOMM Comput. Commun. Rev. 41, 43–48
4. Dreger, H., Feldmann, A., Mai, M., Paxson, V., Sommer, R.: Dynamic application-layer protocol analysis for network intrusion detection. In: Proc. USENIX Security Symposium (2006)
5. Guérin, R., Hosanagar, K.: Fostering ipv6 migration through network quality differentials. SIGCOMM Comput. Commun. Rev. 40, 17–25 (2010)
6. Hinden, B.: Check Point's World IPv6 Day Experience. IETF 81 V6OPS, http://www.ietf.org/proceedings/81/slides/v6ops-2.pptx
7. Kim, J., Schneider, F., Ager, B., Feldmann, A.: Today's Usenet Usage: Characterizing NNTP Traffic. In: Proc. IEEE Global Internet Symposium (2010)
8. Labovitz, C.: Six month, six providers and IPv6. Tech. rep. (March 2011), http://www.monkey.org/~labovit/papers/v6sixmonths.pdf
9. Levy, M.: IETF 81 - World IPv6 Day Operators Review. IETF 81 V6OPS, http://www.ietf.org/proceedings/81/slides/v6ops-19.pdf
10. Limoncelli, T.A., Cerf, V.G.: Successful strategies for ipv6 rollouts. really. Commun. ACM 54, 44–48 (2011)
11. Maier, G., Feldmann, A., Paxson, V., Allman, M.: On dominant characteristics of residential broadband internet traffic. In: Proc. Internet Measurement Conf., IMC (2009)
12. Palmer, C., Thaler, D.: World IPv6 Day at Microsoft. IETF 81 V6OPS, http://www.ietf.org/proceedings/81/slides/v6ops-1.pptx
13. Paxson, V.: Bro: A system for detecting network intruders in real-time. Computer Networks Journal 31, 2435–2463 (1999), Bro homepage: http://www.bro-ids.org
14. InMon: sFlow Toolkit, http://www.inmon.com/technology/sflowTools.php
15. Wijnen, B., Aben, E., Wilhelm, R., Kisteleki, R.: World IPv6 Day—What did we learn? IETF 81 V6OPS, http://www.ietf.org/proceedings/81/slides/v6ops-4.pdf

An End-Host View on Local Traffic at Home and Work

Ahlem Reggani[1], Fabian Schneider[2], and Renata Teixeira[1]

[1] UPMC Sorbonne Universités and CNRS, LIP6, Paris, France
[2] NEC Laboratories Europe, Heidelberg, Germany (work done at UPMC[1])

Abstract. This paper compares local and wide-area traffic from end-hosts connected to different home and work networks. We base our analysis on network and application traces collected from 47 end-hosts for at least one week. We compare traffic patterns in terms of number of connections, bytes, duration, and applications. Not surprisingly, wide-area traffic dominates local traffic for most users. Local connections are often shorter and smaller than Internet connections. Moreover, we find that name services (DNS) and network file systems are the most common local applications, whereas web surfing and P2P, which are the most popular applications in the wide-area, are not significant locally.

1 Introduction

The past couple of decades has seen many studies that characterize Internet traffic [1, 6, 7, 12]. These studies are based on packet traces collected in ISP networks, at border routers of university campuses or enterprise networks. As such, most prior studies focus on wide-area traffic. Little is known about the traffic that stays inside a network, which we call *local traffic*. The main exception is the study of traffic from one enterprise [8, 9], which shows that local traffic is different from wide-area traffic with a significant amount of name service, network file system, and backup traffic. As the authors point out their study is "an example of what modern enterprise traffic looks like" [9]. It is crucial to reappraise such analysis in other enterprises and more important in other types of edge networks. For instance, the spread of broadband Internet has caused an increase in the number of households that have a home network. Yet, there has only been limited analysis of local traffic volumes in three home networks [5], but no in depth characterization of in-home traffic patterns. The challenge of studying local traffic across multiple edge networks is to obtain measurements from *inside* multiple networks.

This paper characterizes local network traffic of multiple networks from the perspective of an end-host that connects inside an edge network. This approach is in contrast with previous work [5, 9], which instruments routers in the local network. Although instrumenting routers could capture all traffic traversing the local network, it is hard to have access to routers at more than a few networks. By monitoring traffic directly at end-hosts, we can sample a larger number of networks, but we can only see the traffic from one of the hosts in the network. For smaller networks (such as home networks) a single host's traffic captures a significant fraction of those networks total traffic, whereas for larger networks (as enterprises) this fraction is less significant.

We rely on data collected at end-hosts using the HostView monitoring tool [4]. HostView records packet header traces and information about applications and user

N. Taft and F. Ricciato (Eds.): PAM 2012, LNCS 7192, pp. 21–31, 2012.

environment. The data we study was collected from 47 users who ran HostView for more than a week each. Given that users move between different networks, this dataset contains end-host traffic from a total of 185 different networks spread over 18 different countries. Section 2 gives an overview of the HostView data. The analysis of local and wide-area traffic from HostView data is challenging, because HostView has no information of which traffic flows are local. Worse, HostView scrapes the end-host IP address from the traces to protect user's privacy, which makes the identification of local traffic more challenging. Therefore, we develop a heuristic to separate local from wide-area traffic. Section 3 describes this heuristic together with our method to categorize environments and applications in the HostView data.

Our analysis (presented in Section 4) asks some high-level questions, for instance: How does the volume of an end-host's local traffic compare to wide-area traffic? Do local and wide-area applications differ? How does traffic vary between home and work? The results show that for most users wide-area traffic dominates local traffic, but that some users have over 80 % of local traffic. Local connections are mostly shorter and smaller than wide-area connections, but sometimes they transfer a larger amount of traffic than large wide-area connections. We find that typical local applications are DNS, ssh, and network file systems (confirming previous findings [9]). Moreover, common applications at work include backup, printing, and web. Yet, these applications are rarely used at home.

2   Summary of HostView Data

In this paper, we use three of the datasets collected by the HostView tool [4]: network packet traces, application labels, and the end-host's network environment. HostView logs all this data directly at the end-host into a trace file, which is periodically uploaded to a server. A new trace is created every four hours or when a change in the network interface or the IP address is detected.

Network traces and application context. HostView logs the first 100 bytes of each packet sent and received by the end-host with libpcap. For DNS packets, it records the whole packet to enable offline hostname to IP address mappings. In this paper, we use the connection summaries generated by previous work [3]. Each connection summary record describes both directions of a TCP or UDP connection and includes (among other fields): The source and destination IP addresses (replacing the host IP address with "0.0.0.0" to comply with French privacy laws), the source and destination port numbers, and the network protocol; The number of bytes, the number of packets, and the duration of the connection; And the name of the process executable that generated the connection.

Network environment. HostView labels each trace file with information describing the network environment the end-host is connected to, including the network interface, a hash of the wireless network SSID and of the BSSID of the access point for wireless networks or a hash of the MAC address of the gateway for wired networks. It also records the ISP, the city, and the country for each trace using the MaxMind GeoIP commercial database from March 2011. When the end-host connects to a new wireless network, HostView asks the user to specify the network type from a pre-defined list: Home, Work, Airport, Hotel, Conference meeting, Friend's home, Public place, Coffee shop or Other (with the possibility to specify). This user tag is used to classify the network the user connects to according to an environment type. Unfortunately, this tag is not available for wired connections and users sometimes skip the questionnaire. Originally, only 40 % of HostView traces had a user tag, but after applying some heuristics (which exploit the fact that users connect to the same network with both wireless and wired, for instance) previous work was able to label 78 % of the traces [3]. Still, the data includes at least one unlabeled trace per user. The next section describes our method to label most of the remaining traces with an environment type.

Dataset characteristics and biases. HostView was announced in networking conferences and researcher mailing lists. Volunteer users downloaded HostView (which is available only for Mac OS and Linux) and ran it during different time intervals between November 2010 and August 2011. In this paper, we use traces from 47 users who ran HostView for at least one week; 32 of these users ran HostView for more than a month.

Because of the way HostView was advertised and its limited operating-system support, the user population is biased towards networking researchers. We acknowledge that networking researchers probably use different applications than the average user and may also work from home. It is still interesting to study examples of the differences between local and wide-area traffic. We do observe a diverse set of applications among different users and our users do use some popular applications like YouTube, Facebook and BitTorrent. Furthermore, this bias influences the types of networks we study. Importantly, "work" is often a university. Overall, we study end-hosts connected to 185 unique networks spread over 18 different countries (Italy: 25, France: 22, Germany: 21, Rest of Europe: 31, Asia: 19, US: 63, Australia: 3, and Brazil: 1); 34 distinct home networks and 38 distinct work environments (29 are universities and 9 enterprises).

Another bias comes from using data collected for a limited time period on only one single end-host in the network. It is well known that traffic characteristics can vary considerably between different networks and over time [10]. HostView can only see a small fraction of the network's traffic and there are some types of traffic that it can never observe. For example, some homes may have a media server that serves content to the TV; this type of traffic traverses the home network, but it is not originated or consumed by an end-host. Despite these shortcomings, we believe that this end-host perspective on local versus wide-area traffic offers the unique opportunity to sample traffic in a relative large number of networks. Whenever appropriate, we also contrast our findings with previous work.

3   Methodology

In this paper, we compare local and wide-area traffic in networks of different types. In addition, we are interested in the traffic application mix. We follow three steps to label HostView traces before our analysis: *(i)* Differentiation of local and wide-area traffic, *(ii)* Extension of the incomplete network type labeling, and *(iii)* Categorization of connection records into application groups.

Table 1. Examples of process names and network services to category mappings. This list is not complete and only intended to give an idea.

Category	Process name (Examples)	Application protocols
Backup	retroclient	amanda
Chat	Skype, iChat, Adium, Pidgin	ircd, SIP, msnp, snpp, xmpp
DistantControl	ssh, sshd, VNC, screen sharing	ssh(22), webmin
Email	Mail, Outlook, Thunderbird	IMAP(S), POP3(S), (S)SMTP
Personal	Media players, games, productivity	rtsp
FileTransfer	ftp, dropbox, svn, git, SW updates	ftp, rsync, svn, cvspserver
Management	traceroute, iperf, nmap, ntpd, uPNP	BOOTP, MySQL, VPN, SNMP, whois
Miscellaneous	perl, python, VirtualBox, openvpn	—
NameService	dns, nmblookup, named, nmbd, nscd	domain(53), mdns, netbios-ns
NetworkFS	smbclient, smbd, AppleFileServer	AFP, AFS, LDAP, netbios, nfs
P2P	amule, uTorrent, transmission	amule, Kazaa, BitTorrent
Printing	cupsd, lpd, HP, Lexmark	ipp, printer
Web	Firefox, Chrome, Safari, Opera, httpd, plugin-container, WebKitPluginHost	HTTP(S)

Local vs. wide-area. HostView does not collect the host IP address, so we cannot identify the local subnet based on the host IP prefix. We develop a number of heuristics to classify traffic as local or wide-area. We define *local* traffic as all the traffic exchanged between an end-user machine and a private IP address, i. e., 192.168/16, 172.16/12, 10/8. We expect this classification to correctly match most local traffic at homes, as those typically connect through a NAT gateway sharing one public IP on the outside. To avoid misclassification when the ISP employs carrier-grade NAT, we develop a second heuristic that analyzes the remote IP addresses of all traffic flows classified as local. When we observe that the remote IP addresses fall in more than five different subnets, we compute the number of connections and bytes for each remote /24 to identify whether there is a "preferred subnet", i.e., a remote subnet that carries most of the traffic (>99.9 %). If there is a preferred subnet, then we leave all traffic classified as local. Otherwise, we flag the network for manual inspection. The HostView data had a total of five home networks which contacted more than five different remote subnets, four of these had a preferred subnet. We manually inspected the remaining home network and found that a large fraction of P2P traffic going to IPs in 10.* networks. In fact, this user's home ISP is known deploy carrier-grade NAT, so we label this 10.* traffic as wide-area and we leave the 192.* traffic as local. For work networks, we might misclassify local traffic as wide-area when hosts connected to the local network have public IP addresses. We address this issue with a third heuristic that labels all traffic to a destination IP address that has the exact same organization name as that of the source network as local. Finally, we classify all broadcast traffic as local. We label all the remaining traffic as *wide-area*.

Extension of network environment labels. As discussed in Section 2, some of the HostView traces have no network type tag (e. g., Home or Work). We manually inspect the ISP, the network interface, and the geo-location of each unlabeled trace and assign a label. For example, we label a trace annotated with *ISP: "University of California"* ;

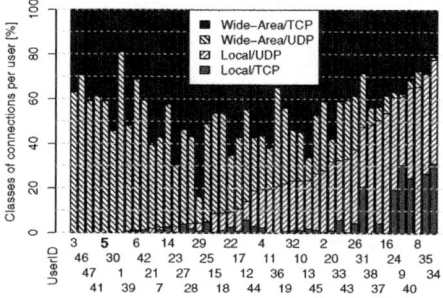
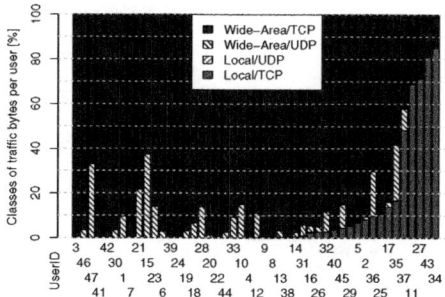

Fig. 1. Local vs. wide-area connections per user (Total number of connections per user varies between 2.5 K and 3 M.)

Fig. 2. Bytes transferred on local vs. wide-area connections per user (Total amount of traffic per user varies between 800 MB and 770 GB)

City: "Santa Cruz, California"; Country: "United States" as *Work*. Another example containing *ISP: "Free"; City: "Paris"; Country: "France"* is labeled *Home*. This manual classification reduced the fraction of unlabeled traces to 2%. Some traces have no information that indicates the type of network.

Application Categorization. For our analysis of popular applications we rely on a two-staged categorization process. First, we assign one of eleven application categories or "unclassified" to each connection based on the process executable name. Second, we label any connection that remains unclassified based on the application protocol as derived from the port number using the IANA mapping. We assign categories to those process names and application protocols that account for the most connections and the most volume. Table 1 lists the eleven categories and gives example process names and application protocols for each of them.

4   Results

This section first compares local and wide-area traffic in general. Then, it studies the split of local and wide-area traffic at home and at work.

Local vs. Internet: Connection and Bytes. Figures 1 and 2 show the fraction of local (two bottom bars) and wide-area (two top bars) traffic for each user (UserIDs are the same across figures for comparison). For each user, we separate UDP (shaded bars) from TCP (solid bars) traffic. We consider the composition of traffic by number of connections (Figure 1) and bytes (Figure 2).

Take the example of the rightmost user in Figure 1, UserID *34*, 77% (46% UDP and 31% TCP) of this user's connections are local. The remaining traffic is directed to the Internet (0% UDP and 23% TCP). In general, we observe that Internet traffic dominates both in number of connections and bytes, although this dominance is much more pronounced for bytes. In total, we classify 780 GB as local and 3 TB as wide-area traffic. Furthermore, we see that UDP dominates local connections for almost 80% of

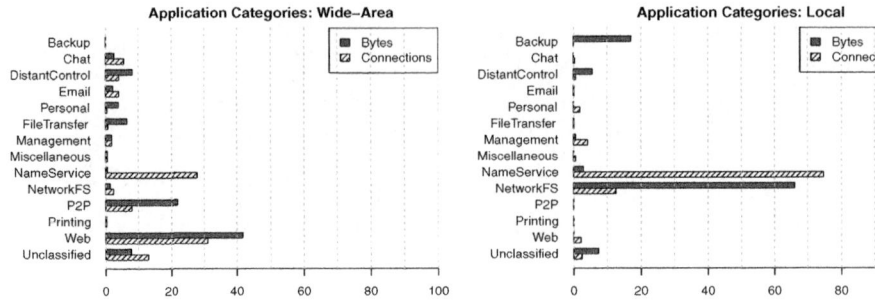

Fig. 3. Application mix for wide-area traffic   **Fig. 4.** Application mix for local traffic

the users. The absence of shaded bars in Figure 2 clearly shows that almost all bytes are transferred in TCP connections (>89 %).

The four rightmost users in Figure 2 transfer more bytes locally than in the wide-area. As we discuss in the next section, most of this traffic corresponds to network file system, so these users could be playing music or watching videos from a local network storage. In Figure 2, more than half of the users exchange almost all traffic with hosts in the wide-area (corroborating previous findings [5]). In the rare cases these users do exchange traffic with hosts in the local network, they mainly perform file transfers.

Local vs. Internet: Application Mix We now study how local and wide-area applications differ. Figures 3 and 4 show the application mix in terms of connections (shaded bars) and data bytes (solid bars). These figures use the application categorization method described in Section 3, which leaves no more than 12 % of connections and 7 % of bytes *unclassified*.

Figure 3 shows the application mix for wide-area traffic. We see that the proportion of bytes per application class agrees with results from previous studies [6, 7]. Web traffic and P2P are the top applications. In addition, we see some file transfers and distant control traffic (ssh and VNC). When we classify in terms of number of connections, the mix changes and name services take the second place behind Web. Chat and Email are also more prevalent in terms of connections than bytes.

Figure 4 shows that name services (e. g., DNS) dominates local traffic in terms of connections, whereas backup and network file systems (e. g., AFP and SMB) in terms of bytes. A previous study of enterprise traffic [9] also found that network file system and name service dominate local traffic, but their study found considerably more local email and web traffic than what we find. A significant part of our data is of home traffic, which may explain this difference. We now split the traffic into home and work.

Traffic at Home and Work Our analysis so far has mixed traffic from multiple network environments, including home, work, airports, coffee shops, or hotels. Based on our extended environment labels (see Section 3) we investigate the differences not only between local and wide-area traffic, but also across different types of network environments. Figure 5 shows the distribution of traffic and users over the different environments. Note that a single user can visit multiple environments. After applying our

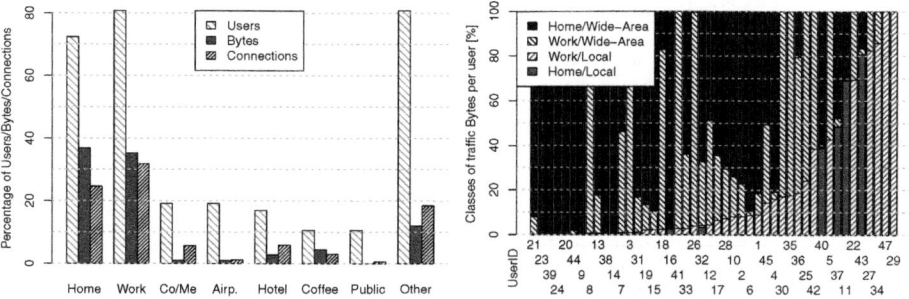

Fig. 5. Percentage of Users, volume, and connections by environment

Fig. 6. Bytes transferred at home vs. work and traffic target per user

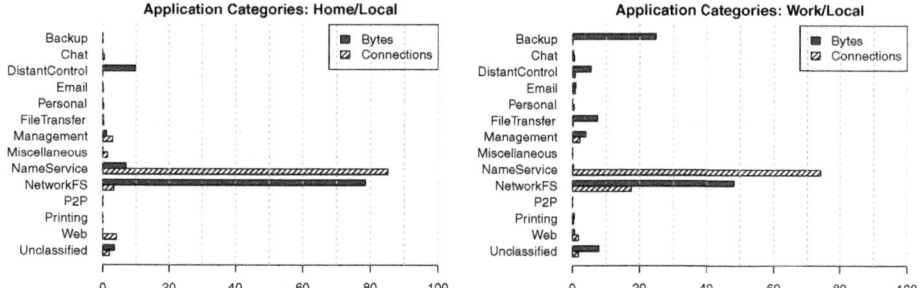

Fig. 7. Application Mix for Home/Local traffic   **Fig. 8.** Application Mix for Work/Local traffic

heuristics the 'Other' category, which includes instances when users labeled the environment as other and when our heuristic could not label the environment, only accounts for 12 % of the bytes and 18 % of the connections. We see that users (light shaded bars) are primarily at home or work, thus we select these two environments for further study. These environments include 56 % of the connections (heavy shaded bars) and 72 % of the bytes (solid bars). Moreover, our analysis of local traffic in different environments (not shown) shows that the fraction of local traffic in all environments but home and work is marginal (<1.25 %).

Figure 6 shows the number of bytes sent and received per user for all four combinations: home/wide-area, work/wide-area, work/local, and home/local. As expected, we see a similar split between local (bottom) and wide-area (top) traffic The differences between Figure 6 and Figure 2 happen because here we only include traffic from home and work. The majority of users has more local traffic at work. Only four users have a significant fraction of local traffic at home.

Application Mix at Home and Work. Now that we established a basic understanding of how traffic differs between home and work as well as local and wide-area, we investigate the application mix in each of these cases. The analysis of wide-area traffic at work (omitted for conciseness) shows almost no P2P traffic, but a considerable fraction

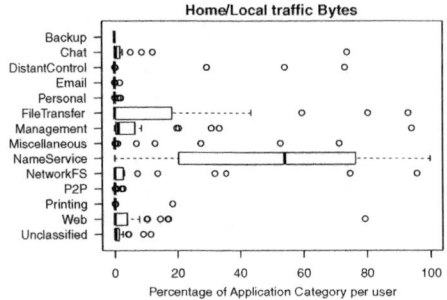
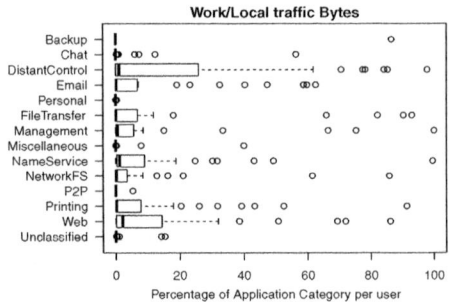

Fig. 9. Boxplot of application mix per user for Home/Local traffic

Fig. 10. Boxplot of application mix per user for Work/Local traffic

of file transfers and distant control traffic. These results are consistent with previous findings by Pang et al. [9].

We study the application mix of local traffic at home in Figure 7 and at work in Figure 8. Local traffic at work includes file transfers and backup traffic, which are not present in home traffic. Different from Pang et al. [9], we see little local email or web traffic at work. Indeed, it turns out that email traffic of most HostView users is wide-area. A possible explanation is that they are typically mobile and hence rely less on local infrastructure.

Another difference is the lack of backup traffic at home, which may reflect users' preference to backup directly at external disks when at home, instead of over the network. The backup traffic at work is mainly from a single user, who is responsible for almost all the bytes of backup traffic in Figure 8. We do also observe some file transfer traffic locally at work. Most of that is transmit (file transfer client for Mac OS) and FTP, but some is Dropbox (a cloud storage/synchronization service). Given it is a cloud service (cloud = wide-area) we did not expect to find Dropbox locally. It turns out that Dropbox is using a direct connection for synchronization across devices in the same LAN. Dropbox constitutes half of the file transfers in our local home traces.

As single users can have a distorting impact on the overall traffic composition, we now calculate the application mix per user. Figures 9 and 10 show boxplots[1] of the application mix per user in terms of bytes. Each row shows the distribution of the individual contribution of the corresponding application category across all users. We find that although network file system traffic dominates local traffic, most users have less than 10 % of traffic in this category both at home and at work. Reversely, although name service represents a small percent of the total number of bytes in Figure 7, the median across all users is over 50 %. We find similar effects for file transfers at home. At work, contrary to Figure 8, we do see web, email, and printing usage.

Connection size and duration. We end our analysis with a study of the characteristics of local and wide-area connections both at home and work. We show the complimentary cumulative distribution of the number of bytes per connection in Figure 11 and

---

[1] The box (line inside the box) shows the quartiles (median); whiskers show nearest values not beyond a standard span from the quartiles; points beyond (outliers) are drawn individually.

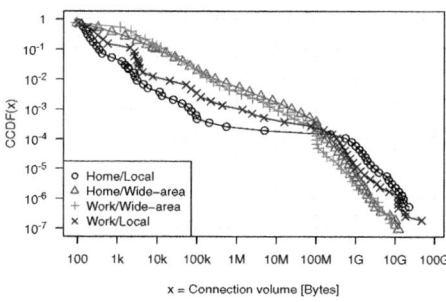

Fig. 11. CCDF of connection volumes

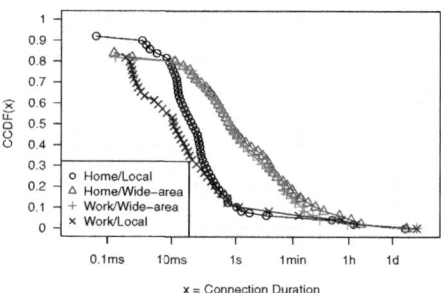

Fig. 12. CCDF of conn. durations (log-linear)

connection durations in Figure 12. For example, the 'work/local' point at x = 10kB in Figure 11 indicates that only 1 % (y-axis) of all the connections are larger that 10kB.

In terms of bytes, we observe in general larger (further to the right) connections for wide-area traffic. Local connections are typically small, but the largest local connections exceed the size and duration of wide-area connections. This observation confirms one previous study showing that home traffic sometimes have short spikes [5]. Although the connection durations in Figure 12 are limited by the 4 hour trace file cutoff, most connections are shorter than this limit. We also see the local connections (circles and crosses) are up to two orders of magnitude shorter than wide-area connections.

5   Related Work

Wide-area traffic measured from *inside* the network has been analyzed from different angles over the past decades [1,6,7,12]. These measurements, however, cannot capture local traffic in networks at the edge. Our study analyzes local traffic and how it compares with wide-area traffic with data collected directly at end-hosts using HostView [4]. Other studies have collected and analyzed similar end-host data in the past [2,11]. In particular, Giroire et al. [2] has compared network traffic from end-hosts across three network environments (inside the company, VPN to company, and outside the company). Different from ours, their study has not characterized local network traffic in depth and although it measured laptops of a larger number of users than HostView measured, they are all employees of a single enterprise.

Most similar to our work are the studies of one enterprise network [8,9] and of three home networks [5]. These prior studies instrument the local network to collect packet traces and can hence observe most local and wide-area traffic. Our study measures one (or at most a couple) of end-host in each network and hence cannot have such a complete view of each of the studied networks, but it can sample a larger number of networks. The home network study focuses mainly on network performance, not on traffic characterization. Their few traffic characterization results show that wide-area traffic dominates local traffic in the three homes, but that there are some, rare spikes of local traffic. The analysis in the enterprise study [9] is most similar to ours and we contrasted their findings with ours throughout this paper. Given that Internet traffic can vary significantly among sites and over time [10], our study contributes to show the diversity of traffic patterns in different network environments.

6   Summary

This paper presented a comparison of local traffic in different network environments from the perspective of end-hosts. The advantage of using end-hosts as vantage points is that we study traffic collected from over one hundred different edge networks. Our results showed that there is a large diversity in importance of local traffic relative to wide-area traffic, but that in general wide-area traffic dominates. In some networks (like airports and coffee-shops), we rarely see any local traffic, the only local traffic is DNS. At home and work, we do observe a non-negligible fraction of local traffic. Most local traffic is composed by short connections, but sometimes local connections transfer an extremely large number of bytes. Besides DNS, the most typical local applications are network file system and backup, but the composition of local traffic depends on the user and the network. The drawback of measuring local traffic from end-hosts is that we can only see a small fraction of each network's traffic. In the future, we plan to collect data directly from home gateways to measure all traffic from a single home over a longer period of time. In fact, home users are already deploying home gateways modified to perform measurements. We are working with the developers of Bismark (http://projectbismark.net/) to collect passive traffic measurements as well.

Acknowledgments.   We thank D. Joumblatt and O. Goga for their help with the HostView data. This work was supported by the European Community's Seventh Framework Programme (FP7/2007-2013) no. 258378 (FIGARO) and carried out at LINCS (www.lincs.fr).

References

1. Cáceres, R., Danzig, P.B., Jamin, S., Mitzel, D.J.: Characteristics of wide-area TCP/IP conversations. In: Proc. ACM SIGCOMM, pp. 101–112 (1991)
2. Giroire, F., Chandrashekar, J., Iannaccone, G., Papagiannaki, K., Schooler, E.M., Taft, N.: The Cubicle vs. The Coffee Shop: Behavioral Modes in Enterprise End-Users. In: Claypool, M., Uhlig, S. (eds.) PAM 2008. LNCS, vol. 4979, pp. 202–211. Springer, Heidelberg (2008)
3. Joumblatt, D., Goga, O., Teixeira, R., Chandrashekar, J., Taft, N.: Characterizing end-host application performance across multiple networking environments. In: Proc. INFOCOM, Mini-Conference (2012)
4. Joumblatt, D., Teixeira, R., Chandrashekar, J., Taft, N.: Hostview: annotating end-host performance measurements with user feedback. SIGMETRICS Perform. Eval. Rev. 38, 43–48 (2011)
5. Karagiannis, T., Christos, G., Key, P.: Homemaestro: Distributed monitoring and diagnosis of performance anomalies in home networks, Tech. Rep. MSR (October 2008)
6. Labovitz, C., Iekel-Johnson, S., McPherson, D., Oberheide, J., Jahanian, F.: Internet interdomain traffic. In: Proc. ACM SIGCOMM, pp. 75–86 (2010)
7. Maier, G., Feldmann, A., Paxson, V., Allman, M.: On dominant characteristics of residential broadband internet traffic. In: Proc. ACM IMC, pp. 90–102 (2009)

8. Nechaev, B., Allman, M., Paxson, V., Gurtov, A.: A preliminary analysis of tcp performance in an enterprise network. In: Proc. INM/WREN 2010, p. 7 (2010)
9. Pang, R., Allman, M., Bennett, M., Lee, J., Paxson, V., Tierney, B.: A first look at modern enterprise traffic. In: Proc. ACM IMC (2005)
10. Paxson, V.: Empirically-derived analytic models of wide- area tcp connections. IEEE/ACM Transactions on Networking 2 (August 1994)
11. Saikat, G., Chandrashekar, J., Taft, N., Papagiannaki, K.: How healthy are today's enterprise networks. In: Proc. IMC, pp. 145–150 (2008)
12. Thompson, K., Miller, G.J., Wilder, R.: Wide-area internet traffic patterns and characteristics. IEEE Network 11(6), 10–23 (1997)

Comparison of User Traffic Characteristics on Mobile-Access versus Fixed-Access Networks

Mikko V.J. Heikkinen[1,2,3] and Arthur W. Berger[3,4]

[1] Aalto University School of Electrical Engineering
mikko.heikkinen@aalto.fi
[2] Helsinki Institute for Information Technology HIIT
[3] Massachusetts Institute of Technology
[4] Akamai Technologies
awberger@mit.edu

Abstract. We compare Web traffic characteristics of mobile- versus fixed-access end-hosts, where herein the term "mobile" refers to access via cell towers, using for example the 3G/UMTS standard, and the term "fixed" includes Wi-Fi access. It is well-known that connection speeds are in general slower over mobile-access networks, and also that often there is higher packet loss. We were curious whether this leads mobile-access users to have smaller connections. We examined the bytes-per-connection and packet loss based on packet retransmissions from a sampling of logs from servers of Akamai Technologies. We obtained 149 million connections, across 51 countries. The mean bytes-per-connection was typically larger for fixed-access: for two-thirds of the countries, it was at least one-third larger. Regarding distributions, we found that the difference between the bytes-per-connection for mobile- versus fixed-access was statistically significant for each of the countries, and likewise for packet loss. However, the difference is typically small. For some countries, mobile-access had the larger connections. As expected, mobile-access often had higher packet loss than fixed-access, but the reverse pertained for some countries. Typically packet loss increased during the busy period of the day, when mobile-access had a larger increase.

1 Introduction

Mobile broadband has become a significant factor in the Internet communications market, and it continues to grow: Cisco [5] forecast that global mobile IP data traffic will double every year through 2014. Informa [7] estimated that there would be globally 670 million mobile broadband subscribers in 2011.

We are interested in comparing Web traffic characteristics of mobile- versus fixed-access end-hosts, where herein the term "mobile" refers to access via cell towers, using for example the 3G/UMTS standard, and the term "fixed" includes Wi-Fi access. Whereas prior work has compared the applications used by mobile- and fixed-access devices [10], here we are interested in the network level, and comparing the size of connections (i.e., number of bytes per connection) for mobile versus fixed devices that are accessing the Web.[1]

---

[1] An extended version of this paper is available as a technical report [6].

N. Taft and F. Ricciato (Eds.): PAM 2012, LNCS 7192, pp. 32–41, 2012.

It is well-known that connection speeds are in general slower over mobile-access networks [2]. Also, and as reported herein, often, though not always, there is higher packet loss with mobile-access, see §4.2. We are curious whether this leads users to have smaller connections, or would they persevere, so to speak, through the more adverse network conditions.

From a sampling of logs from July 2010 from servers of Akamai Technologies, we examine the number of bytes-per-connection, and packet loss based on packet retransmissions. The data for this study were collected prior to the deployment of 4G/LTE, and thus form a baseline for comparison for when 4G/LTE is broadly in use.

The contributions of this study are:

1. The first reported comparison of mobile- versus fixed-access connection-size and packet-loss
2. The comparison of the daily variation in bytes-per-connection and packet loss, for mobile- and fixed-access
3. Results spanning 51 countries

This paper is structured as follows: §2 reviews the related work. §3 describes our data set. §4 contains our results. §5 summarizes and discusses our results.

2 Related Work

Regarding side-by-side comparison of mobile- and fixed-access traffic, Akamai's [2] quarterly "State of Internet" reports connection speeds for both fixed- and mobile-access. Also, Sandvine [10] reported traffic profiles for both fixed- and mobile-access. Complementing these two studies, the present work also makes such a comparison, though in contrast to the prior work, we examine different attributes: the number of bytes per connection and packet loss. Using a data set from the Akamai content distribution servers, our study is global in scope and presents results for over 50 different countries.

In addition to the two previous side-by-side fixed- and mobile-access traffic comparisons at the network level, at least two studies have compared fixed- and mobile-access traffic at the application level: Hossfeld et al. [8] compared the performance of a peer-to-peer file sharing application in both fixed- and mobile-access networks, whereas Svoboda [11] compared the session lengths of online gamers in fixed- and mobile-access networks. Furthermore, Kalden & Ekström [9] compared (non-side-by-side) the results from their analysis of GPRS mobile-access traffic to studies of fixed-access traffic by other researchers.

3 Data Set and Methodology

We used data from log files of Akamai Technologies that contained information that enabled a comparison of mobile- and fixed-access traffic on a per country basis. The data consisted of a global sub-sampling of TCP connections between clients and Akamai servers. These connections are for data that originated at Web sites of medium to large organizations and where the aggregate set of clients is globally distributed. The log lines included the Unix time, the source address of incoming packets seen by the Akamai server, the number of bytes per connection, and the number of retransmitted packets, given Selective Acknowledgment (SACK), which we use as an estimate of packet loss. For the present analysis we used logs from the week of July 25 through 31, 2010.

Our methodology for associating a log line with mobile- or fixed-access is as follows. As the log lines do not contain this association, we started with the source address, which could be the address of the end-device itself, or the public facing address of a mobile access point, etc. We associated this address with an Autonomous System (AS) based on Border Gateway Protocol (BGP) feeds collected by Akamai. We then used the fact that some network operators that offer mobile service dedicate an AS for that purpose, and likewise for fixed-access services; though a complicating factor is that this is not a universal practice, and some ASs contain both mobile and fixed access. For its quarterly "State of Internet" reports [2], Akamai had already identified ASs dedicated for mobile-access, as well as for fixed-access. Some of these ASs had been identified based on prior knowledge, some were identified by their name, and some by contacting the network operator. Additional mobile ASs were found by an initial discriminator of the ASs having a relatively low average connection speed, and then from this pool of ASs, further inquiries were made to confirm whether they were mobile ASs. Given countries in which mobile ASs had been identified, a sampling of fixed-access ASs were also selected to provide a comparison. ASs that could not be identified with high confidence as being in one of these categories were excluded.

We then selected TCP connections in the log files where the client IP address was in one of the selected mobile or fixed ASs. We used the Akamai geo-location service EdgeScape [1] to identify the country in which the client IP address was located. (EdgeScape provides a service-level agreement (SLA) that the association of address to country has 99% accuracy.) We obtained 149 million connections, across 51 countries, where we excluded countries for which the dataset contained less than 1,000 mobile or fixed connections (and some countries with least data to save space, see [6] for results on 57 countries). The median number of mobile-access connections per-country was 48,000, and for fixed-access it was 650,000. As we were interested in comparing the mobile and fixed daily demand, we again used EdgeScape to obtain the latitude and longitude of the client IP address, from which we obtained the local time-zone relative to GMT. This enabled daily demand plots where hour "0" corresponds to midnight for the given client.

4   Results

4.1   Number of Bytes per Connection

Summary Statistics. Table 1 shows the 3rd quartile and mean of the number of KiloBytes-per-connection, partitioned by country and by fixed-access versus mobile-access. (See [6] for an extended version of the table.) The rows are arranged in increasing order of the mean number of KBytes-per-connection for fixed-access. Note that the mean is larger than the 3rd quartile as the distribution of KBytes-per-connection tends to have a small percentage of large connections. There is clear variation across countries in KBytes-per-connection: The 3rd quartile (75% quantile) varies from 6 to 21 for fixed-access, and 7 to 27 for mobile-access; and the mean varies from 38 to 152 for fixed-access, and 19 to 178 for mobile-access. The 3rd quartile of all countries is 17 for fixed-access, and 14 for mobile-access; the mean of all countries is 113 for fixed-access and 47 for mobile-access.

There are also clear differences between fixed-access and mobile-access. For 65% of the countries, the mean bytes-per-connection was at least one-third larger for fixed-access. For most of the countries ($\sim$75% based on the 3rd quartile), the fixed-access connections have more KBytes than mobile-access; and thus there is a minority where the reverse pertains. As an example, in the USA, the 3rd quartile of KBytes-per-connection for fixed-access is larger than mobile-access, being respectively 16 and 12; while in the South Korea the order is reversed, having values 6 and 27, respectively. In the USA, the mean is again greater for fixed-access, 152 versus 44 KBytes-per-connection, while in France the corresponding values are 102 and 178.

Distributions. We also examined the cumulative distribution function (CDF) of KBytes-per-connection for fixed-access and mobile-access. As one might expect for such a large data set as ours, using the non-parametric Kolmogorov-Smirnov test, we found that the null hypothesis that the two sample distributions (fixed- and mobile-access) come from the same population distribution is rejected with high confidence, for all of the countries, typically with p-values much less than 0.01. Although the two sample distributions are statistically distinct, for many of the countries the visual difference in a plot is rather slight. Though, for a minority of countries, the difference is dramatic.

Figure 1 is a sampling of four countries. For both country pairs, we show two plots: a CDF with a linear scale on the axes, and a complementary cumulative distribution function (CCDF) with logarithmic scales. The former is useful for seeing the bulk 90% of the connections, and the latter for the minority of large-size connections, which impact the means reported in Table 1.

For the USA and France, the distributions given fixed-access versus mobile-access are rather similar, at least for the bulk of the connections. The medians are essentially the same. By the 3rd quartile the difference is more noticeable. An interesting contrast between the USA and France is that in the former the distribution given fixed-access connections has a heavier tail, whereas in the latter the mobile-access connections do, up to 10 MBytes. For example, in the USA, 0.7% of the fixed-access connections are at least 1 MBytes, which is greater than the 0.4% of mobile-access connections. In France, again 0.7% of the fixed-access connections are at least 1 MByte, whereas 2.9% of the mobile-access connections are. For connections of 100 MBytes or more, fixed-access dominates (though of course the percentage of connections is quite small).

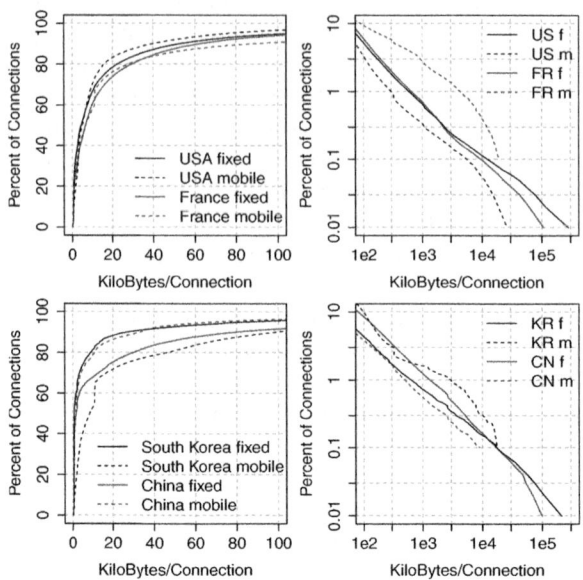

Fig. 1. Distribution for size of connections (left) and complementary distribution for size of connections (right) for the USA and France (top) and South Korea and China (bottom)

In contrast to the USA and France, China and South Korea are two of the minority of countries in Table 1 where the difference in distributions is visually quite evident even for the non-tail portion. Also, as a contrast between South Korea and China, in the former the mobile-access connections are larger (in the sense of the CDF), and in the latter the reverse pertains, even up to connections of 10 MBytes. For example, in South Korea, 22% of the mobile-access connections are greater than 40 KBytes, while fewer (8%) of fixed-access are. In China, 8% of the mobile-access connections are greater than 40 KBytes, whereas more (15%) of fixed-access are.

4.2   Packet Loss Based on Packet Retransmissions

Packet loss on the connection is one of the performance measures of the quality of service provided by the network operator. We were curious how packet loss compared on fixed-access versus mobile-access. Note that this comparison of mobile- and fixed-access packet loss is for clients accessing Web content from Akamai servers. The Akamai server is typically in the same AS as the client, in which case the loss, when it occurs, is within client's AS. And if the server is not in the same AS, then in all likelihood it is in a nearby upstream AS. Thus, in general, the number of packet retransmissions tends to be less as compared to the client accessing Web content directly from an origin site, as then the path is longer, with greater opportunity for experiencing congestion. For each

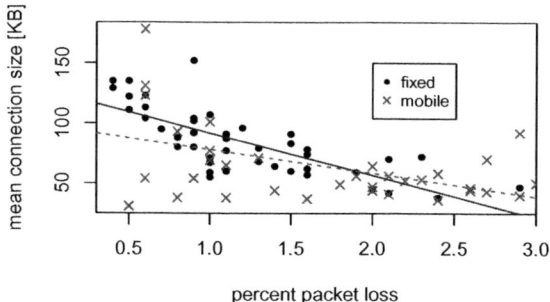

Fig. 2. Mean connection size versus packet loss, per country, for the subset of countries whose mean packet loss is no more than 3%

connection, we compute the percent of packets sent from the server to the client that are duplicate packets, given SACK TCP, which we use as an estimate of lost packets.

Table 2 reports mean per-connection percent packet loss, partitioned by country and by fixed-access versus mobile-access connections. (See [6] for an extended version of the table.) Typically, there is no packet loss: The median per-connection packet loss was 0.0% in all countries; and the 3rd quartile was also 0.0% in many, but not all cases (see [6]). Note that the mean per-connection packet loss gives equal weight to large and small connections. As a comparison, Table 2 also reports the overall, or access-network, packet loss, defined as the total number of duplicate packets, summed across the set of connections, divided by the total number of packets sent. The rows are ordered in increasing value of fixed-access minus mobile-access mean per-connection packet loss. Countries where this difference is positive, the last 13 rows of the table, had higher packet loss on the fixed-access connections. Note that the mean per-connection packet loss is more often greater than the overall access-network packet loss, which indicates that smaller connections tend to have higher loss. The mean per-connection packet loss of all countries is 2.2% for fixed and 2.5% for mobile, whereas the mean access-network packet loss of all countries is 1.1% for fixed and 1.8% for mobile.

4.3 Dependence of Connection Size on Packet Loss

We wanted to examine the heuristic notion that higher packet loss leads to smaller connection sizes. From Table 2 and Table 1, we have the average network packet loss and mean connection size, respectively, per country. Figure 2 displays a scatter plot of these values and a fitted linear regression line. Since the few countries with the upper-end packet loss can be considered atypical, Figure 2 shows the subset of countries whose mean packet loss is no more than 3%. The plot is truly scattered; though, by eye one can sense a downward trend, i.e. smaller mean connection size with higher packet loss, for both fixed- and mobile-access. The regression lines are included not because a linear model is a good fit,

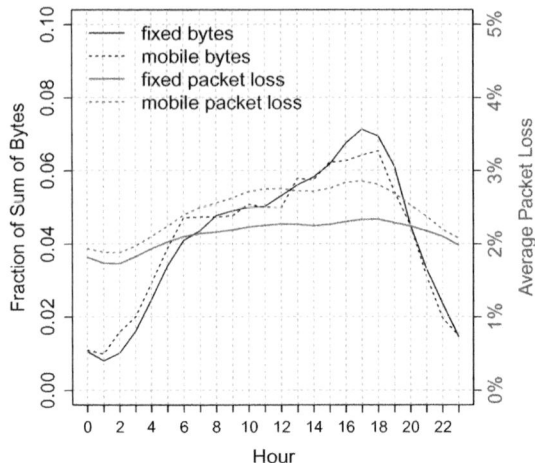

Fig. 3. Daily distribution for size of connections and packet loss, all countries

but to indicate the downward trend. The statistical test on the regression lines having zero slope is rejected with high confidence (p<0.002).

Although the data support the notion that higher packet loss leads to smaller connection size, one's viewpoint of the strength of the trend (-20 KBytes-per-percentage-packet-loss for mobile in Figure 2) is obviously colored by one's prior expectation. Regardless, the plot also clearly shows the great variability. Of particular note are the two countries whose fixed access has high packet loss of at least 4% and relatively high mean connection size of at least 125 KBytes: China and Russia (see Tables 1 and 2).

4.4   Daily Traffic Pattern

We compared the daily demand for both fixed- and mobile-access. Figure 3 shows the fraction of bytes sent in each of the 24 hours of a day, on fixed-access and on mobile-access networks across all countries. Figures for some individual countries are in [6]. We determined the latitude and longitude of the client address, from which we obtained the local time zone relative to GMT, see §3, and thus we could bin the traffic such that the hour "0" corresponds to midnight for the given client. Also shown on the plots is the mean per-connection packet loss in the respective hour. The daily demand pattern for fixed- and mobile-access are very much alike—fixed-access has a slightly higher afternoon peak, and mobile-access has a bit higher proportion the post-midnight early-morning hours. Packet loss on mobile-access is higher than on fixed-access and has a larger increase during the heavy traffic period of the day. As one would expect, the packet loss for both mobile- and fixed-access increases during the busy period of the day. If one considered the regression of the per-hour packet loss on the per-hour fraction of bytes sent, then the hypothesis of zero slope would be rejected with extremely

Table 1. KiloBytes-per-Connection Statistics

Country	3rd Quartile		Mean	
	Fixed	Mobile	Fixed	Mobile
Uruguay	17	16	38	53
Peru	19	19	45	27
Venezuela	18	17	47	39
Sri Lanka	18	16	47	45
El Salvador	18	20	50	44
Pakistan	19	17	52	59
Croatia	18	9	55	19
Malaysia	20	18	55	43
Israel	16	17	57	49
Greece	19	15	59	41
Paraguay	19	17	59	44
Colombia	19	14	59	52
Slovenia	20	9	60	38
Italy	18	17	60	44
Thailand	18	14	62	31
Slovakia	18	17	62	71
Chile	19	17	64	43
Czech Rep.	18	17	67	43
Australia	13	11	68	37
Morocco	20	18	70	50
Hungary	19	16	71	47
South Africa	12	12	72	123
Kuwait	18	20	72	153
Puerto Rico	18	17	74	72
Lithuania	19	18	77	64
Brazil	19	20	78	58
Mexico	18	21	79	36
Spain	16	16	80	49
Singapore	16	15	82	46
New Zealand	16	16	83	40
Hong Kong	18	14	87	65
Portugal	20	19	88	53
Poland	17	16	91	56
Taiwan	13	12	91	77
Ireland	20	17	92	101
Belgium	19	15	95	93
Ukraine	19	14	96	70
France	21	18	102	178
Austria	18	15	104	54
UK	18	16	104	69
Estonia	18	17	107	56
Norway	16	13	111	38
Canada	18	11	113	38
Germany	19	12	122	71
Switzerland	17	11	123	54
Russia	21	16	125	92
Moldova	18	19	129	54
China	19	7	130	64
Netherlands	14	11	135	79
South Korea	6	27	135	131
USA	16	12	152	44

Table 2. Percent Packet Loss Statistics

Country	Mean Packet Loss Per-Connection		Access-Network	
	Fixed	Mobile	Fixed	Mobile
Peru	2.0	5.8	2.0	5.1
Czech Rep.	1.3	4.5	1.0	3.2
Chile	2.0	5.1	1.4	2.7
Moldova	1.1	3.7	0.4	4.7
Colombia	2.3	4.8	1.9	2.2
Poland	1.8	4.2	1.1	1.9
Morocco	3.2	5.4	2.1	3.0
Portugal	1.6	3.7	0.8	3.4
Estonia	1.6	3.7	1.0	2.1
Ukraine	1.6	3.6	1.2	2.7
Hungary	1.8	3.7	1.0	2.0
Brazil	2.3	4.1	1.6	2.4
Croatia	1.4	3.1	1.0	3.8
Norway	1.5	3.2	0.5	3.1
Belgium	1.4	3.1	0.7	0.8
Spain	1.6	3.3	0.9	1.8
Lithuania	1.6	3.3	1.1	2.0
Venezuela	3.6	5.0	2.9	3.7
Greece	1.5	2.9	1.0	2.1
France	1.5	2.9	0.9	0.6
Puerto Rico	3.0	4.3	1.6	4.2
Italy	2.6	3.9	1.5	2.0
Israel	2.1	3.3	1.6	6.8
New Zealand	2.6	3.6	1.5	2.9
Ireland	2.5	3.3	0.9	1.0
Slovakia	2.1	2.9	1.6	1.3
Russia	4.0	4.7	5.2	2.9
South Korea	0.7	1.4	0.4	0.6
Austria	1.4	2.0	0.6	0.9
Canada	1.3	1.9	0.6	1.1
Taiwan	2.1	2.4	1.5	1.0
Hong Kong	1.9	2.4	1.1	1.1
Pakistan	4.8	5.2	4.2	3.5
Germany	1.2	1.6	0.5	4.2
Uruguay	2.9	3.3	2.4	2.3
Australia	2.5	2.9	1.3	1.6
Mexico	2.6	2.8	1.3	2.4
USA	1.9	1.9	0.9	1.4
Sri Lanka	3.5	3.1	3.2	3.3
Switzerland	1.5	1.0	0.6	0.6
Singapore	3.8	3.2	4.8	2.6
Netherlands	1.2	0.6	0.5	0.2
Slovenia	1.7	0.8	1.1	0.8
UK	2.8	1.7	0.9	1.0
Paraguay	5.4	4.0	5.0	3.6
El Salvador	5.1	3.1	5.5	2.6
Kuwait	3.0	0.7	2.3	0.2
South Africa	3.4	1.0	3.5	0.6
Malaysia	6.0	3.5	6.5	4.2
Thailand	3.9	0.3	3.3	0.5
China	7.4	3.8	4.0	3.5

high confidence (p<1e-6) for both mobile- and fixed-access. The correlation of packet loss with the fraction of bytes sent is 0.94 for mobile-access and 0.95 for fixed-access.

5   Conclusions

We examined the number of bytes-per-connection, and packet loss based on packet retransmissions from a sampling of logs from servers of Akamai Technologies. Regarding to the original question of whether the more adverse conditions on mobile-access networks leads to shorter connections, the rough, first-order answer is "yes"; though, a fuller answer is much more nuanced. One caution to keep in mind is that the statistical analysis of the present study does not prove a causal relationship. Tables 1 and 2 do show that on a per-country basis, packet loss is higher and the mean connection size is smaller on mobile-access for most countries; but there are noted exceptions. From the viewpoint of distributions, we found that the difference between the bytes-per-connection for mobile-access versus fixed-access, as well as the packet-loss distributions, was statistically significant, for all countries we analyzed. However, when plotted, the visual difference is typically small. Also, for some countries, the mobile-access had the larger connections.

In a scatter plot of per-country mean connection size versus mean packet loss, there is a statistically significant trend of smaller connections having higher packet loss for both mobile- and fixed-access, though there is great variability. Aggregating across counties, we found that the daily demand variation is about the same for mobile- and fixed-access, and for both, the packet loss does increase during the busy period of the day, though the increase of mobile-access is greater, suggesting greater sensitivity to the increased demand, that is, a greater likelihood of constrained capacity. Though, as reported in [6], some countries have little to no daily variation in packet loss. We also found per-connection packet loss for both fixed- and mobile-access is often greater than the overall access-network packet loss, indicating smaller connections having higher loss.

Similar to our result of negative correlation between connection size and packet loss rate, bit rate had a consistent positive correlation and jitter above certain limit had a negative correlation with the length of Skype VoIP calls [4]. Also, within certain bounds, round-trip time (RTT), queueing delay, and packet loss rate had negative correlations with session lengths of an online multiplayer game [3]. In general, adverse effects on the quality of service (QoS) seem to decrease the intensity of usage of that service.

Self-selection explains partially why mobile-access connections are typically smaller than fixed-access connections. Users may prefer not to stream long video clips, engage in large downloads, or do other high volume transactions over mobile-access connections. Prevalence of high-speed mobile-access connections could lead to more traffic over mobile-access. In other words, a complementary effect would occur, where higher speed of mobile-access would enable more large-volume transactions.

Analyzing the root causes for our results would require investigating in detail the status of network infrastructure together with device and service implementation and usage in each country, which are out of the scope of this study. One could speculate there are significant differences among those factors across countries. The disparity between fixed-access and mobile-access across countries could be used in simulations or modeling of network performance.

Acknowledgments. During this work, MH was a Visiting Student at MIT CSAIL. MH's work was supported by FICNIA and TEKES. We would like to thank Steven Bauer, David Clark, Rubén García, Tuomo Komulainen, William Lehr, Antti Riikonen, Jesse Sowell, Stephen Woodrow, and anonymous reviewers for their assistance and comments. Any opinions expressed, and any errors are solely the responsibility of the authors.

References

1. Akamai: Akamai's Edgescape Geo-Location Service. Tech. rep. (2010)
2. Akamai: State of the Internet 2Q/2010. Tech. rep. (2010)
3. Chen, K.T., Huang, P., Wang, G.S., Huang, C.Y., Lei, C.L.: On the Sensitivity of Online Game Playing Time to Network QoS. In: IEEE INFOCOM (2006)
4. Chen, K.T., Huang, C.Y., Huang, P., Lei, C.L.: Quantifying Skype User Satisfaction. SIGCOMM Comput. Commun. Rev. 36(4), 399–410 (2006)
5. Cisco: Cisco Visual Networking Index: Forecast and Methodology, 2009-2014. Tech. rep. (2010)
6. Heikkinen, M.V.J., Berger, A.W.: Comparison of User Traffic Characteristics on Mobile-Access versus Fixed-Access Networks. Tech. Rep. MIT-CSAIL-TR-2011-028, MIT CSAIL (2011), http://hdl.handle.net/1721.1/62579
7. Hibberd, M.: Mobile Data Traffic Almost Triples Year on Year. Informa (2010)
8. Hossfeld, T., Tutschku, K., Andersen, F.U.: Mapping of File-Sharing onto Mobile Environments: Feasibility and Performance of eDonkey with GPRS. In: IEEE WCNC, pp. 2453–2458 (2005)
9. Kalden, R., Ekström, H.: Searching for Mobile Mice and Elephants in GPRS Networks. SIGMOBILE Mob. Comput. Commun. Rev. 8(4), 37–46 (2004)
10. Sandvine: Fall 2010 Global Internet Phenomena. Tech. rep. (2010)
11. Svoboda, P.: Measurement and Modelling of Internet Traffic over 2.5 and 3G Cellular Core Networks. Ph.D. thesis, Vienna University of Technology (2008)

BackStreamDB: A Distributed System for Backbone Traffic Monitoring Providing Arbitrary Measurements in Real-Time

Christian Lyra[1], Carmem S. Hara[2], and Elias P. Duarte Jr.[2]

[1] Brazilian Research Network (RNP) – Point of Presence at Parana State
P.O.Box 19037 81531-990 Curitiba-PR, Brazil
[2] Department of Informatics – Federal University of Parana
P.O.Box 19081 81531-990 Curitiba-PR, Brazil
`lyra@pop-pr.rnp.br`, {`carmem,elias`}`@inf.ufpr.br`

Abstract. Monitoring the traffic of wide area networks consisting of several autonomous systems connected through a high-speed backbone is a challenge due to the huge amount of traffic. Keeping logs for obtaining measurements is unfeasible. This work describes a distributed real-time strategy for backbone traffic monitoring that does not employ logs and allows arbitrary metrics to be collected about the traffic of the backbone as a whole. Traffic is sampled by monitors that are distributed across the backbone and are accessed by a Stream Processing Engine (SPE). Besides the distributed monitoring architecture, we present an implementation (BackStreamDB) that was deployed on a national backbone. Case studies are described that show the system flexibility. Experiments are reported in which we evaluated the amount of traffic that can be handled.

1 Introduction

Consider a wide area network, consisting of several Autonomous Systems (AS) connected through a high-speed backbone. Obtaining information about the network as a whole and about individual components, in particular traffic information, is the first step for most of network management tasks. Traffic information is important for evaluating the performance, monitoring the security and for generating profiles that can be used by accounting systems. Although a combination of polling and alarms offered by traditional network management protocols can be effectively used in certain limited settings, it does not scale well, and cannot be used for monitoring traffic in large backbones.

One way to gather information about network traffic is by using a sniffer. Sniffers are able to store and decode all network traffic they see. Although this may allow the extraction of any type of traffic information, in order to be deployed at a wide area backbone sniffers should obtain the complete network traffic, and the amount of data to be processed can be overwhelming.

To solve this problem, network vendors have been developing for several years products that are effective in gathering information on network traffic. Protocols like Netflow[1] and Sflow [13] obtain information at the packet flow level. A "flow"

---

[1] `http://www.cisco.com/web/go/netflow`

N. Taft and F. Ricciato (Eds.): PAM 2012, LNCS 7192, pp. 42–52, 2012.

is defined as a set of packets of a given protocol flowing between two endpoints, each consisting of an IP address and transport-layer port. After the flow information is obtained, it is *stored* in secondary memory, and tools like flow-tools[2] and ntop[3] can be employed for obtaining information about the traffic. This approach for network monitoring has several drawbacks. First, the majority of existing tools require flow data to be stored in order to be analyzed. Depending on the volume of traffic, this would demand considerable storage space for keeping logs, and possibly a tool for managing the log size, such as RRD[4]. In addition, since data flows are not processed at the time they are processed by routers, flow measurements are not provided in real-time. This may have an impact on important network administration tasks, such as the detection of traffic anomalies generated by port sweeps or port scans. Second, both ntop and flow-tools are based on a limited set of predefined metrics. Although they are meant to cover a large number of network administration needs, it is quite common for network administrators to develop scripts in order to obtain additional monitoring information. However, this approach does not exempt flow traffic from being stored, and does not provide results in real-time.

In this paper we propose a distributed architecture for integrating Stream Processing Engines (SPE) and flow monitoring tools within a framework developed for large-scale backbones consisting of multiple autonomous systems. SPEs [10] were developed to provide the same basic features found in traditional Database Management Systems, but operations are executed in real time on continuous data streams. In our case the data stream is the network traffic itself. We have implemented a system, called BackStreamDB, based on the proposed architecture. In this system, metrics of interest to the network administrator are expressed in a high level SQL-like language. This allows arbitrary queries to be issued about the traffic that is flowing across the *whole* backbone, in which flow data sources may be geographically distributed. Query results are provided in real time, and can refer to either a particular segment, or to a set of (or all) autonomous systems of the backbone. This approach of defining metrics as queries allows modifications and improvements to be easily made on the fly by just executing a different query.

In addition, one of the most significant contributions of the system is that arbitrary measures can be obtained without storing any traffic logs. As the amount of traffic in these systems is huge, existing passive monitoring strategies that rely on logs [4,8] are hardly able to offer similar functionality. Another key advantage of the proposed strategy is extensibility. In its current implementation, BackStreamDB monitors a backbone using Netflow records as source data. It extends our previous work [11], in which we propose a system to monitor local segments at the packet level. Thus, the system can provide a general framework for monitoring a network, in which the administrator issues queries to gather measurements from both local and wide area networks using the same language.

---

[2] http://www.splintered.net/sw/flow-tools/

[3] http://www.ntop.org

[4] http://ee-sta~ethz.ch/~oetiker/webtools/rrdtool/

BackStreamDB has been tested on the Brazilian RNP backbone[5], showing the feasibility of the proposed approach. Case studies are described that show the system flexibility. Experiments are reported in which we evaluated the amount of traffic that can be handled. The main contributions of this paper are:

- An architecture for distributed traffic monitoring based on a Stream Processing Engine and flow processing protocols, integrated to a multi-AS backbone traffic monitoring framework;
- Development of a distributed traffic monitoring system based on the proposed architecture. It allows arbitrary queries about the traffic on a wide area backbone to be processed in real time;
- Experimental deployment of the system on the Brazilian national RNP backbone and analysis of results on real datasets.

The rest of this paper is organized as follows. Section 2 presents an architecture for traffic monitoring based on SPEs, and BackStreamDB, the system built based on the proposed architecture. Section 3 presents experimental results and Section 4 describes related work. The conclusion follows in Section 5.

2   An Architecture for Backbone Traffic Monitoring

The distributed monitoring architecture we propose allows a network administrator to issue arbitrary queries to obtain network traffic information from a multi-AS backbone. Different granularity are permitted as monitored objects may range from individual segments to the backbone as a whole. Data is obtained from multiple flow data sources that are geographically distributed across the network, and traffic information is obtained and processed in a distributed fashion in real time. This strategy is scalable, as it is possible to accommodate increasingly larger traffic loads by changing the system configuration to distribute data to other existing nodes in the network.

The architecture is shown in Figure 1. SPE (Stream Processing Engine) nodes are deployed for processing queries, and the system has three other main components: *acquisition* modules, *universal receiver (ureceiver)*, and *global catalog*, that are described below. *Acquisition modules* are in charge of receiving flow data and of converting them to SPE conformant format. The data is then sent to one or more SPE nodes for query processing. An SPE node can either process the entire query or forward partial results to be processed by another SPE node. The final query results are sent to *ureceiver*. The *acquisition modules* are thus responsible for the interface between data sources and SPEs. A *ureceiver* (universal receiver) is responsible for the interface between SPEs and visualization tools. Query results can also be stored for historical purposes. In short, *ureceiver* is responsible for consuming data produced by SPEs and forwarding them to appropriate applications. Information about queries that are being processed by SPEs are stored on the third component of the system: the *global catalog*. For each query the catalog maintains the query definition and information specifying the SPE nodes which are executing the query.

---

[5] http://www.rnp.br

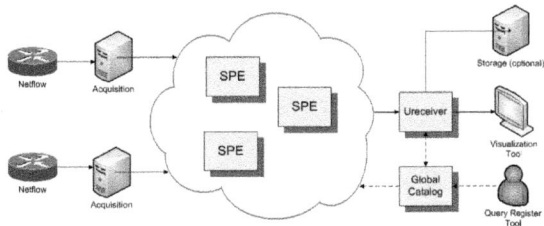

Fig. 1. Architecture for traffic monitoring based on SPE and flow protocol

There is a large spectrum of possible system configurations, ranging from a fully distributed system in which each module is assigned to a distinct node, to a centralized system, in which a single node runs all modules. Ideally, when data sources are geographically distributed, both an *acquisition module* and an SPE node should be deployed close to the source. In this way, source data can be locally filtered by the SPE node, reducing the volume of data to be transmitted among SPE nodes and the *ureceiver*.

Query results can be either accessed in real time by a network administrator with visualization tools, or can also be stored if required. Since the system does not log flow data, but only query results that have been individually specified by the administrator, BackStreamDB can drastically reduce the storage cost. Query definitions are fed to the system by a *Query Register Tool* in a high-level query language, which makes queries easy to maintain.

2.1 BackStreamDB

A distributed monitoring system called BackStreamDB was implemented based on the proposed architecture. Borealis [1] was chosen as the SPE. The main reason for this choice is that its distributed nature enables a set of SPE nodes to be deployed across the network, and in particular, close to data sources. The Borealis component called `BigGiantHead` is used to deploy a query on SPE nodes. The `BigGiantHead` can be executed in either transient or "daemon" mode. In transient mode, the application is invoked only to send control data to SPEs, and then quits. Control data include assignment of query tasks to SPEs, and data flow information. In "daemon" mode it continuously listens for query invocation requests and sends the control data accordingly to SPEs.

Currently, BackStreamDB processes Netflow data. In the current system, the *acquisition module* obtains data using the *New Netflow Collector (NNFC)*[6]. NNFC is a tool for capturing and storing Netflow data sent by a router. An NNFC plugin was developed to allow communication using Internet Process Communication (IPC) with `flowsender`, an application we developed for translating and forwarding data to Borealis SPEs.

BackStreamDB can be easily extended to support other formats besides Netflow. A new input format can be configured in a way that is similar to defining a new schema for databases, or wrappers to exchange data between applications.

---

[6] http://sourceforge.net/projects/nnfc

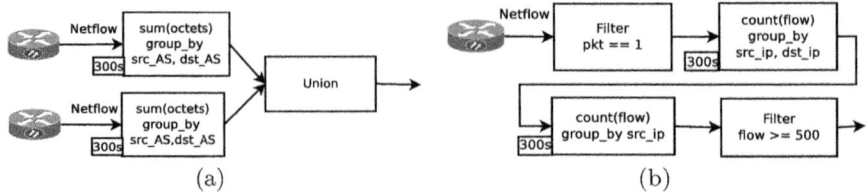

Fig. 2. (a)Query that generates a traffic matrix. (b)Anomaly detection query.

This process involves: specification of the Borealis input format, and development of an application for translating data collected from the source to the new format in the acquisition module.

Query results produced by SPE nodes are sent to a ureceiver. In the standard Borealis distribution it is necessary to develop a new receiver application for each distinct query result format. This is because Borealis outputs results in binary format, and the receiver is responsible for decoding these values into typed output fields. We have changed this approach by coding the ureceiver with the capability to *infer* the output format based on the query definition. As a result, the system does not have to be recompiled when new query results are defined, as in the standard Borealis distribution. When invoked, ureceiver waits for a connection from a Borealis SPE, and when new query results arrive, they are output either in text or graphical form by a visualization tool.

For the query language, we employ the same language adopted by Borealis, in which queries are expressed in an XML document, containing input, output, and query definitions. BackStreamDB's *query register tool* reads the XML document, stores the information in the *global catalog*, and communicates with *BigGiant-Head* through the network in order to deploy the execution of queries on different nodes. For showing the generality of the proposed architecture and system, we next present how one can easily build a traffic matrix and detect traffic anomaly using BackStreamDB.

Traffic Matrix. A traffic matrix shows the amount of traffic transmitted among all possible pairs of nodes of a given network. It provides useful information for defining routing policies and for taking traffic engineering decisions. Building a traffic matrix with BackStreamDB is simply a matter of configuring the system to aggregate the records by source and destination AS while summing up the octets, as depicted in Figure 2(a). Here, we use a graphical representation of a query, in which each box executes an operation supported by the query language. First, the query computes the sum of octets in Netflow records with the same source and destination autonomous systems, src_AS and dst_AS, respectively, generating a result every 300 seconds. Then, a union operator is applied to combine the results in a single output stream.

Traffic Anomaly Detection. It is possible to use BackStreamDB to detect traffic anomalies such as port sweeps or port scans. A very common type of network probing consists of sending packets to all hosts on a given network in order to find the active and working ones. This probe can be characterized by packet flows consisting of one single packet; that is, usually the probing host sends just one ICMP or UDP packet. A query for detecting this kind of anomaly is shown in Figure 2(b). First, flows are filtered, selecting only those that consist of one single packet (pkt == 1). These flows are then grouped by source (src_ip) and destination IPs (dst_ip). In order to count the number of distinct destinations of packet flows sent from a single source, we regroup them considering only the source IP. The result is the number of one packet flows sent by distinct source addresses. This result can then be filtered considering a given threshold. In our example, only source addresses issuing at least 500 probes are considered suspicious, and are reported in the query result.

These two examples show the expressive power of the system's query language, and the flexibility of the proposed system, which has several applications. In the next section, we present experimental results that show that it is feasible to deploy BackStreamDB for monitoring the traffic of a wide area network.

3   Experimental Evaluation

In order to validate BackStreamDB three experiments were executed and are described below. These experiments show the amount of traffic the system is able to handle in terms of Netflow records.

Experiment 1: Single Node, Synthetic Traffic. The first experiment involved a single node processing synthetic traffic, which we fully controlled in order to check whether results generated by BackStreamDB were as expected. This experiment also allowed the evaluation of how much traffic could be processed by an SPE. Two hosts were employed, a processing node and a client node. The processing node was an Athlon XP 2600+ with 1 GB of RAM. We implemented and used a tool (dummysender) for generating synthetic Netflow data. The client node, which executed the BigGiantHead, dummysender, flowsender and ureceiver applications, was a 900MHz Celeron CPU with 2GB of RAM. Both computers were connected to a 100Mbps Ethernet LAN. The traffic rate generated ranged from 1,000 to 4,000 Netflow records per second, using steps of 1,000 records. The SPE executed a simple but useful query which computes the number of packets processed within an interval (window) of 10 seconds. Since we knew the expected results in advance, it was straightforward to verify the results. The experiment was repeated 10 times for each record rate, and the results were accurate for all record rates up to 35,000 records per second, approximately. At rates above this point the SPE entered an error state and crashed. The same experiment was later executed using a faster processor, a 2GHz Core 2 Duo machine with 1GB of RAM. In this case we were able to achieve accurate results for rates up to 60,000 records per second.

Experiment 2: Multiple Nodes, Synthetic Traffic. In order to simulate an environment similar to the Brazilian RNP backbone, with several geographically distributed Autonomous Systems, we have deployed multiple SPE nodes, each of them capturing a distinct stream of Netflow records, as illustrated in Figure 3(a). Similar to the first experiment, we considered a synthetic load generated by dummysender, and employed 3 processing nodes and one client node. The

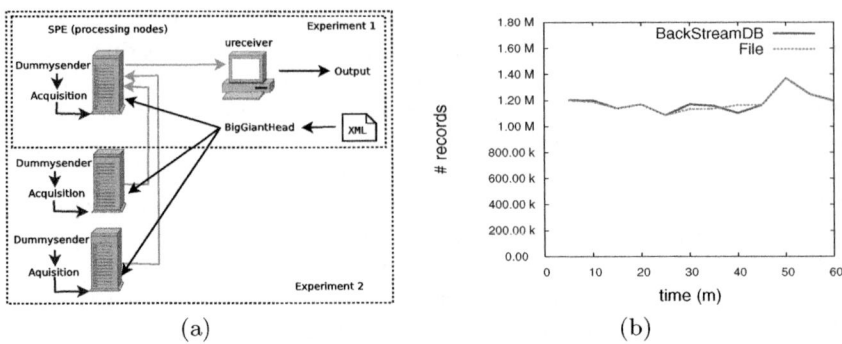

Fig. 3. (a)Experiments with synthetic traffic. (b)Results generated on real traffic.

processing nodes were based on Athlon XP processors (models 2600+, 2400+ and 2200+) each with 1GB of RAM. The client node (executing `BigGiantHead` and `ureceiver` applications) was the same one employed in the previous experiment, featuring a 900MHz Celeron processor with 2GB of RAM. All computers were connected to a 100Mbps Ethernet LAN.

The same query employed in the first experiment was issued in this case: the number of packets processed within 10 seconds window. However, in this experiment each node processes only the locally generated records. Partial results were then sent by each processing node to a node elected to produce the final result. On each processing node we generated traffic at a rate of 30,000 records per second, which was correctly summed up by the elected node, which produced the output of 90,000 records at all repetitions of the experiment. Observe that similar rates are expected for processing queries as the ones illustrated in Figures 2(a) and 2(b). For 2(a), the grouping and sum of octets could be locally executed at each processing node, and only the union of all results at the client node. For distributing the query on Figure 2(b), the filtering and the first grouping and counting operations could be executed locally at each processing node, while the second aggregation and filtering operations at the client. This experiment results show that BackStreamDB scales well, and is capable of processing heavier traffic loads by adding new processing nodes to the system.

Experiment 3: Multiple Nodes, Real Traffic. The goal of the third experiment was to evaluate the tool with a real traffic load. This experiment was conducted at the Brazilian Research Network (RNP), using traffic flow data collected at the Parana state Point of Presence (PoP-PR). Traffic information was collected with `Nprobe`, an application that collects traffic from a mirrored port of a border switch, and outputs a Netflow stream. `Nprobe` was configured to send a copy of the Netflow stream to our *acquisition* application, and also to an application for storing the data. The processor that collects Netflow streams produces output data in intervals of 5 minutes, the standard window size for this kind of application. We have issued queries to generate results in the same window size by BackStreamDB. This allows a straightforward verification of the results, with a direct comparison with the expected results generated from stored data. The real traffic load differs from the synthetic load of Experiments 1 and 2 described above because of its high variance. While the synthetic load is a continuous stream, the real load oscillates from very low rates to occasional bursts containing a large number of packets. Records were sent to BackStreamDB at intervals of 30 seconds.

The traffic processed by Nprobe was around 1Gbps, which corresponds to 100,000 packets per second. When this traffic is transformed to Netflow, about one million records are generated every 5 minutes. We used the same query of the other experiments. The processing node was a 2GHz Core 2 Duo CPU with 1GB of RAM. Figure 3(b) shows the total number of records produced by BackStreamDB and also the values obtained by processing the Netflow files for an interval of one hour. It can be observed that the results are not identical throughout the experiment. There are two reasons for this difference. First, there is a small difference on the total number of records stored on the file, and processed by BackStreamDB. While BackStreamDB processed 14,160,930 records during an hour, the file contained 14,799,980 records, resulting in a difference of 0.1% records, possibly due to the loss of a few UDP packets, which is the transport protocol employed to carry Netflow data. The second reason is that the application that collects Netflow records uses the machine local time to determine its window, while BackStreamDB uses the timestamp from the record itself. So it is possible that the set of records processed in each system on a given time window is not the same. This can be evidenced on the graphic, which shows a smaller number of records in a time frame, followed by a time frame with larger number of records. However, during the entire experiment, this difference was at most 5.2%, which happened around the 40th minute. This experiment showed that BackStreamDB was able to monitor the traffic of a high-speed national backbone, providing real time measurements that were consistent with the ones generated from stored data.

4   Related Work

Several existing network management and traffic monitoring tools can be considered to be related to this work. An extensive list can be found in [6]. Among the tools that process Netflow, one of the first distributed as open source is cflowd[7], which later originated flowscan[8]. In [8] the authors argue that tools for packet analysis do not scale well for high speed networks and propose a framework for monitoring backbones in real time which is based on Netflow. The framework has a centralized architecture, and requires users to write plugins for each monitoring task. In [12], a tool which collects Netflow data and export them in pcap format is described. Such data can then be used as input to Wireshark[9] to obtain analytical information. Ntop[10] is a tool that can be used both for packet analysis and for flow management, using a Netflow/Sflow plugin. It is possible to generate

---

[7] http://www.caida.org/tools/measurement/cflowd
[8] http://www.caida.org/tools/utilities/flowscan/
[9] http://www.wireshark.org
[10] http://www.ntop.org

various types of reports and graphics using Ntop, but they are limited to the predefined metrics provided by the tool, i.e. arbitrary queries are not supported. Another system for traffic monitoring based on Netflow is presented in [4]. That system captures Netflow records which are then stored in an Oracle Database. Databases allow arbitrary queries to be issued on the stored data. However, this approach still requires a considerable amount of storage, as opposed to on-the-fly stream processing. The authors of SMART [15] argue that traditional Netflow tools that store collected data on disk for later processing are not efficient for large-scale network traffic monitoring. They propose an in memory storage in order to process data efficiently. The reported results in terms of Netflow records processed per second - thirty thousand records per second - is very close to what we have achieved using an SPE, as detailed in Section 3.

Borealis is a second generation distributed SPE. Other prototypes have been developed in the context of TelegraphCQ [5] and STREAM [3] projects. Gigas-cope [7] is a system which uses an SPE tailored for high speed network mon-itoring. Although reported results are promising, Gigascope is a proprietary (AT&T's) commercial product. Motivated by the possibility of developing an open source SPE for traffic monitoring, the authors of [14] describe a case study using TelegraphCQ SPE [5]. It involved a functionality analysis to determine whether the SPE can be used to provide the same metrics of T-RAT, a tool developed for analyzing TCP packet traces. The results obtained in terms of traffic volume were modest, but it can be considered a seminal work, in which a single centralized SPE is applied for network management. MaD-WiSe [2] is a distributed monitoring system for managing data streams generated by wire-less sensor networks. Our previous work, PaQueT [11], has been proposed to monitor a single network segment, generating packet level metrics. Moreover, PaQueT has not been designed as a *distributed* system in which modules with specific functionalities can be spread over a wide area network. Some of the main features of BackStreamDB include the following: it allows data gathering from multiple data sources and features distributed processing at multiple nodes. It is also based on an architecture with separate modules for data acquisition and query result treatment, and is able to process data in Netflow format, considering the *whole* backbone.

5   Conclusion

In this paper we proposed an architecture for real time backbone traffic moni-toring that provides arbitrary measurements about individual segments or the backbone as a whole. The strategy is based on both flow protocols and stream processing engines and does not require traffic logs to be stored. The distributed nature of the proposed system is scalable as depending on the amount of traffic, more nodes can be deployed for monitoring tasks. BackStreamDB is an imple-mentation of the proposed strategy, based on Borealis SPE and Netflow. Back-StreamDB was deployed and validated on the Brazilian national RNP backbone. An experimental study involving both synthetic as well as real traffic shows that the approach is feasible and dependable, generating consistent results in both settings. BackStreamDB was able to process a workload of one million Netflow records of real traffic in intervals of five minutes. To highlight the system functionality in order to show how it can help network administrators to fulfill their tasks, case studies were presented for computing a traffic matrix, and detecting traffic signatures.

We are currently developing a version of BackStreamDB to be a service provider in the PerfSONAR framework [9], a service-oriented architecture for multi-domain network monitoring.

Acknowledgments. We thank the Brazilian National Research Network, RNP, for supporting the deployment of the proposed system through Working Group GT-BackStreamDB. This work was partially supported by grant 304013/2009-9 from the Brazilian Research Agency (CNPq).

References

1. Abadi, D.J., Ahmad, Y., Balazinska, M., Çentintemel, U., Cherniack, M., Hwang, J.H., Lindner, W., Maskey, A.S., Rasin, A., Ryvkina, E., Tatbul, N., Xing, Y., Zdonik, S.: The Design of the Borealis Stream Processing Engine. In: Proc. of the Conf. on Innovative Data Systems Research, pp. 277–289 (2005)
2. Amato, G., Chessa, S., Vairo, C.: MaD-WiSe: A Distributed Stream Management System for Wireless Sensor Networks. Software Practice and Experience 40(5), 431–451 (2010)
3. Arasu, A., Babcock, B., Babu, S., Cieslewicz, J., Datar, M., Ito, K., Motwani, R., Srivastava, U., Widom, J.: STREAM: The Stanford Data Stream Management System. IEEE Data Engineering Bulletin 26(1), 19–26 (2003)
4. Bin, L., Chuang, L., Jian, Q., Jianping, H., Ungsunan, P.: A NetFlow-based Flow Analisys and Monitoring System in Enterprise Networks. Computer Networks 52(5), 1074–1092 (2008)
5. Chandrasekaran, S., Cooper, O., Deshpande, A., Franklin, M.J., Hellerstein, J.M., Hong, W., Krishnamurthy, S., Madden, S., Raman, V., Reiss, F., Shah, M.: TelegraphCQ: Continuous Dataflow Processing for an Uncertain World. In: Proc. of the Conf. on Innovative Data Systems Research (2003)
6. Cottrell, L.: Network Monitoring Tools (2011), http://www.slac.stanford.edu/xorg/nmtf/nmtf-tools.html
7. Cranor, C., Johnson, T., Spataschek, O.: Gigascope: A Stream Database for Network Applications. In: Proc. of the ACM SIGMOD Int. Conf. on Management of Data Conference, pp. 647–651 (2003)
8. Dubendorfer, T., Wagner, A., Plattner, B.: A Framework for Real-Time Worm Attack Detection and Backbone Monitoring. In: Proc. of the IEEE Int. Workshop on Critical Infrastructure Protection, pp. 3–12 (2005)
9. Hanemann, A., Boote, J.W., Boyd, E.L., Durand, J., Kudarimoti, L., Lapacz, R., Swany, D.M., Trocha, S., Zurawski, J.: PerfSONAR: A Service Oriented Architecture for Multi-domain Network Monitoring. In: Benatallah, B., Casati, F., Traverso, P. (eds.) ICSOC 2005. LNCS, vol. 3826, pp. 241–254. Springer, Heidelberg (2005)
10. Koudas, N., Srivastava, D.: Data Stream Query Processing: A Tutorial. In: Proc. of the Int. Conf. on Very Large Data Bases, p. 1149 (2003)
11. Ligocki, N., Gomes, C.L., Hara, C.: A Flexible Network Monitoring Tool based on a Data Stream Management System. In: Proc. of the IEEE Symp. on Computers and Communications, pp. 800–805 (2008)

12. Munz, G., Carle, G.: Distributed Network Analysis Using TOPAS and Wireshark. In: Network Operations and Management Symp. Workshops, pp. 161–164 (2008)
13. Phaal, P., Panchen, S., McKee, N.: RFC 3176: InMon Corporation's sFlow: A Method for Monitoring Traffic in Switched and Routed Networks (2001)
14. Plagemann, T., Goebel, V., Bergamini, A., Tolu, G., Urvoy-Keller, G., Biersack, E.W.: Using Data Stream Management Systems for Traffic Analysis – A Case Study. In: Barakat, C., Pratt, I. (eds.) PAM 2004. LNCS, vol. 3015, pp. 215–226. Springer, Heidelberg (2004)
15. Zhou, A., Yan, Y., Gong, X., Chang, J., Dai, D.: SMART: A System for Online Monitoring Large Volumes of Network Traffic. In: Proc. of the IEEE Int. Conf. on Data Engineering, pp. 1576–1579 (2008)

A Sequence-Oriented Stream Warehouse Paradigm for Network Monitoring Applications

Lukasz Golab[1], Theodore Johnson[2], Subhabrata Sen[2], and Jennifer Yates[2]

[1] University of Waterloo, Canada
[2] AT&T Labs - Research, Florham Park, NJ, USA

Abstract. Network administrators are faced with the increasingly challenging task of monitoring their network's health in real time, drawing upon diverse and voluminous measurement data feeds and extensively mining them. The role of database systems in network monitoring has traditionally been that of data repositories; even if an application uses a database, the application logic is implemented using external programs. While such programs are flexible, they tend to be ad-hoc, opaque, inefficient and hard to maintain over time. In this paper, we propose a new way of implementing network monitoring applications: directly within a database as continually updated tables defined using a declarative query language (SQL). We also address a crucial technical issue with realizing this approach: SQL was designed for set-oriented data transformations, but network monitoring involves sequence-oriented analysis. To solve this problem, we propose an extension to SQL that makes sequence-oriented analysis easier to express and faster to evaluate. Using a prototype implementation in a large-scale production data warehouse, we demonstrate how the declarative sequence-oriented query language simplifies application development and how the associated system optimizations improve application performance.

1 Introduction

Managing a complex network requires tools to rapidly detect and troubleshoot issues. This involves monitoring of network topology and configuration, network element status changes (traps) and logs (syslogs), individual network element and end-to-end performance measurements, control plane state and events, traffic measurements and events from other network layers (e.g., layer one) [7,14,16]. Understanding what is happening within the network, particularly during an incident, requires drawing upon data from these diverse sources. Collecting and exploring these data at scale (hundreds of millions of records a day) is extremely challenging [5,6,12,13].

There are many advantages to harnessing database and data warehouse technologies to maintain network data. One operational example is the DataDepot streaming warehouse system [8] that maintains the Darkstar data repository [11]. Darkstar collects a wide variety of data and support many production applications, both for real-time alerting and off-line data mining.

However, data warehouses have traditionally been used only as data repositories. That is, application developers extract data from the warehouse using queries, but place the application logic in external programs. These programs tend to be opaque, inefficient, ad-hoc, and contain many hidden hard-coded links. Repeating such an analysis

N. Taft and F. Ricciato (Eds.): PAM 2012, LNCS 7192, pp. 53–63, 2012.

after a hiatus of a year generally ranges from being difficult to untenable. Since the data are processed outside the warehouse, the complexity of these scripts also increases as data structures and associated logic have to be created for handling data management functions, duplicating what a warehouse can already natively support. Examples include updating relevant data structures and indices with new data, and propagating the impact of new data on any dependent processes.

In this paper, we propose a new approach that deploys real-time network monitoring applications directly *within the warehouse*; note that our notion of real-time refers to processing and reacting to new data as they arrive. The idea is to translate the data processing steps of the application into declarative queries whose results are continually maintained as database tables. This approach can simplify application development and management, and improve performance and availability (more details in Section 3).

The first challenge in realizing this idea is to provide similar performance to an optimized external program. However, while databases can save the results of queries into temporary tables, these tables are static, or, at best, they can only be updated periodically. This is suitable only for off-line operations that take a complete data set as input and return a transformed data set as output. On the other hand, real-time applications operate in stream-in-stream-out mode, incrementally processing new data and producing new results. As we will show, recent advances in DataDepot make it possible to load new data as they arrive and continuously propagate changes throughout the warehouse.

The second issue is to provide a query language for expressing network monitoring applications. The standard SQL database language is geared towards set-oriented data transformations. However, network monitoring is mostly sequence-oriented. For example, we may want to notify users if some metric increases by at least a certain amount relative to its *previous* value, or if it stays above a critical threshold for several consecutive time periods. In this paper, we propose, and experimentally evaluate within a production stream warehouse, a novel extension of SQL to natively support sequence-oriented applications at scale.

While there exist related work on various components of our solution such as stream warehousing and sequence processing, this work is the first to put these together into a large-scale production system that can handle the data rates and latency requirements of real-time network monitoring. To summarize our goals and contributions, 1) we aim to inform the networking community of a new way to implement network monitoring applications that exploits the state-of-the-art in data management technologies, 2) we propose a novel extension of SQL that makes it easier to express and optimize sequence-oriented applications, and 3) as proof of concept, we implement the proposed extensions in DataDepot and build an operational network monitoring application. The application produces real-time alerts when various performance metrics such as end-to-end packet loss exceed specified thresholds for sustained periods of time. We demonstrate how the declarative sequence-oriented language simplifies application development, and we experimentally show a threefold performance improvement as compared to expressing the application logic using the existing set-oriented version of DataDepot.

This work is the outcome of an inter-disciplinary collaboration between networking and database researchers to develop easy-to-manage, scalable, data intensive network monitoring applications. We hope that the ideas and benefits demonstrated in this paper will encourage researchers and practitioners to explore and exploit emerging database technologies in network management.

2   Background and Related Work

A conventional data warehouse provides extensive data storage and analytics facilities, along with the ability to manage deeply nested levels of pre-computed query results (termed *materialized views*). However, view updates are normally performed in a large batch. This enables many optimizations but does not provide the data freshness needed by network monitoring applications. By contrast, a Data Stream Management System (DSMS) operates on data on-the-fly, providing fast response; see, e.g., [4]. However, a DSMS is designed to operate in-memory, and stores only a short segment of the most recent data. Streaming extensions of SQL have also been proposed [10], but they focus on set operations over windows of recent history rather than sequential operations.

DataDepot [8] is a *stream warehouse* that combines aspects of a DSMS and conventional data warehouse by providing very long term storage as well as continuous updates of materialized views. Other stream warehouses include Moirae [3], TelegraphCQ/FastBit [18], and Everest [2]. However, none of these can natively support sequence operators or real-time view updates; Everest enables ad-hoc real-time analysis by loading *raw* data in real-time, but re-computes views periodically, while Moirae and FastBit focus on matching new data against similar historical data. Furthermore, there has been work on sequential operators in the context of event processing (see, e.g., [1]), but it focuses on complex pattern matching rather than guaranteeing high performance.

The data flow through a stream warehouse begins with *raw data*, such as SNMP polls, traffic summaries or system logs, which are loaded into a first level of materialized views often called *base tables*. Updates to the base tables then propagate through the remaining materialized views often called *derived tables*. Since views can store terabytes of data spanning years, an efficient mechanism for updating them is a critical component of a stream warehouse. A common mechanism is to *temporally partition* each view according to a record timestamp. Then, only those partitions which are affected by new data need to be updated. In Figure 1, we illustrate the propagation of new data from a raw source, to a base table, then through two levels of dependent (derived) views. The base and dependent tables are all temporally partitioned by some criteria. We have also determined the flow of data from a source partition to a dependent partition - see [8] for a discussion of how to infer these data flows. New records have arrived in the raw data source, which, when processed, only affect two partitions in the base table (the most recent data, and some late in-the-past data). The two updated partitions in the base table trigger updates only to two partitions in the first materialized view, and transitively to two partitions in the second materialized view.

We have developed a number of features for DataDepot which facilitate near real-time data loading:

– We want to update views frequently, but we do not want queries against the views to be "blocked" by updates. We added an inexpensive Multi-Version Concurrency Control that allows tables to be updated and queried at the same time [17].

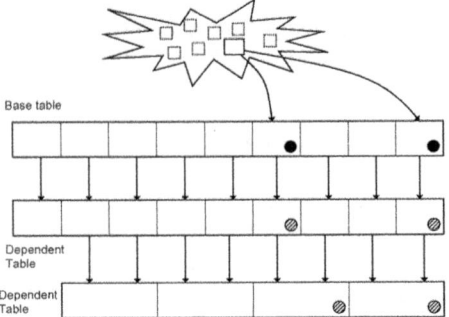

Fig. 1. Update propagation from raw sources to materialized views

- We enabled *multi-granularity* partitions: new data are stored in small, e.g., 5-minute, partitions, while historical data are stored in larger, e.g., 1-day, partitions (unlike RRDTool [15], historical data are not aggregated, only grouped into larger partitions). Since updates typically affect recent partitions, small partitions for recent data reduce the amount of data to bring into memory for updates. Large partitions for historical data allow us to store enough history for off-line data mining.
- We developed a real-time update scheduler that executes updates when new data arrive, scales to hundreds of tables and views with various priorities, and is tuned for minimizing the tardiness of updates to critical tables [9].

3   Implementing Applications Inside a Data Stream Warehouse

The approach we advocate in this paper is to translate the data processing steps of a real-time application into declarative queries, whose results are maintained in a hierarchy of materialized views. The view hierarchy encodes data flow through the application, and each step amounts to a query against the results of the previous step. When new data arrive, they are incrementally processed by each step.

There are many advantages of shifting complex application logic to the database. First, the application designer can rely on the warehouse to efficiently propagate new data through the data flow. Second, the warehouse provides a declarative query language and a suite of efficient query evaluation techniques, including indices on materialized views. Third, results are stored in the database and can be reused and re-processed by other applications. Fourth, the code (queries and partition dependencies) is often more compact, and easier to document, debug and extend than a procedural program.

There are two technical issues in applying the proposed approach to real-time applications: system support for efficient view updates, which we have described in the previous section, and language support for sequence operators, which we propose next.

Relational database systems, including DataDepot, use the well-known SQL language, in which simple queries are expressed as "SELECT f FROM t WHERE p GROUP BY g HAVING h". Here, f is the list of fields and/or aggregate functions to return, t is a list of tables referenced in the query, p is a predicate that must be satisfied by each record in the output, g is a list of fields on which to group the data, such that the aggregate function in f, if any, will be evaluated separately for each group, and h is a predicate on each group defined in g that governs which groups will be reported in the result. Multiple tables and/or views can be *joined* by listing them in t and specifying the joining condition in p. In addition to filtering, merging, joining and aggregating data, SQL includes set operations of the form "SELECT ... WHERE EXISTS (SELECT ...)" or "SELECT ... WHERE NOT EXISTS (SELECT ...)". These return a result only if the result of the query inside the brackets is non-empty or empty, respectively.

Network monitoring applications are often sequence-oriented: comparing current timestamps or sequence numbers to their previous values to compute delays or out-of-order packets, finding consecutive records that exceed a threshold, grouping records with nearby timestamps into flows or sessions, etc. The basic operations required by such queries — e.g., referring to the previous record in the sequence, maintaining a state machine over the data that have arrived so far — are difficult to express using standard SQL and inefficient to execute using standard database algorithms. For example, suppose that we want to remove records from a message stream S that have another record from the same device name within sixty seconds (in order to output only one record per "session"). One way to express this using SQL is with a nested set operator:

```
SELECT name, timestamp FROM S
WHERE NOT EXISTS(
   SELECT S2.name, S2.timestamp FROM S AS S2
   WHERE S2.name=name
   AND timestamp >= S2.timestamp
   AND timestamp <= S2.timestamp + 60)
```

This query correlates S with a copy of itself, $S2$. This construct is not intuitive and hard to optimize – a database may answer it by scanning S, and, for each element in S, scanning S again to ensure that there are no records for the given element name within the past 60 seconds. Instead, we can do better by scanning S only once and remembering the timestamp of the previous record for each network element.

In this paper, we propose a generic extension to SQL that enables a new class of sequence-oriented queries to be easily expressed and optimized: we add an UPDATE BY clause that defines state variables to maintain as data are processed sequentially. Output records are then emitted based on the current record being processed and the values of the state variables. Using the proposed extension, the above query becomes:

```
SELECT name, timestamp FROM S
GROUP BY name, timestamp SEQ
UPDATE BY (timestamp-last[1]>60 ? timestamp : last)
          INITIALLY timestamp AS last
HAVING timestamp = last
```

The GROUP BY clause defines the entities being tracked, with the SEQ keyword denoting an ordered field (timestamp, sequence number, IP address, etc.). Here, grouping by device name and timestamp indicates that each device produces a sequence of records. The state maintained for each group is defined in the UPDATE BY clause. Each entry defines a variable; here, there is one variable named last. Its initial value is defined to be the timestamp (of the first record), and, as specified in the conditional evaluation expression, it is advanced to the next timestamp value whenever the difference between the timestamp and the previous value of last (denoted `last[1]`) is greater than 60 seconds. The (optional) HAVING clause determines whether a record should be output for a given input record. In this query, we want to produce an output record whenever `last` is advanced to the value of the current timestamp.

We argue that defining state variables can express common network monitoring applications that operate on data sequences. With the above SQL extension, we no longer have to simulate sequential operations using set expressions. It is much easier to write sequence queries and efficiently execute them instead of relying on general-purpose set-oriented optimizations provided by the database. In particular, as proof of concept, we have implemented the following execution strategy in DataDepot (which may be incorporated into any SQL-based relational database system). First, we scan the table(s) referenced in the FROM clause and sort the records according to the SEQ field. We then process each record in sequence and update the UPDATE BY variables (which are indexed in a hash table for fast lookup). After processing each record, we evaluate the HAVING clause to determine whether or not to construct an output record.

4   Case Study

Our case study involves an active measurement infrastructure of a large ISP that periodically measures packet loss and delay from each monitor server to a set of destinations (other monitors and routers). To conduct the measurements, a monitor launches a probe train to a destination, which reflects the received packets back to the source. The monitors, their placement, and the set of destinations probed by each monitor are set up such that the union of all the source-destination probe pairs covers all the end-end paths in each network. Globally, this results in thousands of measurements every 15 minutes.

In real time, network operators monitor these measurements, identify serious performance events where the loss (or delay) for a source-destination pair exceeds a critical threshold for sustained time periods, and conduct troubleshooting. Traditionally performed manually, computing these events involves joins across multiple data feeds (multiple types of probes, configuration data), requires tracking many networks, and is time consuming and error prone. Our task is to automate the creation of these incidents to ensure greater accuracy, and to enable operators to move away from tedious number-crunching across multiple screens so they can focus on troubleshooting the outages.

The input consists of loss and delay measurements, and a configuration feed providing various details for each pair, such as the loss/delay thresholds. A source-destination pair causes an *alarm* once the metric (loss or delay) exceeds a critical threshold for four consecutive time intervals. We want to automate the identification of loss and delay alarms of the form (start time, end time, source, destination, average loss/delay). We will only discuss loss alarms from now on, as delay alarms follow a similar logic.

Suppose that the following sequence of (date, time, loss percentage) records is generated by a probe between source S and destination D. Suppose that the loss threshold is one percent. We label measurements exceeding the threshold as red; black otherwise:

```
2011-01-01, 9:00, 0.8, BLACK
2011-01-01, 9:15, 1.5, RED
2011-01-01, 9:30, 1.8, RED
```

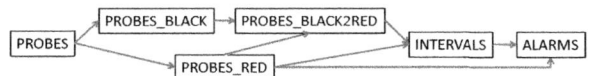

Fig. 2. Implementing a network alerting application using standard SQL views

```
2011-01-01,  9:45,  1.6,  RED
2011-01-01.  10:00,  2.0,  RED
2011-01-01,  10:15,  1.8,  RED
2011-01-01.  10:30,  0.2,  BLACK
```

At time 9:00, the loss percentage is below threshold (black). At 9:15, it rises above the threshold (red), but an alarm is not yet raised; likewise at 9:30 and 9:45. At 10:00, we have four consecutive red measurements and we output the following:

```
2010-01-01 9:15,  2010-01-01 10:00,  S,  D,  1.63.
```

An alarm for this pair continues at 10:15 because the new measurement continues to exceed the critical threshold, and at that time we output

```
2010-01-01 9:15,  2010-01-01 10:15,  S,  D,  1.73.
```

The loss percentage drops below threshold at 10:30, so we do not output anything for this pair at that time.

This logic may be expressed as follows. For each pair, if its current measurement is red, then we compute the time of the first red measurement that occurred after its most recent black measurement. In the above example, the processing at time 10:00 is to look up the most recent black measurement time of 9:00 and conclude that the start of the consecutive red sequence is at time 9:15.

Figure 2 shows the tables that implement loss alarms within DataDepot using standard (non-sequential) SQL. The PROBES table collects loss measurements (and correlates various probe configuration information such as critical loss threshold via a join with the configuration table). PROBES is partitioned into 15-minute time bins so that new data can be loaded into the most recent partition without affecting the rest of the table. The remaining five tables, also partitioned into 15-minute time bins, implement the application logic. PROBES_BLACK and PROBES_RED select black and red measurements, respectively, PROBES_BLACK2RED selects red measurements that occurred immediately after black measurements, INTERVALS constructs intervals with consecutive red measurements, and ALARMS computes intervals that contain at least four red measurements. For each of these tables, we also need to specify the relationship between its partitions and those of its sources (recall Figure 1); this information is crucial to ensuring efficient update propagation. For example, the current partition of PROBES_BLACK2RED can be computed by accessing the current partition of PROBES_RED and the previous-to-current partition of PROBES_BLACK. Without these partition relationships, the database would have no choice but to scan the entire history of PROBES_RED and PROBES_BLACK when computing a single 15-minute partition of PROBES_BLACK2RED. The final piece is a Web-based front end that displays the current alarms and is refreshed by querying the ALARMS table.

With standard SQL, we are forced to simulate sequential analysis with complex and difficult-to-optimize set operations. For example, the INTERVALS table selects the source-destination pairs with currently red measurements (from PROBES_RED) and looks up the most recent record for that pair in PROBES_BLACK2RED using a NOT EXISTS operator:

```
SELECT R.Source, R.Destination, B.Ts, R.Ts
FROM PROBES_RED R, PROBES_BLACK2RED B
WHERE R.Source=B.Source
  AND R.Destination=B.Destination AND R.Ts >= B.Ts
  AND NOT EXISTS{
    SELECT Timestamp FROM PROBES_BLACK2RED B2
    WHERE B2.Source=B.Source
      AND B2.Destination = B.Destination
      AND B2.Ts > B.Ts )
```

That is, we check that there does NOT EXIST another record for that pair in PROBES_BLACK2RED with a larger timestamp (denoted Ts).

In contrast, only one table suffices to implement the loss alarms logic using our sequence-oriented extensions (Ts is the timestamp field and Loss is the loss value; for simplicity, assume that the critical loss threshold is one percent):

```
SELECT Source, Destination, Ts-(red_ct*900), Ts, sum_loss/red_ct
FROM PROBES
GROUP BY Source, Destination, Ts SEQ
UPDATE BY
  (Loss>1% AND first_red[1]<last_black[1] ? Ts : first_red[1])
    INITIALLY (Loss>1% ? Ts : 0) AS first_red,
  (Loss<=1% ? Ts : last_black[1])
    INITIALLY (Loss<=1% ? Ts : 0) AS last_black,
  (first_red>last_black ? red_ct[1]+1 : 0)
    INITIALLY (Loss>1% ? 1 : 0) AS red_ct,
  (first_red>last_black ? sum_loss[1]+Loss : 0)
    INITIALLY (Loss>1% ? Loss : 0) AS sum_loss
HAVING red_ct >= 4
```

The logic is expressed using four UPDATE BY variables. For each pair, first_red, keeps track of the timestamp of the first red measurement after the most recent black one, last_black maintains the time of the most recent black measurement, red_ct counts the number of red measurements in the current alarm interval and sum_loss sums up the loss values over the current alarm interval. In the SELECT clause, we return the Source and Destination points of the given pair, the starting time of the alarm (which is simply the current timestamp minus the number of red measurements times 900 seconds), the current time, and average loss during the alarm interval (computed by diving sum_loss by the number of red measurements). The HAVING clause ensures that we output an alarm only if we have seen at least four consecutive red measurements.

The sequential ALARMS table also needs to specify a partition relationship with PROBES. Assuming that alarms do not last longer than six hours, we only need to scan the most recent six hours of PROBES when computing a new partition of ALARMS.

We note that the real-time features of DataDepot were crucial in enabling this application: views are automatically maintained as new data arrive and use multi-version

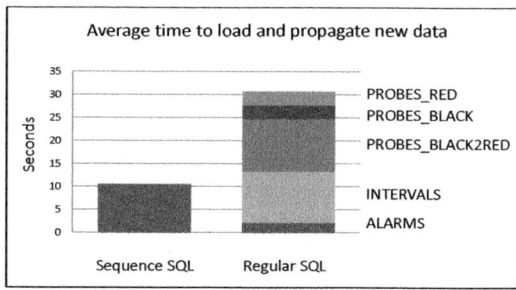

Fig. 3. Comparison of application refresh times

concurrency control so they can be queried at any time, and we have used multi-granularity partitions, with small recent partitions for efficiency and larger historical partitions to store a very long history of alarms.

5   Experiments

We now show that our network monitoring application can be efficiently maintained using the proposed sequence extensions. We also discuss the performance of our solution in the Darkstar warehouse, which is one of several network data warehouses maintained by DataDepot. Darkstar is run by a large ISP, loads over 100 raw data feeds, maintains over 300 tables and materialized views, and ingests more that 340 million raw records per day. Darkstar consists of an application server (2.86 GHz Xeon chip, 4 cores, 48 Gb of RAM, 4Gb fiber channel to secondary storage) and a cluster of database servers.

We begin with a comparison of the update time of our application using the hierarchy of regular SQL views from Figure 2 versus using the single sequential view. To control this experiment, we executed updates on the application server rather than allowing the live warehouse to schedule them. We measured the time to update each table over a period of one day (new data arrive every 15 minutes, so there were 96 updates) and report the average update times in Figure 3. Using regular SQL, it takes over 30 seconds to process a 15-minute batch of data through all the intermediate tables, with PROBES_BLACK2RED and INTERVALS alone taking around 10 seconds each. Using sequential SQL, it only takes an average of ten seconds to update the single view. Our sequence extensions also save space since there is only one view, not five, to store.

We now discuss the performance of the live warehouse. Over a nine-day period, we measured the time to propagate raw probe data to the ALARMS table. We found that the end-to-end update propagation time (which includes waiting times while other tables are being updated) was well under five minutes 97 percent of the time. This is far below the 15-minute inter-arrival time of the raw data. Thus, in spite of the high degree of activity (hundreds of complex views maintained in nearly-real time), we were still able to provide timely updates, with the DataDepot scheduler allocating resources to "stale" tables without starving other tables. Of course, a network firestorm may cause many feeds to produce huge data volumes, in which case we may have to perform load shedding such as sampling.

6   Conclusions

Rather than viewing data warehouses as a convenient way to organize data for higher-level applications, this paper advocated implementing real-time network monitoring applications *within the warehouse* as collections of materialized views. We presented a novel extension to the SQL query language that natively supports sequence-oriented analysis. To illustrate the feasibility of our approach, we presented a network alerting application that we implemented using the proposed method inside a production data warehouse. We experimentally showed a 3-fold performance improvement as well as a significant reduction in application complexity thanks to the proposed sequence-oriented extensions. We hope that this paper stimulates further research on the role of database technologies in network management, and encourages the adoption of these ideas by researchers and practitioners.

References

1. Agrawal, J., et al.: Efficient pattern matching over event streams. In: SIGMOD 2008, pp. 147–160 (2008)
2. Ahuja, M., et al.: Peta-scale data warehousing at Yahoo! In: SIGMOD 2009, pp. 855–862 (2009)
3. Balazinska, M., et al.: Moirae: History-enhanced monitoring. In: CIDR 2007, pp. 375–386 (2007)
4. Cranor, C., et al.: A stream database for network applications. In: SIGMOD 2003, pp. 647–651 (2003)
5. Deri, L., Lorenzetti, V., Mortimer, S.: Collection and Exploration of Large Data Monitoring Sets Using Bitmap Databases. In: Ricciato, F., Mellia, M., Biersack, E. (eds.) TMA 2010. LNCS, vol. 6003, pp. 73–86. Springer, Heidelberg (2010)
6. Desnoyers, P., Shenoy, P.J.: Hyperion: High volume stream archival for retrospective querying. In: USENIX Annual Technical Conference, pp. 45–58 (2007)
7. Eriksson, B., et al.: Basisdetect: a model-based network event detection framework. In: IMC 2010, pp. 451–464 (2010)
8. Golab, L., et al.: Stream warehousing with DataDepot. In: SIGMOD 2009, pp. 847–854 (2009)
9. Golab, L., Johnson, T., Shkapenyuk, V.: Scheduling updates in a real-time stream warehouse. In: ICDE 2009, pp. 1207–1210 (2009)
10. Jain, N., et al.: Towards a streaming SQL standard. Proc. of the VLDB Endowment 1(2), 1379–1390 (2008)
11. Kalmanek, C., et al.: Darkstar: Using exploratory data mining to raise the bar on network reliability and performance. In: DRCN 2009 (2009)
12. Li, X., et al.: Advanced indexing techniques for wide-area network monitoring. In: NetDB 2005 (2005)
13. Maier, G., et al.: Enriching network security analysis with time travel. SIGCOMM Comput. Commun. Rev. 38, 183–194 (2008)
14. Markopoulou, A., et al.: Characterization of failures in an operational ip backbone network. IEEE/ACM Trans. Netw. 16(4), 749–762 (2008)
15. Papadogiannakis, A., Polychronakis, M., Markatos, E.P.: RRDtrace: Long-term raw network traffic recording using fixed-size storage. In: MASCOTS 2010, pp. 101–110 (2010)

16. Qiu, T., et al.: What happened in my network: mining network events from router syslogs. In: IMC 2010, pp. 472–484 (2010)
17. Quass, D., Widom, J.: On-line warehouse view maintenance. In: SIGMOD 1997, pp. 393–404 (1997)
18. Reiss, F., et al.: Enabling real-time querying of live and historical stream data. In: SSDBM 2007, p. 28 (2007)

On Multi–gigabit Packet Capturing
with Multi–core Commodity Hardware

Nicola Bonelli, Andrea Di Pietro, Stefano Giordano, and Gregorio Procissi

CNIT and Università di Pisa, Pisa, Italy

Abstract. Nowadays commodity hardware is offering an ever increasing degree of parallelism (CPUs with more and more cores, NICs with parallel queues). However, most of the existing network monitoring software has not yet been designed with high parallelism in mind. Therefore we designed a novel packet capturing engine, named PFQ, that allows efficient capturing and in–kernel aggregation, as well as connection–aware load balancing. Such an engine is based on a novel lockless queue and allows parallel packet capturing to let the user–space application arbitrarily define its degree of parallelism. Therefore, both legacy applications and natively parallel ones can benefit from such a capturing engine. In addition, PFQ outperforms its competitors both in terms of captured packets and CPU consumption.

1   Introduction and Motivation

Monitoring high performance links on a current network is definitely a challenging task: on one hand the data rate, which is becoming increasingly high, calls for hardware acceleration of the fast data path, while, on the other hand, the complexity of the analysis to be carried out and the need to have it updated according to the emerging applications and threats requires a flexibility and modularity that only software can provide. However, the evolution of commodity hardware is pushing parallelism forward as the key factor that may allow software to attain hardware-class performance while still retaining its advantages. On one side, commodity CPUs are providing more and more cores, while on the other modern NICs are supporting multiple hardware queues that allow cores to fetch packets concurrently (in particular, this technology is known as *Receive Side Scaling*, henceforward RSS). Unfortunately, current network monitoring and security software is not yet able to completely leverage the potential which is brought on by the hardware evolution: even if progress is actually being made (multiple queue support has been included in the latest releases of the Linux kernel), much of current monitoring software has been designed in the pre–multicore era. The aim of our work is to make the full power of parallel CPUs available to both traditional and natively parallel application, through efficient and configurable in–kernel packet flow aggregation. Therefore, we designed a novel packet capturing engine, named PFQ, that allows to parallelize the packet capturing process in the kernel and, at the same time, to split and balance the captured packets across a user–defined set of capturing sockets. This

N. Taft and F. Ricciato (Eds.): PAM 2012, LNCS 7192, pp. 64–73, 2012.
© Springer-Verlag Berlin Heidelberg 2012

way, the application writer can arbitrarily choose its level of parallelism with PFQ, hiding within the kernel the full parallelism of the system. In particular, an application can either use a single capturing socket (as in the case of legacy applications) or have PFQ balance incoming frames across a configurable set of collection points (sockets) or even use a completely parallel setup, where packets follow parallel paths from the device driver up to the application. In all of those cases, PFQ yields better performance than its competitors, while burning a lower amount of CPU cycles. Differently from many existing works for accelerating software packet processing, PFQ does not require driver modification (although a minimal few–lines patch in the driver can further improve performance). Scalability can be achieved through batch processing (which, in turn, leverages the hierarchical cache structure of modern CPUs) and through lockless techniques, which allow multiple threads to update the same state with no locking and minimal overhead. In particular, we designed a novel double buffer multi–producer single–consumer lockless queue which allows high scalability. PFQ is open–source software released under GPL license and can be freely downloaded at [1]. The package consists of a Linux kernel module and of a C++ user–space library. The rest of the paper is organized as follows: section 2 summarizes the state of the art in the topic of packet capturing solutions, while section 3 describes the architecture of our packet capturing engine. Section 4 shows the results of our measurement campaign and the Conclusions section follows.

2   State–of–the–Art in Packet Capturing

Several solutions have been proposed to speed up the packet capturing capabilities of commodity PCs. nCap [2] uses memory mapping to directly expose to the application the memory areas where the NIC copies incoming frames. The same approach is adopted by Netmap [3], a BSD based project which integrates in the same interface a number of modified drivers mapping the NIC transmit and receive buffers directly into user space. Also PF_RING [4] uses a memory mapped ring to export packets to user space processes: such a ring can be filled by a regular sniffer (thus using the standard linux capturing mechanisms) or by specially modified drivers, which skip the default kernel processing chain. Those can be both drivers with minimal patches (aware drivers) or heavily modified ones. Memory mapping has also been adopted by the well-known PCAP capturing libraries [5]. In the past years, the capturing stack of Free-BSD has been enhanced by a double–buffer mechanism, where packets are written into a memory–mapped buffer which is first filled within the kernel and then switched over to the application for reading. This is different from PF_RING, where applications and kernel work on the same ring concurrently. Although our proposed architecture also adopts a double buffer solution, it brings it further by introducing other optimizations (like batch processing) and by explicitly tailoring it to a multi–core scenario. Many works (most of them on software based routers) have obtained good results in accelerating software packet processing by extensively patching the device drivers. TNAPI [6] effectively addressed the topic, but the proposed solution is based on a heavily customized driver, which detaches parallel polling threads instead of relying on NAPI. Besides, its heavy use of kernel level polling leads to high CPU utilization. The authors in [7] focus on how to distribute work across cores in order to build high performance software routers. Although the results are certainly interesting, it relies on the Click modular router [8] and its modified polling driver to deliver good performance. In [10], the authors present Packetshader, an extremely well performing software router, which is built around GPU acceleration of computation intensive and memory intensive functionalities (such as address lookup). Also, it relies on a heavily modified driver which introduces several optimizations, such as using a reduced version of the socket buffer structure and preallocating huge buffers to avoid per–packet memory allocations. Our work is somewhat orthogonal to those based on modified drivers, as PFQ is a general architecture that can be beneficial to both vanilla and modified drivers.

3   PFQ Capturing Engine

The system as a whole is depicted in Figure 1 and is made up by the following components: the packet fetcher, the demultiplexing block and socket queues. The fetcher dequeues the packet directly from the driver, which can be a standard driver or a patched "aware" driver, and inserts it into the batching queue. The next stage is represented by the demultiplexing block, which is in charge of selecting which socket(s) need to receive the packet. The final component of PFQ is the socket queue, which represents the interface between user space and kernel space. All of the kernel processing (from the the reception of the packet up to its copy into the socket queue) is carried out within the NAPI context; the last processing stage is completely performed at user space, thanks to memory mapping. In the following we will describe in more detail each building block.

3.1   Building Blocks

Aware driver. The concept of driver awareness has been first introduced by PF_RING: an aware driver, instead of passing a packet up the standard linux networking stack, highjacks and forwards it directly to the capturing module. This implies that, on one hand, the message does not have to go through the standard network stack processing, thus improving performance. On the other hand, the capturing module has exclusive ownership of the packet, which is invisible to the rest of the kernel (including the sniffers). We developed a patched version of the ixgbe driver that just involves minimal code modifications (around a dozen lines of code); such a simple patch can be easily applied to new and existing drivers. We point out that such a block is completely optional and PFQ shows good performance with vanilla drivers too. Moreover, an aware driver managing multiple interfaces can handle in aware-mode only the packets coming from a monitoring interface, while exposing the others to the kernel stack.

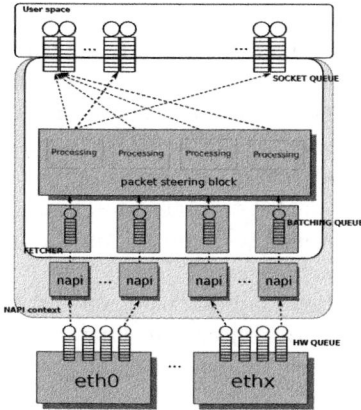

Fig. 1. PFQ scheme at–a–glance

Packet fetcher. The packet fetcher is the only component which acts on a packet by packet basis. It receives the packets and inserts the associated pointer into its *batching queue*. Once such a queue (whose length is configurable) is filled, all of its enqueued packets are processed by the next block in a single batch. Batch processing turns out to be more efficient in that it improves the temporal locality of memory accesses, thus reducing the probability of both cache misses and concurrent access to shared data. In particular, a significant advantage comes from deallocating packets in batches that, according to our measurements, can reduce the deallocation cost by as much as 75%. Our measurements reveal that the optimal queue length is of the order of a hundred of packets. Notice that, as the packet is timestamped before queueing, this component does not influence timing accuracy.

Packet steering block. The main function of the steering block is to select which sockets need to receive the captured packets. Notice that, although it is a single functional block, the steering block processing is completely distributed and does not represent a serialization point (in fact, it only deals with read–only state). Such a block consists of a routing matrix that allows to flexibly dispatch the incoming packets across multiple capturing sockets. In particular, such a matrix associates each reception queue of each handled card with one or more capturing sockets. Such sockets can be independent from each other (thus receiving one copy of the packet each) or can be aggregated into a load balancing group. In this latter case, a hash function is computed for each packet and only one socket in the balancing group is chosen. An additional advantage of such an approach is the possibility of performing a bidirectional load balancing. Indeed, RSS performs its native form of load balancing by computing a hash function over the 5–tuple of incoming packets. However, such a scheme may not be appropriate for some applications, as RSS is not symmetric. For example, applications that monitor TCP connections need to observe packets from both directions which RSS would dispatch to different cores. For this reason, the packet steering block recomputes a symmetric hash function that will rebalance the packets with small overhead. Notice that load balancing and copy are not mutually exclusive: packets from the same hardware queue can be copied to a set of sockets and load–balanced across another one. In greater detail, the demultiplexing block is composed by a bit–field matrix and a load balancing function. The switching matrix stores, for each queue, a bitmap specifying which sockets have to receive its packets. Such a design allows dynamic insertion and removal of sockets with no need for mutexes on the fast data path.

Socket queue. It is the last component of our architecture and the only one which is subject to inter–core contention. Our design shares some similarities with that of the FreeBSD zero–copy packet filter, but it improves the state of the art by introducing a wait–free solution which is optimized for a multi–core environment. Indeed, the whole mechanism implements a multiple producer – single consumer wait–free queue. The main components of this block are two memory mapped buffers: while one of them is being filled with the packets coming from the demultiplexer, the other one is being read from the user application. The two buffers are periodically swapped through a memory mapped variable (named *index* in the pseudocode of algorithm 1) that stores both the index of the queue being written to and the number of bytes that have been already inserted (in particular, its most significant bit represents the queue index). Each producer (i.e. a NAPI kernel thread) reserves a portion of the buffer by atomically incrementing the shared index; such a reservation can be made on a packet by packet basis or once for a batch. After the thread has been granted exclusive ownership of its buffer range, it will fill it with the captured packet along with a short pseudo header containing meta–data (e.g. the timestamp). Finally, it will finalize it by setting a validation bit in the pseudo–header after raising a write memory barrier. Notice that, when the user application copies the packets to a user space buffer, some NAPI contexts may still be writing into the queue. This will results in some of the slots being "half filled" when they reach the application; however, the user–space thread can wait for the validation bit to be set. On the application side, the user thread which needs to read the buffer will first reset the index by specifying another active queue (so as to direct all subsequent writes to it). Subsequently, it will copy to the application buffer a number of bytes corresponding to the value shown by the old index. Such copy will be performed in a single batch, as, from our past measurements, batch copy can be up to 30% faster. Alternatively, packets can be read in place in a zero–copy fashion. The access protocol is described in greater detail by the pseudocode in algorithm 1. Notice that, the first read of the index is not functionally necessary, but prevents the index from overflowing in case the consumer is not swapping for a long period. Finally, we point out that PFQ comes with a C++ user-space library which hides the complexity of the lockless queue while still transferring packets in batches.

Algorithm 1. Pseudo-code for the NAPI context inserting N packets into the double–buffer queue.

function insert_packet(bytes, packet)
1: **if** $QLENGTH(index) < BUFFER\_LEN$ **then**
2:     queue full, exit   ▷ this first read is only to prevent overflow
3: **end if**
4: $curr\_index \leftarrow atomic\_incr(index, bytes + PSEUDO\_HEADER\_LENGTH)$
5: $curr\_bytes \leftarrow QLENGTH(curr\_index)$
6: $curr\_buffer \leftarrow QACTIVE(curr\_index)$
7: **if** $curr\_bytes < BUFFER\_LEN$ **then**
8:     $queue full, exit$
9: **end if**
10: $my\_buffer \leftarrow buffer\_pointer[curr\_buffer] + curr\_bytes - (bytes + PSEUDO\_HEADER\_LENGTH)$
11: copy packet and compile pseudo header
12: $write\_memory\_barrier()$
13: set pseudo header validity bit

function read_packets()
1: $active\_queue \leftarrow QACTIVE(index)$
2: $next\_index \leftarrow complement(acive\_queue) << INDEX\_BITS - 1$
3: $index \leftarrow next\_index$ ▷ atomic swap
4: $my\_buffer \leftarrow buffer\_pointer[active\_queue]$
5: **for all** packet in my_buffer **do**
6:     wait for valid bit to be set
7:     read packet and pseudo header
8: **end for**

4 Experimental Results

We assessed the performance of our system under several configurations and we compared it mainly against that of PF_RING. The latter is the obvious competitor for PFQ, in that it is a general architecture that increases the capturing performance with both vanilla and modified drivers. Unfortunately we could not consider PF_RING TNAPI [6] in the comparison as it is not publicly available for download. We also show some results obtained by the well–known PCAP library (version 1.1.1 with memory mapping enabled), that only works with vanilla drivers; however, as PCAP does not explicitly support hardware queues, its results can be shown in a few layouts only. We wrote a simple packet counting application for PFQ, while for PF_RING we used the *pfcount* application that comes with the project distribution. We took two main performance metrics into consideration: number of captured packets and average CPU consumption. While the first one is the most obvious performance index, the second one is important as well: if the capturing engine is consuming a very high fraction of CPU cycles, a monitoring application will hardly have resources to do any significant processing. The testbed for experiments is made up of two identical machines, one for generating traffic, the other in charge of capturing. Both of them come with a 6 cores Intel X5650 Xeon (2.66 Ghz clock, 12Mb cache), 12 GB of DDR3 RAM, and an Intel E10G42BT NIC, with the 82599 controller on board. In order to test our system with the maximum degree of parallelism, we kept Intel Hyperthreading enabled, thus carrying out the experiments with 12 virtual cores. We will show that such a choice yields performance improvement in all scenarios. Both servers run Linux with the lates 3.0.1 kernel and the *ixgbe* 3.4.24 NICs driver. Due to the high cost of hardware based traffic generators and to the limited performance of software based ones, we chose, as the authors also did in [10], to write our own generator. Such a software [12] which, again, leverages platform parallelism, is able to generate up to 12 Millions minimum–sized packets per second. We validated its performance by means of a borrowed Napatech hardware based traffic analyzer (courtesy of Luca Deri). In particular, we verified that the maximum generated rate advertised by the generator itself was the same rate measured by the Napatech board. Moreover, in order to leverage the RSS load–balancing mechanism, we randomized the IP addresses of each packet.

Finally, we remark that due to the use of hyperthreading, we can display up to 12 capturing cores; however, from the performance point of view, this is not the same of having 12 real CPUs. The CPU numbers are arranged as follows: real core number x corresponds to two virtual cores x and $6+x$, respectively. Therefore, if we increase the set of capturing cores in a linear manner starting from 0, we expect the contribution of the first six cores to be significantly higher than that of the others (as it actually appears in our results). Therefore, we expect an ideal graph to scale linearly from 1 to 6 and to show a discontinuity in 6 and to grow linearly again, but with a much less steep slope, from 7 to 12 cores.

4.1   One–Thread Setup

In this first layout, which is the most relevant for legacy applications, we used a variable number of hardware queues for fetching packets and we only used one socket to bring them to user space. Indeed, we hid the system parallelism within the kernel while still exposing a standard interface to the application. In particular we used a layout that we showed to be beneficial in [13]: we captured the packets on all the physical cores but one, and on that one we bound the user–space process. The results shown in Figure 2 report the number of captured packets for both modified and aware drivers: the behavior of PFQ with an increasing degree of parallelism is piece–wise linear (due to the expected discontinuity around 6) while PF_RING, that handles contention through traditional lock–based mechanisms, and PCAP do not manage to scale with the number of cores. Besides, the scalability of our architecture does not depend on the driver: using an aware or a vanilla driver just reflects on the slope of the graph, but linearity is preserved. Notice that, as anticipated, we did not capture packets on the physical core where the user space process is bound: therefore, the number of available capturing cores is limited to 10.

Figure 3 reports the bit rate of the captured traffic for several packet sizes and by using 12 hardware queues. PFQ always captures all of the traffic our generator can provide (although this does not always correspond to the nominal maximum bit rate).

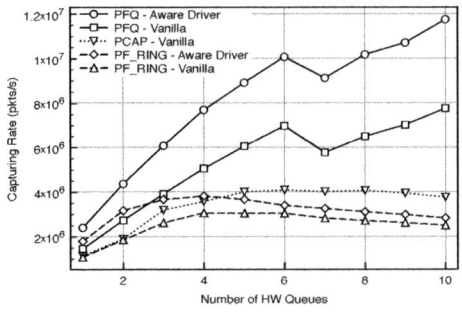

Fig. 2. One capturing thread

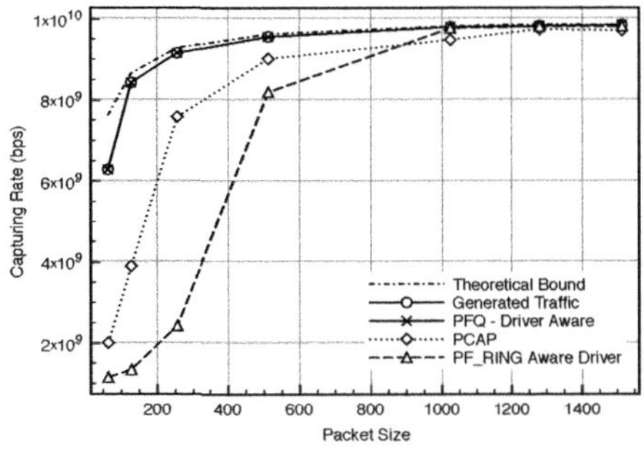

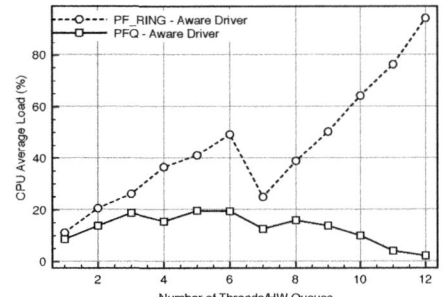

Fig. 3. Throughput vs. Packet Size

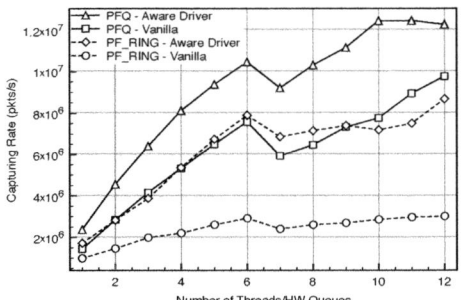

Fig. 4. Completely parallel processing paths

Fig. 5. Completely parallel processing paths: CPU consumption

4.2 Parallel Setup

In this scenario each hardware queue is associated with its own user space thread, so that the processing paths of packets are completely parallel. Notice that in this scenario we used PF_RING with the recently introduced *quick mode* option, which allows avoiding per–queue locks. The results are shown in Figure 4 and show that, although PF_RING manages to achieve good performance by preventing locking, PFQ still outperforms it. Besides, PFQ shows the same behavior with both vanilla and aware drivers (apart from a scale factor), while PF_RING only scales well with aware drivers. Notice that PFQ is able to capture all of the incoming packets with 10 cores (its throughput steadies because there is no additional traffic to capture); unfortunately, our generator is not able to produce more input traffic and, therefore, we can only obtain a lower bound of PFQ's performance.

We also report the CPU utilization (in the case of aware drivers) in Figure 5: while PF_RING saturates the CPU, the global CPU consumption in the case of PFQ is roughly constant and well below 20%.

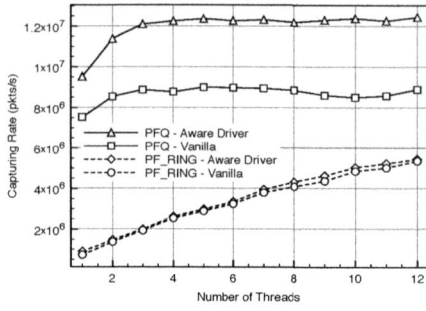 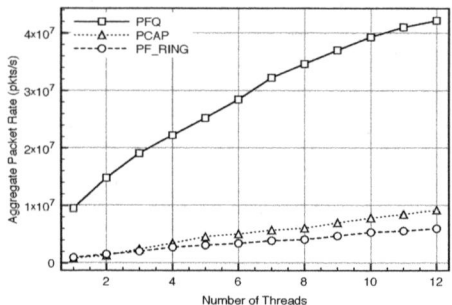

Fig. 6. Load balancing across a variable number of user–space threads

Fig. 7. Copying traffic to a variable number of user–space threads

4.3   Multiple Capture Sockets

Besides high performance, one of the strengths of PFQ is the ability of decoupling parallelism between the application level and the kernel level. In this set of tests we measure the performance of such a feature by always using the maximum number of available contexts in the kernel (i.e. 12) and by varying the number of parallel user–space threads. First, we report the overall throughput when incoming packets are load–balanced across the application threads. In order to have a benchmark, we compare our result with that of PF_RING using the recently introduced RSS rehash functionality. However, the balancing functionality in PF_RING slightly differ from that of PFQ. The results are reported in Figure 6 and show that, with an aware driver, PFQ is able to capture all of the incoming traffic with just 3 user–space threads while, with a vanilla driver, the behavior is the same but the overall throughput is lower.

We also evaluate a scenario where multiple applications are requesting a copy of the same packet: the results are shown in Figure 7 and show the *cumulative* number of packets brought to user–space. In this case, we also show the results for PCAP. Ideally this graph should scale linearly, as the same traffic is being copied to more and more threads; however the overhead of copy and concurrent access to the socket queues has a relevant impact on performance when the number of copies is high. Notice, however, that such a large number of copies is unlikely in a practical setup. Interestingly, this figure also provides an upper bound of the number of packets the system may be able to process with a faster driver with no allocations or multiple capturing cards: PFQ is able to enqueue and make available to user space over 42 Mpps, thus outperforming by far both competitors.

5   Conclusions

In this paper we presented PFQ, a novel packet capturing engine that allows to flexibly decouple user space and kernel space parallelism with negligible performance overhead. Thanks to a careful multi–core aware design, PFQ outperforms its competitors in all of the different use cases that we used for testing. In the future, we plan to develop a flexible framework for application–aware packet steering and classification to be integrated within the engine architecture.

Acknowledgments. The authors wish to thanks Luca Deri for his support towards this research. This work was partially supported by the Italian project IMPRESA and by EU project DEMONS (contract-no. 257315). The views and conclusions contained herein are those of the authors and should not be interpreted as necessarily representing the official policies or endorsements, either expressed or implied, of the DEMONS project or the European Commission.

References

1. http://netserv.iet.unipi.it/software/pfq/
2. Deri, L.: ncap: wire-speed packet capture and transmission. In: End-to-End Monitoring Techniques and Services on 2005, pp. 47–55. IEEE Computer Society, Washington, DC (2005)
3. Rizzo, L.: http://info.iet.unipi.it/~luigi/netmap/
4. Deri, L.: http://www.ntop.org
5. Libpcap MMAP mode on linux Phil Woods, http://public.lanl.gov/cpw/
6. Fusco, F., Deri, L.: High speed network traffic analysis with commodity multi-core systems. In: IMC 2010, pp. 218–224 (2010)
7. Egi, N., Greenhalgh, A., Handley, M., Hoerdt, M., Huici, F., Mathy, L., Papadimitriou, P.: Forwarding path architectures for multicore software routers. In: Proc. of PRESTO 2010, pp. 3:1–3:6. ACM, New York (2010)
8. Kohler, E., Morris, R., Chen, B., Jannotti, J., Frans Kaashoek, M.: The click modular router. ACM Trans. Comput. Syst. 18, 263–297 (2000)
9. Dobrescu, M., Egi, N., Argyraki, K., Chun, B., Fall, K., Iannaccone, G., Knies, A., Manesh, M., Ratnasamy, S.: Routebricks: exploiting parallelism to scale software routers. In: ACM SIGOPS, pp. 15–28. ACM, New York (2009)
10. Han, S., Jang, K., Park, K., Moon, S.: Packetshader: a gpu-accelerated software router. In: Proceedings of the ACM SIGCOMM 2010 Conference on SIGCOMM, SIGCOMM 2010, pp. 195–206. ACM, New York (2010)
11. Han, S., Jang, K., Park, K., Moon, S.: Building a single-box 100 gbps software router. In: IEEE LANMAN (2010)
12. Bonelli, N., Di Pietro, A., Giordano, S., Procissi, G.: Flexible high performance traffic generation on commodity multi-core platforms. In: To appear in Traffic Monitoring and Analysis (TMA 2012) Workshop (2012)
13. Bonelli, N., Di Pietro, A., Giordano, S., Procissi, G.: Packet capturing on parallel architectures. In: IEEE Workshop on Measurements and Networking (2011)

SyFi: A Systematic Approach for Estimating Stateful Firewall Performance

Yordanos Beyene, Michalis Faloutsos, and Harsha V. Madhyastha

Department of Computer Science and Engineering, UC Riverside
{yordanos,michalis,harsha}@cs.ucr.edu

Abstract. Due to the lack of a standardized methodology for reporting firewall performance, current datasheets are designed for marketing and provide inflated throughput measurements obtained under unrealistic scenarios. As a result, customers lack usable metrics to select a device that best meets their needs.

In this paper, we develop a systematic approach to estimate the performance offered by stateful firewalls. To do so, we first conduct extensive experiments with two enterprise firewalls in a wide range of configurations and traffic profiles to identify the characteristics of a network's traffic that affect firewall performance. Based on the observations from our measurements, we develop a model that can estimate the expected performance of a particular stateful firewall when deployed in a customer's network. Our model ties together a succinct set of network traffic characteristics and firewall benchmarks. We validate our model with a third enterprise-grade firewall, and find that it predicts firewall throughput with less than 6-10% error across a range of traffic profiles.

1 Introduction

Which firewall will meet the throughput requirement of our network?

Currently, a customer shopping for a firewall cannot find a good answer to this basic question. Since there is no systematic methodology for evaluating and reporting firewall performance, firewall vendors report (a) unrealistically high performance obtained with unspecified or arbitrarily chosen traffic profiles [1], and (b) performance metrics that can be easily "gamed" [2] as we discuss later. As a result, customers have to either rely on word-of-mouth recommendations or go through the laborious process of testing each firewall themselves.

Thus far, characterizing firewall performance has received limited attention from both industry and researchers. To counter approaches taken by firewall vendors to report unrealistic high throughput numbers (e.g., by using maximum-sized UDP packets), third-party testing agencies such as NSS [23] measure firewall performance using a more realistic pre-defined traffic mix. Though a step in the right direction, this approach is limited in that its results are not applicable for a customer with a different traffic mix. Traffic characteristics vary from site to site, and as we examine later, firewall throughput significantly varies across traffic profiles. On the other hand, the focus of the research community

N. Taft and F. Ricciato (Eds.): PAM 2012, LNCS 7192, pp. 74–84, 2012.

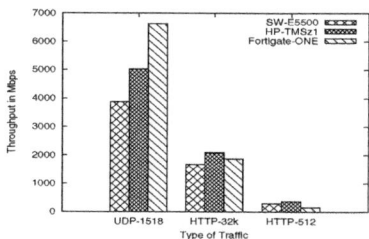
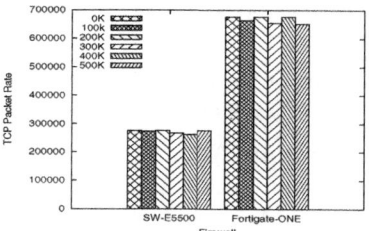

Fig. 1. Variation in maximum throughput across firewalls on different traffic profiles

Fig. 2. Effect of the number of active concurrent sessions on maximum packet rate

has mainly been on improving firewall performance by optimizing the firewall rule set [7,12,17], detecting firewall rule conflicts [18,9,8], and developing firewall architectures that make firewalls efficient and prevent such rule conflict errors from occurring [16,15,19,20].

Our goal instead is to develop a meaningful way to characterize the performance of stateful firewalls. Our approach is motivated by the observation that the performance a customer can expect from a firewall depends on characteristics of both network traffic at the customer's site and the firewall's hardware and software. For example, Figure 1 shows the throughput obtained with three enterprise-grade firewalls with three different traffic profiles. We see that the choice of the best firewall depends on the traffic profile, and there is no firewall that performs best in all cases.

In this paper, we first experiment with two enterprise firewalls to determine the characteristics of network traffic that impact their performance. We find that packet sizes and the number of active firewall sessions have minimal impact on the firewall's performance. On the other hand, our measurements show that the protocol and packet type make a significant difference; both firewalls incur much higher processing overhead with 1) TCP packets as compared to UDP, and 2) packets that create new sessions on the firewall compared to data packets that belong to an existing session.

We use these observations to develop a simple model of stateful firewall performance. Our model ties together two inputs—1) a profile of the traffic at the customer's network, and 2) computational costs incurred by a firewall on different types of packets. We prescribe the format for the first input based on our observations of the resource requirements imposed on firewalls by different types of packets. We believe firewall vendors should be specifying the latter input in their datasheets.

We validate our model with a third firewall, different from the two used to derive our model. We apply our model to a range of traffic profiles and find that in each case, our model's estimate of the throughput is within 6% of measured values. We also evaluate our model's ability to predict the firewall's performance when subjected to a SYN flood attack, and here too, its throughput estimates are within a 10% error across traffic profiles.

2   Understanding Firewall Performance

In this section, we provide a brief background on stateful firewalls and then describe our measurement-based approach to characterize them.

Background: A stateful firewall secures a private network by keeping track of flows and enforcing security policies. We use the term flow (interchangeably with session) in its commonly used sense—a stream of packets with the same five tuple: source and destination IP address, source and destination port, and protocol type. A stateful firewall inspects all incoming and outgoing packets and decides to discard or accept a packet based on the sequence of rules in the firewall rule set and its session table. A packet that belongs to a new session is allowed to enter the network if permitted by the firewall rule set, whereas packets corresponding to previously established sessions are let through by looking up the session table.

Measurement-driven characterization. Here, we examine which factors affect the performance of a stateful firewall in practice. We conduct focused experiments for each factor in isolation on two commercial enterprise-level firewalls: (a) SonicWall E5500 [6], and (b) Fortinet Fortigate-ONE [3]. Though both devices come with additional security features such as intrusion detection, here we focus on one of the common deployment scenarios for these devices where they are configured to run as a stateful firewall. This reflects the current status quo in which most customers rely on separate application-aware filtering devices to sit behind stateful firewalls [5], rather than bundling both features on the same device. Note that the devices are not selected based on cost or hardware specification, and hence the purpose of this study is not to compare the firewalls, but rather to ensure that our observations are not unique to any one firewall.

Traffic generator: We use the traffic generation tool from BreakingPoint Systems (BPS) [10] to generate synthetic traffic for our experiments. BPS is a powerful test tool used to measure and analyze the performance, security, and stability of network devices. The BPS version that we use can generate up to 30 million simultaneous sessions, 1.5 million sessions per second, and 16 Gbps of stateful blended application traffic with over 130 application protocols, sufficient to stress-test all the firewalls we considered. It provided us enormous flexibility to simulate conditions needed to characterize the products.

Test setup: In our experiments, we used eight 1 Gbps interfaces on each firewall, matched in pairs as input and output. Our aggregate maximum rate of 8 Gbps sufficed to reach the processing capacity of either firewall. Our test traffic generator serves as the source and destination for all generated flows, and keeps track of the number of transmitted and received packets and reports packet drops. We adopt the industry-wide convention to calculate the performance as the sum of the packets and bytes across all interfaces, irrespective of their direction (i.e. from inside the network going outside or vice versa). Though a firewall's performance can be affected by its rule set (ACL) size, given the operation on an ACL (it only affects the first packet of every flow) and the optimizations that one can

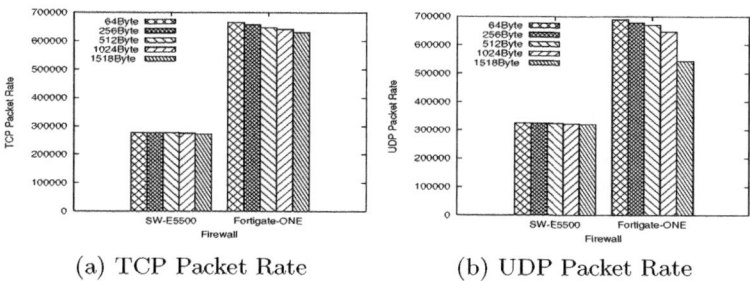

(a) TCP Packet Rate   (b) UDP Packet Rate

Fig. 3. Maximum packet rate with different packet sizes

perform on these rules (e.g., reordering of rules) to lower the number of ACL hits, we isolate the performance of the firewall from the ACL as a first order of approximation. We do a separate series of experiments in Section 4 to identify the effect that the firewall's ruleset has on its performance.

Impact of concurrent sessions. First, we investigate whether the number of concurrently active firewall sessions affects a firewall's performance. To study this, we introduce a set of *background* sessions; these are flows on which we do not send any packets once they are setup. These flows occupy space in the firewall's session table without adding traffic flowing through the firewall. We ensure that the session timeout on the firewall is long enough that these background sessions do not expire early. In addition, we have *regular* sessions on which we do send packets after they are created.

In each test, we start with one flow that sends 10,000 packets/second, and every 60 seconds we add a new flow that sends 10,000 packets/sec. Note that every flow stays active until the experiment stops, so the number of packets increases every 60 seconds. We need to add new flows to increase packet rate because our traffic generating tool can at most generate 10,000 packets/sec per flow. We stop creating more flows when the device can handle no more load, i.e., when we see an onset of persistence packet drops, and record the maximum packet rate that the firewall can handle. We found that the specific numbers used here (1 flow every 60 seconds, 10k packets/sec/flow) provide enough granularity and time for the system to stabilize and allows us to detect the point of load saturation with reasonable accuracy.

We measured the maximum packet rate as above with the creation of the background sessions and the regular sessions interspersed, with the background sessions created first, and with the background sessions created last to capture the performance impact of the order in which sessions are created. In each case, we experimented with varying number of background sessions ranging from 0 to 500K in increments of 100K. In all cases, as shown in Figure 2, we found that the number of active sessions in the firewall table had minimal impact on the maximum packet rate on either device.

Impact of packet size on packet rate. Next, we measure the impact of packet size on firewall performance. We vary the packet size across 64, 256, 512,

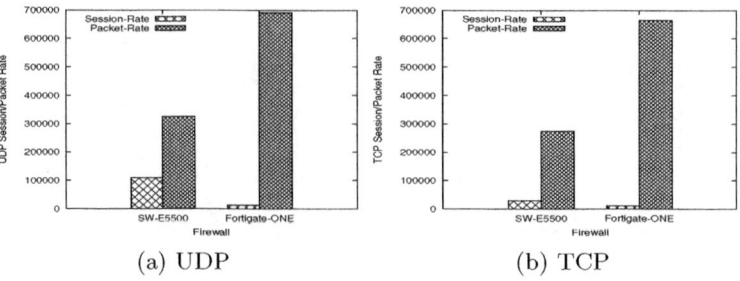

(a) UDP   (b) TCP

Fig. 4. Session rate versus packet rate

1024 and 1518 bytes, and in each case, measure the maximum packet rate as above. Figures 3a and 3b illustrate the maximum packet rates for TCP and UDP packets. Both figures show that packet size has negligible impact; the maximum packet rate declines by less than 3% for TCP and by less than 5% for UDP when packet size increases from 64 bytes to 1518 bytes. Thus, packet size has minimal impact on packet rate; *a firewall vendor can inflate the throughput in bytes/second by using the maximum packet size possible.*

We also note that though our approach is agnostic to the specific bottleneck resource as it treats the firewall as a black box, we observed the CPU to be the bottleneck in all cases and packet loss occurred when CPU utilization reached nearly 100%. We observed an isolated incident with Fortigate-ONE where maximum packet rate with UDP drops by nearly 20% when the packet size is 1518 bytes. This could be due to an implementation inefficiency in the tested firmware version.

Cost of creating a session. We next compare the overhead of processing packets that create sessions on the firewall with that of processing subsequent packets that belong to an active session. We do this by computing the maximum session rate as described next and comparing it with the previously measured maximum packet rates. We begin by creating 5K new flows every second and increase the rate by 1K flows every 60 seconds until the firewall resources are exhausted and we start observing persistent packet drops. Thus, the firewall establishes 5K new sessions every second in the first cycle, 6K new sessions every second in the second cycle, and so on. For every flow, we stop sending packets after it is created. We also lowered the session timeout on the firewall to force it to flush sessions regularly; packet loss is thus caused due to the firewall's resource limitation, and not because the session table is full. We record the maximum session rate as the maximum rate of session creation reached before we start observing packet drops.

Figures 4a and 4b compare the maximum session rates and packet rates for UDP and TCP. The large difference between the session and packet rates is indicative of the much higher cost of establishing a session compared to processing subsequent packets. Though the extent of variation between creating sessions and processing subsequent packets varies across the two firewalls, this is to be expected since each firewall runs its own proprietary software.

Impact of transport protocol. We make two other observations from our measurements of maximum packet and session rates. First, we see that establishing a TCP session is more expensive than a UDP session. Second, we find that processing a TCP data packet is more expensive than a subsequent UDP packet. These findings show that packet processing costs depend on the transport protocol of packets.

Finally, we varied application level properties, such as the generating application or sender and receiver port numbers, but we observed no significant performance impact. Note that the application type may have significant impact for security devices that inspect payload which is beyond the scope of this paper.

3 SyFi: Model for Firewall Performance

Based on the insights from our measurements, we develop a systematic approach for estimating the performance of any stateful firewall. As summarized in Figure 5, given a firewall and a traffic profile as input, our model outputs the maximum throughput that the firewall can sustain.

Traffic profile. First, our model represents any input traffic profile as the mix of four packet types, which we denote with T_t, $t = 1, 2, 3, 4$. These four packet types are: a) packets associated with establishing TCP sessions (TCP SYN packets), (b) TCP data packets, (b) the first packets of a UDP flow, and (d) the subsequent packets of a UDP flow [1]. Thus, we represent a traffic profile with the probability P_t that a packet of type T_t is seen. These probabilities can be directly computed from a traffic trace gathered at the target network. There may be some challenges in isolating UDP packets that create sessions from those that belong to an existing session as firewalls clear sessions that have been inactive for longer than the firewall time-out. The subtle but reasonable assumption that can be made is to consider flow with inter-packet intervals longer than firewall time-outas the beginning of a new flow. On the other hand, if the traffic description is in terms of the application layer (e.g., 80% HTTP and 20% FTP), it is straightforward to calculate the probabilities if (a) the fraction of flows per application, and (b) the average number of packets per flow is known.

Firewall profile. Second, based on the measurements we described in Section 2, we measure the overhead or cost of each packet type T_t, denoted as C_t. In our case, we use the CPU utilization associated with processing each packet type as the cost, but more generally, this is the utilization of the firewall bottleneck. We compute the cost C_t for each of the four packet types T_t as $\frac{1}{Max_t}$, where Max_t is the maximum rate measured using the steps described in Section 2. Though this step of characterizing costs is resource intensive, it needs to be performed only once for each firewall device and the measurements can be reused across all traffic scenarios. Recall that packet sizes, firewall session table size, and application level protocol type were seen to have minimal effect on performance.

---

[1] We focus on UDP and TCP packets as they account for over 95% of Internet traffic [25], but the model can be extended to include packets such as ICMP.

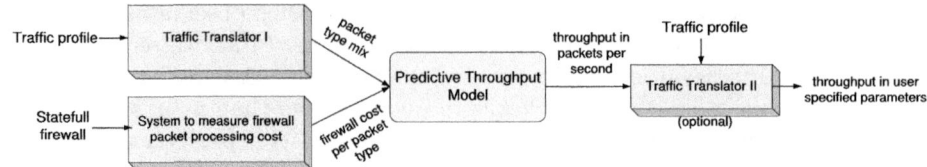

Fig. 5. Systematic Firewall Throughput Approach

3.1   Analytical Model

Finally, we calculate the expected throughput of the firewall on the input traffic profile in terms of packets per second, which we denote by N. Given the probability P_t and the cost C_t for each of the four packet types, we compute the cost (CPU utilization) for N packets per second as follows.

$$CPU = N \times \sum_{t=1}^{4}(C_t \times P_t) \tag{1}$$

The maximum number of packets occurs when the CPU is fully utilized, i.e., when CPU utilization is 1 (= 100%). Thus, we compute the maximum number of packets per second as follows.

$$N = \frac{1}{\sum_{t=1}^{4}(C_t \times P_t)} \tag{2}$$

Though the final equation that lies at the heart of our model may appear simple, note that the simplicity of the model stems from our experimental observations, before which how to estimate a firewall's performance was unclear. For example, the facts that packet size and number of concurrent sessions have minimal impact on performance are key observations that enables our approach to be simple, yet highly accurate (as we show later in Section 4).

Once we have the firewall performance in packets per second, it is straightforward to calculate the throughput in any metric that the user prefers. For example, the Traffic Translator II in our approach can be used to compute firewall throughput in bytes per second, as long as average packet size is available.

4   Validation of the Model

In this section, we validate the accuracy of our model by comparing its predictions with actual measurements. We perform this validation when using the model in two scenarios—1) to estimate a firewall's performance on normal traffic, and 2) to estimate a firewall's performance when under a SYN flood attack.

In the first part of our validation, we present here results from the HP TM-Szl firewall [4]—a different device from the ones we used to develop our model in Sections 2 and 3; we measure packet processing costs using the mechanism described in Section 2 for the four types of packets considered in our model.

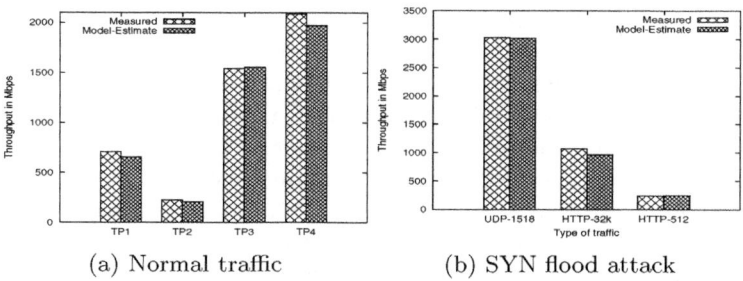

(a) Normal traffic   (b) SYN flood attack

Fig. 6. Comparison of measured throughput with throughput estimates from our model

We evaluate our model on four disparate profiles of normal traffic, which test different variations with respect to protocol type, packet size, and packet counts per flow. In the second part, we evaluate on the ability of our model to predict the performance of the SonicWall firewall when under a SYN flood attack.

Normal traffic. The four traffic profiles we consider are as follows. In our baseline traffic profile *TP1*, 20% of flows correspond to TCP traffic and the remaining 80% of flows are UDP. UDP flows send 100 packets/second and the average packet size is 64 bytes, while TCP flows send 1000 packets/second, and the average packet size is 512 bytes. In our second traffic profile *TP2*, we keep all parameters the same as in *TP1* but make all flows shorter; we decrease the number of packets per TCP and UDP flow to 10 and 1, respectively. Shorter flows result in a higher rate of session creation, which as we have shown earlier is an expensive operation for stateful firewalls. Third, in *TP3*, we change the average packet sizes in our baseline profile to make packets larger; we make average packet sizes for TCP and UDP flows to be 1024 bytes and 512 bytes respectively. Lastly, we use the standard HTTP-32K traffic profile generated by our BPS traffic generation tool. We analyzed the packets generated by our test tool and found that every HTTP flow contains 52 packets which includes 3 packets each for TCP connection setup and teardown, 1 HTTP GET, 1 ACK for the HTTP GET, 22 TCP data packets, and 22 TCP ACK packets. We use this information to compute the probabilities for our fourth traffic profile *TP4*.

For each of the four traffic profiles, we measure the maximum throughput that the HP TMSzl firewall can support by generating the corresponding traffic from our traffic generation tool and scaling up the rate of the traffic until we begin to observe packet drops. We then compare the measured values with the corresponding estimates provided by our model. Figure 6 shows that our model's estimates are within 6% of the measured values for all four traffic profiles. These results highlight our model's ability to correctly predict the effects of variations in flow duration, packet sizes, and protocol types.

Attack traffic. Beyond estimating the throughput that a firewall can support on the normal traffic at a customer's site, customers may also want to ensure that the firewall they choose can support their traffic even when under attack. To evaluate the utility of our model in such a scenario, we consider the problem of estimating firewall throughput in the face of a SYN flood attack. For this experiment, we consider three different standard traffic patterns in our traffic generation tool—UDP flows with 1518 bytes of data, HTTP flows with 32 KB of data, and HTTP flows with 512 bytes of data on average. We subject the SonicWall firewall to these traffic patterns in turn, and in each case, use our traffic generation tool to launch 10K SYN packets per second in parallel. Figure 6(b) compares the measured values of the throughput sustained by the firewall with the corresponding estimates from our model. Our model's estimates are accurate with less than 10% error in all three traffic profiles.

The experiments reveal significant throughput change when traffic profile varies. Thus the 5 Gbps data sheet through for the HP TMSzl [4], and the 3.9 Gbps throughput for SonicWall [6] is over-optimistic.

Finally, we performed a preliminary investigation of the effect of the firewall's ruleset, i.e., the set of ACLs used to filter traffic, on session rate. We ran an experiment wherein we populated the firewall's ruleset with several DENY rules that do not match our test traffic, and added a single rule at the bottom to permit the test traffic. We repeated this experiment on all three firewalls, varying the number of rules and the test traffic. In all cases, we found that the maximum session rate significantly declines with an increase in the number of rules.

5   Related Work

RFC 2544 [11] is the industry leading network interconnecting device benchmarking methodology since 1999. RFC 2647 [22] extends the terminology established with definitions specific to firewalls. It specifies device throughput to be tested with frames sized 64, 128, 256, 512, 1024 and 1518 bytes. Firewall vendors exploit RFC 2544 by publishing throughput measurements in bytes/sec conducted with full-sized (1,518 bytes) UDP packets only. Clearly, this does not reflect a typical enterprise traffic mix, which involves different protocols and packet sizes.

Third-party testing agencies such as NSS [23] have challenged vendors by evaluating and comparing firewalls with respect to their performance, security, and stability. NSS measure throughput using a more realistic traffic mix. Though a step in the right direction, it doesn't address a customer's basic question of how the firewall will perform in her network since the firewall's throughput varies significantly across traffic profiles.

The focus of the research community has been on 1) optimizing firewall rules either by reordering rules or removing redundant rules [7,12,17], 2) detecting policy errors in a firewall's ruleset [21,18,9], 3) detecting anomalies and vulnerabilities in firewalls [9,24,14], and 4) improving firewall design [16,15] to prevent the policy errors and anomalies from happening in the first place.

To the best of our knowledge, there is no prior work to answer the question—*what is the performance a given customer can expect from a particular firewall?* Customers may therefore end up buying a low performing device which could potentially introduce a bottleneck into their network, or a high performing device that is more expensive than necessary. In this paper, we resolve this issue in a systematic way, and our model accurately computes the expected performance of a firewall using a profile of the traffic profile from the deployment environment.

Perhaps the most closely related work in terms of resource based performance analysis is that of Dreger et al. [13]. They developed `nidsconf`, a tool that examines Intrusion Detection Systems resource utilization on a sample traffic profile and derives configurations that prevent bursts of packet drops due to spikes in CPU and memory utilization.

6 Conclusions

Since performance numbers in the datasheets of firewalls are often inflated, customers of stateful firewalls today are left needing to rely on word of mouth recommendations to choose a firewall. To make the process more scientific, in this paper, we examined two state-of-the-art enterprise-level stateful firewalls to highlight the factors that affect their performance. Based on our observations that protocol and packet type matter for performance but packet sizes and number of concurrent sessions do not, we developed a model of firewall performance that takes as input characteristics of the particular firewall and the traffic at a target network. Our evaluations on a third firewall showed that our model can estimate throughput across different traffic profiles with over 90% accuracy. In the future, we will study the performance impact of payload inspection and connection teardown packets.

References

1. Comparison shopping for scalable firewall products, `http://tinyurl.com/7smaqet`
2. Data sheets lie: How to measure the performance, security and stability of network devices,
   `http://resources.breakingpoint.com/acton/form/567/0024:d-0004/0/`
3. Fortinet FortiGate-ONE,
   `http://www.fortinet.com/products/fortigate/one.html`
4. HP Threat Management Services zl module,
   `http://h20195.www2.hp.com/v2/GetPDF.aspx/4AA2-6512ENN.pdf/`
5. Next Generation Firewalls not ready to replace all legacy firewalls,
   `http://searchnetworking.techtarget.com/news/1520651/`
   `Next-generation-firewalls-not-ready-to-replace-all-legacy-firewalls/`
6. SonicWALL E-class network security appliance E5500,
   `http://www.firewalls.com/sonicwall/`
   `sonicwall-firewall/sonicwall-e-class-series/`
7. Acharya, S., Wang, J., Ge, Z., Zane, T.F., Greenberg, A.: Traffic-aware firewall optimization strategies. In: ICC (2006)
8. Al-Shaer, E., Hamed, H., Boutaba, R., Hasan, M.: Conflict classification and analysis of distributed firewall policies. In: IEEE JSAC (2005)
9. Baboescu, F., Varghese, G.: Fast and scalable conflict detection for packet classifiers. In: IEEE ICNP (2002)
10. BreakingPoint firewall performance testing,
    `http://www.breakingpointsystems.com/solutions/firewall-testing/`

11. Bradner, S., McQuaid, J.: Benchmarking methodology for network interconnect devices. RFC 2544 (1999)
12. Cohen, E., Lund, C.: Packet classification in large ISPs: Design and evaluation of decision tree classifiers. In: ACM SIGMETRICS (2005)
13. Dreger, H., Feldmann, A., Paxson, V., Sommer, R.: Predicting the Resource Consumption of Network Intrusion Detection Systems. In: Lippmann, R., Kirda, E., Trachtenberg, A. (eds.) RAID 2008. LNCS, vol. 5230, pp. 135–154. Springer, Heidelberg (2008)
14. El-Atawy, A., Al-Shaer, E., Tran, T., Boutaba, R.: Adaptive early packet filtering for protecting firewalls against DoS attacks. In: IEEE INFOCOM (2009)
15. Gouda, M.G., Liu, A., Jafry, M.: Verification of distributed firewalls. In: IEEE GLOBECOM (2008)
16. Gouda, M.G., Liu, A.X.: Structured firewall design. Computer Networks (2007)
17. Hamed, H., Al-Shaer, E.: Dynamic rule-ordering optimization for high-speed firewall filtering. In: ASIACCS (2006)
18. Hari, A., Suri, S., Parulkar, G.: Detecting and resolving packet filter conflicts. In: IEEE INFOCOM (2000)
19. Liu, A.X.: Change-impact analysis of firewall policies. In: European Symp. Research Computer Security (2007)
20. Liu, A.X.: Firewall policy verification and troubleshooting. In: ICC (2008)
21. Liu, A.X., Gouda, M.G.: Firewall policy queries. IEEE Trans. on Parallel and Distributed Systems (2009)
22. Newman, D.: Benchmarking terminology for firewall devices. RFC 2647 (1999)
23. NSS Labs. IPS, UTM, Web application firewall testing lab, http://nsslabs.com
24. Shaer, E.A., Hamed, H.: Discovery of policy anomalies in distributed firewalls. In: IEEE INFOCOM (2004)
25. Caceres, R.: Measurements of Wide-Area Internet Traffic, UCB/CSD.89/550, Univ. CA, Berkeley (1989)

OFLOPS: An Open Framework
for OpenFlow Switch Evaluation

Charalampos Rotsos[1], Nadi Sarrar[2], Steve Uhlig[3],
Rob Sherwood[4,*], and Andrew W. Moore[1]

[1] University of Cambridge
[2] TU Berlin / T-Labs
[3] Queen Mary, University of London
[4] Big Switch Networks

Abstract. Recent efforts in software-defined networks, such as OpenFlow, give unprecedented access into the forwarding plane of networking equipment. When building a network based on OpenFlow however, one must take into account the performance characteristics of particular OpenFlow switch implementations. In this paper, we present OFLOPS, an open and generic software framework that permits the development of tests for OpenFlow-enabled switches, that measure the capabilities and bottlenecks between the forwarding engine of the switch and the remote control application. OFLOPS combines hardware instrumentation with an extensible software framework.

We use OFLOPS to evaluate current OpenFlow switch implementations and make the following observations: (i) The switching performance of flows depends on applied actions and firmware. (ii) Current OpenFlow implementations differ substantially in flow updating rates as well as traffic monitoring capabilities. (iii) Accurate OpenFlow command completion can be observed only through the data plane. These observations are crucial for understanding the applicability of OpenFlow in the context of specific use-cases, which have requirements in terms of forwarding table consistency, flow setup latency, flow space granularity, packet modification types, and/or traffic monitoring abilities.

1 Introduction

OpenFlow[1], an instance of software-defined networking (SDN), gives access deep within the network forwarding plane while providing a common, simple, API for network-device control. Implementation details are left to the discretion of each vendor. This leads to an expectation of diverse strengths and weaknesses across the existing OpenFlow implementations, which motivates our work.

OpenFlow is increasingly adopted, both by hardware vendors as well as by the research community [9,19,16]. Yet, there have been few performance studies: to our knowledge, OFLOPS is the first attempt to develop a platform that is able to provide detailed measurements for the OpenFlow implementations. Curtis *et al.* [6] discuss some design limitations of the protocol when deployed in large network environments. We consider OFLOPS, alongside [7], as one of a new generation of measurement systems

---

* The majority of the work was completed while at Deutsche Telekom Inc. R&D Lab.
[1] http://www.openflow.org/

N. Taft and F. Ricciato (Eds.): PAM 2012, LNCS 7192, pp. 85–95, 2012.

that, like the intelligent traffic and router evaluators [10,2], go beyond simple packet-capture.

We present OFLOPS[2], a tool that enables the rapid development of use-case tests for both hardware and software OpenFlow implementations. Using OFLOPS, developers can simulate specific usage scenarios and understand the impact of switch implementations in performance. We use OFLOPS to test publicly-available OpenFlow software implementations as well as several OpenFlow-enabled commercial hardware platforms, and report our findings about their varying performance characteristics. To better understand the behavior of the tested OpenFlow implementations, OFLOPS combines measurements from the OpenFlow control channel with data-plane measurements. To ensure sub-millisecond-level accuracy of the measurements, we bundle the OFLOPS software with specialized hardware in the form of the NetFPGA platform[3]. Note that if the tests do not require millisecond-level accuracy, commodity hardware can be used instead of the NetFPGA [3].

The rest of this paper is structured as follows. We first present the design of the OFLOPS framework in Section 2. We describe the measurement setup in Section 3. We describe our measurements in Section 4. We provide basic experiments that test the flow processing capabilities of the implementations (Section 4.1) as well as the performance and overhead of the OpenFlow communication channel (Section 4.2). We follow with specific tests, targeting the monitoring capabilities of OpenFlow (Section 4.3) as well as interactions between different types of OpenFlow commands (Section 4.4). We conclude in Section 5.

2   OFLOPS Framework

Measuring OpenFlow switch implementations is a challenging task in terms of characterization accuracy, noise suppression and precision. Performance characterization is not trivial as most OpenFlow-enabled devices provide rich functionality but do not disclose implementation details. In order to understand the performance impact of an experiment, multiple input measurements must be monitored concurrently. Furthermore, measurement noise minimization can only be achieved through proper design of the measurement platform. Current controller designs, like [8], target production networks and thus are optimized for throughput maximization and programmability, but incur high measurement inaccuracy. Finally, high precision measurements after a point are subject to loss due to unobserved parameters of the measurement host, such as OS scheduling and clock drift.

The OFLOPS design philosophy is to enable seamless interaction with an OpenFlow-enabled device over multiple data channels without introducing significant additional processing delays. The platform provides a unified system that allows developers to control and receive information from multiple control sources: data and control channels as well as SNMP to provide specific switch-state information. For the development of measurement experiments over OFLOPS, the platform provides a rich, event-driven,

---

[2] OFLOPS is under GPL licence and can be downloaded from
  http://www.openflow.org/wk/index.php/Oflops
[3] http://www.netfpga.org

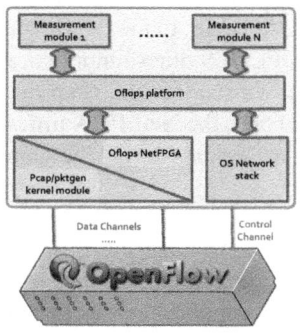

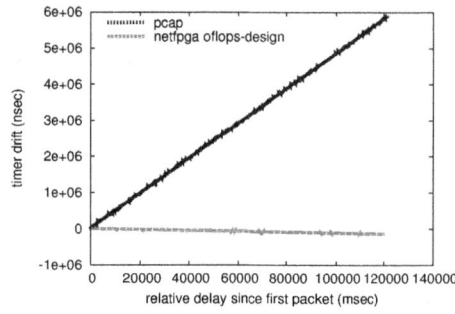

Fig. 1. OFLOPS design schematic

Fig. 2. Evaluating timestamping precision using a DAG card

API that allows developers to handle events programatically in order to implement and measure custom controller functionality. The current version is written predominantly in C. Experiments are compiled as shared libraries and loaded at run-time using a simple configuration language, through which experimental parameters can be defined. A schematic of the platform is presented in Figure 1. Details of the OFLOPS programming model can be found in the API manual [4].

The platform is implemented as a multi-threaded application, to take advantage of modern multicore environments. To reduce latency, our design avoids concurrent access controls: we leave any concurrency-control complexity to individual module implementations. OFLOPS consists of the following five threads, each one serving specific type of events:

1. Data Packet Generation controls data plane traffic generators.
2. Data Packet Capture captures and pushes data plane traffic to modules.
3. Control Channel translates OpenFlow packets to control events.
4. SNMP Channel performs asynchronous SNMP polling.
5. Time Manager manages time events scheduled by measurement modules.

OFLOPS provides the ability to control concurrently multiple data channels to the switch. By embedding the data channel within the platform, it is possible to understand the impact of the measurement scenario on the switching plane. To enable our platform to run on multiple heterogeneous platforms, we have integrated support for multiple packet generation and capturing mechanisms. For the packet generation functionality, OFLOPS supports three mechanisms: user-space, kernel-space through the pktgen module [13], and hardware-accelerated through an extension of the design of the NetFPGA Stanford Packet Generator [5]. For the packet capturing and timestamping, the platform supports both the pcap library and the modified NetFPGA design. Each approach provides different precisions and different impacts upon the measurement platform.

A comparison of the precision of the traffic capturing mechanisms is presented in Figure 2. In this experiment we use a constant rate 100 Mbps probe of small packets for

---

[4] http://www.openflow.org/wk/images/3/3e/Manual.pdf

a two minute period. The probe is duplicated, using an optical wiretap with negligible delay, and sent simultaneously to OFLOPS and to a DAG card. In the figure, we plot the differences of the relative timestamp between each OFLOPS timestamping mechanism and the DAG card for each packet. From the figure, we see that the pcap timestamps drift by 6 milliseconds after 2 minutes. On the other hand, the NetFPGA timestamping mechanism has a smaller drift at the level of a few microseconds during the same period.

3   Measurement Setup

The number of OpenFlow-enabled devices has slowly increased recently, with switch and router vendors providing experimental OpenFlow support such as prototype and evaluation firmware. At the end of 2009, the OpenFlow protocol specification was released in its first stable version 1.0 [1], the first recommended version implemented by vendors for production systems. Consequently, vendors did proceed on maturing their prototype implementations, offering production-ready OpenFlow-enabled switches today. Using OFLOPS, we evaluate OpenFlow-enabled switches from three different switch vendors. Vendor 1 has production-ready OpenFlow support, whereas vendors 2 and 3 at this point only provide experimental OpenFlow support. The set of selected switches provides a representative but not exhaustive sample of available OpenFlow-enabled top-of-rack-style switching hardware. Details regarding the CPU and the size of the flow table of the switches are provided in Table 1.

OpenFlow is not limited to hardware. The OpenFlow protocol reference is the software switch, OpenVSwitch [14], an important implementation for production environments. Firstly, OpenVSwitch provides a replacement for the poor-performing Linux bridge, a crucial functionality for virtualised operating systems. Secondly, several hardware switch vendors use OpenVSwitch as the basis for the development of their own OpenFlow-enabled firmware. Thus, the mature software implementation of the OpenFlow protocol is ported to commercial hardware, making certain implementation bugs less likely to (re)appear. In this paper, we study OpenVSwitch alongside our performance and scalability study of hardware switches. Finally, in our comparison we include the OpenFlow switch design for the NetFPGA platform [12]; a full implementation of the protocol, limited though in capabilities due to hardware platform limitations.

In order to conduct our measurements, we setup OFLOPS on a dual-core 2.4GHz Xeon server equipped with a NetFPGA card. For all the experiments we utilize the NetFPGA-based packet generating and capturing mechanism. 1Gbps control and data

Table 1. OpenFlow switch details

Switch	CPU	Flow table size
Switch1	PowerPC 500MHz	3072 mixed flows
Switch2	PowerPC 666MHz	1500 mixed flows
Switch3	PowerPC 828MHz	2048 mixed flows
OpenVSwitch	Xeon 3.6GHz	1M mixed flows
NetFPGA	DualCore 2.4GHz	32K exact & 100 wildcard

channels are connected directly to the tested switches. We measure the processing delay incurred by the NetFPGA-based hardware design to be a near-constant 900 nsec independent of the probe rate.

4   Evaluation

In this section we present a set of tests performed by OFLOPS to measure the behavior and performance of OpenFlow-enabled devices, by simulating a set of simple usage scenarios. These tests target (1) the OpenFlow packet processing actions, (2) the update rate of the OpenFlow flow table along with its impact on the data plane, (3) the monitoring capabilities provided by OpenFlow, and (4) the impact of interactions between different OpenFlow operations.

4.1   Packet Modifications

The OpenFlow specification [1] defines ten packet modification actions which can be applied on incoming packets. Available actions include modification of MAC, IP, and VLAN values, as well as transport-layer fields and flows can contain any combination of them. The left column of Table 2 lists the packet fields that can be modified by an OpenFlow-enabled switch. These actions are used by network devices such as IP routers (e.g., rewriting of source and destination MAC addresses) and NAT (rewriting of IP addresses and ports). Existing network equipment is tailored to perform a subset of these operations, usually in hardware to sustain line rate. On the other hand, how these operations are to be used is yet to be defined for new network primitives and applications, such as network virtualization, mobility support, or flow-based traffic engineering.

To measure the time taken by an OpenFlow implementation to modify a packet field header, we generate from the NetFPGA card UDP packets of 100 bytes at a constant rate of 100Mbps (approx. 125 Kpps). This rate is high enough to give statistically significant results in a short period of time. The flow table is initialized with a flow that applies a specific action on all probe packets and the processing delay is calculated using the transmission and receipt timestamps, provided by the NetFPGA.

Evaluating individual packet field modification, Table 2 reports the median difference between the generation and capture timestamp of the measurement probe along with its standard deviation and percent of lost packets.

We observe significant differences in the performance of the hardware switches due in part to the way each handles packet modifications. Switch1, with its production-grade implementation, handles all modifications in hardware; this explains its low packet processing delay between 3 and 4 microseconds. On the other hand, Switch2 and Switch3 each run experimental firmware providing only partial hardware support for OpenFlow actions. Switch2 uses the switch CPU to perform some of the available field modifications, resulting in two orders of magnitude higher packet processing delay and variance. Switch3 follows a different approach: All packets of flows with actions not supported in hardware are silently discarded. The performance of the OpenVSwitch software implementation lies between Switch1 and the other hardware switches. OpenVSwitch fully implements all OpenFlow actions. However, hardware switches outperform OpenVSwitch when the flow actions are supported in hardware.

Table 2. Time in μs to perform individual packet modifications and packet loss. Processing delay indicates whether the operation is implemented in hardware ($<10\mu$s) or software ($>10\mu$s).

Mod. type	Switch1			OpenVSwitch			Switch2			Switch3			NetFPGA		
	med	sd	loss%	med	sd	loss%	med	sd	loss%	med	sd	loss%	med	sd	loss%
Forward	4	0	0	35	13	0	6	0	0	5	0	0	3	0	0
MAC addr.	4	0	0	35	13	0	302	727	88	-	-	100	3	0	0
IP addr.	3	0	0	36	13	0	302	615	88	-	-	100	3	0	0
IP ToS	3	0	0	36	16	0	6	0	0	-	-	100	3	0	0
L4 port	3	0	0	35	15	0	302	611	88	-	-	100	3	0	0
VLAN pcp	3	0	0	36	20	0	6	0	0	5	0	0	3	0	0
VLAN id	4	0	0	35	17	0	301	610	88	5	0	0	3	0	0
VLAN rem.	4	0	0	35	15	0	335	626	88	5	0	0	3	0	0

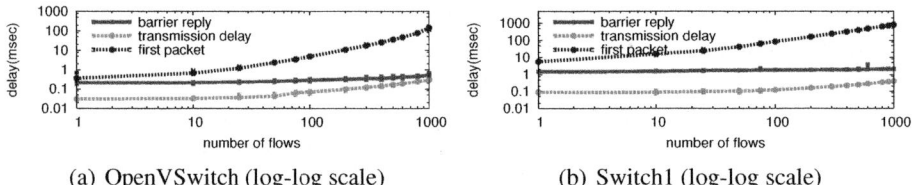

(a) OpenVSwitch (log-log scale)   (b) Switch1 (log-log scale)

Fig. 3. Flow entry insertion delay: as reported using the `barrier` notification and as observed at the data plane

We conducted a further series of experiments with variable numbers of packet modifications as flow actions and probe rates. We observed, that the combined processing time of a set of packet modifications is equal to the highest processing time across all individual actions in the set. For higher probe rates, we report that all software-implemented actions increase latency and packet loss, while hardware-supported actions are not affected.

4.2 Flow Table Update Rate

The flow table is a central component of an OpenFlow switch and is the equivalent of a Forwarding Information Base (FIB) on routers. Given the importance of FIB updates on commercial routers, e.g., to reduce the impact of control plane dynamics on the data plane, the FIB update processing time of commercial routers provide useful reference points and lower bounds for the time to update a flow entry on an OpenFlow switch. The time to install a new entry on commercial routers has been reported in the range of a few hundreds of microseconds [15].

OpenFlow provides a mechanism to define barriers between sets of commands: the `barrier` command. According to the OpenFlow specification [1], the barrier command is a way to be notified that a set of OpenFlow operations has been completed. Further, the switch has to complete the set of operations issued prior to the barrier before executing any further operation. If the OpenFlow implementations comply with the specification, we expect to receive a barrier notification for a flow modification once the flow table of the switch has been updated, implying that the change can be seen from the data plane.

We check the behavior of the tested OpenFlow implementations, finding variation among them. For OpenVSwitch and Switch1, Figure 3 shows the time to install a set of entries in the flow table. The NetFPGA-based switch results (not reported) are similar to those of Switch1, while Switch2 and Switch3 are not reported as this OpenFlow message is not supported by the firmware. For this experiment, OFLOPS relies on a stream of packets of 100 bytes at a constant rate of 10Mbps on the data plane that targets the newly installed flows in a round-robin manner. The probe achieves sufficiently low inter-packet periods in order to measure accurately the flow insertion time, without packet loss.

In Figure 3, we show three different times. The first, *barrier notification*, is derived by measuring the time between when the **first insertion command** is sent by the OFLOPS controller and the time the barrier notification is received by the PC. The second, *transmission delay*, is the time between the first and last flow insertion commands are sent out from the PC running OFLOPS. The third, *first packet*, is the time between the **first insertion command** is issued and a packet has been observed for the last of the (newly) inserted rules on the data plane. For each configuration, we run the experiment 100 times and Figure 3 shows the median result as well as the 10th and 90th percentiles (variations are small and cannot be easily viewed).

From Figure 3, we observe that even though the *transmission delay* for sending flow insertion commands increases with their number, this time is negligible when compared with data plane measurements (*first packet*). Notably, the *barrier notification* measurements are almost constant, increasing only as the transmission delay increases (difficult to discern on the log-log plot) and, critically, this operation returns before any *first packet* measurement. This implies that the way the *barrier notification* is implemented does not reflect the time when the hardware flow-table has been updated.

In these results we demonstrate how OFLOPS can compute per-flow overheads. We observe that the flow insertion time for Switch1 starts at 1.8ms for a single entry, but converges toward an approximate overhead of 1ms per inserted entry as the number of insertions grows.

Flow insertion types. We now distinguish between flow insertions and the modification of existing flows. With OpenFlow, a flow rule may perform exact packet matches or

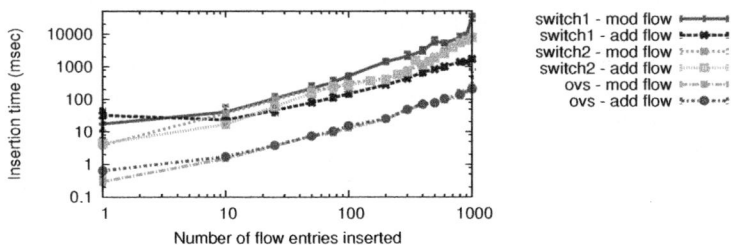

Fig. 4. Delay of flow insertion and flow modification, as observed from the data plane (log-log scale)

use wild-cards to match a range of values. Figure 4 compares the flow insertion delay as a function of the number of inserted entries. This is done for the insertion of new entries and for the modification of existing entries.

These results show that for software switches that keep all entries in memory, the type of entry or insertion does not make a difference in the flow insertion time. Surprisingly, both Switch1 and Switch2 take more time to modify existing flow entries compared to adding new flow entries. For Switch1, this occurs for more than 10 new entries, while for Switch2 this occurs after a few tens of new entries. After discussing this issue with the vendor of Switch2, we came to the following conclusion: as the number of TCAM entries increases, updates become more complex as they typically requires re-ordering of existing entries.

Clearly, the results depend both on the entry type and implementation. For example, exact match entries may be handled through a hardware or software hash table. Whereas, wild-carded entries, requiring support for variable length lookup, must be handled by specialized memory modules, such as TCAM. With such possible choices and range of different experiments, the flow insertion times reported in Figure 4 are not generalizable, but rather depend on the type of insertion entry and implementation.

4.3   Flow Monitoring

The use of OpenFlow as a monitoring platform has already been suggested for the applications of traffic matrix computation [17,4] and identifying large traffic aggregates [11]. To obtain direct information about the state of the traffic received by an OpenFlow switch, the OpenFlow protocol provides a mechanism to query traffic statistics, either on a per-flow basis or across aggregates matching multiple flows and supports packet and byte counters.

We now test the performance implications of the traffic statistics reporting mechanism of OpenFlow. Using OFLOPS, we install flow entries that match packets sent on the data path. Simultaneously, we start sending flow statistics requests to the switch. Throughout the experiment we record: the delay getting a reply for each query, the amount of packets that the switch sends for each reply and the departure and arrival timestamps of the probe packets.

Figure 5 reports the time to receive a flow statistics reply for each switch, as a function of the request rate. Despite the rate of statistics requests being modest, quite high CPU utilization results for even a few queries per second being sent. Figure 5 reports the switch-CPU utilization as a function of the flow statistics inter-request time. Statistics are retrieved using SNMP. Switch3 is excluded for lack of SNMP support.

From the flow statistics reply times, we observe that all switches have (near-) constant response delays: the delay itself relates to the type of switch. As expected, software switches have faster response times than hardware switches, reflecting the availability of the information in memory without the need to poll multiple hardware counters. These consistent response times also hide the behavior of the exclusively hardware switches whose CPU time increases proportionally with the rate of requests. We observe two implementation approaches for the hardware switches: the switch has a high CPU utilization, answering flow-stats requests as fast as possible (Switch2), or the switch applies a pacing mechanism on its replies, avoiding over-loading its CPU (Switch1).

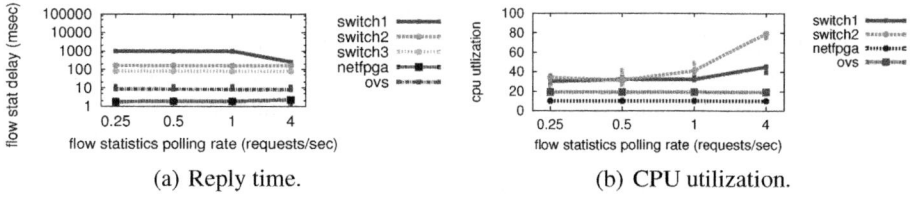

(a) Reply time.   (b) CPU utilization.

Fig. 5. Time to receive a flow statistic (median) and corresponding CPU utilization

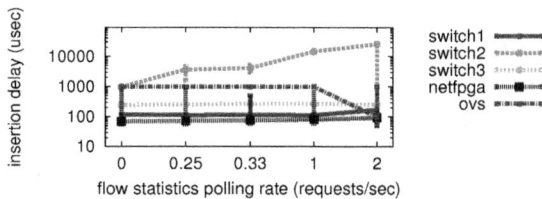

Fig. 6. Delay when updating flow table while the controller polls for statistics

Specifically, at low polling rates Switch1 splits its answer across multiple TCP segments: each segment containing statistics for a single flow. As the probing rate increases, the switch will aggregate multiple flows into a single segment. This suggests that an independent processing mechanisms is used to handle flow statistics requests. Finally, neither software nor NetFPGA switches see an impact of the flow-stats rate on their CPU, thanks to their significantly more powerful PC CPUs (Table 1).

4.4   OpenFlow Command Interaction

An advanced feature of the OpenFlow protocol is its ability to provide applications with, e.g., flow arrival notifications from the network, while simultaneously providing fine-grain control of the forwarding process. This permits applications to adapt in real time to the requirements and load of the network [9,18]. Under certain OpenFlow usage scenarios, e.g., the simultaneous querying of traffic statistics and modification of the flow table, understanding the behavior of the data and control plane of OpenFlow switches is difficult without advanced measurement instrumentation such as the one provided by OFLOPS.

Through this scenario, we extend Section 4.2 to show how the mechanisms of traffic statistics extraction and table manipulation may interact. Specifically, we initialize the flow table with 1024 exact match flows and measure the delay to update a subset of 100 flows. Simultaneously, the measurement module polls the switch for full table statistics at a constant rate. The experiment uses a constant rate 10Mbps packet probe to monitor the data path, and polls every 10 seconds for SNMP CPU values.

In this experiment, we control the probing rate for the flow statistics extraction mechanism, and we plot the time necessary for the modified flows to become active in the flow table. For each probing rate, we repeat the experiment 50 times, plotting the median, 10th and 90th percentile. In Figure 6 we can see that, for lower polling rates, implementations have a near-constant insertion delay comparable to the results of

Section 4.2. For higher probing rates on the other hand, Switch1 and Switch3 do not differ much in their behavior. In contrast, Switch2 exhibits a noteworthy increase in the insertion delay explained by the CPU utilization increase incurred by the flow statistics polling (Figure 5(b)). Finally, OpenVSwitch exhibits a marginal decrease in the median insertion delay and at the same time an increase in its variance. We believe this behavior is caused by interactions with the OS scheduling mechanism: the constant polling causes frequent interrupts for the user-space daemon of the switch, which leads to a batched handling of requests.

5   Summary and Conclusions

We presented, OFLOPS, a modular tool to test the capabilities and performance of OpenFlow-enabled software and hardware switches. OFLOPS combines advanced hardware instrumentation, for accuracy and performance, and provides an extensible software framework. We use OFLOPS to evaluate five different OpenFlow switch implementations, in terms of OpenFlow protocol support as well as performance.

We identify considerable variation among the tested OpenFlow implementations. We take advantage of the ability of OFLOPS for data plane measurements to quantify accurately how fast switches process and apply OpenFlow commands. For example, we found that the barrier reply message is not correctly implemented, making it difficult to predict when flow operations will be seen by the data plane. Finally, we found that the monitoring capabilities of existing hardware switches have limitations in their ability to sustain high rates of requests. Further, at high rates, monitoring operations impact other OpenFlow commands.

We hope that the use of OFLOPS will allow better understanding of the performance impact of OpenFlow implementations in network systems and trigger improvements in the OpenFlow protocol as well as its implementations by various vendors.

References

1. Openflow switch specification (version 1.0.0) (December 2009)
2. Agilent. N2X router tester, http://advanced.comms.agilent.com/n2x/
3. Arlos, P., Fiedler, M.: A Method to Estimate the Timestamp Accuracy of Measurement Hardware and Software Tools. In: Uhlig, S., Papagiannaki, K., Bonaventure, O. (eds.) PAM 2007. LNCS, vol. 4427, pp. 197–206. Springer, Heidelberg (2007)
4. Balestra, G., Luciano, S., Pizzonia, M., Vissicchio, S.: Leveraging router programmability for traffic matrix computation. In: Proc. of PRESTO Workshop (2010)
5. Covington, G.A., Gibb, G., Lockwood, J.W., Mckeown, N.: A packet generator on the NetFPGA platform. In: FCCM (2009)
6. Curtis, A.R., Mogul, J.C., Tourrilhes, J., Yalagandula, P., Sharma, P., Banerjee, S.: Devoflow: scaling flow management for high-performance networks. In: ACM SIGCOMM (2011)
7. Freedman, D.A., Marian, T., Lee, J.H., Birman, K., Weatherspoon, H., Xu, C.: Exact temporal characterization of 10 gbps optical wide-area network. In: IMC 2010 (2010)
8. Gude, N., Koponen, T., Pettit, J., Pfaff, B., Casado, M., McKeown, N., Shenker, S.: Nox: towards an operating system for networks. SIGCOMM Comput. Commun. Rev. (July 2008)

9. Handigol, N., Seetharaman, S., Flajslik, M., McKeown, N., Johari, R.: Plug-n-Serve: Load-Balancing Web Traffic using OpenFlow. ACM SIGCOMM Demo (August 2009)

10. Ixia. Interfaces, http://www.ixiacom.com/

11. Jose, L., Yu, M., Rexford, J.: Online measurement of large traffic aggregates on commodity switches. In: Proc. of the USENIX HotICE Workshop (2011)

12. Naous, J., Erickson, D., Covington, G.A., Appenzeller, G., McKeown, N.: Implementing an openflow switch on the netfpga platform. In: ANCS (2008)

13. Olsson, R.: Pktgen the linux packet generator. In: Proceedings of Linux Symposium (2005)

14. Pettit, J., Gross, J., Pfaff, B., Casado, M., Crosby, S.: Virtualizing the network forwarding plane. In: DC-CAVES (2010)

15. Shaikh, A., Greenberg, A.: Experience in black-box ospf measurement. In: ACM IMC (2001)

16. Sherwood, R., Gibb, G., Yap, K.-K., Cassado, M., Appenzeller, G., McKeown, N., Parulkar, G.: Can the production network be the test-bed? In: OSDI (2010)

17. Tootoonchian, A., Ghobadi, M., Ganjali, Y.: OpenTM: Traffic Matrix Estimator for Open-Flow Networks. In: Krishnamurthy, A., Plattner, B. (eds.) PAM 2010. LNCS, vol. 6032, pp. 201–210. Springer, Heidelberg (2010)

18. Yap, K.-K., Kobayashi, M., Underhill, D., Seetharaman, S., Kazemian, P., McKeown, N.: The stanford openroads deployment. In: Proceedings of ACM WINTECH (2009)

19. Yu, M., Rexford, J., Freedman, M.J., Wang, J.: Scalable flow-based networking with difane. In: ACM SIGCOMM (August 2010)

Probe and Pray: Using UPnP for Home Network Measurements

Lucas DiCioccio[1,2], Renata Teixeira[2,3], Martin May[1], and Christian Kreibich[4]

[1] Technicolor
[2] UPMC Sorbonne Universites
[3] CNRS
[4] ICSI

Abstract. Network measurement practitioners increasingly focus their interest on understanding and debugging home networks. The Universal Plug and Play (UPnP) technology holds promise as a highly efficient way to collect and leverage measurement data and configuration settings available from UPnP-enabled devices found in home networks. Unfortunately, UPnP proves less available and reliable than one would hope. In this paper, we explore the usability of UPnP as a means to measure and characterize home networks. We use data from 120,000 homes, collected with the HomeNet Profiler and Netalyzr troubleshooting suites. Our results show that in the majority of homes we could not collect any UPnP data at all, and when we could, the results were frequently inaccurate or simply wrong. Whenever UPnP-supplied data proved accurate, however, we demonstrate that UPnP provides an array of useful measurement techniques for inferring home network traffic and losses, for identifying home gateway models with configuration or implementation issues, and for obtaining ground truth on access link capacity.

1 Introduction

The network measurement community increasingly focuses attention on measuring and characterizing broadband Internet access and home networks. For example, measurements from end-hosts connected to home networks have highlighted the "buffer bloat" problem of oversized buffers found in a wide range of home gateways, which hurt interactive applications [8]. In addition, a number of measurement efforts infer the speed of residential Internet access networks from different vantage points: servers in the Internet [7], end-hosts connected to home networks [2,8], or home gateways [9]. Some research groups advocate instrumenting home gateways for measuring both access network performance and properties of home networks, because all traffic between the home network and the Internet traverses the home gateway [3–5,9]. On the other hand, measurement suites such as Netalyzr [8] and Ono [2], which run on the end-hosts, face a lower start-up cost and have demonstrated the potential to reach a large number of homes quickly.

Universal Plug and Play (UPnP) [10] offers great opportunities for home network measurement. The UPnP standard provides a suite of protocols for home

N. Taft and F. Ricciato (Eds.): PAM 2012, LNCS 7192, pp. 96–105, 2012.

network devices to automatically discover one another, retrieve operational parameters, and configure themselves. Hence, a tool running on an end-host connected to the home network can directly query the home gateway. For instance, the tool can obtain the manufacturer and the model of the home gateway to then pinpoint devices that suffer from particularly oversized buffers. As another example, end-hosts can obtain the capacity of the access link and the volume of traffic traversing the gateway, which can help explain measured link speeds. Despite UPnP's promises, the few measurement studies that have leveraged UPnP to date have focused on only a handful of home gateways [1,5], and so the general degree of UPnP adoption and the usability of its implementations has so far remained unclear.

This paper explores the opportunities and pitfalls of using UPnP to measure home networks using data collected with Netalyzr [8] and HomeNet Profiler [6]. Our analysis combines and contrasts end-to-end link capacity and buffer delay measurements with additional information obtained from UPnP queries to local gateway devices (§2). While our dataset covers over 120,000 home networks, we only succeed in obtaining UPnP measurements in around 35% of these homes (§3). Worse, when UPnP implementations do produce responses, they sometimes turn out to be misleading or simply wrong (§4).

When the UPnP responses prove accurate, however, they provide considerable value. We show how practitioners can leverage the information for a range of interesting measurements and troubleshooting tasks (§5). First, we use the UPnP data to determine the real access link capacity and find that the protocol overhead is about 14% in most home network deployments. Then, we use the data from the UPnP reports together with end-to-end measurements to determine the amount of cross-traffic from the home traversing the gateway. Furthermore, we quantify packet losses occurring in the home and in the wide area network by comparing the end-to-end measurements with the local information available at UPnP-enabled home gateways. Finally, we leverage UPnP-provided information in order to tie measured buffer sizes and other device characteristics to specific gateway models.

We hope that this paper will inspire researchers to include UPnP in their home network measurement testsuites, and to encourage gateway vendors to improve their UPnP implementations.

2   Measurement Method

We base our analysis on measurement data collected by the Netalyzr [8] and HomeNet Profiler [6] testsuites. Both run on end-hosts, frequently within a home network, and perform a series of measurements when prompted by the user. This section discusses only the subset of measurements we study in the rest of this paper. To get a common baseline for buffer delays, up/downlink capacities, and round-trip times both tools execute the same code: HomeNet Profiler runs Netalyzr via its command-line API. The main Netalyzr paper [8] presents the details of these measurements. In the following we describe UPnP's basic operation, and present the UPnP measurements we implemented in Netalyzr and HomeNet Profiler.

UPnP protocol. UPnP provides mechanisms for LAN-level discovery and control of a wide range of services specified by the UPnP standards. Discovery employs multicast UDP requests in order to contact peers matching a specific service class, expressed in HTTP header-like plaintext. The responses, if any, contain HTTP URLs via which the client may obtain a device's full description, expressed in XML. This description contains a list of APIs the client may subsequently invoke via the HTTP SOAP protocol. The UPnP standard specifies security levels for the APIs to limit the threat of rogue clients accessing sensitive APIs. We employ only non-sensitive APIs.

UPnP measurements. Given our focus on services offered by home gateways, we first discover any 'WANCommonInterfaceConfig' services. We then retrieve the device description from responding devices, and collect four non-sensitive gateway configuration parameters: (1) the device model name and version, (2) the device's WAN interface type (e.g., DSL, Cable), (3) the physical connection rate (e.g., 10 Mbps/1 Mbps), and (4) unidirectional byte/packet counters maintained by the gateway. To test the accuracy of these counters, we retrieve them immediately before and after sending known-size packet trains to a server in the Internet. HomeNet Profiler's train consists of 20 ICMP pings over 10 seconds, Netalyzr's of UDP bursts making up its bandwidth test. Comparing the actual before/after counters to the expected values allows us to gauge cross-traffic. HomeNet Profiler also obtains traffic counters from the local system to account for other cross-traffic from the local host.

In addition to the client-side measurements, both Netalyzr's and HomeNet Profiler's servers log the client's AS number and geographical location based on the public IP address that reports the measurements. Both tools include a survey that explicitly asks users whether they ran the tests from their home. We use this information to identify runs from home networks as opposed to tests conducted from public or office networks. When users did not complete the survey, we apply a heuristic to detect home networks: we first identify all ASes belonging to home access providers (for details, see our technical report [6]). Our analysis considers only a single run from each home network.

3   Dataset

We employ three datasets, summarized in Table 1. The HomeNet Profiler dataset ("HNP") included UPnP measurements from the beginning. Netalyzr added UPnP measurement incrementally. The first version with UPnP, which we call "Netalyzr-1," performed only the device identification. More recent versions, "Netalyzr-2," implement all UPnP measurements discussed in Section 2.

The table indicates that we only obtain UPnP measurements in 35% of all homes. An explanation for the differences in the fraction of homes with UPnP

Table 1. Dataset description (UPnP refers to the percent of homes with UPnP gateways)

Dataset	Start date	End date	Homes	UPnP	Countries	ASes
HNP	4/4/2011	12/15/2011	2209	54%	43	208
Netalyzr-1	3/23/2011	8/29/2011	95417	22%	131	1373
Netalyzr-2	8/30/2011	12/15/2011	30243	47%	114	949

gateway may come from the population bias of each dataset. HNP is biased towards France, Netalyzr-2 towards Germany, whereas Netalyzr-1 is more balanced. This value does not necessarily mean that the home gateways do not implement UPnP. We identify three possible reasons for failing UPnP measurements, which we cannot distinguish in the data: (1) some gateways do not actually implement UPnP; (2) others implement it, but keep UPnP disabled by default; (3) host-level firewalling prevents the end-host from issuing UPnP's multicast discovery query [6] or seeing the responses. The rest of this paper analyzes the homes in which at least one gateway responded to the service discovery query. We first discuss measurements artifacts and how we eliminate them from our dataset, then we present the results with the rest of the data.

4   Measurement Artifacts

When the client manages to receive UPnP responses, the reported values may still be misleading or simply wrong. This section discusses the issues we encountered in practice and explains how we clean the dataset from these measurement artifacts. We first discuss the challenge of interpreting UPnP data correctly without additional information about the home network configuration. Then, we report UPnP specification and implementation problems.

4.1   Misleading Home Network Configurations

Gateways connected over Ethernet. We find 10% of homes with UPnP where the gateway reports Ethernet WAN connectivity. While some homes might connect to the Internet via Ethernet, only few ISPs offer this kind of service. In fact, the top ISPs with gateways that reported Ethernet connectivity in our measurements were Vodafone, Verizon, and Comcast, which do not provide this type of connectivity. We thus believe that most of these cases correspond to homes where the UPnP gateway connects to a modem via Ethernet and the modem connects to the ISP. The reported synchronization rate is then the speed of the Ethernet link between modem and UPnP gateway (e.g., 100 Mbps), which does not reflect the access link speed. When comparing UPnP link speeds with measured link capacity, we therefore eliminate all cases where the gateway claims Ethernet connectivity.

Homes with more than one UPnP gateway. We detect that 3% of the homes with UPnP have more than one UPnP gateway in Netalyzr-2 and 4% homes in HNP.

Such configurations occur in large homes, where it becomes necessary to install multiple access points to cover the entire place. In these deployments, the primary gateway connects to the access link and the others connect to this primary gateway via Ethernet. Since our data cannot reveal the actual primary gateway, we remove these homes from the rest of the analysis. In Netalyzr-1, we only have UPnP queries to the first device that responded as a gateway. Hence, Netalyzr-1 may contain outliers. Given the number of homes with multiple gateways is small, this artifact should not bias our results.

4.2   UPnP Design and Implementation Issues

Inconsistent UPnP discovery. HomeNet Profiler uses two distinct queries to discover UPnP services: one query searches explicitly for gateways (as described in §2), the other queries for any UPnP service with a wildcard option. We compare the number of UPnP gateways found by these two queries as a sanity check. Among the 2186 homes with both measurements, the two queries agree in 85% of the homes; in 14% of the homes, the gateway only answers to the specific search, and in 1% of the homes the gateway only answers the wildcard search. We found no correlation between the gateway model or the ISP and these inconsistent responses, so if the differences stem from implementation errors, these problems only manifest rarely. Lost query packets could likewise offer an explanation for the differences. In the rest of the paper, we only analyze data from devices we discovered via explicit requests for gateway devices.

Incomplete identifiers. UPnP provides two fields to identify devices: name and model. In practice, these fields are not always specified. In some cases, we only get the device name, but not the model. In others, the device name has the UPnP profile name or a vague description such as "Wireless Router" and not the device name.

Inaccurate connection type. We find 25% of homes in the French ISP SFR where the gateway reports Cable connectivity. This ISP does not offer cable Internet. In addition, the same homes all report a symmetric synchronization rate of 4.2 Mbps, which the ISP does not actually offer. We conjecture that some SFR's gateways have a hardcoded UPnP configuration. We find a similar configuration in other models but at a lower frequency.

Inaccurate synchronization rates. We identified three cases of access link synchronization rates reported inaccurately. First, in 1% of homes, the synchronization rate is reported in wrong units. The gateway reports a synchronization rate lower than 64 Kbps, even for ADSL or Cable users. Given the values, we believe that these UPnP implementations report values in Kilobits/s or KiloBytes/s, instead of bits per second (as specified in UPnP specification). This problem affects 30 models by three distinct vendors. Second, in 7% of homes, the gateway reports a synchronization rate of zero in both directions, which clearly cannot be the case given we could contact servers outside the home. Most of these inaccurate values occurred with Sagem and Fritzbox gateways. Finally, some ISPs

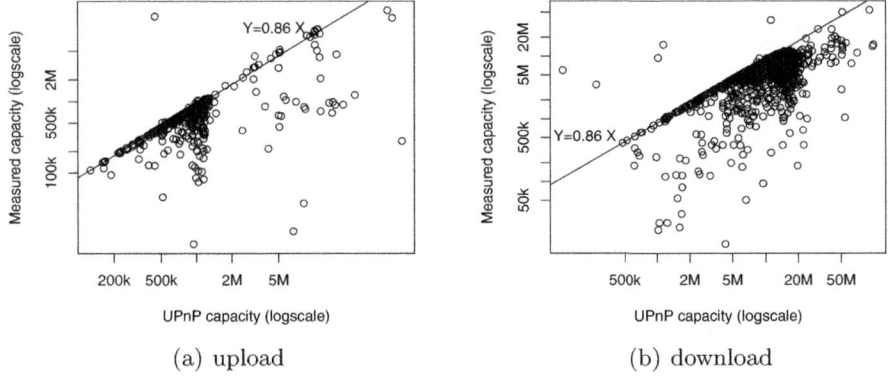

(a) upload   (b) download

Fig. 1. UPnP reported capacities versus active capacity measurements (This figure presents results for 1,084 homes in HNP, Netalyzr-1, and Netalyzr-2)

configure the gateway to report a hardcoded synchronization rate, which often corresponds to the rate the ISP advertises commercially and not the rate negotiated between the modem and the DSLAM or CMTS. In particular, almost all customers of the French ISP Free have the exact same synchronization rate.

Inaccurate traffic counters. The UPnP gateway does not respond to the traffic counter queries in 22% of the homes of Netalyzr-2 and HNP datasets. In 3% homes, UPnP gateways answer the query for traffic counters, but always report the exact same value.

We remove all inaccurate reports (on connection types, synchronization rates, and traffic counters) from the relevant analysis in the rest of this paper.

5   Analysis

This section illustrates four practical examples where UPnP queries help enhance end-host based measurements.

5.1   UPnP Link Capacity Versus Measured Capacity

We compare the upload and download capacities measured by Netalyzr with the capacity reported by UPnP. Figure 1(a) presents the measured upload rates versus the reported upload rates per home. Most points in this figure fall on a straight line with slope 0.86 and zero intercept (72% of the points are within a 5% interval). This linear relationship comes from the protocol overhead of PPP encapsulation. This result means that UPnP reports the raw rates, whereas Netalzyr measures IP rates. We observe a cluster of points with upload rates around 1.2 Mbps, which is a common commercial uplink limitation. Measured upload rates are consistently close to the 0.86 line, which indicates that the uplink is the bottleneck in the end-to-end path and that there is little cross-traffic from the home competing for uplink bandwidth.

Figure 1(b) compares the measured download rates with the download rates UPnP reports per home. Again, we see few points above the $Y = 0.86X$ line, indicating the same overhead as for uploads, and clustering along the line. However, download rates exhibit more variance than upload rates. In general, most Internet applications (such as web surfing or media streaming) consume more downlink than uplink bandwidth. The higher variance in the downstream direction thus

suggests that cross-traffic may affect downstream bandwidth measurement accuracy more than in the upstream direction, despite upstreams frequently possessing smaller available bandwidths. This result reaffirms previous measurements of residential broadband Internet access in the United States [9].

5.2   Inferring Cross Traffic

A measurement tool running on an end-host inside the home can estimate the cross traffic from other hosts connected to the home network by querying the gateway's UPnP traffic counters. We study traffic counters in the HNP dataset, because it logs both UPnP counters and traffic counters in the local host. In this dataset, we obtain realistic traffic counter measurements in a total of 461 homes. Homes in the dataset have different access link capacities, so to compare results across homes we normalize the number of bytes observed by the gateway (computed from UPnP counters) by Netalyzr's measured uplink capacity; we perform the same normalization to the number of bytes sent by the local host.

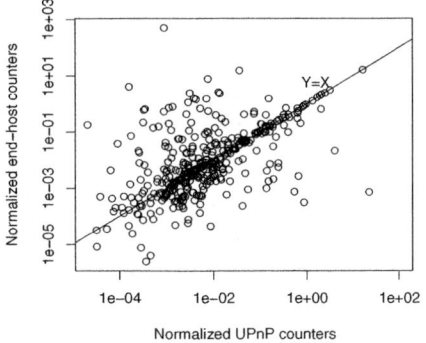

Fig. 2. Access link uplink usage from the localhost and at the gateway (This figure presents results for 461 homes in HNP)

Figure 2 plots the normalized traffic observed at the gateway on the x-axis versus the normalized traffic sent by the host in the y-axis. When x=y, the gateway and the host observe the same traffic, which implies that there is no other traffic in the home network or to the Internet. For points below the diagonal line, the gateway saw more traffic than the end-host, which indicates that other devices in the home network were sending traffic to the Internet. For points above this line, the host was sending traffic to other local destinations (note that the UPnP counter only reports traffic to and from the WAN interface). This plot shows that in most of the homes there was mainly local traffic (from the host to other devices in the home) during our measurements. This case accounts for 53% of the points in Figure 2, whereas the case with cross-traffic from other devices to the Internet represents 38% of points. It may seem surprising to have more traffic to the local network than the Internet. This result is just an artifact of our measurement methodology. When users run HomeNet Profiler or Netalyzr, they often just wait for the results instead of running other Internet applications on the side. In this scenario, the background traffic in the home network (of protocols such as DHCP) composes most of the cross-traffic. In fact, the volume of local cross-traffic is less than 18 KB in 90% of HomeNet Profiler's test.

5.3   Quantifying Loss in the Home vs. The Wide Area

The UPnP traffic counters also prove useful for distinguishing packet loss in the home network from that in the wide area, a use case often mentioned by proponents of gateway-driven measurements. We can conduct the same measurement with a passive UPnP-enabled gateway by extending Netalyzr's bandwidth test, as follows. The test consists of UDP packet roundtrips from the client to Netalyzr's servers and back. Small upstream packets with large downstream responses measure downstream bandwidth and vice versa. The measurement records the number of packets sent by the client (P_c), received by the server (P_s), and responses received back at the client ($P_{c'}$). The packet counters provided by UPnP gateways (P_g) add an extra loss tracking point, which allows locating dominant loss directionally: for the uplink, $P_c \gg P_g \sim P_s$ indicates loss in the home, while $P_c \sim P_g \gg P_s$ reflects loss in the wide area. The downlink follows analogously. This inference could misreport if the local network drops packets while traffic from another home device to the Internet increments the UPnP counters. To avoid false identification, we only consider cases with at least 5% packet loss.

Table 2 breaks down the location of packets losses in Netalyzr-2. We have correct traffic counter measurements for 11508 homes. We keep 6887 homes for which UPnP traffic counters report cross-traffic less than 10% of the estimated uplink capacity. There was no loss in only 2% of tests. This result is expected because Netalyzr's capacity test sends a high rate of packets to fill the pipe, which induces loss. In 47% of tests, losses occur in the wide-area (possibly at the access link, but we cannot pinpoint where in the wide-area exactly). In total, we observe losses in the home network in 28% of tests. It is expected that well provisioned local networks will have less losses. In our future work, we will study whether these losses correlate with wireless home networks.

Table 2. Location of losses (This table presents results for 6,887 homes in Netalyzr-2)

		WAN	
		No loss	Loss
LAN	No loss	2 %	48 %
	Loss	28 %	22 %

5.4   Buffer Sizes

The effects of over-sized buffers, so-called "buffer bloat", have recently received renewed attention by our community. Common wisdom holds that most end-to-end buffering occurs at the gateway, but many different places could introduce buffering, for example the operating system on the end host; wireless access

Table 3. Buffer sizes in KB of UPnP models, Ethernet only

Model	Homes	Buffer size (KB)	Median (KB)
FRITZ Box 6360 Cable	39	365	363
WNDR3700 router	46	234	256
DIR 615	43	197	246
D-Link Router	91	156	98
WRT54G	61	159	74
DIR 300	51	121	73
FRITZ Box 7390	243	48	46
BRCM963xx	34	60	44
Thomson TG	39	22	23

points; or other equipment in the access link. We use UPnP's gateway model information together with Netalyzr's upload capacity and RTT-under-load measurements to infer the buffer sizes of individual gateway models. To avoid any bias in our inferences because of buffering happening on the wireless link, we only conduct this analysis for homes where our measurements run over a wired link. For each home, we infer the amount of buffering from the RTT under load and the measured upload capacity. We then plot the probability density function of these buffering values for all homes with a given gateway model. We take the point of highest density in this plot as the inferred buffer size for this gateway model. In most cases, we see one clear spike in the density function. The consistency of the gateway buffer measurements for all homes with a given model confirms that most current gateways have a fixed buffer size, irrespective of the uplink capacity. Ideally, the buffer size should be proportional to the uplink capacity, which determines the buffer draining rate.

Table 3 presents the inferred buffer sizes and the median buffering values for gateway models that appeared in at least 30 homes. For conciseness, we only present one model per vendor if several models from the same vendor have similar buffer sizes (for example, other models of Fritzbox have similar buffer sizes to the Fritzbox 7390). Buffer sizes vary from 22 to 365 KB. For a typical uplink rate of 1.2 Mbps, any buffer larger than 150 KB will introduce more than one second delay under load, which is prohibitively large for interactive applications. This delay would increase to 2.3 seconds for a 512 Kbps uplink.

6   Conclusion

This paper showed the potential of UPnP as a tool to complement end-host measurements in home networks. UPnP queries can determine the ground-truth access link capacity, pinpoint cross-traffic from the home network, differentiate local from wide-area losses, and identify gateway characteristics per model (as we did for the buffer size). The caveat is that in the majority of homes we measured the end-host could not find an UPnP gateway. To make matters worse, when we were able to find an UPnP gateway, the responses were sometimes hard to interpret and other times simply wrong. Our hope is that as UPnP starts getting used in practice, gateway vendors will enable UPnP by default and improve their implementation. Given that UPnP standards are still evolving, there is an opportunity for the measurement community to influence the standards and determine what future gateways should report to assist in analysis and diagnosis.

Acknowledgements. This work was supported by the Agence National de la Recherche grant C'MON and by the European Community's Seventh Framework Programme (FP7/2007-2013) no. 258378 (FIGARO). We thank Amazon for supporting our EC2 deployment and acknowledge support by the National Science Foundation under grant NSF CNS-0905631, with additional support from Google and Comcast.

References

1. Aggarwal, B., Bhagwan, R., Das, T., Eswaran, S., Padmanabhan, V.N., Voelker, G.M.: NetPrints: Diagnosing Home Network Misconfigurations Using Shared Knowledge. In: Proc. NSDI (April 2009)
2. Bischof, Z.S., Otto, J.S., Sanchez, M.A., Rula, J.P., Choffnes, D.R., Bustamante, F.E.: Crowdsourcing ISP Characterization to The Network Edge. In: ACM SIGCOMM Workshop on Measurements Up the Stack (2011)
3. Calvert, K.L., Edwards, W.K., Feamster, N., Grinter, R.E., Deng, Y., Zhou, X.: Instrumenting Home Networks. In: ACM SIGCOMM Workshop on Home Networks (August 2010)
4. Chetty, M., Halsem, D., Baird, A., Ofoha, U., Summer, B., Grinter, R.E.: Why Is My Internet Slow?: Making Network Speeds Visible. In: Proc. ACM CHI (May 2011)
5. DiCioccio, L., Teixeira, R., Rosenberg, C.: Impact of Home Networks on End-to-End Performance: Controlled Experiments. In: ACM SIGCOMM Workshop on Home Networks (August 2010)
6. DiCioccio, L., Teixeira, R., Rosenberg, C.: Characterizing Home Networks With HomeNet Profiler. Technical Report CP-PRL-2011-09-0001, Technicolor (September 2011)
7. Dischinger, M., Haeberlen, A., Gummadi, K.P., Saroiu, S.: Characterizing Residential Broadband Networks. In: Proc. IMC (October 2007)
8. Kreibich, C., Weaver, N., Nechaev, B., Paxson, V.: Netalyzr: Illuminating the Edge Network. In: Proc. IMC (October 2010)
9. Sundaresan, S., de Donato, W., Feamster, N., Teixeira, R., Crawford, S., Pescapè, A.: Broadband Internet Performance: A View From the Gateway. In: Proc. ACM SIGCOMM (August 2011)
10. UPnP Forums. UPnP Specifications, http://www.upnp.org/

Detecting Pedophile Activity in BitTorrent Networks

Moshe Rutgaizer, Yuval Shavitt, Omer Vertman, and Noa Zilberman

School of Electrical Engineering, Tel-Aviv University, Israel

Abstract. The wide spread of Peer-to-Peer networks makes multimedia files available to users all around the world. However, Peer-to-Peer networks are often used to spread illegal material, while keeping the source of the data and the acquiring users anonymous. In this paper we analyze activity measurements in the BitTorrent network and examine child sex abuse activity through the Mininova web portal. We detect and characterize pedophilic material in the network, and also analyze different aspects of the abusers activity. We hope our results will help law enforcement teams detecting child molesters and tracking them down earlier.

1 Introduction

Peer-to-peer networks are being widely used around the world by millions of users for sharing content. The anonymity provided by these networks makes them prone to sharing illegal contents, from simple copyright protected material to highly dangerous material, as will be discussed next.

The BitTorrent file sharing network was responsible for 27% to 55% of internet traffic (depending on geographic location) in 2009 [13]. The BitTorrent protocol allows to download large files without loading a single source computer, rather the downloading users join a group of hosts that download and upload from each other, simultaneously. Every BitTorrent file is uniquely defined by a descriptor file called a torrent, which is distributed via email or http websites. This torrent file allows the downloading and uploading users, called leechers and seeders, to share the content file.

Pornography is one of the major content consumption area in the Internet. In 2006, over \$2.84 billion were spent in the United States alone on Internet pornography, with 4.2 million websites dedicated for this purpose alone, accounting for 12% of all websites at that time [14]. Child pornography is a subset of this activity, earning over three billion dollars a year (including non-online activity as well), with over 100K websites offering child pornography and with over 116K daily queries in Gnutella network for "child pornography" [14,15].

Many works try to fight Internet child sex abuse. The most common approach is CBIR, Content Based Image and video Retrieval, which tries to detect and retrieve visual files based on previously studied characteristics from similar files. The retrieval techniques have been thoroughly studied in many works, such as

N. Taft and F. Ricciato (Eds.): PAM 2012, LNCS 7192, pp. 106–115, 2012.

[10]. Chopra *et al.* [2] have tried to address the problem at the network level. They suggested adapting classification techniques to allow network infrastructure, such as routers, to detect illegal file transfer. Projects, such as FIVES [3], combine efforts on multiple domains, from efficient file fragment matching, through means to evaluate large amounts of data, to improved capabilities of linking new illegal multimedia material to old one. For video analysis they use not only image features but also motion information [7]. Research related to child sex abuse in P2P networks is scarce,with few exceptions such as MAPAP [11], which focuses on the eDonkey network, or Huges *et al.* [5], studying the Gnutella network. Liberatore *et al.* [9] discussed legal issues involved in investigating child pornography in the Gnutella and BitTorrent networks. They also developed Roundup, used by Internet Crimes Against Children (ICAC) Task Forces to detect child sex abusers in the Gnutella network, given a list of known child pornography files.

In this paper we present a study of child sex abuse activity in the BitTorrent network, examining behavioral patterns in both queries and downloads. The results presented in this paper may be employed by law enforcement forces to detect and track pedophiles in the BitTorrent network, e.g. using the given analysis new illicit files can be detected.

2   MiniNova Data Set

The Mininova website [12] was for a long time a very popular BitTorrent portal, until a court order forced it to remove all copyrighted torrents at the end of 2009. According to Alexa [1] at the end of 2009 the site was ranked 90 of all worldwide websites, with 1.07% of all internet users visiting it, and first of all torrent websites, ahead of portals such as The Pirate Bay (ranked 105),Torrentz.com (ranked 190) and isoHunt (ranked 196). The average visitor to the website is a young male without children, age 18 to 34, browsing from home and staying in the website for 4.3 minutes (based on [1]). Torrents on the website can be found by browsing, or more frequently by searching the website. The torrents are located under categories and subcategories on the website, with over 950 subcategories. A new torrent uploaded to the website is placed under a subcategory selected by the originator; the website moderators rarely change a torrent's location.

The dataset used in this work was obtained from the Mininova website[1], and covers two time periods in 2009: the first from September 2nd to September 25th, and the second from October 15th to December 7th; a total of 67 days. The dataset was anonymized before it was provided to us, with the users IP addresses removed from the dataset. The dataset is comprised of queries and downloads.

– Queries: The query dataset holds 453 million queries. A query registry contains the query text, a timestamp, and its city of origin.

---

[1] We thank E. Dubbelboer and the Mininova team for the database and clarifications.

- Downloads: The downloads dataset holds 515 million torrent downloads, with over 1.3 million distinct torrents. A download entry contains the torrent's name, torrent's subcategory, file size, a timestamp, and the city of the user.

The most popular subcategories (by downloads) on the Mininova website are action and comedy movies, games for Windows, TV shows (miscellaneous) and ebooks. Pornography is not very common in the Mininova website and there is no subcategory dedicated for such torrents. Adult material is often placed under different subcategories, such as "Asian" or "Movies - Other".

2.1   Data Set Limitations

The Mininova data set analysis has several limitations. First of all, this data set covers only one Torrents website. While it can be argued that this site was clearly the leading Torrents site[1] at the sample time, it might not be representative of child sex activity in the entire BitTorrent network. Another difficulty is users anonymity, with only user's city available. This means that the activity of a specific user can not be pinpointed, e.g. there is no clear distinction between users and activity sessions. The downloads database also lacks metadata information, making it difficult to classify the file and correlate between queries and downloads. Last, there is no ground truth database for child sex abuse that can be referenced. We believe that basing our dictionary assumptions on previous work (See Section 1) that corroborate researchers from multiple fields, including social sciences, provide an adequate baseline for our analysis.

3   Results

3.1   General Statistics

We divide the queries and downloads in the database to six groups: movies, music, pictures, applications, documents, and unknown. The distinction is based on keywords for queries, and keywords and torrent category for downloads. Discarding queries and downloads of an unknown type, most of the downloads from Mininova, over 80%, are of movies. Next are music files (about 14%) and pictures (3%). Considering general queries, 53% are for movies, 21% for programs, 14.4% music and 8.5% pictures. Looking at pedophile material, the queries for them divide approximately two thirds movies and one third pictures. The amount of detected distinct pedophile files in the database is too small to set a baseline for pedophile downloads statistics.

3.2   Collected Queries Statistics

Keywords Ranking. To identify pedophile related material, a dictionary of related words is created. The dictionary relies on previous works in this area [17,8] as well as popular online sources [16][2]. The dictionary of pedophile-related

---

[2] We attempted to collect additional information from sources such as InHope (www.inhope.org), but failed to collaborate or retrieve information.

Table 1. Statistics of Pedophilic Queries

Query	Occurrences	% of Pedo. Queries	% of Queries
Lolita	26668	25.20%	0.0059%
Incest	26290	24.84%	0.0058%
Preteen	17910	16.93%	0.0039%
PTHC	10617	10.03%	0.0023%
Pedo	8406	7.94%	0.0018%
Underage	4756	4.49%	0.0010%
R@ygold	1594	1.50%	0.0003%
Hussyfan	1388	1.31%	0.0003%
Yamad	1325	1.25%	0.0003%
12yo	685	0.64%	0.0002%

words that was used for this study includes 47 words. Each of these words on its own has a pedophilic meaning, but in context may become innocent. For example, "Lolita" on its own versus the combination of "Lolita" and "Nabokov", which refers to the known novel. In all our results, we apply a filter to all such known combinations, which add up to over 40 combinations. We note that the created dictionary may not be full, but we show that these words alone are enough to portray a worrying picture.

Table 1 presents the top-10 most used terms in pedophilic queries. The table contains for each word, the number of occurrences, percentage out of pedophilic queries, and percentage out of total number of queries. The words "lolita" and "incest" are the most popular terms used. We recognize that these two words may also relate to non-pedophilic contexts, but claim that at least some of these queries are still related, as we show in the next section. We see that about 50% of all queries are the top 2 words, which we suspect not to be completely filtered, still only four or five more words are dominant in the queries. It is also observed that these words appear in one of every 25K to 100K queries out of all queries, which is considered high.

We compare these results with Gish et al.[4] which looked at popular queries in the Gnutella network. The term "PTHC" ranked fifth in their most popular constant phrases, appearing in approximately 0.1% of all queries, while the term incest ranked tenth, appearing in 0.05% of all queries. In the Mininova database these two terms are not as frequent as in Gnutella, however the use of Gnutella and Mininova by users is not identical; While in the Gnutella network the most popular queries are pornographic or music related [4] in Mininova the popular categories are movies and applications. The same observation also applies when comparing the results to MAPAP's eDonkey based research [11]: the term "PTHC" is ranked first, with the second term being "Pedo", both searched considerably more than any other term. Other popular terms in BitTorrent, such as "Lolita", are less popular in eDonkey, while terms such as "Preteen" and "Underage" are not ranked at all.

The most frequent queries are also compared with isoHunt's top searches list [6][3]. isoHunt's list does not provide information about the number of queries

---

[3] IsoHunt was ranked second amongst torrent websites [1] at the sampling time.

per term, rather it ranks them by their popularity. In addition, isoHunt provides different ranking for filtered and unfiltered terms, with all pedophilic terms, except "lolita", being filtered out. Compared to the Mininova top-10 list, the term "PTHC" is ranked highest (83), followed by "Preteen"(119), "Lolita"(135), "Incest"(143), "Pedo"(257), "12yo"(275), "Underage"(284), and "Hussyfan"(955). The terms "R@ygold" and "Yamad" are not amongst the top 1000 searches. We see an additional difference from our top-ranked list, as terms such as "7yo", which was not amongst our top-30 queries, being placed high in the global search list (290), and with the term "9yo" being ranked higher(274) than "12yo".

Another aspect that should be considered here is the time that passed between datasets collections: two years between the Gnutella and eDonkey collection to the Mininova dataset, and two additional years from Mininova to isoHunt.Over this time, the awareness to P2P networks usage for ill purposes has grown, thus users "vocabulary" has widened and altered in order to avoid tracking.

Correlation Between Keywords. Queries identified as pedophile-related often include more than a single term that is pedophilic in nature. Figure 1 presents a heatmap of keywords appearing together in the same queries. Only the highest-ranked keywords are shown. It is evident from the figure that the six highest ranking keywords are well connected: each one of them appears tens to hundreds of times in queries with the other five keywords. We strongly believe that such queries are being issued with the intent to find torrents of child pornography. The percentage of queries where two terms are used in conjunction is only 3.8%, with some of the keywords, such as PTSC and Hussyfan, co-occurring with other term in over 10% of their appearances. The keyword Yamad, on the other hand, appears in only 3 queries together with other terms.

On some occasions, connection can be made between pedophile terms and ordinary words. By ranking words that co-appear in the same queries as pedophile terms, some interesting insights surface. For all keywords, except for one case, there is no dominant single word that appears with them: a word never

	Lolita	Incest	Preteen	PTHC	Pedo	Under age	R@y gold	Hussyfan	Yamad	12yo
Lolita		61	304	68	91	109	4	31	0	9
Incest	61		131	73	81	26	2	1	0	8
Preteen	304	131		107	93	113	3	11	0	12
PTHC	68	73	107		75	37	106	64	2	17
Pedo	91	81	93	75		23	8	9	1	11
Under age	109	26	113	37	23		2	5	0	0
R@y gold	4	2	3	106	8	2		18	0	0
Hussyfan	31	1	11	64	9	5	18		0	0
Yamad	0	0	0	2	1	0	0	0		0
12yo	9	8	12	17	11	0	0	0	0	

File Indic-ator	Total Down-loads	Looked Up	Lifetime [Hours]
P1	948	397	194.5
P2	136	25	1727.9
P3	44	2	1.4
V4	2446	29	1740.1

Fig. 1. Heatmap of keywords appearance in the same queries

Fig. 2. Pedophilic Torrents Downloads

appears in more than 10% of the queries were a keyword appears. We distinguish between 3 main types of words that appear together with keywords: media type, pornography related words, and names. Words that fall under the category "media type" include, for example, "video", "pics" and "stickam", representing three type of media files: movies, still pictures and streaming media. We note that the term "video" is most common amongst such queries, as can be expected from torrents. Words that fall under the category "pornography" include terms such as "sex","xxx", and "porn". When a keyword occurs together with one of these words in a query, the ill intent of the issuing user is clear, for example, co-occurrences of "lolita" and "porn" or of "12yo" with "sex". The last group of words includes personal names, is of highest concern. This category includes names such as "Vicky", "Jenny" and "Daphne", issued together with keywords "PTSC" and "PTHC". The most troubling aspect is when these words appear together in queries with age indication, like "9yo jenny". While this may sound as a naive query, a quick search of this term on the web leads to tens of pedophile forums discussions with a clear description of the movie contents as well as other sources that include the illicit content. We thus deduce that this method can be used also outside the BitTorrent network to track and discover pedophile contents.

Extending The Dictionary. An important contribution is detecting new terms that relate to child sex abuse, which is a hard task in an anonymous database. For this end, we analyze separately queries from each city, and define **a busy period** as a sequence of queries with no gaps longer than a given threshold. In large cities with many users the busy period is an aggregation of many users and may be quite long. We are looking for cities with sparse accesses to Mininova, where the probability that two user sessions will fall into the same busy period is negligible.

We analyze the busy periods length in cities with an average of 500 queries a day or less and found that in 98.5% of the cases the length is no longer than five minutes and the number of queries is no more than ten. We thus assume that these busy periods are due to a single user activity and define **a single user busy period (SUBP)** as a busy period up to five minutes long and with up to ten queries . This is in line with Alexa [1] finding that the average site visit time was 4.3 minutes. For further analysis we used only cities that contain only distinct SUBPs, at least 10 SUBPs and that registered at least one pedophile query. This resulted in 692 cities.

We find the SUBPs where pedophile terms were used in queries and create a list of potential new keywords. This list has initially about two thousand words. We screen out of these words numbers, conjunctions and terms that are highly ranked in the global queries list (such as "Harry Potter"). This process was also accompanied by a manual inspection, in order to avoid filtering required terms. This leaves us with 140 words. We classify those to four groups: 51 General sex related words, 29 names of potential victims, 54 pedophile keywords, and 7 words that may refer to either general pornography or child sex abuse. The 54 new words include 19 words that have either a spelling error or a different spelling than an existing keyword in the database, such as "lolyta", 18 familiar terms that are written a bit differently, e.g., 10yr or kingspass, and 17 completely new terms. The new terms were checked using Urban Dictionary [16] and Google websearch, without entering any site with an illicit material. The list of ignored phrases is updated in accordance. This thus extended the dictionary by 115%. Four of the words in the extended dictionary are also ranked within a new top 12 pedophile query terms, with 842 to 3317 queries each.

One issue in extending the dictionary is the definition of child sex abuse terms. As definitions differ between countries, it is unclear whether terms such as "teensex" should be added or not. The heuristic discovers six such new terms, that relate to teens pornography.

Frequency. The frequency of pedophile queries is relatively high, approximately 0.04% of all queries to the database. The queries are distributed across all hours of the day, with least queries being sent at 6am and most queries sent at 1am (user's local time). The pedophile queries frequency graph generally follows the global queries graph, with minor deviations, mainly caused by a slightly higher rate of pedophile queries during night hours and early morning. The high rate of pedophile queries is also interesting as the site scarcely contains child sex abuse torrents, yet we did not observe a decline in queries rate over time, as may be expected when pedophiles find out the contents of the site.

3.3   Downloads Analysis

Distinct Pedophile Downloads. We detect in the Mininova database only 5 files (out of over a million) that include in their filename keywords taken from our dictionary and are not of a legal nature. These files are also manually checked and verified to be potential illicit material and not innocent ones[4]. We note that some files, such as torrents called "PTHC" are often used to target their leechers and spread viruses, however our focus here is the leechers and not the seeders.

The distinct 5 files contain five of the words included in our dictionary, and they are downloaded 1432 times within the dataset timeframe.

Correlation Between Downloads And Queries. Tracking down pedophile activity in the Mininova dataset is a hard task, both in identifying child sex abuse material and processing the large database. A different challenge stems from the fact that while the dataset provides a torrent name, the meta data connected to this torrent, such as a description of the file and users comments, are not visible to us. As a result, it is difficult to correlate between queries and downloads, since the connection may reside in the hidden data. We use three parameters to overcome this obstacle: time, city and repetition pattern. We say that the query and download correlate if they both originate from the same city and the download is seen shortly after the query. If a suspected filename includes one of the dictionary terms, or if the set of downloads resulting from the restrictions on time and city include only a single entry, then the task is simple.

---

[4] based on filenames and web search, without viewing the actual file contents.

however, this is not the common case. We thus say that a file is included in a set of suspected pedophile files if for multiple pedophile queries it is included in the resulting downloads set. Using our heuristic, we find a ratio of 1:30 between queries and downloads, while using a set of over 90K pedophile queries.

The first observation is that 7.2% of the queries result in no matched download. Another indication of success of the heuristic is that it detects downloads of the pedophile torrents with known keywords (as described in Section 3.3). We note in this group of downloads the reoccurrence of keywords with kids names, such as a torrent called "pthc 9yo jenny". It also detected pedophile torrents that contain in their filenames words with sexual connotation. We note that the majority of these files is pictures and not other types of multimedia. We last detect a group of files with innocent names, that can easily be tracked back to pornographic material. An attempt to discover child pornography files with innocent names has failed so far.

We take some of the files with pedophile related keywords in their filenames and further investigate them. while most considered torrents include distinctive keywords, some torrents known to include child pornography may be the result of an occasional pornography search (for example, a nudist family movie whose content was verified). Figure 2 shows the number of downloads of four of these torrents as a result of a pedophilic query, compared to their overall number of downloads. The first three files, marked P1 through P3, have distinct pedophilic words in their names, such as PTHC and Raygold. File V4 is pedophilic in the wide sense, meaning its name includes pornographic but not pedophilic keywords in it, but its content is known to include a video of nude children. The selected files are downloaded only within the duration that we check the database, meaning their first and last downloads are in the timeframe our dataset was collected. V4 is the only exception, as its first download may have occurred before we started logging.

We take these downloads and cross them back to the queries generating from the same location in the time period before the file was downloaded. We find that many of the downloaded files are as a result of direct access to the page. For P3 only two queries were submitted that contain a pedophilic or a sex related word. For other files, we see that most of the downloads are also the result of direct access, either because no query was submitted from the origin city before the download time or because no pedophilic or pornographic related query was issued. For all four torrents, 23% to 67% of the downloads had no prior query, 15% to 34% of the downloads followed a query with a word from the torrent's name and 5% to 14% of the downloads can be related to a pedophilic or pornographic keyword in a previous query (except for P3). As in large cities, such as Chicago, Paris or London, there are tens of queries every minute, we can not track the query directly to its source despite filtering out innocent queries.

Figure 3 shows for the same four files the download time distribution. Each sub-figure shows for one of the files the number of downloads every hour since the file was first downloaded. As the behavior differs significantly between files, the axis values are different. For file P1 and P3, the downloads peak in the first

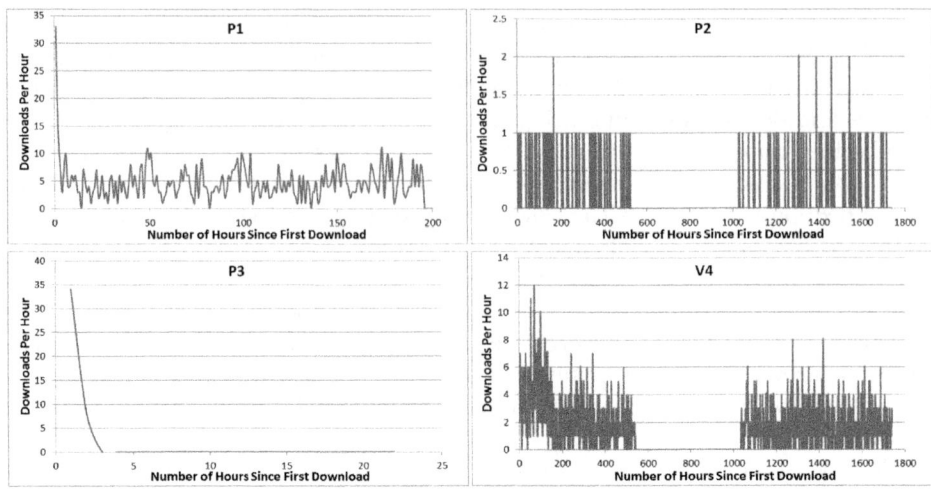

Fig. 3. Number of File Downloads per Hour

hour that the file is distributed, and decline afterwards (P3 is downloaded over 2 hours only). File P2 and V4 are downloaded over a long period of time, at a relatively constant low rate, with the gap during this time period caused by a gap in the data. interestingly, File V4 peaks after 3-4 days since the measurement begins, as opposed to the previous cases.

Geographic Aspects. The geographic distribution of illicit downloads is spread around the world, in all continents. We take the four files discussed in the previous section and further investigate their download pattern. Following their trend in time, the downloads are spread across four continents from the time of the first download to the last.

Another interesting result checks the time difference between downloads from the same city. While the lifetime of P3 is not long enough to examine this, in P1 the time gap between two downloads from the same city is less then one day, for cities with more than a couple of downloads. In torrents P2 and V4, on the other hand, the gap between two downloads is often over a week and even over a month. The density of downloads from the same city is lower as well. We assume that this may be as the contents of P1 and P3 may be of "high quality", while P2 and V4 may be bogus or of lower interest, hence this result.

3.4   Behavior Analysis

We use the small cities heuristic described in 3.2 to explore the behavior of pedophile users in the Mininova database. We note that small cities behavior may be different than a global view, but we believe that due to the large number of cities included in this analysis, it has a value.

The average number of queries in a standard visit to Mininova is measured (in the set of small cities) to be 2.6. In comparison, a visit which includes a pedophile term in it has on the average only 1.5 queries. The average gap between queries in such a visit is 32 seconds.

4 Conclusion

In this paper we presented an analysis of pedophilic activity in Mininova, a portal used by the BitTorrent network. We discussed how child pornography is spread through multimedia files and how the files can be detected on the BitTorrent network. The paper focused on the characteristics of the molesters looking for illicit material, as they manifest in their web activity, by time and content. We also suggest a way to expand the list of known pedophile keywords, and succeed to more than double our initial list. A repetitive run of this heuristic on recent peer-to-peer databases can assist law enforcement teams to detect pedophiles more efficiently.

References

1. Alexa, http://www.alexa.com (accessed: November 17, 2009)
2. Chopra, M., Martin, M.V., Rueda, L., Hung, P.C.K.: Toward new paradigms to combating internet child pornography. In: CCECE 2006, pp. 1012–1015 (2006)
3. Fives. Forensics Image and Video Examination Support, http://fives.kau.se/
4. Gish, A.S., Shavitt, Y., Tankel, T.: Geographical statistics and characteristics of p2p query strings. In: IPTPS 2007 (2007)
5. Hughes, D., Gibson, S., Walkerdine, J., Coulson, G.: Is deviant behaviour the norm on p2p file sharing networks? IEEE Distributed Systems Online 7 (2006)
6. isoHunt. isoHunt Zeitgeist, http://ca.isohunt.com/ (accessed: April 2011)
7. Jansohn, C., Ulges, A., Breuel, T.: Detecting pornographic video content by combining image features with motion information. In: Proceedings of the International Conference on Multimedia. ACM (October 2009)
8. Latapy, M., Magnien, C., Fournier, R.: Quantifying paedophile queries in a large p2p system. In: IEEE Infocom Mini-Conference (2011)
9. Liberatore, M., Erdely, R., Kerle, T., Levine, B.N., Shields, C.: Forensic Investigation of Peer-to-Peer File Sharing Networks. In: Proc. DFRWS Annual Digital Forensics Research Conference (August 2010)
10. Lynn, C.: Image Recognition Takes Another Step Forward. Seybold Report (2004)
11. MAPAP. Measurement and Analysis of P2P activity Against Paedophile content, http://ec.europa.eu/information_society/activities/sip/ projects/completed/illeg_content/index_en.html
12. Mininova, http://www.mininova.org/
13. Mochalski, K., Schulze, H.: Ipoque internet study 2008/2009 (2009)
14. Ropelato, J.: Internet pornography statistics. TopTenReviews (2007)
15. TopTenReviews. Porn industry statistics (February 6, 2004), http://www.toptenreviews.com/2-6-04.html
16. Urban Dictionary, http://www.urbandictionary.com/ (accessed: February 2011)
17. Vehovar, V., Ziberna, A., Kovacic, M., Mrvar, A., Dousak, M.: An empirical investigation of paedophile keywords in edonkey p2p network. tech. report (2009)

Re-wiring Activity of Malicious Networks

Maria Konte and Nick Feamster

Georgia Institute of Technology
{mkonte,feamster}@cc.gatech.edu

Abstract. This paper studies the AS-level *re-wiring dynamics* (changes in the connectivity) of malicious networks. Anecdotal evidence suggests that some malicious ASes that are primarily involved in nefarious activities on the Internet, were sequentially de-peered by providers before their final cut-off (as occurred in the well-publicized cases of Atrivo/Intercage). We present the first systematic study of the re-wiring dynamics of malicious ASes. We tracked the ASes that were listed by Hostexploit over the last two years and compared their AS-level re-wiring dynamics with non-reported ASes. Using a publicly available dataset of Customer-Provider (CP) relations in the Internet's AS graph, we studied how interconnection between autonomous systems evolves, both for ASes that provide connectivity for attackers and ASes that were not reported as malicious. We find that malicious networks are more aggressive both in forming links with providers and changing their upstream connectivity than other ASes. Our results indicate that the re-wiring dynamics of the networks that host attacks are stable over time, despite the evolving nature of the attacks themselves, which suggests that existing defense mechanisms could benefit from incorporating these features.

1 Introduction

Securing the Internet's routing system has been a concern for both network operators and protocol designers for nearly fifteen years. One of the frequently stated reasons for securing the Internet's interdomain routing protocol, the Border Gateway Protocol (BGP), is that attackers may use BGP to launch their attacks and hide their traces. Previous work has exposed some specific techniques that attackers use; for example, Ramachandran *et al.* observed that some attackers send spam from short-lived prefixes [13]. Nevertheless, little is known about how ASes that host these attackers exploit BGP to provide them with further protection. There have been some publicized cases of malicious ASes—major hubs of illegal activity—namely Atrivo/Intercage and VolgaHost, that were observed to get frequently de-peered. Eventually they were officially reported and cut off by all providers in September 2008 and January 2011, respectively. This practice of frequent change in upstream connectivity and eventual cut-off may constitute a feature that potentially characterizes malicious ASes, regardless of the type of attacks they launch which varies across time. We refer to the activity that is related with change of connectivity of an AS as *re-wiring activity* of this AS.

This paper presents the first systematic study of the re-wiring activity of malicious ASes, with the goal of improving our understanding of how malicious networks exploit interconnection through different upstream ASes to cover their tracks. Rather than attempting to detect any individual type of attack (e.g., spam, denial of service), we

N. Taft and F. Ricciato (Eds.): PAM 2012, LNCS 7192, pp. 116–125, 2012.
© Springer-Verlag Berlin Heidelberg 2012

characterize the re-wiring activity of malicious networks that are primarily responsible for attacker activities. We identify features of the re-wiring behavior that may be more stable across time than the characteristics of any single attack. We believe that ultimately certain aspects of routing behavior may serve as invariants for detecting malicious infrastructure, even as the attacks themselves evolve.

We draw the following conclusions from our study:

- *Malicious Enterprise Customers (ECs) on average change their upstream connectivity more aggressively than non reported ECs.* We offer a new class of observations on the AS-level re-wiring activity of malicious ECs. ECs are typically stub networks (Section 3). We find that, on average, malicious ECs change their upstream connectivity more frequently and link with a larger set of providers throughout their lifetime than non-reported ECs. We observe that malicious ECs link on average with a total of twelve providers from 1998–2010, whereas the rest of ECs link with only about four providers on average. Also, malicious ECs' peering sessions last for less time; the top 5% of CP links formed by malicious ECs are observed for 14–31 consecutive snapshots of the AS graph, whereas the top 5% of the CP links formed by the rest of ECs are observed for 27–51 consecutive snapshots.
- *Malicious ECs prefer to attach to popular providers as non reported ECs do when they first appear, but they attach to less popular providers when they re-wire later in their lifetime.* In 2009–2010, all malicious ECs that were observed for the first time used the *most-preferred providers* (the providers that are responsible for the most CP links generated by non-reported ECs at that snapshot) for transit, as the rest of the ECs did (Section 4). During the same time period, the malicious ECs that were observed to re-wire, attached to providers from which only a fraction of 30–50% were among the top providers preferred by non-reported ECs.

Our results highlight some findings that have implications for the design of more effective defense mechanisms against Internet attacks, which we discuss in more detail in Section 5. Even though an AS may be acting maliciously, network administrators in other networks may not be aware of it. Instead, if AS rewiring activity is monitored and potential malfeasance is reported, then this information may be useful to network administrators. For example, in the case of AS-Atrivo, even if not all network administrators knew that AS-Atrivo was acting maliciously or the details of the attacks, it may have been helpful to know that its re-wiring activity was suspicious, in case they receive suspicious traffic originating from that AS or if AS-Atrivo tries to connect directly with them. The re-wiring features are independent of the evolving nature of the attacks and also more difficult for the attackers to tamper, incorporating them may provide significant gains over existing defense mechanisms or complement them.

The rest of this paper is organized as follows. In Section 2, we give an overview of related work. In Section 3, we describe the datasets we used in our analysis. Section 4 presents our findings and Section 5 offers some observations about the implications of our findings with regard to existing defense mechanisms. We conclude in Section 6.

2   Related Work

Previous studies have investigated various types of malicious activity in isolation such as worms, botnets, spam, and Internet scam infrastructure [2, 6, 7, 9–12, 15, 18] to propose detection solutions. Kim *et al.* [9] designed a system that generates worm signatures based on the analysis of the prevalence of portions of flow payloads. Xie *et al.* [19] analyzed a three-month sample of emails to characterize spamming botnets, properties of botnet IP addresses, sending patterns and developed a system called AutoRE that generated regular expression signatures for detection of botnet-based spam emails and botnet membership. Anderson *et al.* [1] developed a measurement system called Spamscatter that mines emails in real-time, follows the link embedded at the email, and clusters the destination Web sites using image shingling to capture graphical similarity between rendered sites. In contrast, we focus on networks whose primary purpose is to instrument these activities, and we attempt to understand their re-wiring behavior at the AS level.

There exists a limited number of studies that have investigated spammers' use of the routing infrastructure to facilitate their activities [16, 17]. These studies have provided evidence of the fact that spammers advertise routes to hijacked IP prefixes for short amounts of time. Ramachandran *et al.* [13, 14] performed a large-scale study on the network-level properties of spam and quantified the extent to which spammers use this technique of short-lived BGP announcements to send spam. Also, Feamster *et al.* [4, 5] studied route advertisements for private or unassigned ("bogon") IP addresses. Our work investigates the re-wiring activity of networks that have been reported as malicious, and we compare them with non-reported networks.

3   Data

Our primary dataset consists of a list of networks that are reported as top in Internet criminal activities, in a period of three years (2009–2011) according to Hostexploit. There are a total of 129 distinct ASes. We hypothesize that malicious ASes have different business functions and incentives than most ASes, which may be reflected on the links they form with other ASes in the Internet. To understand the re-wiring behavior of these networks we obtain a publicly available dataset of customer-provider links formed among ASes over ten years (available here [3]), over which we track them. We considerASes that have not ever been reported by Hostexploit to be legitimate.

Hostexploit reports. To study the behavior of malicious networks that are mostly engaged in Internet nefarious activities, we collected the list of ASes reported as most malicious networks by Hostexploit in global Internet activity reports issued in quarters of 2009–2011. Hostexploit is an open organization of international volunteers who are Internet professionals within the areas of web hosting, server management, DNS, Internet security, and intrusion detection systems, with a focus on creating awareness of cybercrime activity. Hostexploit integrates and correlates data from multiple sources such as spam, malware, malicious URLs, spam bots, botnet command and control servers, phishing servers, exploit servers, and cyber-warfare intelligence provided by industry

AS Number	Name	Country
AS41947	WEBALTA-AS OAO Webalta	RU
AS29073	ECATEL-AS AS29073, Ecatel Network	NL
AS16138	INTERIAPL INTERIA.PL Autonomous System	PL
AS10297	ENET-2 - eNET Inc.	US

Fig. 1. A quarterly report from Hostexploit from the 1st quarter of 2011. The report ranks ASes by an index (HE) based on the activity of the AS, weighted by the size of its allocated address space.

partners. To provide a list of the worst networks, they rate each AS with a Hostexploit Index (HE), based on the activity of the AS weighted by the size of its allocated address space. HE is a proportional rather than an absolute index of AS maliciousness. Hostexploit has been issuing reports on top networks by their HE index periodically since 2009.

Figure 1 shows an example Hostexploit report for the first quarter of 2011. The report is accompanied by an analysis of the quarterly results. For example, they compare the new ranking results with the previous quarterly ranking, show the top worst networks by sector (spam, botnet hosting, etc.), show an analysis by country, etc.

Historic AS relationships. To understand the re-wiring behavior of malicious networks, we tracked these ASes' rewiring activity over a ten years. Dhamdhere *et al.* [3] collected BGP AS paths from BGP table dumps obtained from repositories at RouteViews and RIPE. They collected snapshots of AS paths; a snapshot refers to a period of 21 days (not an instant). During each snapshot, they collected at five different times the unique AS paths from all active monitors. Then, to obtain the primary Internet links (used most of the time) and to filter out the backup links (used during failures or overload conditions), they kept only the AS paths that appeared in the majority of the samples and ignored the rest (majority filtering algorithm). Then, they used the AS paths in each snapshot (those that had passed the majority filtering process) to infer the underlying AS topology and the relationships between adjacent ASes. Finally, they used the well-known algorithm proposed by Gao [8]. Gao's algorithm resulted in four types of AS relationships: Customer-Provider (CP), peering, sibling, and unknown. To understand the evolution of the Internet ecosystem they classified ASes into types depending on their function and business type, based on their observable topological properties. They classified ASes into Enterprise Customers (ECs), small transit provider, large transit provider, content access and hosting provider.

In this study, we focus only on the CP links of ECs (62 in total). We note that based on the method that the classes were derived, ASes of the same class are close in terms of the number of customers and peers they link with at each snapshot. As far as the number of providers they link with at each snapshot there is larger variability among

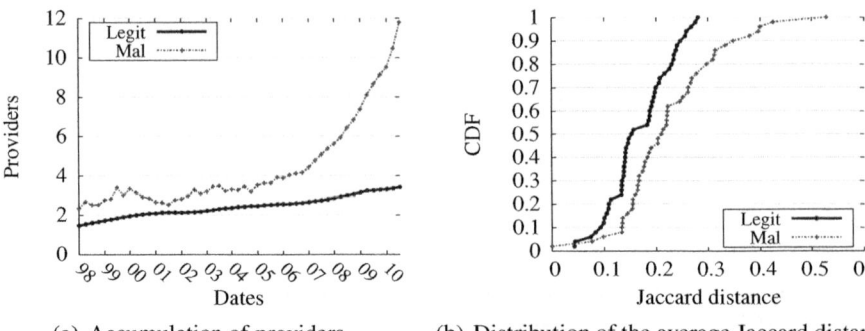

(a) Accumulation of providers.

(b) Distribution of the average Jaccard distance between two consecutive snapshots of links with providers.

Fig. 2. Malicious ECs on average attach to more providers and change their providers more frequently than legitimate ECs

the ASes, but our analysis is not relying on this metric. Instead, we are looking at the accumulation of distinct providers across time, the CP link duration and other features (see Section 4).

Dataset limitations. Our data has the following limitations: (1) The Hostexploit data may be inaccurate. (2) The methods that were used to infer the AS graph [3] have been shown to to be inadequate. Most ASes are detected but a significant fraction of peering and backup links at the edges of the Internet are missed. (3) Dhamdhere *et al.*'s AS classification algorithm may introduce errors.

4   Results

We hypothesize that malicious ASes have different business functions and incentives than the rest of the ASes, and that these differences may be reflected on their re-wiring activity. For example, we suspect that malicious ASes may get frequently de-peered from their providers and that they need to re-wire more frequently than legitimate ASes. To test our hypothesis, we survey the wiring trends of malicious networks; (1) re-wiring frequency and (2) attachment preference. To determine whether our findings may be suitable for characterizing network re-wiring activity, we compare the behavior of malicious ASes to that of non-reported ASes over a ten-year period. We present the results of our analysis for Enterprise Customers (ECs) only.

4.1   Re-wiring Frequency

To understand the re-wiring dynamics of malicious networks and, more specifically, how these networks change their upstream connectivity, we examine three features; (1) the number of providers they link with throughout their lifetime, (2) how frequently they change providers and (3) how long their CP links last. To determine whether these features may be suitable for characterizing the re-wiring activity of malicious ECs, we compare the behavior of malicious ECs to that of the rest of the ECs over ten years.

Malicious ECs on average connect to more providers than legitimate ECs Do. To investigate how malicious ECs link with their providers we first look at the total number of providers they link with throughout their lifetime. To compute the cumulative number of providers that an EC has, on average, first we track each EC for the duration of its lifetime; we add the total number of providers it links with to the total number of providers for its group (malicious or rest of EC). Then, for every snapshot, we compute the average by dividing the cumulative total number of providers of the EC group with the number of ASes in the EC class. We note that across time the size of the group increases as new ECs appear, and as does the cumulative number of providers for the group of EC. The rate with which the two numbers increase does not stay the same across time, so some snapshots exhibit a small decrease in the average cumulative number of providers. Figure 2(a) shows the cumulative number of providers that ECs attach to, on average, for two cases: malicious ECs and the rest of ECs. On average, malicious ECs link with more providers throughout their lifetime than the rest of the ECs do.

Malicious ECs link on average with a total of twelve providers during the period 1998–2010, whereas the rest of ECs link on average with only about four providers. The top ECs by the total number of providers are AS 3, which connected to 83 distinct providers; AS 26415, which linked with a total of 68 providers; and the private AS 65000, linked to 20 different providers. On the other hand, the malicious EC that we observed to link with the most providers (a total of 83) through its lifetime was AS 23456. We note that this AS is reserved by IANA and is used for backward compatibility between old (2-byte AS support) and new (4-byte AS support) BGP speakers. Because it is reserved for backwards compatibility, this AS is likely not a single AS, but rather a group of ASes; we must investigate this further to better understand the individual ASes that are perpetrating suspicious activity.

Malicious ECs on average change upstream providers more frequently than legitimate ECs. To quantify the aggressiveness of an EC in changing its upstream connectivity, we consider the distance between the set of the AS's providers for two consecutive snapshots. We use the Jaccard distance as a metric of distance between the set of providers of two consecutive snapshots. For example, a Jaccard distance of 0.8 indicates that 80% of the links seen in the two snapshots are observed in one of the two snapshots but not in both. We calculated the Jaccard distance between two consecutive snapshots for each AS throughout its lifetime. Figure 2(b) shows the distribution of the Jaccard distance values for malicious ECs and the rest of the ECs throughout their lifetime. We observe that malicious ECs are more aggressive on average in changing their upstream connectivity than the rest of ECs.

The fact that malicious ECs change their upstream connectivity more frequently than legitimate ECs may be a reflection of the following: (1) malicious ECs are noticed by their providers regarding their attacker activities, they get de-peered and they are forced to change upstream connectivity more frequently than legitimate ECs, (2) malicious ECs attempt to find providers with less strict restrictions, which may make it easier for

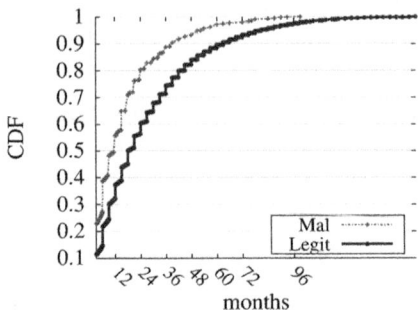

Fig. 3. Distribution of the average duration of CP links formed by ECs with their providers. Malicious ECs on average form shorter duration links than the rest of the ECs.

them to launch their attacks, (3) malicious ECs attempt to avoid accountability or legal consequences of their activities.

Malicious ECs on average form shorter duration CP links than legitimate ECs. To better understand the behavior of malicious ECs, we consider the duration of the links they form with their providers. To compute the CP link duration, we proceed as follows: First, for every snapshot, we determine the links that are present. Second, for each link, we determine whether it is present in the previous snapshot. Finally, for each link, we measure the total number of consecutive snapshots it was present. In cases where a link appears multiple times throughout 1998–2010 we consider the average duration of that link. Figure 3 shows the distribution of average CP link duration of malicious ECs and the rest of ECs. We observe that malicious ECs on average form CP links that are shorter in duration than the CP links that legitimate ECs form.

Figure 3 shows that approximately 22% of the CP links formed by malicious EC and about 10% of CP links formed by the rest of ECs were observed for only one snapshot. For example ASes in AS 23456, which linked with the largest number of providers, formed CP links with ASes 30083, 5617, and 7643, which appeared for only one snapshot. Examples of short-lived CP links formed by non-malicious ECs include AS 20195–AS 6395, AS 39709–AS 28870, and AS 3748–AS 4554. These links were observed for only one snapshot. On the other hand, as far as long-lived CP links, the top 5% of CP links formed by malicious ECs are observed for 14–31 consecutive snapshots, whereas the top 5% of the CP links formed by non-malicious ECs are observed for 27–51 consecutive snapshots. The most long-lived CP links by malicious ECs are links AS 14280–AS 6327 which was observed for 33 consecutive snapshots, AS 17974–AS 7713 for 31 consecutive snapshots and AS 13174-AS 1299 for 30 consecutive snapshots. The most long-lived CP links by legitimate ECs were observed for 51 consecutive snapshots (i.e., the entire period from 1998 to 2010); some examples are: AS 8581–AS 5408, AS 2508–AS 2907, AS 7065–AS 701, AS 10357–AS 7066, and AS 1104–AS 1103.

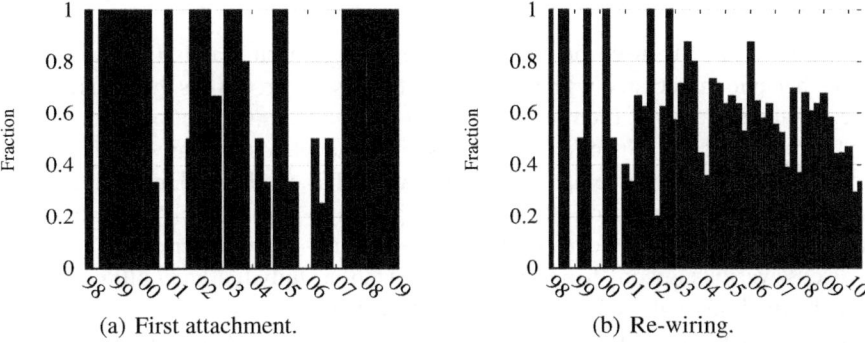

(a) First attachment.   (b) Re-wiring.

Fig. 4. Fraction of malicious ASes providers' that belong to the most preferred providers of all ECs for each snapshot. Malicious ECs in some cases attach to the most popular providers when they first appear, but not when they rewire. This is especially true for the more recent years.

4.2 Attachment Preference

In this section, we study the providers that malicious ECs connect to. Our goal is to determine whether malicious ECs have different attachment preferences than the rest of the ECs. We define the *most preferred providers* as the providers that are responsible for the most CP links generated by non-reported ECs at that snapshot. We find that malicious ECs do not connect to the most preferred providers as non-reported ECs do.

First, at each snapshot, we determine the most preferred providers as follows: we calculate the total number of CP links generated by non-reported ECs at each snapshot and we extract the providers that are responsible for at least 60% of the total at that snapshot. This set comprises the most preferred providers of non-reported ECs at each snapshot. Second, for each snapshot, we determine the providers that malicious ECs link with and whether those links are first-time attachments or re-wirings. Finally, at each snapshot, we calculate the fraction of the providers that malicious ECs link with that also belong to the most preferred providers of non-reported ECs. We calculate this fraction separately for the cases of first-attachment (when an EC is observed for the first time) and re-wiring (when an EC re-wires).

Figure 4 shows the fractions of the providers of malicious ECs that belong to the most preferred providers of non-reported ECs, for the cases of first attachment and re-wiring across time. We observe that for the case of first attachment, all or almost all of the providers they link with are also among the most preferred providers of non-reported ECs. In contrast, for the case of re-wiring, only a percentage of the providers that malicious ECs link with are also among the most preferred providers of non-reported ECs. We observe that for the years 2009–2010, approximately 30–50% of the providers that malicious ECs link with are also among the most preferred providers of non-reported ECs.

5   Recommendations and Future Work

Although we have focused on *characterization* of re-wiring activity, we believe that routing behavior associated with malicious networks has properties that can lead to both better protection against Internet attacks and more efficient detection of the networks that host the attackers. Specifically, because it is independent of any particular attack, routing behavior may serve as invariant behavior that can help identify networks that perpetrate a wider variety of attacks. Routing data is also publicly available and can complement other types of detection mechanisms. In the remainder of this section, first we discuss various lessons from this characterization study that may ultimately inform detection methods and second we discuss future work.

We first note that networks that consistently host malicious activity have re-wiring behaviors that are distinct from other networks. This may point to possibilities for stemming the tide of attack traffic in the future. In the past, we have seen dramatic de-peering events of a single AS (e.g., Atrivo/Intercage), which have resulted in a precipitous drop in spam traffic, which returned at a later date, likely as the spammers re-established upstream connectivity with other upstream ASes. Our analysis shows that the stub ASes that tend to originate a significant amount of attack traffic tend to re-wire with upstream ASes that are not "preferred" upstream ASes. In the future, more effective AS reputation systems might incorporate information not only about the AS itself that originates the traffic, but also the *upstream ASes to which the network connects*. Given the aggressive re-wiring in which malicious ASes participate, another possible way forward might be to encourage some type of registration or verification process by which an AS (or its upstream) is vetted as a reputable provider.

In future work, we plan to evaluate (1) the possibility to classify malicious ASes using re-wiring activity features we observed in this study and (2) the efficacy of using routing information as input to an AS reputation system. We also plan to investigate the re-wiring activity of malicious ASes by class (e.g., small transit providers, large transit providers and content providers) and also by the type of attack they appear to be engaged with (e.g., some malicious ASes may appear mostly to send spam during a specific period of time whereas other ASes may appear to be hosting command-and-control infrastructure). It remains to be seen whether a blacklisting system that is based on re-wiring behavior would be sufficiently different than one that uses observations of the attacks themselves as input.

6   Conclusion

Although limited empirical studies have suggested that attackers exploit BGP routing to help cloak their attacks, there has been no detailed longitudinal study of how malicious networks may interconnect differently from other ASes. In this paper, we have analyzed more than ten years of BGP data in conjunction with reports of malicious ASes from Hostexploit and found that ASes that are known to host malicious traffic consistently exhibit different re-wiring behavior than other ASes. We believe that our findings may ultimately serve as useful features for other reputation or attack detection mechanisms. The fact that routing dynamics are a property of the network hosting the attack, rather than of any specific attack, may ultimately prove advantageous in this regard. In particular, using BGP routing data as an input to such an AS-based reputation system is a promising area for future work.

References

1. Anderson, D.S., Fleizach, C., Savage, S., Voelker, G.M.: Spamscatter: Characterizing Internet scam hosting infrastructure. In: 14th Conference on USENIX Security Symposium (2007)
2. Chiang, K., Lloyd, L.: A case study of the Rustock rootkit and spam bot. In: The First Workshop in Understanding Botnets (2007)
3. Dhamdhere, A., Dovrolis, C.: Ten Years in the Evolution of the Internet Ecosystem. In: Proceedings of ACM SIGCOMM/USENIX Internet Measurement Conference, IMC (2008)
4. Feamster, N.: Open problems in BGP anomaly detection. In: CAIDA Workshop on Internet Signal Processing (2004)
5. Feamster, N., Jung, J., Balakrishnan, H.: An Empirical Study of Bogon Route Advertisements. ACM Computer Communications Review (2004)
6. Fetterly, D., Manasse, M., Najork, M., Wiener, J.L.: A large-scale study of the evolution of web pages. Softw. Pract. Exper. (2004)
7. Li, F., Hsieh, M.H.: An empirical study of clustering behavior of spammers and group-based anti-spam strategies. In: CEAS 2006: Proceedings of the 3rd Conference on Email and Anti-Spam (2006)
8. Gao, L.: On Inferring Autonomous System Relationships in the Internet. IEEE/ACM Transactions on Networking (2001)
9. Kim, H.A., Karp, B.: Autograph: Toward automated, distributed worm signature detection. In: The 13th Conference on USENIX Security Symposium (2004)
10. Kreibich, C., Crowcroft, J.: Honeycomb: Creating intrusion detection signatures using honeypots. In: 2nd Workshop on Hot Topics in Networks, HotNets-II (2003)
11. Li, Z., Sanghi, M., Chen, Y., Kao, M.Y., Chavez, B.: Hamsa: Fast signature generation for zero-day polymorphic worm with provable attack resilience. In: IEEE Symposium on Security and Privacy (2006)
12. Newsome, J., Karp, B., Song, D.: Polygraph: Automatically generating signatures for polymorphic worms. In: Proceedings of the 2005 IEEE Symposium on Security and Privacy (2005)
13. Ramachandran, A., Feamster, N.: Understanding the network-level behavior of spammers. In: Proceedings of SIGCOMM (2006)
14. Ramachandran, A., Feamster, N., Vempala, S.: Filtering spam with behavioral blacklisting. In: Proceedings of the 14th ACM Conference on Computer and Communications Security (2007)
15. Singh, S., Estan, C., Varghese, G., Savage, S.: Automated worm fingerprinting. In: OSDI (2004)
16. Spammer-X. Inside the Spam Cartel. Syngress (2004)
17. Todd, J.: AS number inconsistencies (2002),
    http://www.merit.edu/mail.archives/nanog/2002-07/msg00259.html
18. Xie, Y., Yu, F., Achan, K., Gillum, E., Goldszmidt, M., Wobber, T.: How dynamic are IP addresses?. In: ACM SIGCOMM (2007)
19. Xie, Y., Yu, F., Achan, K., Panigrahy, R., Hulten, G.: Spamming botnets: signatures and characteristics. In: SIGCOMM (2008)

Difficulties in Modeling SCADA Traffic: A Comparative Analysis

Rafael R.R. Barbosa, Ramin Sadre, and Aiko Pras

University of Twente Design and Analysis of Communication Systems (DACS)
Enschede, The Netherlands
{r.barbosa,r.sadre,a.pras}@utwente.nl

Abstract. Modern critical infrastructures, such as water distribution and power generation, are large facilities that are distributed over large geographical areas. Supervisory Control and Data Acquisition (SCADA) networks are deployed to guarantee the correct operation and safety of these infrastructures. In this paper, we describe key characteristics of SCADA traffic, verifying if models developed for traffic in traditional IT networks are applicable. Our results show that SCADA traffic largely differs from traditional IT traffic, more noticeably not presenting diurnal patters or self-similar correlations in the time series.

1 Introduction

Modern critical infrastructures, such as water distribution and power generation, are large facilities that are distributed over large geographical areas. Supervisory Control And Data Acquisition (SCADA) networks are deployed to continuously monitor these infrastructures in order to guarantee correct operation and safety. Originally, SCADA networks were isolated networks running proprietary protocols, but there is an increasing trend toward the usage of IP protocols and the interconnection with other networks and even the Internet.

Intuitively, we expect SCADA to present traffic patterns much different to those of "traditional" Information Technology (IT) networks. This is due to a number of reasons. First, SCADA networks are expected to be more stable over time, in the sense that new nodes are not expected to join or leave frequently. Second, traditional networks usually support a multitude of protocols, such as HTTP, instant messaging and Voice over IP, while the number of services in SCADA networks is expected to be more limited. Finally, most of the SCADA traffic is expected to be generated in a periodical fashion, due to the polling mechanism used to gather data. In consequence, traffic patterns should not be so dependent on human activity as in traditional IT networks.

Apart from the assumptions given above, not much more is publicly known about the behavior of SCADA traffic. This is partly caused by the sensitivity of the data. In fact, publications on SCADA networks generally do not rely on empirical data as obtained from real-world measurement [1,2,3]. In contrast,

N. Taft and F. Ricciato (Eds.): PAM 2012, LNCS 7192, pp. 126–135, 2012.

traditional networks have been intensively studied, sometimes leading to surprising insights. As an example, we refer to the seminal work in [4] and [5] on the self-similar nature of network traffic and, connected to that, to studies on the presence of long-range dependency and heavy-tailed distributions [6,7,8,9]. The research has resulted in models and tools employed in, for example, the design and dimensioning of network equipment and the parametrization of management algorithms. Naturally, the question arises whether the existing models are also valid for SCADA networks.

The goal of this paper is *to verify if models used to describe traditional network traffic can also be applied to SCADA traffic.* We achieve this by comparing a traditional IP traffic trace with *real-world* SCADA measurements done by us. However, network behavior can be compared in a virtually infinite number of ways, starting from the above mentioned characteristic of self-similarity to topological properties [10] and application specific aspects [11]. In order to provide information that is of interest for a wide range of readers, we base our analysis in this first work on a list of "invariants", i.e., behaviours that are empirically shown to hold for a wide range of environments, proposed in the well known paper of Floyd and Paxson [12]. We revise this list and test our datasets for the invariants applicable to our context.

In a separate, but closely related work, we perform a series of tests to characterize SCADA traffic at the IP level, while drawing a comparison with Simple Network Management Protocol (SNMP) traffic [13]. Our analysis confirms that most hosts (including user workstations) generate data in a periodical way, resulting in a remarkably constant traffic time series. Surprisingly, we observe that changes in the IP level connectivity matrix are common.

The rest of this paper is organized as follows. In Section 2, we describe the datasets used in this paper. In Section 3, we give a short description of the invariants and we briefly explain how the tests are performed. The results are presented in Section 4. Finally, conclusions are given in Section 5.

2   Datasets

The datasets that we use in this paper consist of four network packet traces in pcap format [14], collected at three different locations: two water treatment and distribution facilities that use SCADA networks and one research institute network with "ordinary" IP traffic. From the pcap traces we generate flow information by aggregating packets that are no more than 300s apart, based on the traditional 5-tuple of protocol number, source and destination IP addresses and port numbers. In this section, we give more insight into the data.

The two SCADA locations have different topologies, as shown in Figure 1. Both topologies have a *corporate network* that does not have direct access to the other parts of the network and is, in general, connected to the Internet. In the three-layer topology (Figure 1a) , the remaining part of the network consists of the *field network* and the *control network*. The field network contains the Programmable Logic Controllers (PLC) and the Remote Terminal Units (RTU)

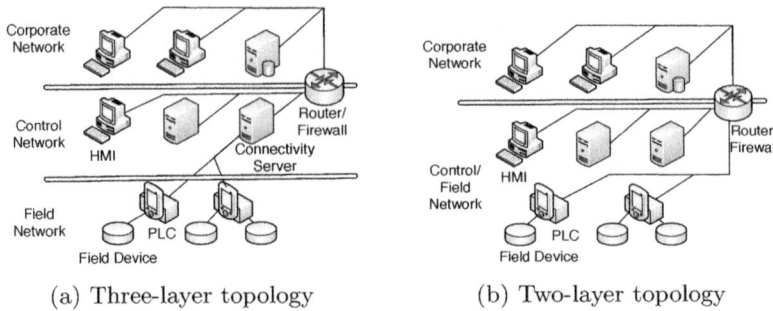

(a) Three-layer topology   (b) Two-layer topology

Fig. 1. SCADA topologies of the monitored networks

Table 1. Datasets overview

Name	Number of hosts	Duration	Average pkts/s	Average KBytes/s
2layer	45	13 days	504.1	82.5
3layer-control	14	10 days	28.7	5.1
3layer-field	31	10 days	75.7	28.2
IT	100	7.5 days	81.9	65.3

that monitor (and possibly issue commands to) the field devices. The control network contains several servers with different purposes, such as automatically polling of field nodes and performing the access control; and the Human-Machine Interfaces (HMI). The latter are operator workstations that provide an user interface to the field nodes. The communication between the control network and the field network passes through a single node, the connectivity server. In contrast, there is no such explicit (physical) separation between the control network and the field network in the two-layer topology (Figure 1b).

For the SCADA location following the 2-layer topology, we have captured the traffic in the joint control/field network. We refer to the collected dataset as *2layer* in the following. For the 3-layer SCADA location, we have captured the traffic in the control network as well as in the field network. The so obtained two packet traces are referred to as *3layer-control* and *3layer-field*. In both locations, the data capture was done through a switch's *mirror port*, that replicated all traffic in a given network. No data loss was reported. Finally, we have ignored the traffic in the corporate networks since they do not transport SCADA traffic.

In order to provide a comparison with a traditional IT environment, we have selected a publicly available traffic trace from the network of an educational organization: Location 6 from [15]. The organization is relatively small with around 36 employees and 100 students. Its network is comparable to the above SCADA networks in the number of hosts as well as in the average bandwidth and, hence, is an adequate candidate for the following studies. We use only a portion of the available data, approximately the first 7.5 days of the trace. We refer to this dataset as *IT*. An overview of all four datasets is given in Table 1.

3   Invariants

In [12], seven invariants in Internet traffic are presented. Not all of them are suitable for the datasets considered in this paper. In Sections 3.1 through 3.3, we give a short description of those four invariants that we test in Section 4 and we briefly explain how the tests are performed. In Section 3.4 we discuss the remaining three invariants and the reasons why we have not considered them.

3.1   Diurnal Patterns of Activity

Network activity is strongly correlated with human activity. As a consequence, it starts increasing around 8–9 AM local time, peaks around 11 AM and 3–4 PM and decreases as business day ends at 5 PM. Moreover, the amount of traffic during the weekends tends to be considerably smaller than during week days. In order to verify if SCADA traffic also follows this pattern, we plot time series for three different measures: the number of active flows, *packets/sec* and *bytes/sec*.

3.2   Self-similarity

Self-similarity is the quality that the whole resembles its parts. In network traffic, it can be observed as bursty periods being present at different timescales, from milliseconds to a few hours. This property violates the assumptions of traditional Markovian modeling that predicts that longer-term correlations are weak. Since the initial findings in the early 90's [4,5], self-similarity of network traffic has remained an active field of research (see, e.g., [9]).

For this paper, we have decided to employ three popular visual methods to test self-similarity [4,6]: the R/S analysis, variance-time plots and periodograms. The visual representation of their results allows to detect anomalies and to estimate the degree of self-similarity in the data:

R/S analysis: For a given set of observations $X = X(t), 0 < t \leq N$, consider a subset with starting point t_i and size n. Let $\overline{X}(t_i, n)$ and $S(t_i, n)$ be, respectively, the mean and the standard deviation of a subsample of X calculated over the interval $[t_i, t_i+(n-1)]$. The *rescaled adjusted range* plot (or *R/S pox diagram*) can be obtained by dividing a set of observations X into K non-overlapping subsets of size N/K with starting points $t_i = i(N/K) + 1$. One selects logarithmically spaced values of n and plots $\log(R/S(t_i, n))$ as a function of $\log(n)$, where R/S is the *R/S statistic*. The Hurst parameter can be estimated from the slope of a line fitted to the resulting curve.

Variance-time plots: Self-similar time series do not become "smoother" at larger time scales, i.e., the variance decreases slowly for increasing aggregation levels. Let $X^{(m)}$ be the aggregated process, defined as $X^{(m)}(t) = m^{-1} \sum_{t=1}^{t+(m-1)} X(t)$. The variance-time plot shows the variance of the aggregated process, $S^2(X^{(m)})$ versus the aggregation level m in a log-log scale. A line is least-squares fitted to the resulting curve, ignoring small values of m. A slope $-1 \leq \beta \leq 0$ suggests self-similarity, and the Hurst parameter can be estimated as $H = 1 - \beta/2$.

Periodograms: The last method consists of fitting a least-squares line to the low-frequency part of a periodogram, typically the lowest 10%. The Hurst parameter can be estimated as $H = (1 - \beta)/2$, with β being the slope of the fitted line.

3.3 Log-Normal Connection Sizes and Heavy-Tail Distributions

Log-normal distributions are a good fit to the body of connection size distributions, while the tails of network-activity related distributions are often heavy-tailed. Since the original list of invariants was published, a debate started over which of these models better describe connection size distributions: heavy-tail (e.g., [6]) or log-normal (e.g., [7]). Recently, Gong et al. [8] argued that there is never sufficient data to support any analytical form summarizing the tail behavior, therefore the research efforts should focus instead on studying the complex nature of traffic generation and its implications.

In this work, we do not attempt to fit our measurements to theoretical distributions. We simply show, through widely used Complementary Cumulative Distribution Functions (CCDFs) [7], that measurements from the *IT* dataset generally match the results reported in the literature and point out the differences to the connection size distributions in SCADA networks.

3.4 Invariants Not Tested in This Work

In addition to the above four invariants, [12] also defines three invariants that we do *not* further study in this paper for reasons explained in the following:

Session arrivals: A "session" refers to the period of time a human uses the network for a specific task. There is evidence that session arrivals are well-modeled by a Poisson process, e.g., FTP, TELNET [5] and HTTP [16]. Since the concept is highly protocol specific, it is hard to develop a general method to group network packets to sessions. This is especially true for our SCADA datasets, as most of the protocols are closed. Hence, we do not attempt to test this invariant in this work. Note that *flows* are *not* well-modeled by a Poisson process.

Telnet packet generation: Packets generated by keystrokes, e.g., in a Telnet session, obey a Pareto distribution. Since this invariant mostly concerns human behavior and a single specific protocol, we have not considered it in this work.

Characteristics of the global topology: Some behaviors appear due to characteristics of the Earth. For example, the delay in inter-continental connections is bounded by the propagation delay. Such characteristics are not relevant for the relatively small networks considered in this paper.

4   Analysis Results

In this section we discuss the results of our analysis regarding the four selected invariants.

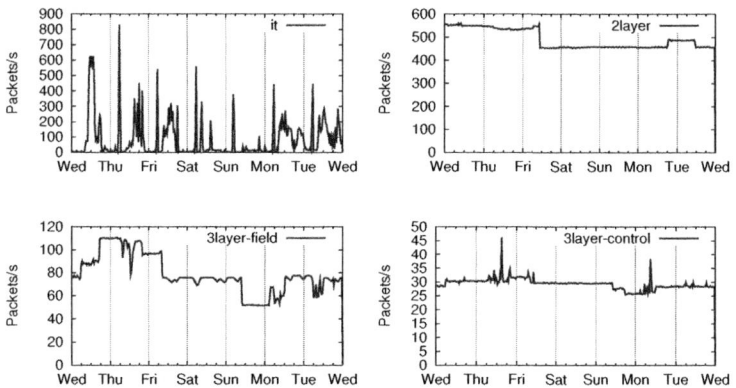

Fig. 2. Looking for diurnal traffic patterns

4.1   Diurnal Patterns of Activity

Diurnal patterns in network activity are widely reported in the literature [12]. In contrast, most of the traffic of a SCADA environment is generated periodically by the polling mechanism used to retrieve data, and as a consequence, it should have a very regular throughput. To verify this, we plot three different time series: *packets/s*, *bytes/s* and *number of active flows*, calculated over 30-minute bins for our four datasets. To ease the comparison, we align the time series based on weekdays. Figure 2 show the results for *packets/s*. The results for the other metrics are analogous, thus not shown due to space constraints.

As can be seen, the SCADA traffic does not present day and night patterns. Instead, all time series remain stable over large periods of time, to which we refer as *baselines*. Note, however, that the throughput is not constant. Notably, datasets *2layer* and *3layer-field* present a considerable drop in the packet rate at around Friday noon and Sunday noon respectively. Such stability combined with the fact that most sources generate traffic in a periodical way [13] indicates that *ON/OFF* models might provide a good approximation for the general shape of the time series.

A closer inspection of the data reveals three major causes for the deviations from the baseline: (i) the start or end of flows with large throughput, (ii) the increase (or decease) in the rate in which variables are pooled and (iii) the increase (or decrease) in the number of variables pooled. We speculate that the changes are mostly caused by certain changes in the physical process that the SCADA systems control, e.g., tanks becoming full or an increase in the water demand. Another possible cause is a manual access to the PLCs, for either retrieving data or uploading a new configuration. Further research is necessary to establish if these changes can be predicted.

As expected, the *IT* dataset shows diurnal patterns of activity, with lower throughput during the nights and weekends. The daily peaks seen in the early morning (around 5.25 AM) are caused by a single large flow between the same

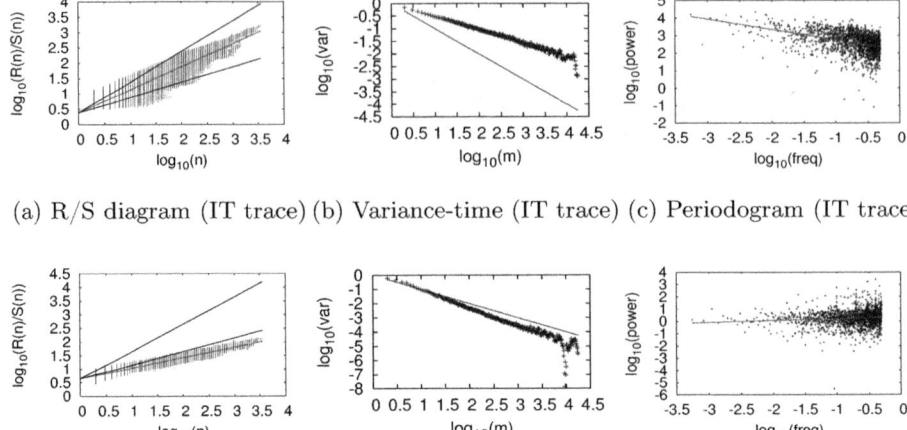

(a) R/S diagram (IT trace) (b) Variance-time (IT trace) (c) Periodogram (IT trace)

(d) R/S diagram (3c trace) (e) Variance-time (3c trace) (f) Periodogram (3c trace)

Fig. 3. Self-similarity tests on the IT trace and the 3layer-control (3c) trace

two hosts. We assume it to be related to some automated activity, such as backup, but we did not attempt to verify which.

4.2   Self-similarity

One of the requirements for a random variable to be self-similar is that it must be wide-sense stationary [4], which implies, among other things, a constant mean over time. Therefore, due to the diurnal patterns of activity, network traffic is not truly self-similar [8]. However, network measurements with durations up to a few hours *do* present self-similar time series [4,6]. Other sources of non-stationarity are singular events that cause drastic changes in the network behavior, such as a maintenance operation or changes in physical processes (see Section 3.2). For the following analysis, we have taken periods of a few hours from our datasets where the stationarity requirement is satisfied.

The self-similarity analysis is performed for the *pkts/s* and *bytes/s* time series with 100 millisecond bins for all datasets. The results for the *bytes/s* are analogous to the ones from *pkts/s* and, therefore, are omitted. Figure 3 depicts the R/S pox diagram, the variance time plots and the periodograms for *IT* in the first row (Figures 3a, 3b and 3c respectively) and *3layer-control* in the second row (Figures 3d, 3e and 3f respectively). The results for the other SCADA datasets are analogous, thus also omitted.

The R/S pox diagram of a self-similar random variable should have an asymptotic slope between 0.5 and 1 (represented by the black dotted lines). The slope is typically estimated by least-square fitting (represented by the red dotted line). It is clear from Figures 3a and 3d that *IT* presents self-similar behavior, while *3layer-control* does not. A comparable result is obtained using the variance-time

Table 2. Hurst parameter estimations

dataset	bytes/s			pkts/s		
	R/S	var-time	period	R/S	var-time	period
IT	0.73	0.72	0.79	0.75	[0.71-0.72]	0.79
2layer	0.17	[0.09,0.11]	0.13	0.17	[0.32,0.42]	0.22
3layer-control	0.38	[0.38,0.44]	0.43	0.39	[0.36,0.37]	0.44
3layer-field	0.02	[0.27,0.31]	0.29	0.44	[0.35,0.42]	0.04

plot test, where the slope of the resulting curve should be shallower than -1 (black dotted line). This test shows that the variance of the SCADA time series decays much faster than the expected for a self-similar process. In contrast, the *IT* dataset result is consistent with the traditional network measurements. The same conclusion can be drawn from the periodogram test. When applying this method, we obtain a estimative of $H = 0.79$ for the *IT* dataset and of $H = 0.44$ for *3layer-control*. Note that the Hurst parameter of a self-similar process should be in the interval $H \in [0.5, 1)$.

Table 2 summarize the results of our analysis, reporting the estimates for the Hurst parameter from the R/S analysis (*R/S*), variance-time plots (*var-time*) and periodograms (*period*). All estimates for the SCADA datasets indicate a non-self-similar behavior, although the estimates are not consistent between tests. In contrast, the *IT* dataset shows more consistent estimate of the Hurst parameter, which is in agreement with a self-similar behavior. Note also that, while the R/S analysis and periodograms yield a single estimate, the variance-time plots produce a small range of estimates. This happens because for both small and large aggregation levels m there is a considerable amount of variance that should not be taken into account when performing the least-square fit. In our analysis we remove up to 15% of either end of the variance-time plot to obtain the Hurst estimates.

4.3   Distributional Aspects of Connection Sizes

As explained in Section 3.3, there is a debate in the research community around which distribution best fits the tail behavior of connections sizes[1], heavy-tail (usually Pareto-distributed) or log-normal. We can illustrate both behaviors for the *IT* trace. In the case of the number of packets per flow, plotted in Figure 4a, the CCDF presents an almost constant slope, indicating that a Pareto model might provide a good fit. In the case of flow duration, plotted in Figure 4b, the behavior is closer to that of an log-normal distribution, with an increasing slope when approaching extreme values in the tail.

For the SCADA datasets, the results are not always conclusive. For instance, consider again the connection size in packets plotted in Figure 4a. The tail for dataset *2layer* could be modeled as Pareto, if one considers the tail to consist of

---

[1] In this paper we use the terms connection and flow interchangeably. For the definition of flow we refer to Section 2.

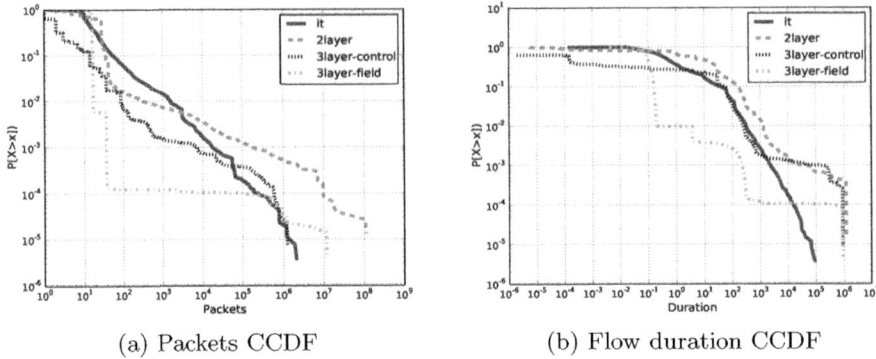

(a) Packets CCDF   (b) Flow duration CCDF

Fig. 4. Flow size Complementary CDF's

values above 10^2. In the case of *3layer-control*, the CCDF presents large variations and cannot be approximated by either model. When considering duration,
2layer and *3layer-control* CCDFs present different slopes at different ranges.
See for instance the CCDF of *3layer-control* in Figure 4b. The slope is relatively
small up to $10s$, it sharply increases in the interval $[10, 10^3]$ after which it sharply
reduces. Finally, the tail of dataset *3layer-field* for both metrics is dominated by
a small range of values, which produces the nearly vertical lines in both plots.

Irrespective of which is the best model to represent the connection size distribution, all datasets share a common characteristic: the connection size distribution is always *positively skewed*, i.e, it has a body containing the majority of
the values in the distribution and a tail with extreme values in the right.

5   Conclusions

The goal of this paper was to verify if models used to describe traditional network
traffic can also be applied to SCADA traffic. To this end, we have analyzed
SCADA traffic traces collected at two water treatment and distribution facilities
and compared their characteristics with those of traditional network traffic. Our
analysis has been based on a list of network traffic invariants widely observed in
network measurements.

We draw the following conclusions from our results. First, SCADA networks do
not present the diurnal patterns of activity common to traditional IT networks, as
most of the traffic is generated by automated processes with little human interaction. More important, self-similar correlations in the time series are not present.
Our results suggest that simple *ON/OFF* models might provide a good approximation for the time series. Finally, neither heavy-tail nor log-normal models seem
to provide a good fit for the connection sizes. In summary, our results indicate that
the existing traffic models can not be easily applied to SCADA traffic.

To our best knowledge, we provide the first study on real-world SCADA traces
in this paper. Since existing publications on SCADA networks generally do not

rely on empirical data, we believe that our findings are a first step towards constructing realistic SCADA traffic models to support future research in the area. In future work, we intend to extend our analysis of SCADA traffic, including the characterization of the flow arrival process and the extraction of periodical patterns.

References

1. Kobayashi, T.H., Batista, A.B., Brito, A.M., Pires, P.S.M.: Using a packet manipulation tool for security analysis of industrial network protocols. In: IEEE Conference on Emerging Technologies and Factory Automation (ETFA), pp. 744–747 (2007)
2. Cheung, S., Skinner, K., Dutertre, B., Fong, M., Lindqvist, U., Valdes, A.: Using model-based intrusion detection for SCADA networks. In: Proceedings of the SCADA Security Scientific Symposium, pp. 1–12. Citeseer (2007)
3. Valdes, A., Cheung, S.: Communication pattern anomaly detection in process control systems. In: IEEE Conference on Technologies for Homeland Security, HST 2009, pp. 22–29. IEEE (May 2009)
4. Leland, W.E., Willinger, W., Taqqu, M.S., Wilson, D.V.: On the self-similar nature of Ethernet traffic. ACM SIGCOMM Computer Communication Review 25(1), 202–213 (1995)
5. Paxson, V., Floyd, S.: Wide area traffic: the failure of Poisson modeling. IEEE/ACM Transactions on Networking 3(3), 226–244 (1995)
6. Crovella, M.E., Bestavros, A.: Self-similarity in World Wide Web traffic: evidence and possible causes. IEEE/ACM Transactions on Networking 5(6), 835–846 (1997)
7. Downey, A.: Lognormal and Pareto distributions in the Internet. Computer Communications 28(7), 790–801 (2005)
8. Gong, W.-B., Liu, Y., Misra, V., Towsley, D.: Self-similarity and long range dependence on the internet: a second look at the evidence, origins and implications. Computer Networks 48(3), 377–399 (2005); Long Range Dependent Traffic
9. Loiseau, P., Goncalves, P., Dewaele, G., Borgnat, P., Abry, P., Primet, P.V.-B.: Investigating Self-Similarity and Heavy-Tailed Distributions on a Large-Scale Experimental Facility. IEEE/ACM Transactions on Networking 18(4), 1261–1274 (2010)
10. Vázquez, A., Pastor-Satorras, R., Vespignani, A.: Large-scale topological and dynamical properties of the internet. Physical Review E 65 (2002)
11. Sadre, R., Haverkort, B.R.: Changes in the Web from 2000 to 2007. In: De Turck, F., Kellerer, W., Kormentzas, G. (eds.) DSOM 2008. LNCS, vol. 5273, pp. 136–148. Springer, Heidelberg (2008)
12. Floyd, S., Paxson, V.: Difficulties in simulating the Internet. IEEE/ACM Transactions on Networking 9(4), 392–403 (2001)
13. Barbosa, R.R.R., Sadre, R., Pras, A.: A First Look into SCADA Network Traffic. In: Network Operations and Management Symposium, NOMS (to appear, 2012)
14. Jacobson, V., Leres, C., McCanne, S., et al.: Tcpdump (1989)
15. Barbosa, R.R.R., Sadre, R., Pras, A., van de Meent, R.: Simpleweb/university of twente traffic traces data repository. Technical report, Centre for Telematics and Information Technology, University of Twente (April 2010)
16. Nuzman, C., Saniee, I., Sweldens, W., Weiss, A.: A compound model for TCP connection arrivals for LAN and WAN applications. Computer Networks 40(3), 319–337 (2002)

Characterizing Delays in Norwegian 3G Networks

Ahmed Elmokashfi, Amund Kvalbein, Jie Xiang, and Kristian R. Evensen

Simula Research Laboratory

Abstract. This paper presents a first look at long-term delay measurements from data connections in 3 Norwegian 3G Networks. We have performed active measurements for more than 6 months from 90 voting locations used in a trial with electronic voting during this fall's regional elections. Our monitors are geographically spread across all of Norway, and give an unprecedented view of the performance and stability of the total 3G infrastructure of a country. In this paper, we focus on delay characteristics. We find large differences in delay between different monitors. More interestingly, we observe that the delay characteristics of the different operators are very different, pointing to operator-specific network design and configurations as the most important factor for delays.

1 Introduction

We are witnessing a revolution in the way people access and use the Internet. The advent of mobile devices such as smartphones and tablets, combined with the almost universal coverage of 3G networks, has radically changed how we access, share and process information. A stable and resilient 3G network connection has become a necessity for the daily operations of individuals and organizations. Yet, we have little knowledge of the long-term stability and performance of 3G data networks, beyond the coverage maps provided by network operators. This gives a very limited basis for comparing and evaluating the quality of the offered services. To alleviate this, there is a need for long-term measurements of the stability, availability and quality experienced by users in each network.

This paper presents a first look at long-term measurements of mobile broadband (MBB) data connections from 3 different network operators in Norway, with an emphasis on delay characteristics. The measurements are carried out over a period of more than 6 months from 90 locations in 10 municipalities spread across Norway. The measurements are performed using *ping* and *traceroute* from our monitor nodes to servers placed at two different locations. These measurements were collected in connection with a trial of electronic voting during the Norwegian regional elections in fall 2011. Hence, all monitors are placed in voting locations. The number of voting locations in each municipality varies between 4 and 15. Voting locations are geographically spread according to habitation patterns in the participating municipalities, which vary in size and population density.

Our measurements have a unique combination of features:

N. Taft and F. Ricciato (Eds.): PAM 2012, LNCS 7192, pp. 136–146, 2012.

- They are taken from a large number of geographically diverse measurement points, giving a representative view of the quality of MBB data connections experienced by customers across Norway.
- They are measured over a long period of over 6 months, giving a good basis for capturing both short-term and long-term variations in the experienced performance.
- They are performed simultaneously in 3 different cellular networks, giving a unique possibility to directly compare and correlate the performance of different networks.

In this paper, we present the measurement setup, and use the data to take a first look at an important performance metric: delay. More specifically, we focus on RTTs measured by *ping*. We characterize delay along several axis, and compare the delays experienced in different networks and at different locations. We find that there are large differences between operators with respect to both absolute delays and variations, and that each operator has its own "signature" in the delay characteristics. Interestingly, we also find that the delay characteristics are mainly network-dependent rather than monitor-dependent, indicating the key role played by network design decisions in deciding delay characteristics.

2   Measurement Setup and Data

We have built a measurement infrastructure consisting of 90 measurement hosts in 10 municipalities across Norway as shown in Fig. 1a. Our measurement nodes are hosted in separate locations within each municipality; the average distance between two monitors in a municipality is 7.7 km. The infrastructure also includes two servers, one is located in the middle of Norway (Brønnøysund) and the other one is located in the south east of Norway (Fornebu)[1].

Our measurement node is a Dell Latitude E6510 laptop running Ubuntu 10.04. As shown in Fig. 1b, each node is multi-homed to four ISPs, three of them are MBB providers. The fourth operator is which ever fixed broadband provider that is available on-site. This connection will have varying quality, from high-speed fiber connection in some locations to nothing at all in other. In this paper, we use fixed broadband measurements as a reference point for comparing the performance of the MBB providers. Operators 1 and 2 offer a High Speed Packet Access (HSPA) based data service, an evolution of Wide-band Code Division Multiple Access (WCDMA). In locations where the HSPA service is not available, the connection reverts to EDGE/GPRS. In the following, we refer to these operators as $HSPA_1$ and $HSPA_2$. Operator 3 offers a CDMA2000 1xEV-DO (Evolution-Data Optimized) based data service, we refer to this operator as EV-DO. Our measurement node connects to these 3G operators through the following devices. Dell built-in wireless 5540 HSPA mobile broadband mini-card ($HSPA_1$), ZTE MF636 USB modem ($HSPA_2$), and Huawei EC506 wireless router (EV-DO).

---

[1] For more information about our measurement setup please refer to http://nevada.simula.no/

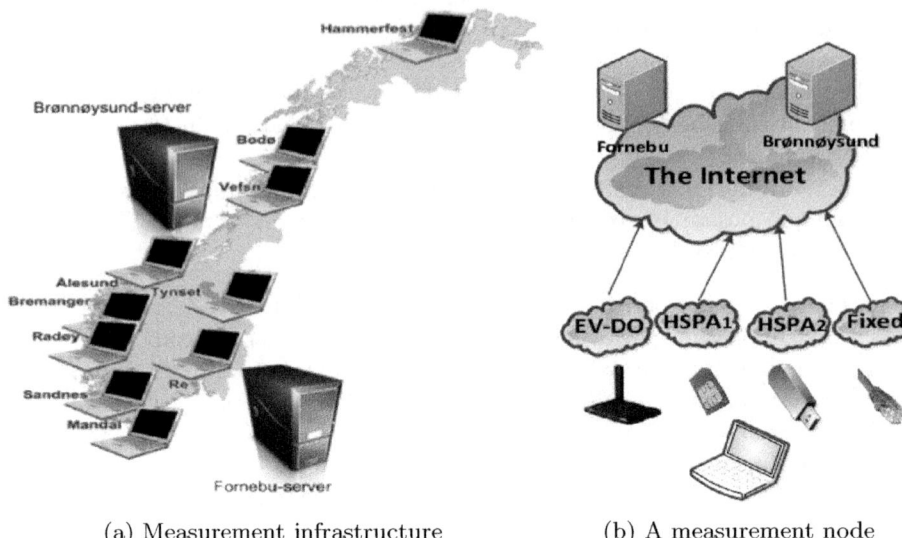

(a) Measurement infrastructure   (b) A measurement node

Fig. 1. Measurement setup

We discuss the impact of the different modems on the measured delays in the next section.

Each node periodically runs *ping* and *traceroute* measurements through each of its four interfaces to the two servers indicated above. Ping measurements are performed every second through the fixed connection and every 5 seconds through the wireless networks. Traceroute measurements are performed every 10 minutes. We use a modified version of Paris traceroute [2], where we have added support for specifying which interface to use for each run. We also use AT commands every minute to measure the received signal strength. Our measurements cover the period from February to August 2011, but in this paper we often use only a subset of the data collected as long as this does not influence the results. Most of our analysis is based on data collected during July 2011.

The scale and complexity of our infrastructure poses several challenges regarding its management and operation. To minimize the administration overhead (e.g. traveling to remote sites), we have designed our monitors to be as self-administered as possible. Each host maintains a reverse SSH session with our Fornebu server, to be used by the host for uploading its measurement data, and by the server for pushing new configurations and remote management when needed. Further, each node stores measurement data locally and uploads it every day to the server at around 3 AM. A monitor periodically checks the status of the SSH session and all four network interfaces and automatically tries to restore any failing session or interface. IT personnel at remote municipalities help when on-site intervention is needed on a voluntary basis. Thus, long response times are expected when a node is permanently down. Another challenge that we have faced is the instability of $HSPA_2$'s 3G USB modems; the majority of them require frequent physical removal and re-plugging. Due to these challenges we use measurements from around 60 hosts out of 90 in this study, and only 17 $HSPA_2$ monitors.

3   Delay Characteristics of Norwegian 3G Networks

In this study, we use the IP-layer tools *ping* and *traceroute* to measure the end-to-end delay between the measurement nodes and our servers. This means that we are not able to dissect the contribution of the different components in the 3G access networks (such as the base station and the Radio Network Controller) to the total delay. Using *traceroute*, we are still able to compare the RTT in the first IP-hop to that of the end-to-end path. The first IP hop in 3G networks will typically be the Gateway GPRS Service Node (GGSN).

In this section, we present our findings regarding delay characteristics in the measured MBB networks.

There are large differences in delay between operators. The left panel in Fig. 2 illustrates a typical CDF of RTTs measured at one of our monitoring points during July 2011. All MBB networks exhibit roughly an order of magnitude higher delay than the fixed network. Delay varies significantly between networks; we note that $HSPA_1$'s delay is higher than that of *EV-DO* and $HSPA_2$, and varies in a wider range between 200ms and 600ms.

The right plot in in Fig. 2 shows the 5th percentile, median, and 95th percentile of RTTs measured in July 2011 between each monitor and the Fornebu server[2]. This figure shows that there are large and consistent differences in delay between operators. $HSPA_1$ shows the highest delay (median RTT $\sim$ 300ms across all monitors). Then follows *EV-DO* (median RTT $\sim$ 180ms), before $HSPA_2$ (median RTT $\sim$ 104ms). Note that, as explained in Sec. 2 we have fewer monitors of type $HSPA_2$. The fixed line RTTs are significantly smaller (median RTT $\sim$ 16ms) than all MBB operators.

We also record large variations between monitors in the same operator and even within a single connection. $HSPA_1$'s RTTs in a single connection shows large variations reaching up to two orders of magnitude. In some cases, the round trip delay can reach several seconds, even tens of seconds. Across monitors, *EV-DO*'s RTTs are more stable than those of $HSPA_1$ and $HSPA_2$. It's median RTT varies between 162ms and 297ms across monitors. The same metric varies between 82.5ms and 1691ms in $HSPA_1$; and between 71.2ms and 740ms in $HSPA_2$.

The observed differences cannot be explained by different modems alone. As described in Sec. 2, we use different modems to connect to the different operators. It is therefore natural to ask whether the choice of modem can explain the observed differences. To investigate this, we have run controlled experiments with different modems for each operator. Table 1 shows the median

---

[2] Measurements to the other server show similar results.

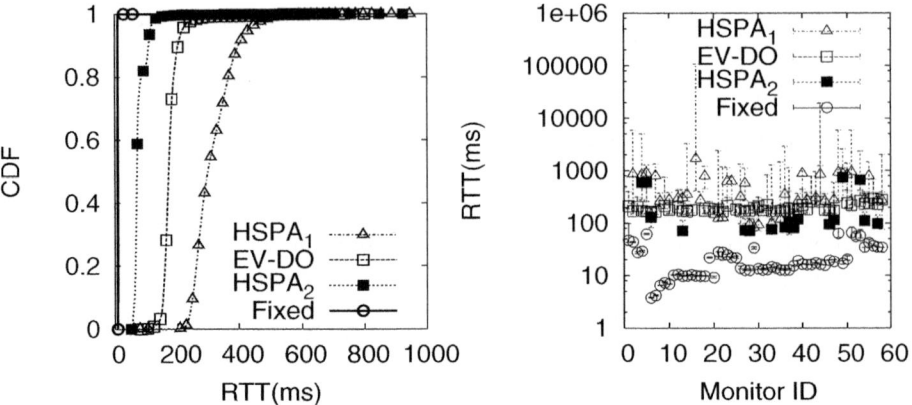

Fig. 2. Example of a typical RTT CDF (left), RTTs statistics (right)

delay recorded over a 24 hour period using different modems[3]. The measurements for each operator are taken in parallel during the same 24 hour period. All modems are USB sticks, except the internal modem and Huawei EC506 (which is a standalone wireless router). The values marked with a star represent the modem that was used in the long-term measurements. We observe that the choice of modem has a marked influence on delay, but that it is far from the dominant factor. We plan to do more systematic evaluations of the role of the modem in future studies.

Table 1. Comparing Modems

Operator	Internal	ZTE MF636	Huawei E1752	Huawei EC506	C-motech D50
$HSPA_1$	282 ms*		368 ms		
$HSPA_2$	57 ms	72 ms*	64 ms		
$EV\text{-}DO$				164 ms*	81 ms

While there are sometimes large differences between monitors of the same operator, they mainly belong to the same population. Our previous observations sometimes show large variations in delay between monitors of the same operator, thus it is interesting to check whether these differences are inherent in MBB networks or just reflect local effects near an affected monitor (e.g. poor wireless coverage). To answer this we investigate differences between delay distributions of monitors that belong to the same operator.

To compare two different delay samples as to whether they belong to the same population, we need to pick an appropriate statistical test that suits our data.

---

[3] Due to the different technologies and provider locks, we are not able to test all modems across all operators.

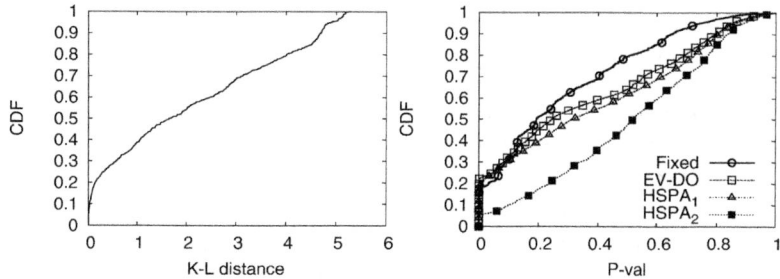

Fig. 3. KL distance distribution (left), Resulting P-values distribution (right)

First, it is reasonable to avoid parametric tests (e.g. t-test), since we cannot make assumptions about the underlying probability distribution of the RTT data. One possibility is to apply the two-sample Kolmogorov-Smirnov test [5] for comparing continuous, one dimensional distributions. But, RTT distributions are not continuous, thus we decide to employ the Kullback-Leibler (K-L) divergence test instead [7]. The K-L divergence is a measure for the closeness between two samples P and Q in terms of extra information bits required to encode a message based on P instead of Q. Note that the K-L divergence in general is not symmetric.

K-L divergence by itself cannot determine whether the two tested delay samples are drawn from the same population at a certain confidence level. Hence, we construct a hypothesis test that is inspired by the approach used in [10]. In the following, we present this hypothesis test; our null hypothesis H_0 is that the tested samples have identical underlying distribution.

For each interface and monitor, we draw 30 random mutually exclusive samples of equal sizes from RTT measurements in July'11. We then calculate the K-L divergence for each pair, that results in 870 values. These values are then used to estimate the corresponding empirical CDF of K-L divergence. The left panel in Fig. 3 presents an example of such CDF estimated for one of our *EV-DO* monitoring interfaces, in the following we call this interface X. If we want to compare the distribution of RTTs measured at another *EV-DO* interface Y to that of X, we first measure the K-L divergence between Y and X. Let's assume that K-$L(Y, X) = 2$. We use the empirical CDF of K-L divergence values at X to find $F(K$-L distance $= 2)$. This value represents the probability that such divergence can occur between two samples drawn from the RTT population of interface X. The P-value of our test is then calculated as $1 - F(K$-L distance $= 2)$, we accept H_0 if P-$value > 0.05$, i.e. the probability that such divergence occurs between two samples from the same population is at least 5%. In our example, the P-value is 0.46 thus we accept H_0.

Using our constructed hypothesis test we compare all pairs of distributions from the same operator. The right plot in Fig. 3 shows the CDF of the calculated P-values. We observe that a large fraction of pairs in all interfaces is characterized by a P-value larger than 0.05, meaning that the majority of RTT distributions come from the same population. Our results show that at least 75% of all monitor pairs from the same operator belong to the same population. We also compare RTT distributions across operators and find that a significant fraction of pairs do not belong to the same population. For example, only 49% of all pairs are of the same population, when comparing EV-DO to $HSPA_1$. This is in agreement with our earlier observations in Fig. 2.

The fact that delay distribution in most monitors of the same operators mainly come from the same population is quite interesting. First, recalling the large differences between operators, it seems that each operator has its own "signature" in the delay characteristics. Second, it shows that the delay characteristics of a connection is mainly network-dependent rather than monitor-dependent.

3G access network plays a central role in deciding delay characteristics. The 3G access network seems to play a central role for the delay characteristics. We cannot directly measure this (since there are no IP hops in this network), so we investigate this by looking at delay correlations between monitors at different geographical distances. We first calculate the temporal correlation between all pairs of RTT time series from the same operator. To construct these time series, we use one month of delay measurements per monitor, divide it to five-minute bins, and calculate the average RTT in each bin. Second, we examine how temporal correlation between two time series varies in relation to the geographical distance between the respective monitors. To estimate correlations between monitors, we use the non-parametric Kendall's τ rank correlation coefficient [5]. τ takes value between -1 and 1, and it represents the difference between the probability that the observed data are in the same order in both samples and the probability that they are not.

The left panel in Fig. 4 depicts τ's CDFs for monitors that are at most 100km apart for all operators. The MBB operators demonstrate stronger correlation than the fixed network. In the middle panel, we plot the τ's CDFs corresponding to our fixed line monitors. Each curve represents correlations between monitors that are within a specific distance range from each other. We observe that the temporal correlation between the fixed line monitors is generally low ($\tau \leq 0.3$ in almost 80% of the cases). Furthermore, *distance between monitors has a negligible impact on their correlations.*

Interestingly, we observe a quite different behavior in the MBB networks. *Monitors that are up to 300km apart are strongly correlated. Beyond that the correlation properties are similar to those of fixed line monitors.* The right panel in Fig. 4 illustrates this for $HSPA_1$. Monitors in EV-DO and $HSPA_2$ behave similarly. It is natural to relate this behavior to the architecture of 3G networks, where geographically close base stations share the same Radio Network Controller (RNC). This result shows that the 3G access network is an important contributor to the overall delay characteristics, and indicates that queuing at the Base Station Controller (BSC) level plays an important role.

The access network is a decisive factor for delay, but is not responsible for outliers. The common wisdom is that last mile delay constitutes a large fraction of end-to-end delay in wireless networks. The last mile

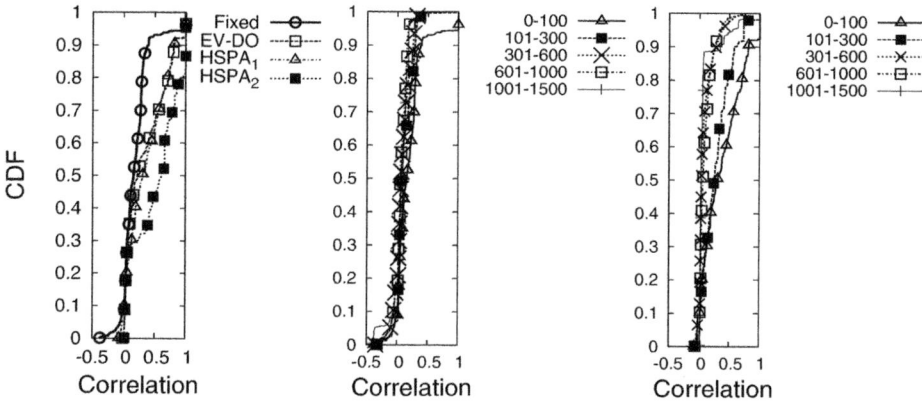

Fig. 4. Delay correlation between monitors in relation to their geographical distance. Monitors that are up to 100 km apart (left), Fixed (middle), $HSPA_1$(right)

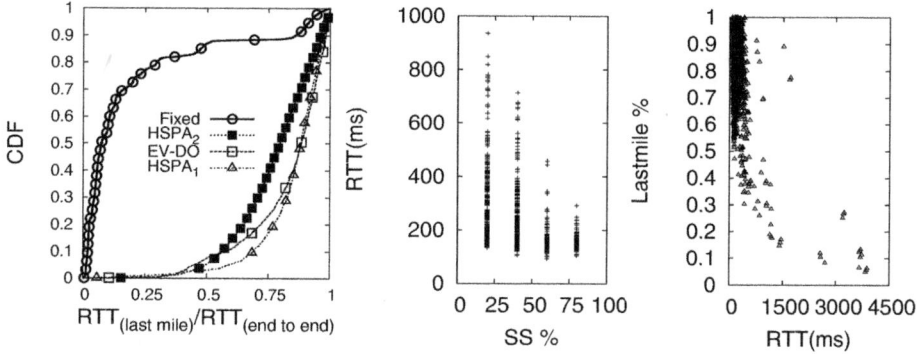

Fig. 5. Last mile delay characteristics

includes the part of the 3G network between an end device and the first IP hop in the respective provider's cloud (i.e. the GGSN). In a wired network, the last mile corresponds to all physical infra-structure that lies between a customer's access device (e.g. ADSL modem) and the first gateway in her ISP's network.

In order to quantify the contribution of the access network to observed RTTs, we consider the ratio (r) of the last mile RTT to the end to end RTT. We employ our traceroute measurements to estimate the last mile latency (i.e. by extracting the RTT to the first IP hop in the respective provider's network). The left panel in Fig 5 illustrates r's CDF, each curve is estimated by combining r values from all monitors of the corresponding operator. As expected, we observe a clear difference between the fixed network and the three wireless interfaces. In the fixed network, r is less than 10% in 50% of the cases, but in the wireless networks it is more than 50% in 90% of the cases. We also note that the contribution of the

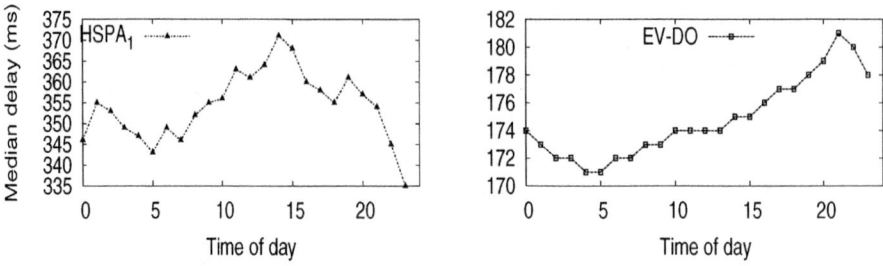

Fig. 6. Delay variation during the day

access network to observed RTTs is higher in $HSPA_1$ than in EV-DO than in $HSPA_2$. The last observation is in accordance with our earlier findings.

Several factors contribute to the last mile latency including modem performance, signal quality, queuing in the access network beyond the first wireless hop, and the impact of different components in the access network (e.g. RNC). The middle panel in Fig. 5 shows the relation between last mile RTTs, measured in all EV-DO monitors, and the received signal strength (SS) represented as a percentage of the best attainable signal quality. Note that, the SS we measure only covers the received signal. We observe that *last mile RTTs increase as SS deteriorates.* In our future work, we plan to investigate the impact of other factors (e.g. queuing in the access network beyond the first wireless hop) on the last mile delay.

Finally, we ask whether the access network is responsible for the very high delay values that we sometimes experience. The right panel in Fig. 5 depicts the relation between r and RTTs aggregated across all $HSPA_1$ monitors. Surprisingly, *we observe that r decreases as RTT increases*, suggesting that such large RTTs are caused by performance degradation beyond the access network, i.e., in the GGSN or at the IP path from the GGSN to the measurement servers. EV-DO and $HSPA_2$ show a similar behavior.

3G delays exhibit clear diurnal patterns. To indirectly measure coarse-grained traffic patterns, we explore how delay varies throughout the day. The plots in Fig. 6 shows the median delay of $HSPA_1$ and EV-DO as a function in the time of the day. To calculate for operator X at hour H, we collect all RTTs from all measurements from X that are recorded at hour H throughout May'11 and then find their median[4].

Not surprisingly, we find clear diurnal patterns in delay. This has earlier been reported in many studies from fixed networks [3]. Interestingly, delay peaks at different hours in our measured networks. While $HSPA_1$ delays are highest during business hours, EV-DO shows a different pattern with higher delays in the evening. We have been in contact with EV-DO, and they confirm that they see more traffic in their network at these hours, probably because they have a large number of home and recreational users.

---

[4] July data show similar patterns.

4 Related Work

Laner et. al [8] measured 3G uplink delay in an operational HSPA network and showed that the average delay is strongly dependent on the packet size. Further, they found that last mile delay constitutes a large fraction of measured delays. The authors in [4] analyzed packet delay in UMTS networks and identified ARQ loss recovery mechanisms as the main cause behind the high variability in packet delay. Arlos and Fiedler [1] measured the influence of the packet size on the one-way delay (OWD) in 3G networks in three different operators in Sweden. They showed that choosing an optimal packet size significantly reduces OWD. In contrast with previous work that measured delay in 3G networks, we provide a more complete study that involves two different 3G technologies, three operators and about 60 monitoring points.

Other papers (e.g. [6,9]) measured different set of performance metrics in 3G networks; including TCP and UDP performance, throughput, and network resource allocation.

5 Conclusions

This work presents a first look on long-term measurements of MBB data connections from 3 different network operators in Norway. More specifically, in this paper, we investigate the characteristics of round trip delays with a focus on the role of the 3G access network. We observe large differences between operators with respect to both absolute delays and variations. Access network latency constitutes a significant part of the total delay. However, its share drops at large RTTs. We also observe that delays in 3G networks exhibit clear diurnal patterns that peak at different hours during the day depending on the operator.

Interestingly, we find that the delay characteristics in different 3G networks are mainly network-dependent rather than monitor-dependent, and that each operator has its own "signature" in the delay characteristics. These findings indicate that differences between MBB operators are mainly dictated by the way their access networks are designed and configured. The important role played by the 3G access network in deciding delay characteristic is further confirmed through analyzing correlations between monitors of the same operator. The identified strong correlation between geographically close 3G monitors indicates the presence of significant infrastructure aggregation within each operator access network.

References

1. Arlos, P., Fiedler, M.: Influence of the Packet Size on the One-Way Delay in 3G Networks. In: Krishnamurthy, A., Plattner, B. (eds.) PAM 2010. LNCS, vol. 6032, pp. 61–70. Springer, Heidelberg (2010)
2. Augustin, B., Cuvellier, X., Orgogozo, B., Viger, F., Friedman, T., Latapy, M., Magnien, C., Teixeira, R.: Avoiding traceroute anomalies with Paris traceroute. In: IMC (2006)

3. Brownlee, N., Claffy, K.: Understanding Internet Traffic Streams: Dragonflies and Tortoises. IEEE Communications, 110–117 (July 2002)
4. Cano-Garcia, J.M., Gonzalez-Parada, E., Casilari, E.: Experimental Analysis and Characterization of Packet Delay in UMTS Networks. In: Koucheryavy, Y., Harju, J., Iversen, V.B. (eds.) NEW2AN 2006. LNCS, vol. 4003, pp. 396–407. Springer, Heidelberg (2006)
5. Hollander, M., Wolfe, D.A.: Nonparametric statistical methods, 2nd edn. Wiley (1999)
6. Jurvansuu, M., Prokkola, J., Hanski, M., Perala, P.: HSDPA performance in live networks. In: ICC (2007)
7. Kullback, S., Leibler, R.A.: On information and sufficiency. Ann. Math. Statist. 22(1), 79–86 (1951)
8. Laner, M., Svoboda, P., Hasenleithner, E., Rupp, M.: Dissecting 3G Uplink Delay by Measuring in an Operational HSPA Network. In: Spring, N., Riley, G.F. (eds.) PAM 2011. LNCS, vol. 6579, pp. 52–61. Springer, Heidelberg (2011)
9. Tan, W.L., Lam, F., Lau, W.C.: An Empirical Study on the Capacity and Performance of 3G Networks. IEEE Transactions on Mobile Computing 7(6) (2008)
10. Tariq, M.M.B., Dhamdhere, A., Dovrolis, C., Ammar, M.: Poisson versus periodic path probing (or, does PASTA matter?). In: IMC (2005)

On 60 GHz Wireless Link Performance in Indoor Environments

Xiaozheng Tie[1,*], Kishore Ramachandran[2], and Rajesh Mahindra[2]

[1] University of Massachusetts, Amherst, MA
[2] NEC Laboratories America, Princeton, NJ

Abstract. The multi-Gbps throughput potential of 60 GHz wireless interfaces make them an attractive technology for next-generation gigabit WLANs. For increased coverage, and improved resilience to human-body blockage, beamsteering with high-gain directional antennas is emerging to be an integral part of 60 GHz radios. However, the real-world performance of these state-of-the-art radios in typical indoor environments has not previously been explored well in open literature.

To this end, in this paper, we address the following open questions: how do these radios perform in indoor line-of-sight(LOS) and non-line-of-sight (NLOS) locations? how sensitive is performance to factors such as node orientation or placement? how robust is performance to human-body blockage and mobility? Our measurement results from a real office setting, using a first-of-its-kind experimental platform (called Presto), show that, contrary to conventional perception, state-of-the-art 60 GHz radios perform well even in NLOS locations, in the presence of human-body blockage and LOS mobility. While their performance is affected by node (or more precisely, antenna array) orientation, simply using a few more antenna arrays and dynamically selecting amongst them shows potential to address this issue. The implications of these observations is in lowering the barriers to their adoption in next-generation gigabit WLANs.

1   Introduction

Emerging radios in the unlicensed 57-66 GHz spectrum (colloquially known as "60 GHz" radios) [23,6,22,9,1] offer the opportunity to enable throughput-intensive, short-range wireless networks (e.g. [8]) and new services (such as sync-and-go file transfers). By leveraging a wide channel bandwidth ($\sim$2 GHz), these radios can support over-the-air multi-Gbps data transfers. A caveat, however, is that 60 GHz radios need high-gain directional communication to leverage their throughput potential at distances greater than a few meters [4]. In addition, signals at these millimeter-wavelength frequencies are blocked by human bodies [3,20] and attenuated by obstacles (e.g. walls) (see Table III in [23]).

To overcome these challenges, state-of-the-art 60 GHz radios use high-gain, switched-beam directional antennas [21,16]. High antenna gain helps increase

---

* Work done during internship at NEC Labs America, Inc.

N. Taft and F. Ricciato (Eds.): PAM 2012, LNCS 7192, pp. 147–157, 2012.
© Springer-Verlag Berlin Heidelberg 2012

the coverage range and overcome attenuation by obstacles while the ability to switch beams at run-time (i.e. beamsteering) can help steer signals "around" human-body blockage. A natural follow-up question is whether it is feasible to build *general-purpose, gigabit wireless LANs* using these state-of-the-art 60 GHz radios? Unlike existing use of this technology restricted to point-to-point, LOS scenarios [8,17,19], is it possible to extend its applicability to environments with NLOS blockage from walls/cubicles, human-body blockage, and user mobility?

Towards determining this feasibility, we measure 60 GHz link performance in an indoor enterprise environment. Through experiments in a realistic setting, this paper answers the following set of basic and important questions: *What is the effect of LOS or NLOS node location on performance? How sensitive is the performance to node (or more precisely, antenna array) orientation? How robust is the performance to human-body blockage and mobility?* To our knowledge, we are not aware of any other network-layer measurements that address all these generic questions in the indoor context. Prior efforts in this domain focused mainly on PHY-layer channel characterization [23,3].

To conduct these measurements, due to the lack of availability of 60 GHz wireless interfaces for PCs, we build a first-of-its-kind experimental platform called **Presto**. Presto enables IP-over-60-GHz communication by leveraging commercial off-the-shelf (COTS) 60 GHz wireless HDMI radios and interfacing them with PCs via readily-available FPGAs.

In theory, high antenna gain can help overcome attenuation losses due to wall or cubicle blockage. Further, multipath reflections in indoor environments could present alternate paths that beamsteering can take advantage of in the presence of human-body blockage or while adapting to user mobility. We study how effective state-of-the-art 60 GHz radios are in dealing with these real-world situations. In particular, we make the following key observations: (1) 60 GHz radios are able to overcome NLOS blockage due to walls and cubicles; their coverage range is reduced relative to LOS scenarios but could still be enough to satisfy the needs of dense WLANs. (2) Antenna array orientation has a significant effect on performance even in the presence of indoor multipath reflections; mitigation strategies that add to the single antenna array at each node and dynamically select amongst them show potential to address this issue. (3) Finally, beamsteering is effective in dealing with low levels of human-body blockage and LOS mobility at walking speeds; existing implementations need to react faster in the presence of high levels of dynamically-occurring human-body blockage.

The rest of the paper is organized as follows. Background on state-of-the-art 60 GHz radios and beamsteering is presented in §2. Our experimental platform, Presto, is described in §3. §4 describes our experimental methodology and §5 presents our results and interpretations from our experiments. §6 concludes.

2   Background

Need for Directionality & Beamsteering: With omni-directional antennas, 60 GHz radios cannot support distances greater than a few meters (see Figure

1 in [4]). The millimeter(mm) wavelengths at these frequencies lead to reduced antenna aperture areas, which in turn lead to much higher path loss [6] and susceptibility to blockage [20].

Fortunately, antenna directionality can be used to overcome these limitations since directionality is inversely proportional to the square of the wavelength (Chap. 15, [12]). The mm-wavelengths also enable antenna arrays with tens of elements on a single die thus promoting beamsteering [13,14].

With the realization that directionality and beamsteering are essential, the WirelessHD [2] and WiGig [22] specifications, as well as the IEEE 802.11ad draft standard [9] for 60 GHz radios include the necessary mechanisms and protocol support at the MAC and PHY layers (see further details in Appendix in [10]).

Antenna Realization for Beamsteering: Typically, beamsteering is enabled by *switched-beam directional antennas* that provide a good trade-off among the available antenna technologies; they are less bulky than a collection of *fixed-beam antennas* [15] and simpler to implement and incorporate than *adaptive-beam antennas* [14]. A common way of realizing switched-beam antennas is by using *phased array antennas.* Phased array antennas consist of an array of antenna elements, the signals sent to which are weighted in both magnitude and phase. The applied weights help reinforce energy in a particular direction, thereby producing an antenna beam pattern with high Signal-to-Noise-Ratio (SNR) over an omni pattern in the desired direction contributing to a *directional/array* gain. *To realize beamsteering, several such beam patterns are generated with a phased array antenna such that they cover the entire azimuth (360°), and a specific beam pattern is dynamically chosen from the available set during run-time operation.*

Practical realizations in state-of-the-art 60 GHz radios use square or a rectangular array of elements in planar patch form [7]. These planar patch arrays are typically polarized in the horizontal or vertical direction (i.e. can steer beams in one of these directions), and have a limited angular range (< 180 degrees) [16,21] over which beams can be steered. These characteristics raise questions as to how sensitive performance will be to real-world factors like relative node location, antenna array orientation, temporary blockage by human bodies and user mobility? These questions motivate our measurements in an indoor enterprise environment. Due to the unavailability of 60 GHz wireless interfaces for PCs, we first build a new experimental platform called Presto.

3 The Presto Platform

Presto currently contains two simplex 60 GHz links (see Figure 1(a)). The nodes hosting the 60 GHz transmitter (TX) and receiver (RX) are 2.8 GHz quad-core general-purpose PCs running Linux. The wireless TX and RX connect to the PCs through customized HDMI interface boards (HIB). Figure 1(b) shows a picture of the HIB, and Figure 1(c) shows the 60 GHz transceivers.

60 GHz Wireless Transceivers: We use the Vizio XWH200 wireless HDMI TX-RX pairs [21]. These TX-RX pairs can support a peak MAC throughput of

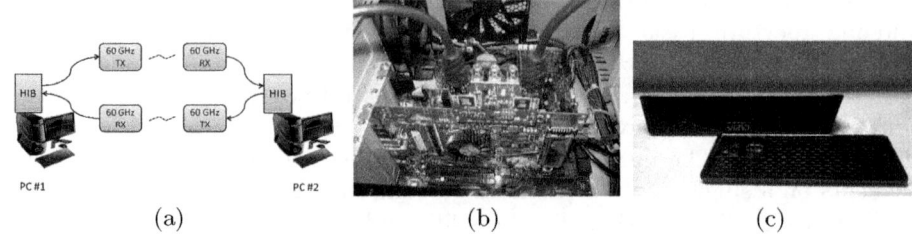

(a)   (b)   (c)

Fig. 1. The Presto Platform. (a) Setup Overview, (b) HIB on the PCIe interface on a quad-core PC, and (c) Vizio 60 GHz Transceivers.

3Gbps (at the peak PHY rate of 3.8Gbps) and are based on Silicon Image, Inc.'s 2nd-generation WirelessHD 60 GHz radios [18] (see further details in Appendix in [10]). These devices are traditionally designed to support *uncompressed* HD video transfer from a Blue-ray player to an HDTV. While the 60 GHz MAC and PHY specifications have sufficiently matured [9,2], the *protocol adaptation layer (PAL)* to interface the TCP/IP networking stack with 60 GHz transceivers is still under development [9,2]. Consequently, only an HDMI interface is provided. Hence, our first challenge is to interface these transceivers with the PC to support IP-over-wireless-HDMI packet data communications.

HDMI-Interface Board (HIB): To enable IP-over-wireless-HDMI, we use a HDMI interface board (HIB) that interfaces with the PC over the PCIe bus. The HIB is an Altera Aria II GX FPGA development board [5] with Microtronix [11] HDMI transmitter and receiver daughter-cards. The HIB has two HDMI interfaces, one for transmit and one for receive. We consider two design options for the placement of the IP-to-HDMI conversion functionality on the FPGA: (a) placing full functionality in the FPGA, (b) splitting the functionality between the FPGA and the host processor.

In the first approach, the FPGA can hide all the complexity of IP-over-HDMI and expose an Ethernet interface to the networking stack. While this enables ease of experimentation, sufficient processing power and memory are needed on the FPGA in order to support multi-Gbps speeds, which can increase its cost significantly. In the second approach, the FPGA efficiently transfers raw data (in bytes) between the HDMI interface and the PC's RAM. The software on the host CPU can then interface with the RAM, create the abstraction of a network interface and implement data-link layer functionality (like framing). By offloading most of the functionality to the host PC, such an approach is cost-effective. But it needs fast CPUs to enable network processing at multi-Gbps speeds. Presto adopts the second approach to keep the FPGA simple and cost-effective, while relying on the ready availability of fast CPUs.

FPGA Logic: The software on the FPGA uses scatter-gather DMA (sgdma) logic to take data spread over memory and transfer it over PCIe to or from the Avalon memory-mapped bus on the FPGA. Additional logic transfers data

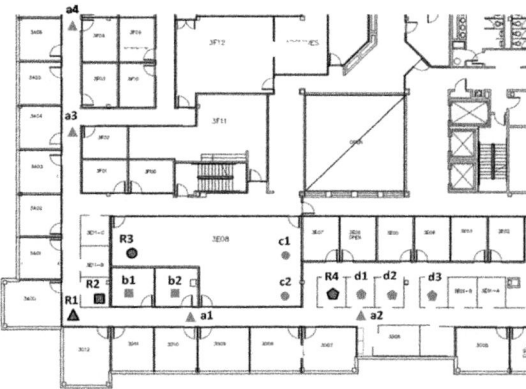

Fig. 2. Indoor Testbed; R1-R4: receivers, a1-d3: transmitters

between the Avalon bus and the HDMI transmit/receive ports. Such an approach enables high-speed transfers from RAM over PCIe to the HDMI ports.

To transfer binary IP traffic over the Vizio adapters, they are modified to use RGB mode to avoid data corruption due to color-space conversion (to YCrCb). This allows us to measure data corruption due to channel-induced errors alone. Among the RGB lines, we use the R-line to indicate that "valid" data from the PC is available on the G- and B-lines. This control-data split is needed since, HDMI video data, unlike IP traffic, is always flowing on the connection. *This split means that our current prototype can provide at most 2/3 of the raw capacity supported by these 60 GHz radios, i.e. 2/3 of 3 Gbps.* We plan to reduce this overhead in future versions of Presto.

Kernel-space Device Driver: To expose a byte-level file abstraction (primarily for ease and efficiency), the FPGA works in unison with a custom-built Linux device driver that hides the complexity of transferring data directly over the PCIc bus by exposing a standard POSIX API (i.e. open, read, write, close system calls). Once the driver is loaded, a `/dev/sgdma` device is created.

As a first case-study with Presto, we measure uni-directional (simplex), 60 GHz wireless link performance in an indoor enterprise environment.

4   Experimental Methodology

We conduct our measurements in a typical indoor enterprise environment with offices, cubicles, and corridors. Figure 2 shows our testbed deployed using Presto nodes. We consider four scenarios in eleven different TX, RX locations to capture different environmental effects, as summarized in Table 4(a).

To account for sensitivity to the TX/RX antenna array orientation, we divide the 360 degree X-Y plane into four orientations and vary them for each TX/RX location. This results in 16 TX/RX orientation combinations for each TX/RX location. We index each combination in Table 4(b) to ease our result description.

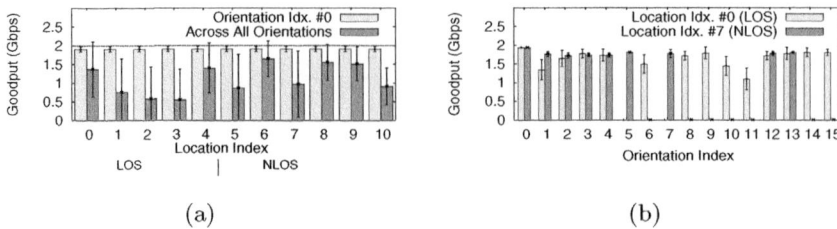

Fig. 3. 60 GHz link goodput at (a) all locations and (b) two specific locations

Traffic and Metrics: We generate backlogged traffic at 2 Gbps by using simple transmit and receive modules that directly write to and read from /dev/sgdma 32KB chunks of data in a loop for a specified amount of time[1]. Each experiment runs for 20 seconds and is repeated four times. We remove data from the start and end of experiments to avoid edge effects. We use *link goodput* as the metric to quantify performance. Link goodput is measured as the average number of correctly received bits-per-second. Note that we account for both byte corruption (we send a known sequence of bytes) as well as loss.

5   Evaluation

In this section, we present several results that demonstrate in indoor environments: (a) the ability of 60 GHz radios to overcome wall/cubicle blockage, (b) their sensitivity to node (or antenna array) orientation, and (c) their robustness to human-body blockage and walking-speeds mobility (preliminary).

Loc. Idx	Scenario	RX/TX	Distance	Blockage
0	Corridor	R1/a1	8m	LOS
1		R1/a2	20m	LOS
2		R1/a3	10m	LOS
3		R1/a4	25m	LOS
4	Lab	R3/c1	12m	LOS
5		R3/c2	12m	NLOS
6	Office	R2/b1	3m	NLOS (1 wall)
7		R2/b2	5m	NLOS (2 walls)
8	Cubicle	R4/d1	3m	NLOS (1 wall)
9		R4/d2	5m	NLOS (2 walls)
10		R4/d3	6m	NLOS (4 walls)

(a) Eleven TX/RX locations

Ori. Idx	RX	TX	Ori. Idx	RX	TX
0	→	←	8	←	←
1	→	↓	9	←	↓
2	→	→	10	←	→
3	→	↑	11	←	↑
4	↑	←	12	↓	←
5	↑	↓	13	↓	↓
6	↑	→	14	↓	→
7	↑	↑	15	↓	↑

(b) Sixteen TX/RX orientations

Fig. 4. Measurement location characteristics and TX/RX orientations tested

Effect of LOS/NLOS Node Location: For each of the eleven locations, Figure 3(a) shows the goodput when the nodes are aligned (i.e. Orientation

---

[1] We observe that when using lower than 32KB chunks, the PCs cannot fully utilize the available link capacity. Note that we use blocking reads and writes.

Idx. #0) and across all X-Y orientations. When the nodes are aligned, goodput performance remains ~2 Gbps consistently irrespective of the LOS/NLOS nature of the location. *Thus, contrary to conventional perception, 60 GHz radios are able to overcome persistent blockage by walls and cubicles.* While the mean goodput does drop when we consider all orientations, it is still $> 0.5 Gbps$ even in locations with persistent wall/cubicle blockage.

To investigate the high standard deviation in goodput across orientations, we plot the goodput for each orientation in two sample locations in Figure 3(b). A binary goodput behavior (i.e. either $> 1 Gbps$ or zero) is revealed due to our use of a fixed PHY bit-rate. Overall, Figures 3(a) and 3(b) reveal that *performance is very sensitive to node orientation.* We study this effect in detail next.

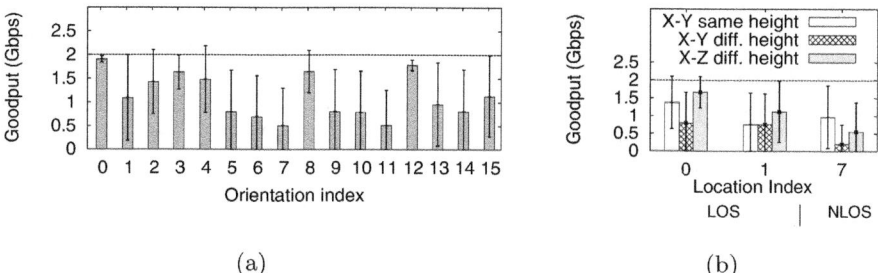

(a)   (b)

Fig. 5. Goodput (a) per-orientation across locations and (b) per-location across heights and orientations

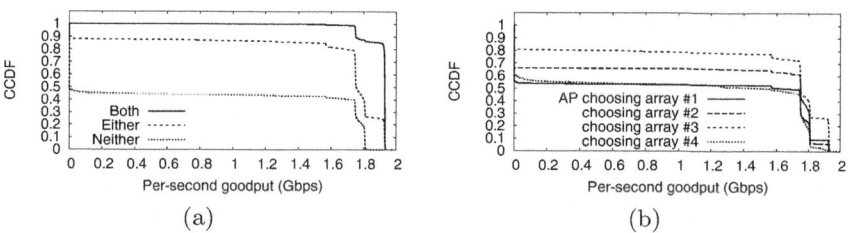

(a)   (b)

Fig. 6. Complementary CDF of (a) per-second link goodput across locations when both, either or neither side is aligned with the other, and (b) per-second link goodput when one side chooses from multiple fixed antenna arrays

Sensitivity to Node or Antenna Array Orientation: In real-world deployments, antenna array orientation on either TX/RX can be along any one of three dimensions. To account for this, we study the performance for different fixed orientations in the X-Y plane. We also consider the effect of relative height differences and orientations in the X-Z plane.

X-Y plane: Figure 5(a) shows for each TX/RX orientation, the mean and standard deviation in goodput across all locations. Mean goodput of all orientations is above 0.5 Gbps and 50% of the orientations have a goodput of above

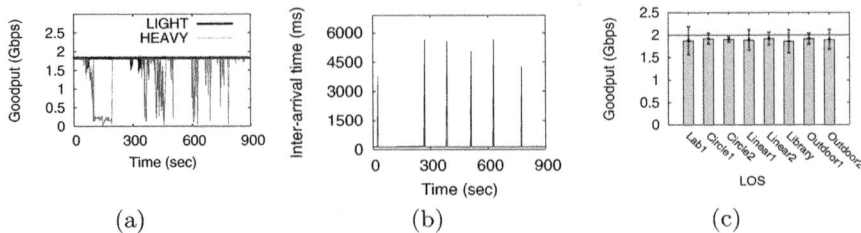

Fig. 7. Goodput with (a) light and heavy human activity. (b) Re-beamforming delay and (c) goodput with LOS mobility at walking-speeds.

1 Gbps. However, *performance of individual orientations varies widely across locations: standard deviation in goodput is > 0.5Gbps for a majority (14 out of 16) of orientations and the mean goodput between different orientations differs by up to 1.3 Gbps.* Thus, an orientation that works well in one location need not work well in another. This behavior is also visible in Figure 3(b): nine orientations (#5-11 and #14-15) provide > 1*Gbps* mean goodput in one location while providing zero goodput in the other location.

Different heights and the X-Z plane: In many real-world deployments (e.g. indoor enterprise WLANs), communicating entities are at different heights. Further, the antenna array can be oriented in the X-Z plane as well. This prompts us to place the TX and RX at different heights at three locations and measure the performance when the TX and RX antenna arrays are oriented in the X-Y and X-Z planes. In Figure 5(b), we compare these measurements with those when the TX and RX were at the same height, across orientations in the X-Y plane. When the nodes are at different heights, mean goodput with X-Y plane orientation is much lower than that with X-Z orientation. In fact, even when the nodes are at the same height, for some locations (Idx. #0 and #1), this is the case. Thus, sensitivity to X-Z plane orientations should also be considered.

Importance of orienting towards the other side: To expand on the benefit of using orientation index #0 (see Figure 3), Figure 6(a) breaks down link goodput across all locations into when (a) both, (b) at least one, and (c) neither antenna array(s) are pointing towards the other side. Even when one antenna array is oriented towards the other side, goodput is greater than 1.5 Gbps 85% of the time with a median goodput of 1.7 Gbps. Further, when neither antenna array is aligned, goodput is 0 over 50% of the time!

Benefit of using multiple antenna arrays: One way of mitigating antenna array orientation mis-match is to use multiple antenna arrays at each node and dynamically selecting amongst them at run-time. Figure 6(b) shows the feasibility of such an approach by plotting the link goodput across all locations when one side (e.g. access point (AP)) chooses from amongst four antenna arrays corresponding to the four TX/RX orientations in the X-Y plane. Note that the other side (e.g. the client) can choose any orientation. *By choosing antenna array #3, the AP can recover a significant portion of performance loss due to antenna array orientation mis-match in the X-Y plane.*

Robustness to Human-body Blockage: We also design two experiments to study the behavior of 60 GHz transmissions in the presence of light and heavy human activity. The first experiment is conducted in a corridor with light human activity (occasional blockage by 1-2 human bodies). The second experiment is conducted during an informal tea-time gathering of people in a room (10m x 6m x 3m); on average 25-30 people were moving/standing in the room between the TX and the RX that were placed at two diagonally opposite corners of the room, oriented towards each other. The TX-RX channel is LOS in the absence of people. In each case, the transfer was done for 15 minutes and people were kept unaware of the experiments to avoid influencing the results. Goodput results for both experiments are shown in Figure 7(a)). *Beamsteering is quite robust to light human activity. With heavy human activity, while goodput fluctuates significantly in Figure 7(a), it is still high for long periods of time with a mean of 1.68Gbps.* When connectivity is lost, the transceivers perform re-beamforming and restart transfers. To measure the re-beamforming delay, we repeat the experiment in the absence of people but with explicit manual re-alignment of the receiver from time to time. Figure 7(b) shows the re-beamforming delay for the current hardware implementation takes upto six seconds. Due to limited access to the 60Ghz transceivers at this level, we cannot completely justify the reason for such high delay to re-adjust the beam. However, we believe that the current implementation is primarily designed for static settings and that future implementations will react faster and reduce these delays significantly.

Robustness to Mobility (Preliminary): In Figure 7(c), we report goodput performance with walking mobility in nine locations (indoor and outdoor) with LOS between the TX and RX that have up to ~20m distance between them. In each location, the RX moves at about 0.5 m/s, starting at the TX, and had LOS. In the "Circle1" and "Circle2" cases, TX-RX distance was ~5m, and we do not see any negative effects of orientation mis-match. For simplicity, in all other cases the TX and RX were oriented towards each other. *Results indicate that 60 GHz radios can adapt to walking mobility with LOS.*

Implications for Next-Generation Gigabit WLANs: Presto currently uses 60 GHz radios from one manufacturer restricting our evaluation to a single implementation of beamsteering and PHY-layer configuration. This is primarily due to the unavailability of COTS 60 Ghz radios from other manufacturers. However, our preliminary experiments reveal a LOS range of 25m amd NLOS range of ~6m in an indoor enterprise setting. Since the current implementation uses the highest PHY bit-rate, we anticipate that both ranges should improve via the use of lower bit-rates (via more robust modulation and coding). Taken together with the rest of our results, 60Ghz radios show strong potential for use in either (a) high-density gigabit WLANs (where APs are placed tens of meters apart) and/or (b) WLANs in conjunction with Wifi to increase capacity.

Moreover, since Presto is designed to work with any 60 Ghz wireless HDMI radio, it can be used to measure performance for radios from multiple vendors once they are available, and we expect to see similar results. This work opens up interesting and challenging questions for future work: (a) what about adaptation to mobility and human-body blockage in light of sensitivity to orientation?, (b) how well can these radios deal with co-channel interference? (c) while MAC scheduling [22,9] may mitigate deafness concerns in single-cell WLANs, what about coordinated/uncoordinated multi-cell networks?

6   Conclusion

In this paper, we study the link-level performance of state-of-the-art 60 GHz radios in the context of robustness to blockage by walls, cubicles, and human-bodies, adaptation to walking-speeds mobility, as well as sensitivity to antenna array orientation. We make the following key observations: (1) 60 GHz radios are able to overcome NLOS blockage due to walls and cubicles; their coverage range is reduced relative to LOS scenarios but could still be enough to satisfy the needs of dense WLANs. (2) Antenna array orientation has a significant effect on performance even in the presence of indoor multipath reflections; mitigation strategies that add to the single antenna array at each node and dynamically select amongst them show potential to address this issue. (3) Finally, beamsteering is effective in adapting to low levels of human-body blockage and LOS mobility at walking speeds; existing implementations need to react faster in the presence of high levels of dynamically-occurring human-body blockage.

References

1. MAC and PHY Specifications for High Rate WPANs, mm-wave-based alternative PHY extension. IEEE Std 802.15.3c-2009 (Amendment to IEEE Std 802.15.3-2003), pp. 1–187 (October 2009)
2. WirelessHD Specs (August 2009), http://tinyurl.com/2ehkq6f
3. Collonge, S., Zaharia, G., Zein, G.: Influence of the Human Activity on Wide-band Characteristics of the 60 GHz Indoor Radio Channel. IEEE Trans. on Wireless Commun. 3(6), 2396–2406 (2004)
4. Cordiero, C.: Evaluation of Medium Access Technologies for Next Generation Millimeter-Wave WLAN and WPAN. In: ICC (2009)
5. Corp, A.: Arria II GX FPGA Development Kit,
   http://www.altera.com/products/devkits/altera/kit-aiigx-pcie.html
6. Doan, C., et al.: Design considerations for 60 GHz CMOS radios. IEEE Communications Magazine 42(12), 132–140 (2004)
7. Gao, J., Li, K., Sato, T., Wang, J., Harada, H., Kato, S.: Implementation considerations of patch antenna array for 60 GHz beam steering system applications. In: Radio and Wireless Symposium, San Diego, CA, USA, pp. 31–34 (2009)
8. Halperin, D., Kandula, S., Padhye, J., Bahl, P., Wetherall, D.: Augmenting data center networks with multi-gigabit wireless links. In: ACM SIGCOMM (2011)
9. IEEE TGad. PHY/MAC Complete Proposal Spec (approved as D0.1) (May 2010), http://tinyurl.com/2fqlkxx
10. Ramachandran, K., et al.: On 60 GHz Wireless Link Performance in Indoor Environments, NECLA TR (2011), http://www.nec-labs.com/~rajesh/60G.pdf

11. Microtronix Datacom. HDMI Receiver, Transmitter HSMC daughter card (2011), http://tinyurl.com/4re97a5
12. Orfanidis, S.: Electromagnetic Waves and Antennas. Rutgers University (2008)
13. Park, M., Gopalakrishnan, P.: Analysis on spatial reuse and interference in 60-ghz wireless networks. IEEE J. Sel. A. Commun. 27, 1443–1452 (2009)
14. Ramachandran, K., et al.: Adaptive Beamforming for 60 GHz Radios: Challenges and Preliminary Solutions. In: ACM mmCom, pp. 33–38 (2010)
15. Ramachandran, K., Kokku, R., Mahindra, R., Maruhashi, K.: On the Potential of Fixed-Beam 60 GHz Network Interfaces in Mobile Devices. In: Spring, N., Riley, G.F. (eds.) PAM 2011. LNCS, vol. 6579, pp. 62–71. Springer, Heidelberg (2011)
16. Rocketfish, Inc. Rocketfish - WirelessHD Adapter, http://tinyurl.com/4pdzqac
17. SiBeam. OmniLink60 (2010), http://www.sibeam.com/
18. SiBeam. SB9220/SB9210 WirelessHD Chip (2010), http://tinyurl.com/2535v8u
19. Singh, S., Mudumbai, R., Madhow, U.: Interference analysis for highly directional 60-ghz mesh networks: The case for rethinking medium access control. IEEE/ACM Transactions on Networking PP(99), 1 (2011)
20. Singh, S., Ziliotto, F., Madhow, U., Belding, E.M., Rodwell, M.: Blockage and Directivity in 60 GHz Wireless PANs. IEEE JSAC 27(8), 1400–1413 (2009)
21. Vizio, Inc. Universal Wireless HD Video and Audio Kit (XWH200), http://www.vizio.com/accessories/xwh200.html
22. WiGig Alliance. WiGig Specs (May 2010), http://tinyurl.com/29sql4q
23. Xu, H., Kukshya, V., Rappaport, T.: Spatial and Temporal Characteristics of 60 GHz Indoor Channels. IEEE JSAC 20(3), 620–630 (2002)

Geolocating IP Addresses in Cellular Data Networks

Sipat Triukose[1], Sebastien Ardon[1], Anirban Mahanti[1], and Aaditeshwar Seth[2]

[1] NICTA, Locked Bag 9013, Alexandria, NSW, Australia
{sipat.triukose,sebastien.ardon,anirban.mahanti}@nicta.com.au
[2] IIT Delhi, New Delhi, India
aseth@cse.iitd.ernet.in

Abstract. Smartphones connected to cellular networks are increasingly being used to access Internet-based services. Using data collected from smartphones running a popular location-based application, we examine IP address allocation in cellular data networks, with emphasis on understanding the applicability of IP-based geolocation techniques. Our dataset has GPS-based location data for approximately 29,000 cellular network assigned IP addresses in 50 different countries. Using this dataset, we provide insights into the global deployment of cellular networks. For instance, we find that Network Address Translation (NAT) is commonplace in cellular networks. We also find several instances of service differentiation with operators assigning public IP addresses to some devices and private IP addresses to other devices. We also evaluate the error of geolocation databases when determining the position of the smartphones, and find that the error is 100km or more for approximately 70% of our measurements. Further, there is potential for errors at the scale of inter-country and inter-continent distances. We believe this dataset may be of value to the research community, and provide a subset of the dataset to the community.

1 Introduction

Estimating the geographical location of Internet hosts has many applications including targeted marketing, user profiling, fraud detection, regulatory compliance, digital rights management, and server or content distribution network performance tuning. For instance, to comply with region-specific licensing arrangements, many streaming media services restrict content access based on the user's geographic location. One popular approach to geolocation is the use of database services such as Maxmind [2] and IPinfoDB [1] that maintain an exhaustive table of IP prefix to location matches. However, dynamic assignment of IP addresses, increased fragmentation of IP address blocks, and extensive use of middleboxes make IP-based geolocation extremely challenging.

In this paper, we examine IP address allocation in cellular data networks, with emphasis on understanding the feasibility of IP-based geolocation techniques. We believe this is an important problem as smartphones connected to cellular networks are increasingly being used to access Internet-based services. Of course,

N. Taft and F. Ricciato (Eds.): PAM 2012, LNCS 7192, pp. 158–167, 2012.

customized smartphone applications can use the built-in Global Position Systems (GPS) receiver to obtain accurate location information. However, in cases where a service is accessed through the phone's browser[1] or when GPS-based tracking is disabled (e.g., by the user because of privacy concerns), alternative geolocation techniques are necessary. The IP geolocation problem has not received much attention in the context of cellular data networks, and we fill this void by instrumenting a popular location-based iOS application to collect and subsequently analyze a dataset that has GPS-based location data for approximately 29,000 cellular network assigned IP addresses, obtained from several thousand individual smartphones spread across 50 countries.

This paper offers several contributions. First, we characterize the dataset and offer insights on the global deployments of cellular data networks. For instance, we find that NAT and other middleboxes are widely deployed in cellular networks worldwide. We also provide evidence of service differentiation, where a provider assigns publicly visible IP addresses to some users, while other users are behind NAT boxes. Second, we study whether or not geolocation databases provide good location estimates and show that the error is 200km or more in 50% of our measurements. Further, we observe some large errors, owing to mobile operator's implementation of roaming functionality. This can be expected to become a commonplace problem as roaming traffic charges drop. Finally, we provide an original dataset to the community, with an unprecedented number of ground truth measurements of IP to geolocation mapping for cellular data networks.

The remainder of this paper is organized as follows. Section 2 present an overview of related work. Our data collection method and a preliminary analysis of the dataset is present in Section 3. An analysis of the IP addresses observed in our dataset is presented in Section 4. Section 5 presents concluding remarks.

2   Related Work

The problem of geolocating hosts in networks has been widely studied [8]. Techniques range from measuring packet latencies to landmark nodes and then estimating their location relative to these nodes [6–8], applying machine learning to ground truth datasets [5], or using tabular storage of IP prefixes and associated locations ('GeoIP databases') [1, 2]. The accuracy of GeoIP databases has also been debated [9, 10]. For instance, Poese et al. [9] recently evaluated the accuracy of several GeoIP databases using ground truth information from several POP locations from one European wired ISP and found that while most GeoIP databases can claim accuracy at the country level, their databases are heavily biased towards few countries.

---

[1] The HTML5 Geolocation API [3] allows browsers to report a device's position. The source of location data is implementation-dependent, and can be obtained from GPS receivers, WiFi network location databases, or other means. It is still early days for this solution, and geolocation databases are likely to be a popular method for many reasons, including privacy concerns associated with fine-grained location tracking.

Table 1. Dataset details

Data	Description
Unique ID	Per device, unique id (fully anonymised)
Timestamp	Time at server when measurement was recorded
Interface IP Address	IP address assigned to the Cellular Data interface
Observed IP Address	Device IP address, as observed at the application's server
Location	Latitude / Longitude coordinates
Horizontal Accuracy	Accuracy, in meters, of the location measurement

Closely related to our work are recent studies by Balakrishnan et al. [4], Xu et al. [12], and Wang et al. [11]. For mobile devices connected through 3G networks, Balakrishnan et al. [4] studied the accuracy of GeoIP databases, the client/server latencies, and the IP address 'stickiness'. Their study, while comprehensive, is based on three datasets with a maximum of about 100 devices, over a single mobile operator network in the US. Xu et al. [12] combined several data sources to discover cellular network infrastructure. Their work relied on server logs, DNS request logs, and publicly available routing updates to characterize four major US cellular carrier networks. Xu et al. evaluated the cellular network diameter, and demonstrate how this could affect content placement strategies. Wang et al. [11] characterized NAT, firewall, and other security policies deployed in more than 100 cellular IP networks.

We believe our work complements these recent efforts [4, 11, 12]. Our novel dataset has ground truth information on the location of mobile devices, and thus allows us to evaluate how well GeoIP databases may perform for IP addresses assigned by cellular networks. Further, our dataset provides an opportunity to study IP address assignment at a larger scale than that of previous studies, and across carriers in many different countries.

3 Dataset and Preliminary Analysis

3.1 Dataset

Use of third-party smartphone applications has exploded in recent years, owing to the phenomenal success of the 'App Store' model. These third-party applications present an unprecedented opportunity for crowd-sourcing network measurements from mobile networks. For this work, we partnered with the developer of a location-based iOS application[2] to add minimal instrumentation code such that the application's Internet-based server logs reported the device's local IP address. This reporting is only done when the device is using the 3G/GPRS interface for communication.

---

[2] The application is available only on Apple devices running the iOS operating system, and has been downloaded by 140,000 users from 50 countries, and is particularly popular in Germany and Australia.

The application developer provided us with processed data from their server logs. In particular, the raw dataset consists of 29,043 measurement points, collected from 11,230 unique smartphones between May and August 2011. The information available is detailed in Table 1.

This dataset may be obtained by contacting the authors. For privacy reasons, the released dataset will not provide the location data and instead provide the corresponding country and city-level information available from the Google reverse geocoding service. In addition, the released dataset will include the observed IP address but not the Interface IP address. Instead, we include a set of two boolean flags, to indicate respectively whether the device IP address was in the private IANA space, and whether it was different from the observed IP address. Finally the device id and horizontal accuracy are also removed. This transformation on the data improves the users privacy while providing the information required to confirm the key results of this paper, and develop many new findings.

3.2   Geographical Coverage

Before analyzing the collected data, we applied a few simple filtering rules. Note that the number of measurements from a particular device depends on the frequency with which the owner of the device interacts with the application. As we are not interested in recording multiple instances of identical information, for each smartphone we discard a measurement point only if all the following conditions are met, with respect to the previous measurement point: i) both the device and observed IP address are unchanged, ii) the distance between the measurements locations is less than 1km^3, and iii) the time elapsed since the previous measurement is less than 3 hours. Following this preprocessing, we are left with 27,328 measurements. Next, we applied the Google reverse-geocoding service to obtain city and country information from the GPS coordinates. We successfully looked up 26,566 dataset entries. The remainder of this paper focuses on this filtered dataset. In total, we have measurements from 1,924 cities in 50 different countries as summarized in Table 2 and illustrated in Figure 1.

Devices running iOS use a proprietary 'Assisted GPS' method to optimize the device location computation, using a combination of GPS data and a proprietary WiFi geo-database. The 3G iPhone's Assisted GPS typically has horizontal accuracy errors of 10-15 m [13]. The iOS application programmer can retrieve the accuracy level, in meters, associated with any GPS location measurement. This horizontal accuracy value was available for 97% of our measurement points, and these indicate that 78% of the GPS location information are accurate to 100m, and 93% are accurate to at least 1km.

---

^{3} Condition (ii) captures mobility and uses 1km as the threshold since more than 90% of the measurements have horizontal accuracy of at least 1km.

Table 2. Reverse geocoding of measurement locations

Continent	Countries	# of Cities	Total Entries
Australia (2)	AU,NZ	166	18,211
Europe (26)	DE,FR,SE,AT,CH,GB,ES,IT,PL TR,LU,DK,BE,GR,NL,HU,RO RS,FI,CZ,HR,NO,IE,LI,PT,SK	1482	7,036
Asia (14)	TW,SG,JP,MY,CN,HK,KW KH,CY,OM,IN,AE,KR,LB	158	991
America (3)	US,CA, CR	104	282
Others (5)	MO,AR,CO,PR,ZA	14	46

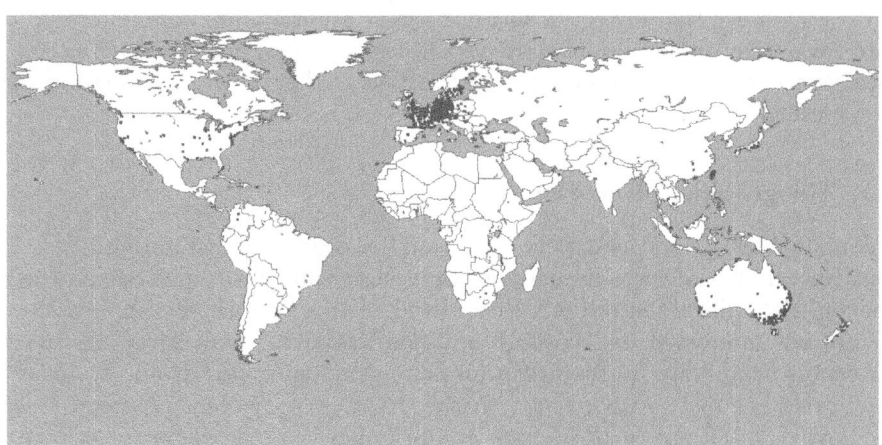

Fig. 1. All measurement locations

3.3   Limitations

Our dataset constitutes a sample of smartphone locations worldwide, the IP address assigned by the cellular data network to these smartphones, and the IP address from which these devices are visible on the Internet. The main drawback of this application-driven measurement method is the spatial and temporal sampling bias introduced as the measurement occurrences are driven by: i) the adoption rate of the smartphone type/OS on which the application is available, ii) the application adoption rate and the spatial distribution of its adopters, and iii) the application usage rate and spatial pattern, which is dependent on the application's intended use. This dataset is, however, to our knowledge, the first of its kind to be available to the research community.

4   Cellular Networks: View from the IP Level

4.1   Public IPs, Private IPs, and Middleboxes

With the number of Internet-enabled smartphones exploding, and the increased scarcity of available IPv4 address space, mobile operators are likely to rely on

Table 3. IP allocation statistics for the top 15 networks in the dataset

Network Name	Country	total devices	# devices with only private IP	# devices with only public IP
OPTUSINTERNET-AU	AU	2039	11	1958
CUSTOMERS-DE	DE,IT,HR, FR,PT,NL	1337	1134	135
TELSTRAINTERNET42-AU	AU	1122	1119	0
VODAFONE	AU	1101	1029	59
H3GAIPNET	AU	789	783	1
DE-D2VODAFONE	DE,ES,NL,CH, FR,IT,DK,GR	702	692	8
VODAFONE-PACIFIC-AU	AU,NL	486	479	0
E-PLUS-MOBILES-BLOCK-6	DE	342	341	0
o2-Germany-NAT-Pool2-FRA	DE	300	299	0
o2-Germany-NAT-Pool1-DUS	DE,ES	283	282	0
o2-Germany-NAT-Pool1-BER	DE	265	264	0
DE-D2VODAFONE-20101118	DE	217	216	1
ORANGE-FR	FR	183	183	0
SFR-INFRA	FR,BE	163	163	0
EMOME-NET	TW	162	3	159

Network Address Translation (NAT) solutions. This section quantifies, for our dataset, the prevelance of public IP address assignment, NAT solution, and other middleboxes.

We observe 18,949 measurements, or roughly 70% of the measurements, where the smartphone's device interface is assigned a private IP address. Assignment of an address from IANA's reserved IP address space indicates the use of NAT solutions between the user's device and the application server. Further, we identify 478 instances where the phone's cellular interface address is assigned a public IP address but it does not match the observed IP address at the application server, thus indicating the presence of middleboxes between the device and the application server.

Table 3 illustrates the diversity of networks seen in our dataset. For each measurement point, we determine the network operator by querying the WHOIS service. The query uses the interface IP address if it is public or the observed IP address if the interface is assigned a private IP address. The table ranks networks based on the number of unique smartphones matched to a network. We notice that most operators use some form of NAT. Further, among these top 15 networks, we find several instances where a network assigns private IP addresses to some devices and public IP addresses to other devices, indicating service differentiation within operators: some devices benefit from publicly routable IP addresses, but most do not. We also find a few instances where a smartphone is assigned a private IP address at one point in time, and a public IP address at another point in time.

Table 4. /24 IP blocks with hosts in more than one country

/24 IP block	# Countries	# Measurement	Country List
77.24.0	7	246	DE,FR,NL,DK,IT,ES,CH
80.187.96	4	174	DE,NL,IT,FR
193.247.250	4	88	FR,IT,NL,CH
80.187.107	3	303	DE,HR,PT
203.20.35	2	792	AU,NL
80.187.106	2	360	DE,IT
89.204.153	2	359	DE,ES
80.187.110	2	310	DE,FR
80.187.111	2	281	DE,FR
80.187.97	2	180	DE,IT

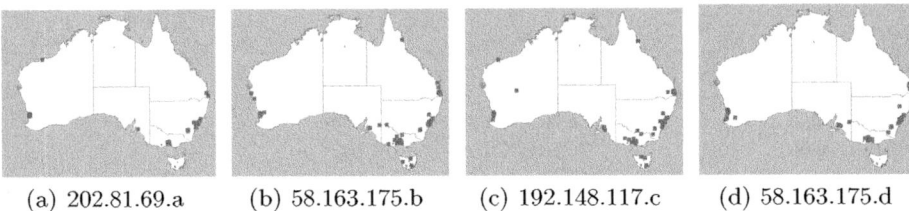

(a) 202.81.69.a   (b) 58.163.175.b   (c) 192.148.117.c   (d) 58.163.175.d

Fig. 2. Dispersion of hosts around the top four mobile gateways in the dataset

4.2   Spatial Allocation of IP Blocks

We investigated the geographical span of devices belonging to the top /24 IP subnets in the dataset. This indication can be useful when building GeoIP databases,
especially when longest prefix matching strategies are used. We identified the top
10 /24 subnets that account for the most measurements from unique devices,
and used Google's reverse-geocoding service to lookup the country location for
each measurement in this set. Using a WHOIS service, we verified that all IPs in
each /24 subnet does indeed belong to the same network provider. Table 4 summarizes our results, and illustrates that devices physically present in different
countries may be assigned an address from the same IP block.

4.3   Spatial Coverage of Gateways

When a cellular network uses middleboxes, the application's server will receive
connections from several distinct devices, all originating from a single IP address
(which we refer to as the mobile gateway IP address). Here, we study the spatial
dispersion of devices around mobile gateways, as observed in our dataset. This
has implications on the accuracy of GeoIP databases as multiple, potentially
far apart, devices have the same IP address from the point-of-view of Internet
servers.

Table 5. Top 10 observed gateway addresses with hosts in more than one country

Observed IP	# Country	Country (# Measurement)
77.24.0.a	3	DE(28),IT(1),NL(1)
77.24.0.b	3	DE(21),ES(2),NL(1)
193.247.250.c	3	CH(2),FR(1),NL(1)
203.20.35.d	2	AU(532),NL(1)
77.24.0.e	2	DE(47),ES(1)
77.24.0.f	2	DE(34),CH(1)
77.24.0.g	2	DE(27),DK(1)
77.24.0.h	2	DE(24),FR(1)
202.175.20.i	2	MO(8),CN(3)
89.204.153.j	2	DE(8),ES(1)

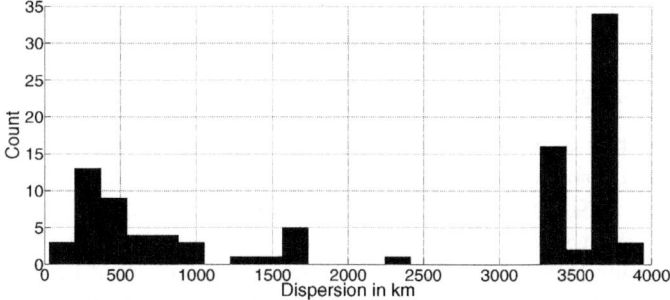

Fig. 3. Geographical dispersion of mobile hosts around the top 100 gateways

Figure 2 illustrates the dispersion of hosts attached to some example mobile gateway IP addresses[4], for one country (Australia). It is interesting to note that each gateway has hosts roughly in all major Australian cities. In addition, we found one device in the Netherland with the observed IP of 203.20.35.d, which is most likely a roaming user. Table 5 quantifies the spatial diversity for the top 10 gateways with hosts in more than one country, in our dataset. Our dataset suggests that mobile networks allocate IP addresses at a country-level granularity: mobile hosts exit the operator's network through a few gateways within the country, and these exit points may also be maintained while roaming.

We quantify the geographic spread of hosts served by a gateway by computing the maximum distance between any two hosts that are connected to the Internet through the same gateway. Figure 3 shows the histogram of the maximum dispersion values (in KM), for the top 100 gateways in our dataset. We notice that there are three clusters: one at approximately 500km, one at about 1500 km, and another at about 4000km. These clusters approximately correspond to the average inter-city, inter-state, and inter-country or inter-continental distances in our dataset. We also observed an outlier at 17,000km (not shown on the plot) which correspond to an Australian user roaming in the Netherlands.

---

[4] The host number part of the IP addresses is truncated.

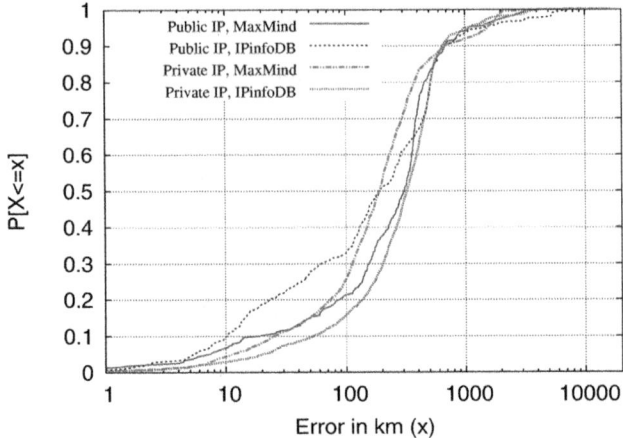

Fig. 4. Geolocation error when using GeoIP databases

4.4 Accuracy of IP Geolocation Databases

We also tested the ability of GeoIP databases to return host location based on IP addresses seen by the application's server. For this analysis, we use two commercial GeoIP databases, namely MaxMind [2] and IPinfoDB [1], and compute the error as the distance between the geographical location returned by the GeoIP database and our measurement location. As previously mentioned, application-level measurements introduce sampling bias: as each measurement occurrence depends on a user starting the application and the user's current position, more popular areas or areas where the service is more popular will have more measurement points. To address this spatial sampling bias, we normalize the error at the city scale, by computing the average error for each city (identified using Google's reverse geocoding service).

Figure 4 shows the distribution of the computed errors, for the GeoIP databases considered, with results presented separately for public and private IP addresses. (Note that for devices with private IPs we use their gateway address as visible to the server on the Internet.) For our dataset, depending on the database used, errors of 100km or more are observed in at least 70% of the measurements although 90% of the errors are under 1000km. The errors are typically larger for devices assigned private IP addresses. This is not surprising as we have previously noted that one mobile gateway could potentially cover an entire country, including countries as large as Australia.

5   Concluding Remarks

We studied cellular data networks from the point-of-view of IP clients, covering both spatial and IP-layer aspects. Our work is based upon a comprehensive dataset of several thousand mobile device locations and IP addresses. Our dataset suggests that mobile operators worldwide are using some form of

NAT or middlebox. This has implications for application designers (e.g., difficulty of implementing peer-to-peer communication, performance implications). As hosts behind NATs appear from a few IP addresses per country, we shown how these IP addresses can cover hosts physically present in entire countries, across international borders, and even continents. We also evaluated the accuracy of GeoIP database in the mobile domain, and found that, for our data, the distance error between the GeoIP database determined location and the GPS determined location is at least 100km for approximately 70% of our measurements, with a few errors being substantially larger.

Acknowledgements. This work was supported by the Commonwealth of Australia under the Australia-India Strategic Research Fund.

References

1. IPInfoDB, http://ipinfodb.com
2. Geolocation and Online Fraud Prevention from MaxMind (2011), http://www.maxmind.com/ (accessed September 14, 2011)
3. Geolocation API specification (2011), http://www.w3.org/TR/geolocation-API/ (accessed September 14, 2011)
4. Balakrishnan, M., Mohomed, I., Ramasubramanian, V.: Where's that Phone?: Geolocating IP Addresses on 3G Networks. In: Proceedings of ACM SIGCOMM Internet Measurement Conference, Chicago, IL, pp. 294–300 (November 2009)
5. Eriksson, B., Barford, P., Sommers, J., Nowak, R.: A Learning-based Approach for IP Geolocation. In: Proceedings of Passive and Active Measurement Conference, Zurich, Switzerland, pp. 171–180 (April 2010)
6. Katz-Bassett, E., John, J.P., Krishnamurthy, A., Wetherall, D., Anderson, T., Chawathe, Y.: Towards IP Geolocation using Delay and Topology Measurements. In: Proceedings of ACM SIGCOMM Internet Measurement Conference, Rio de Janeiro, Brazil, pp. 71–84 (October 2006)
7. Laki, S., Mátray, P., Hága, P., Csabai, I., Vattay, G.: A Model-based Approach for Improving Router Geolocation. Computer Networks 54(9), 1490–1501 (2010)
8. Padmanabhan, V., Subramanian, L.: An Investigation of Geographic Mapping Techniques for Internet Hosts. In: Proceedings of ACM SIGCOMM, San Diego, CA, pp. 173–185 (August 2001)
9. Poese, I., Uhlig, S., Kaafar, M.A., Donnet, B., Gueye, B.: IP Geolocation Databases: Unreliable? ACM SIGCOMM Computer Communication Review 41(2), 53–56 (2011)
10. Shavitt, Y., Zilberman, N.: A Geolocation Databases Study. IEEE Journal on Selected Areas in Communications 19(10), 2044–2056 (2011)
11. Wang, Z., Qian, Z., Xu, Q., Mao, Z., Zhang, M.: An Untold Story of Middleboxes in Cellular Networks. In: Proceedings of ACM SIGCOMM, Toronto, ON, pp. 374–385 (August 2011)
12. Xu, Q., Huang, J., Wang, Z., Qian, F., Gerber, A., Mao, Z.M.: Cellular Data Network Infrastructure Characterization and Implication on Mobile Content Placement. In: Proceedings of ACM SIGMETRICS, San Jose, CA, pp. 317–328 (June 2011)
13. Zandbergen, P.A.: Accuracy of iPhone Locations: A Comparison of Assisted GPS, WiFi and Cellular Positioning. Transactions in GIS 13(S1), 5–25 (2009)

Speed Measurements of Residential Internet Access

Oana Goga and Renata Teixeira

CNRS and UPMC Sorbonne Universités, Paris, France

Abstract. The spread of residential broadband Internet access is raising the question of how to measure Internet speed. We argue that available bandwidth is a key metric of access link speed. Unfortunately, the performance of available bandwidth estimation tools has rarely been tested from hosts connected to residential networks. This paper compares the accuracy and overhead of state-of-the-art available bandwidth estimation tools from hosts connected to commercial ADSL and cable networks. Our results show that, when using default settings, some tools underestimate the available bandwidth by more than 60%. We demonstrate using controlled testbeds that this happens because current home gateways have a limited packet forwarding rate.

1 Introduction

Broadband Internet Service Providers (ISPs) often advertise a maximum download and upload Internet speed, but home users have no reliable means to verify if the performance they get is even close to these maximum values. Government agencies and regulatory bodies are stepping in to help broadband users. For instance, the UK communications regulator (Ofcom) and the American Federal Communications Commission (FCC) are working with SamKnows to distribute routers for home users to test their broadband speed. Regulation bodies are actively seeking better standards to measure Internet speed (take as example the recent FCC challenge [1]). In this context, the Internet measurement community needs to answer the question: How to accurately measure Internet access speed?

The Internet measurement literature defines three metrics of network speed [20]. *Capacity* is the maximum rate at which a link can transmit packets. It is not a good metric for regulating access speed, because it does not capture network speed variations that would occur if, for instance, an ISP assigned too many subscribers to the same link. *TCP achievable throughput* is the maximum throughput obtained by a single TCP connection [12]. It captures the speed users get, but it cannot be used alone to regulate ISPs because the throughput of a single TCP depends on many factors that are exogenous to the access ISP (such as TCP advertised window or RTT). Finally, *available bandwidth* is the residual capacity of a link. Available bandwidth better reflects what ISPs can guarantee to home users and is therefore an essential metric for regulating ISPs. Available bandwidth, however, is not well defined because of the elasticity of TCP cross traffic.

Popular speed tests today such as Speedtest.net or SamKnows mainly estimate the available bandwidth by performing large parallel TCP transfers and post-processing the measurements to minimize the bias of TCP [4]. These tools flood the access link, so we refer to them as *flooding-based tools*. The large parallel TCP transfers will cause other TCP cross traffic to back off in the same way that the home users' traffic would.

N. Taft and F. Ricciato (Eds.): PAM 2012, LNCS 7192, pp. 168–178, 2012.

Thus, flooding-based tools measure the effective available bandwidth. The drawback of this technique is that flooding the link with probes introduces a large overhead. This overhead may not be a problem when a user occasionally runs a speed test, but it will disrupt some of the applications users may run during the test and it will consume network resources. Hence, this overhead may prevent users from signing up for initiatives that run periodic tests over a long period of time such as SamKnows (in particular in cases where home subscribers are limited by monthly bandwidth caps).

Over the last decade, the research community has developed numerous tools to estimate available bandwidth with reduced overhead and in the presence of diverse types of cross traffic [5, 11, 13, 22, 25]. We call these tools *optimized-probing tools*. These tools, however, have not been adopted in current speed tests. Only few of these tools were even tested in residential access networks. In particular, abwprobe [5] was designed and tested for ADSL networks [5], and pathload [13] and spruce [25] were tested in cable networks [16]. Comparative evaluations of available bandwidth estimation have been in core or academic networks and do not include flooding-based tools [3, 8, 19, 23, 25]. Thus, it is unclear how these tools compare in general when running in residential access networks, where bandwidth is asymmetric, traffic is often subject to a token bucket rate shaping [26], residential gateways have limited capacity [10] and very large buffers [15].

This paper studies the performance of available bandwidth estimation in residential access networks. We select tools that are known to work well in backbone and academic networks (§2). Then, we compare the accuracy and overhead of these tools in a setting where hosts are connected to commercial ADSL and cable providers for which we know the access link capacity and we can control cross traffic from the home (§3). This setting ensures that tools experience real access network behavior and yet we can estimate expected bounds of available bandwidth.

Findings. We find that optimized-probing tools that use small probes such as pathload systematically underestimate the bandwidth of residential networks (§4.1). We show using fully controlled testbeds that this underestimation happens because home gateways cannot sustain the high probing rate of these optimized-probing tools (§4.2). Further, we identify poor hardware and overhead of network-address translation as the main limiting factors. Our results show that pathload modified to send large probes, spruce and parallel TCP are the most accurate in estimating the available bandwidth of residential networks (§4.1). Finally, we show that the probing overhead of optimized-probing tools can be as much as 72 times smaller than that of flooding-based tools (§5).

2   Internet Speed Measurements

This section briefly describes the techniques to measure speed: first the flooding-based tools used in most popular speed tests, then the tools and techniques designed by the research community to measure available bandwidth.

2.1   Flooding-Based Tools

Flooding-based tools use multiple parallel TCP connections and compute the combined rate of all connections. Multiple TCP connections are preferred over a single connection because they are more robust to loss [2]. This method also gives more accurate estimates when hosts advertise a small TCP receiver window [4].

SamKnows uses three parallel connections and performs a warm-up transfer to avoid measuring during slow-start [26]. Speedtest.net executes a small download to estimate the connection speed. Based on the result, it selects the size of the transfer file and the number of parallel connections for the test (up to eight). It reports the average throughput achieved during the test after removing the lowest 30% and the highest 10% samples [4]. Netalyzr [15] is a more general tool, but as part of its tests it also reports the line speed. Netalyzr sends a single stream of UDP probes with rates increasing in a slow-start fashion to flood the link. A study of residential broadband capacity used a flood-based technique to infer the capacity of a large number of cable and DSL lines [7].

We use *iperf* to emulate flooding-based tools, because it allows us to set the number of parallel connections, the duration or the size of the transfer among other parameters.

2.2 Optimized-Probing Tools

Optimized-probing tools use two main techniques: the Probe Gap Model (PGM) and the Probe Rate Model (PRM) [25]. Here, we summarize the tools that are already known to perform well in backbone and academic networks [3, 8, 19, 25].

PGM tools send back-to-back probes and estimates the available bandwidth based on the dispersion observed at the receiver. They require an a priori knowledge of the capacity of the bottleneck link. We test *Spruce* [25] and *igi/ptr* [11] from these tools.

PRM tools send probes at different rates. If the probe rate is higher than the available bandwidth, then the probes are received at a lower rate (the packets are buffered at the bottleneck link). The available bandwidth is the maximum rate at which the sending rate matches the receiving rate. PRM tools are usually more accurate but have higher overhead than PGM tools, due to the iterative nature [9]. *Pathload* [13] uses one-way delays of consecutive packets to estimate the available bandwidth. The algorithm outputs the maximum rate at which consecutive one-way delays do not increase. Yaz [24] is a calibrated version of pathload, which minimizes the overhead. We choose to test pathload over Yaz, because pathload has been tested in many different settings and is hence an important comparison point. Moreover, pathload's code is more stable. *Pathchirp* [22] reduces probing overhead with respect to pathload by sending a train of packets with exponentially-reduced inter-packet gaps that probes a large range of rates.

Abwprobe [5] was designed especially for ADSL links. It is based on pathload, but it only requires access to the sender because it uses RTTs instead of one-way delays to estimate the available bandwidth. In our tests, however, abwprobe performs poorly because the high asymmetry between downlink and uplink capacities causes congestion in the uplink. When abwprobe detects that the uplink is congested it aborts the test. The authors discuss the fact that high asymmetry may be a problem and propose some heuristics to address this issue [5], but these heuristics are not implemented yet. Therefore, we do not present the results of abwprobe.

3 Measurement Method

Our goal is to evaluate the tools discussed in the previous section for residential access networks, yet we need enough control to be able to interpret the results. Thus, we opt

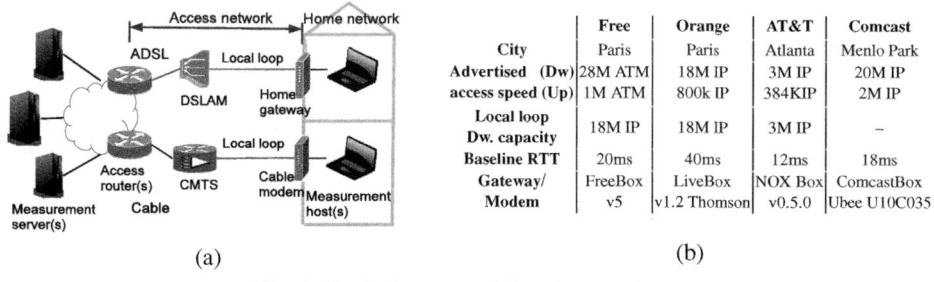

	Free	Orange	AT&T	Comcast
City	Paris	Paris	Atlanta	Menlo Park
Advertised (Dw)	28M ATM	18M IP	3M IP	20M IP
access speed (Up)	1M ATM	800k IP	384KIP	2M IP
Local loop Dw. capacity	18M IP	18M IP	3M IP	–
Baseline RTT	20ms	40ms	12ms	18ms
Gateway/ Modem	FreeBox v5	LiveBox v1.2 Thomson	NOX Box v0.5.0	ComcastBox Ubee U10C035

(a)	(b)

Fig. 1. Testbed setup and line characteristics

for a semi-controlled testbed. Tests run over commercial ADSL and cable lines from different ISPs, where we know the line characteristics and we control both end-hosts as well as the traffic coming from the home. Hence, we can estimate expected bounds of available bandwidth. Our testbed includes two lines in France (ADSL from Free and Orange) and three lines in the United States (two cable lines from Comcast and one ADSL line from AT&T). Fig. 1(b) summarizes the properties of each line. The results for both Comcast lines (one in Atlanta and the other in Menlo Park) were equivalent, for space constraints we only present the properties and results for the Menlo Park line.

Setup. The testbed, illustrated in Fig. 1(a), can be divided in four parts. First, the *measurement servers*, a $2 \times$ Six-Core AMD Opteron (in Paris, UPMC), an Intel Core2 Quad (in Atalanta, Georgia Tech) and an Intel Pentium 4 (in Mountain View, UCSC) connected to the Internet through Gigabit Ethernet (GbE) links. Second, the network between the measurement server and the access router is out of our control, but we issue traceroutes every 5 minutes to verify that the RTT and number of hops of the end-to-end path remain stable. Third, the *access network* connects the home network to the access router. In ADSL networks, the link between the DSL modem or gateway and the DSL Access Multiplexer (DSLAM) is dedicated to a subscriber, whereas the link between the DSLAM and the access router is shared with other subscribers. In cable networks, subscribers connect via a shared medium (typically coaxial cable) to a Cable Modem Termination System (CMTS). In cable networks, the service plan rate limit is configured at the cable modem and is typically implemented using a token bucket rate shaper. The physical connection between the home and the DSLAM or the CMTS is called *local loop* or *last mile*. Fig. 1(b) also shows the local loop capacity we estimate for each tested ADSL line.[1] We know that the access links are the bottlenecks in our tests, because our tests show that the available bandwidth from the measurement server to the access router is always higher than the end-to-end available bandwidth. Finally, the *home network* is connected to the Internet through a home gateway or ADSL/cable modem. The *home gateway* combines the functionalities of an ADSL/cable modem and a router/access point. Fig. 1(b) presents the home gateway model for each line. All lines have a home gateway, except for Comcast, which has a cable modem. The *measurement host*, a ThinkPad T60, is directly connected to the home gateway via a GbE link. We connect the measurement host over Ethernet to emulate a setup similar to SamKnows,

---

[1] We query the line characteristics from the gateway or ISP page (depending on the line) and obtain the estimated capacity using the Kitz site
(http://www.kitz.co.uk/adsl/max_speed_calc.php).

where bandwidth is measured directly from home gateways. Since our goal is to study access performance, placing measurements directly at the gateway avoids interference from wireless or cross traffic in the home [26].

Configuration of Tools. To emulate the flooding-based tools we used iperf with 10 parallel connections and a transfer of 10 s which is enough in our case to even out the slow start. We run all the optimized-probing tools with default settings, unless stated otherwise. Interrupt coalescence (the network card waits to have multiple packets before interrupting the CPU) reduces the accuracy of optimized-probing tools because it alters the dispersion of packet pairs and the one-way delays of packet trains [14, 21]. §4.1 presents results with interrupt coalescence disabled.

Testing Method. A *test* measures the available bandwidth with each different configuration of every tool back-to-back. During all tests we collect packet traces using tcpdump at the measurement server and the host. For each line we perform tests with all three servers. The results presented in §4.1 are for the closest server (in terms of RTT, see Fig. 1(b) for precise values) for each line. Results for the other servers are similar.

Cross Traffic. Previous work has already studied how cross traffic impacts available bandwidth estimation [3, 8, 9, 16, 19, 23, 24]. Hence, we perform our tests during the night (from 11PM to 6AM) and with no cross traffic from the home network to minimize any congestion in the access link. In this scenario, results are easier to interpret, because the available bandwidth matches the capacity.

4   Accuracy

This section evaluates the accuracy of available bandwidth estimation in the residential access links described in the previous section. We first compare the tools using default settings. We find that tools that use small packets underestimate the available bandwidth. Then, we show that the home gateways are to blame because they cannot sustain the high packet rate that results from sending small probe packets.

4.1   Comparison

Tab. 1 presents the available bandwidth inferred by iperf with parallel TCP transfers ('parallel TCP'), spruce, pathload, pathchirp, and igi/ptr for each tested access link. We run 15 tests with each line. The inferred bandwidth is stable across all tests of a given tool, so we summarize the results with the averages and the standard deviations (STDs). Pathload gives intervals as estimations rather than single values, so we present the averages of the minimum and of the maximum value. Pathchirp gives several instantaneous samples of bandwidth for each test. We present the average of the samples per test.

Benchmark. The first line of Tab. 1 helps us interpret the results in this section. It shows the UDP capacity obtained when flooding the link with iperf in UDP. The UDP capacity is computed using a tcpdump trace, as the total amount of bytes (including the IP and UDP headers) going through the link per time unit. The *UDP capacity* represents the maximum achievable IP rate for each line. These values are consistent with the capacity of ADSL local loops and advertised speeds for Comcast in Fig. 1(b). Comcast offers

Table 1. Accuracy of available bandwidth estimation. (*) 10s/6s(Powerboost)

Tool	Pckt. Size	Free Avg (Mbps)	STD	Orange Avg (Mbps)	STD	Comcast Avg (Mbps)	STD	AT&T Avg (Mbps)	STD
UDP capacity	1440B	16.30	0.16	15.80	0.10	20.60/22.93*	0.04/0.06*	2.85	0.004
parallel TCP	1440B	15.41	0.15	15.04	0.15	19.20/22.00*	0.33/0.18*	2.70	0.10
spruce	1440B	16.67	0.69	15.77	0.55	23.35	0.7	2.43	0.01
pathchirp	1000B	17.51	0.43	16.48	1.32	33.40	1.59	2.68	0.12
ptr	500B	11.09	1.70	11.76	2.52	19.45	2.90	1.88	0.15
igi	500B	10.73	1.03	12.52	2.69	26.10	10.62	2.04	0.06
pathload	200B	6.09 – 6.27	0.12	12.29 – 12.81	0.36	21.88 – 22.02	0.5	2.39 – 2.41	0.08
pathload	1440B	16.29 – 16.32	0.10	15.52 – 15.66	0.06	22.87 – 23.10	0.15	2.87-2.91	0.12

Powerboost, which allows users to download at higher rates at the beginning of the connection. The UDP capacity during the Powerboost period is 22.93 Mbps, whereas the sustainable rate is 13.04 Mbps. Hence, for Comcast, Tab. 1 presents UDP capacity and parallel TCP tests averaging the rate during 10 s (which includes 7 s of Powerboost and 3 s in the sustainable rate) and during only the first 6 s (which only measures the Powerboost rate). Optimized-probing tools can only measure the Powerboost rate. In our tests, where the local loop is the bottleneck and there is no cross traffic from the home, available bandwidth estimates should match the UDP capacity.

Results. The top part of Tab. 1 compares optimized-probing tools using the default configuration. *Spruce* gives the most accurate estimates when using default settings. Spruce had lower accuracy when interrupt coalescing was turned on. Although previous work shows that the probe-gap model underlying spruce works poorly under multiple bottlenecks [17, 18, 27], this scenario does not arise in our tests. The results for other optimized-probing tools are not accurate. Consistent with previous observations [8, 19], *pathchirp* overestimates the available bandwidth for most lines. Pathchirp's algorithm is extremely sensitive to interrupt latency variations and timer accuracy [14]. *Igi/ptr* underestimate the available bandwidth by 3 to 5 Mbps for Free and Orange and has large standard deviations. More surprisingly, *pathload*, which is known to report accurate estimates [3, 19, 24], significantly underestimates the available bandwidth in some cases (for instance, for Free by more than 60%).

The inspection of packet traces collected during the tests helps explain these results. We observe that both pathload and igi/ptr use small packets by default, whereas spruce and pathchirp use large packets. For igi/ptr, our tests showed that increasing the packet size does not improve a lot the estimation accuracy. Indeed, igi/ptr estimation algorithm is tuned to work best with 500 bytes to 800 bytes packets. However, for pathload, the bottom part of Tab. 1 shows that a larger probe size (1440 bytes) greatly improves the accuracy for all lines. Pathload's estimation with large probes matches perfectly the UDP capacity. We conclude that the use of small packets is the main cause of the poor performance of pathload with default parameters and we investigate this further in §4.2.

Parallel TCP is able to fully utilize all links and reports values that are close to the UDP capacity. The value is slightly below the UDP capacity because the rate computed by flooding-based tools is calculated as the total amount of data sent divided by the transfer time, which does not include TCP/IP headers and retransmissions. We perform few tests with a concurrent TCP connection from another computer in the home as cross traffic. In this experiment, parallel TCP reports values around 80% of the capacity, whereas pathload with large probes and spruce report available bandwidth close to zero.

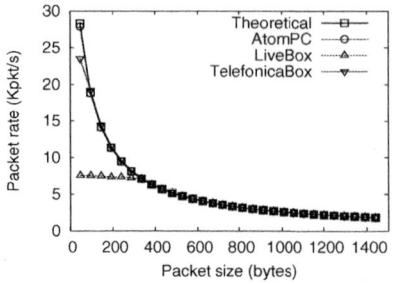
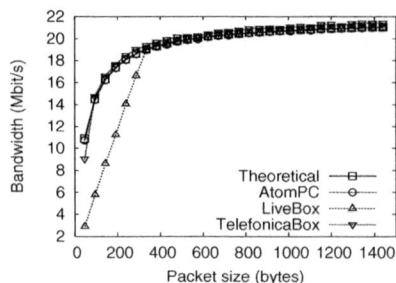

Fig. 2. Maximum packet rate for different packet sizes and different gateways

Fig. 3. Maximum bandwidth for different packet sizes and different gateways

Both techniques are accurate in this case, this disparity comes from the difference in the definition of available bandwidth between flooding-based and optimized-probing tools. Parallel TCP captures the effective bandwidth available for home subscribes, but pathload and spruce capture the residual capacity. A system that uses a combination of these two types of tools can give a better understanding of broadband speed.

Takeaway. Spruce, pathload with large probes, and parallel TCP are the most accurate tools to estimate available bandwidth.

4.2   Explanation of Bandwidth Limit with Small Probes

We investigate the reasons for tools that use small packets to underestimate the available bandwidth in some cases. The main difference between the tests with small packets versus tests with large packets is the probing rate. For a probing bandwidth of 16 Mbps, pathload sends 10,000 probes/s when using 200-bytes probes; this rate is only 1,389 probes/s for 1440-bytes probes. Given that pathload works well in other scenarios [3, 9, 24], our hypothesis is that one of the equipments between the access router and the measurement host in Fig. 1(a) limits or cannot sustain high probing rates.

Testbed description. To identify the limiting equipment we use a fully controlled testbed made of an Avicenia-L DSLAM, a measurement server, a measurement host, and three gateways: a *LiveBox*, the same used for Orange line in the previous section; a *TelefonicaBox* (Thomson TG797), with the same hardware as the LiveBox but with a proprietary real-time OS designed to minimize interrupt latency, instead of a plain linux; and the *AtomPC*, a more powerful Intel ATOM Z530 computer equipped with an ADSL card. The other gateways cannot be used in this testbed. The measurement server and host are Pentium PCs. The gateways are directly connected to the DSLAM and their ADSL links are configured at 24 Mbps ATM downlink and 1.2 Mbps ATM uplink. The measurement server is connected directly to the DSLAM via a GbE link. The measurement host is directly connected to the gateway via a GbE link.

We test the maximum achievable packet rate between the measurement server and the measurement host using all gateways. If the packet rate limitation comes from the DSLAM, then all gateways should achieve similar packet rates; otherwise, if the limitation is at the gateway, then different gateways will reach different packet rates.

Table 2. Maximum packet rate of home gateways

Vendor/Model	Maximum pkts/s	Vendor/Model	Maximum pkts/s
FreeBox/ v5	3,344	D-Link/DIR-300	10,844
LiveBox/Thomson v1.2	6,859	D-Link/DIR-615	40,983
TelefonicaBox/Thomson TG797	22,021	Linksys/BEFSR41v2	2,228
ComcastBox/Ubee U10C035	45,312	Linksys/WR54G	10,225
Belkin/Enhanced N150	3,126	Netgear/WNR2000-100PES	659
Belkin/Wireless G Plus	6,777	Netgear/WGT624 v3	20,208

We test the packet-rate achieved for different packet sizes using iperf/UDP and varying the IP packet size from 40 bytes to 1488 bytes with 48 bytes increments (to avoid ATM padding). We collect packet traces at the receiver to compute the packet rate.

Livebox and Freebox cannot achieve high packet rates. Fig. 2 presents the average packet rate of iperf/UDP across the ten runs for the LiveBox, the TelefonicaBox, and the AtomPC (the coefficient of variation is less than 0.01 for each packet size). This figure also shows the theoretical packet rate, which takes into account the ATM download speed, the encapsulation into cells, and layer-2 overhead, 40 bytes in our case. The lines of AtomPC and the TelefonicaBox closely follow the theoretical line. The AtomPC behaves according to the theoretical limit even when packets are very small. On the other hand, the LiveBox cannot sustain packet rates higher than 6,859 pkts/s. Such low achievable packet rates limit the maximum achievable throughput for small packets. Fig. 3 shows the achieved throughput for the corresponding tests. The Live-Box cannot fully utilize the link when packets are smaller than ≈400 bytes, because it cannot process packets fast enough. Hence, the speed decreases linearly as packets become smaller. For pathload's default of 200-bytes packets, Fig. 3 shows that the LiveBox's average throughput reaches only 12.6 Mbps. Pathload with small packets underestimates the available bandwidth, because it measures the LiveBox's maximum achievable packet rate. Now that we identified that gateways limit the packet rate, we can test the maximum packet rate of the FreeBox with iperf/UDP and 40-bytes packets using the setup of §3. The FreeBox limit is even lower: 3,344 pkts/s. Hence, the FreeBox can only reach an average of 6.1 Mbps for 200-bytes packets.

Other home gateways have similar limits on maximum achieved packet rates. We study the maximum achieved packet rate for a number of popular home gateways using the testbed deployed by Hatonen et al. [10]. In this testbed, gateways are connected to the server and the measurement host via a 100 Mbps Ethernet, so there is no limitation that comes from ADSL or cable technologies, just from the gateway hardware or software. We perform the iperf/UDP test with 40-bytes packets for 38 gateways tested in their study [10]. Tab. 2 presents the maximum packet rates for a selection of the gateways (due to space constraints, we only present the gateway model with lowest and highest maximum packet rate for the four main vendors). Tab. 2 also shows the maximum packet rates for each of the gateways tested earlier in this section. Although the maximum packet rate varies considerably even for gateways of the same vendor, most gateways do have a packet rate limit which is lower than pathload's probing rate.

Network-address translation slows down packet forwarding. In general, home gateways are known to have limited resources [10], but these achievable packet rates are

Table 3. Overhead of available bandwidth estimation. (*) 10s/6s(Powerboost)

Tool	Pckt. Size	Free (Kbytes)	Orange (Kbytes)	Comcast (Kbytes)	AT&T (Kbytes)
parallel TCP	1440B	20,769	20,908	26,844/19,177*	3,587
pathload	1440B	15,992	8,528	12,582	14,160
pathload	200B	2,053	622	2,041	2,067
spruce	1440B	288	288	288	288
pathchirp	1000B	1,140	1,140	1,140	1,105
igi/ptr	500B	414	475	457	475

extremely low. We see that either more powerful hardware (as in the AtomPC) or optimized operating system (as in the TelefonicaBox) can improve the maximum packet rate. We also observe that the ComcastBox achieves much higher packet rates. For Comcast, the measurement host is directly connected to the modem and has a public IP address. Hence, in this context there is no network-address translation (NAT). We conjecture that NAT explains at least part of the per-packet processing overhead. All the gateways in Tab. 2 but the ComcastBox perform address translation. To test this hypothesis, we run tests in the same Comcast line with the measurement host connected to the modem via a Belkin N1 Wireless Router. In this scenario, when NAT is disabled we achieve 31,458 pkts/s, whereas when NAT is enabled we achieve only 17,430 pkts/s.

Takeaway. Home gateways can have low packet forwarding rates. Hence, measurements of available bandwidth from homes need to ensure that the probing rate is lower than the gateway limit.[2]

5   Overhead

Each of the tools we study uses a different probing method with varying overhead. Tab. 3 presents the overhead for each tool. We define the overhead as the total number of bytes on the forward and reverse path during a test. We measure overhead by capturing all packets at the measurement host.

Parallel TCP's flooding-based approach is extremely invasive. For Free and Orange where the access link capacity is approximately 16 Mbps, parallel TCP will send over 20 Mbytes of probes during a 10-seconds test. Pathload with large packets also has significant overhead, which varies with the number of steps needed to converge. In fact, pathload by default uses small packets precisely to control the overhead (see pathload with 200-bytes packets). It is possible to reduce pathload's overhead by selecting the smallest probe size that leads to a probing rate lower than the packet rate limitation. Alternatively, one may use a tool such as Yaz [24], designed to reduce pathload's overhead. Spruce's overhead is independent of the access link capacity, because it always sends 100 pairs of probe packets. As access link capacity increases, the overhead of parallel TCP transfers becomes even higher. For instance, the overhead of parallel TCP is only 12 times higher than spruce's for AT&T, but it is 72 times higher for Orange.

Takeaway. Spruce has the lowest overhead of all tools. The overhead for flooding-based techniques is significantly higher than for optimized-probing tools.

---

[2] To find the gateway limit, measurement tools only need to perform the same iperf/UDP test with 40-bytes packets that we use here.

6   Conclusion

This paper showed that current home gateways have low packet forwarding rates, which hurts the accuracy of some existing available bandwidth estimation tools. We found that spruce can accurately estimate the available bandwidth with minimum overhead. Spruce takes the capacity as input and requires interrupt coalescing to be turned off. In a setting like SamKnows, where measurements run from a fully controlled router, it is possible to turn off interrupt coalescing. Moreover, SamKnows tests download and upload speeds every two hours, so it is important to minimize the probing overhead and the initial test to measure the link capacity can be amortized over time. When turning off interrupt coalescing is not possible, pathload with a probe size optimized to cope with the gateway limitation is the best choice to measure available bandwidth. These optimized-probing tools, however, cannot fully replace flooding-based tools, because of the elasticity of TCP cross traffic. An approach that combines frequent measurements with spruce or pathload and less frequent flooding-based measurements will give the best compromise between accuracy and overhead.

Acknowledgements. We thank Technicolor for the access to the DSLAM testbed and P. Le Guyadec and L. Di Cioccio for their technical help; S. Hatonen, M. Kojo, A. Nyrhinen, and L. Eggert for the access and help with the gateway testbed; and S. Sundaresan for the access to the AT&T and the Comcast lines. We also thank I. Cunha, N. Feamster, D. Joumblatt, P. Loiseau, F. Schneider, and S. Sundaresan for the helpful comments. This work was conducted at the LINCS and supported by the ANR grant C'MON.

References

1. FCC Challenge (2011),
   http://challenge.gov/FCC/114-fcc-open-internet-apps-challenge
2. Altman, E., Barman, D., Tuffin, B., Vojnovic, M.: Parallel TCP sockets: Simple model, throughput and validation. In: Proc. IEEE INFOCOM (2006)
3. Angrisani, L., D'Antonio, S., Esposito, M., Vadursi, M.: Techniques for available bandwidth measurement in IP networks: a performance comparison. Computer Networks 50(3) (2006)
4. Bauer, S., Clark, D., Lehr, W.: Understanding broadband speed measurements. MITAS project white paper (2010)
5. Croce, D., En Najjary, T., Urvoy Keller, G., Biersack, E.W.: Non-cooperative available bandwidth estimation towards ADSL links. In: The 11th Global Internet Symposium on IEEE INFOCOM Workshops 2008 (2008)
6. Croce, D., En-Najjary, T., Urvoy-Keller, G., Biersack, E.W.: Fast Available Bandwidth Sampling for ADSI Links: Rethinking the Estimation for Larger-Scale Measurements. In: Moon, S.B., Teixeira, R., Uhlig, S. (eds.) PAM 2009. LNCS, vol. 5448, pp. 67–76. Springer, Heidelberg (2009)
7. Dischinger, M., Haeberlen, A., Gummadi, K.P., Saroiu, S.: Characterizing Residential Broadband Networks. In: IMC (2007)
8. Goldoni, E., Schivi, M.: End-to-end available bandwidth estimation tools, an experimental comparison. In: Proc. Traffic Monitoring and Analysis Workshop (2010)
9. Guerrero, C.D., Labrador, M.A.: On the applicability of available bandwidth estimation techniques and tools. Computer Communications 33(1) (2010)
10. Hatonen, S., Nyrhinen, A., Eggert, L., Strowes, S., Sarolahti, P., Kojo, M.: An experimental study of home gateway characteristics. In: IMC (2010)

11. Hu, N., Steenkiste, P.: Evaluation and characterization of available bandwidth probing techniques. IEEE J. Selected Areas in Communications 21(6) (2003)
12. Jacobson, V., Braden, R., Borman, D.: A Framework for Defining Empirical Bulk Transfer Capacity Metrics Status of this Memo. RFC 3148 (2001)
13. Jain, M., Dovrolis, C.: End-to-end available bandwidth: Measurement methodology, dynamics, and relation with TCP throughput. In: Proc. ACM SIGCOMM (2002)
14. Jin, G., Tierney, B.L.: System capability effects on algorithms for network bandwidth measurement. In: IMC (2003)
15. Kreibich, C., Weaver, N., Nechaev, B., Paxson, V.: Netalyzr: Illuminating the edge network. In: IMC (2010)
16. Lakshminarayanan, K., Padmanabhan, V.N., Padhye, J.: Bandwidth estimation in broadband access networks. In: IMC (2004)
17. Lao, L., Dovrolis, C., Sanadidi, M.Y.: The probe gap model can underestimate the available bandwidth of multihop paths. ACM CCR 36(5) (2006)
18. Liu, X., Ravindran, K., Loguinov, D.: Multi-hop probing asymptotics in available bandwidth estimation: stochastic analysis. In: IMC (2005)
19. Shriram, A., Murray, M., Hyun, Y., Brownlee, N., Broido, A., Fomenkov, M., Claffy, K.: Comparison of Public End-to-End Bandwidth Estimation Tools on High-Speed Links. In: Dovrolis, C. (ed.) PAM 2005. LNCS, vol. 3431, pp. 306–320. Springer, Heidelberg (2005)
20. Prasad, R., Dovrolis, C., Murray, M., Claffy, K.: Bandwidth estimation: metrics, measurement techniques, and tools. IEEE Network Magazine 17(6) (2003)
21. Prasad, R., Jain, M., Dovrolis, C.: Effects of Interrupt Coalescence on Network Measurements. In: Barakat, C., Pratt, I. (eds.) PAM 2004. LNCS, vol. 3015, pp. 247–256. Springer, Heidelberg (2004)
22. Ribeiro, V.J., Riedi, R.H., Baraniuk, R.G., Navratil, J., Cottrell, L.: pathChirp: Efficient available bandwidth estimation for network paths. In: PAM (2003)
23. Shriram, A., Kaur, J.: Empirical evaluation of techniques for measuring available bandwidth. In: Proc. IEEE INFOCOM (2007)
24. Sommers, J., Barford, P., Willinger, W.: Laboratory-based calibration of available bandwidth estimation tools. Microprocessors and Microsystems Journal 31 (2007)
25. Strauss, J., Katabi, D., Kaashoek, F.: A measurement study of available bandwidth estimation tools. In: IMC (2003)
26. Sundaresan, S., de Donato, W., Feamster, N., Teixeira, R., Crawford, S., Pescapè, A.: Broadband internet performance: A view from the gateway. In: Proc. ACM SIGCOMM (2011)
27. Urvoy-Keller, G., En-Najjary, T., Sorniotti, A.: Operational comparison of available bandwidth estimation tools. ACM CCR 38(1) (2008)

One-Way Traffic Monitoring with `iatmon`

Nevil Brownlee

CAIDA, UC San Diego, and
The University of Auckland, New Zealand
`nevil@auckland.ac.nz`

Abstract. During the last decade, unsolicited one-way Internet traffic has been used to study malicious activity on the Internet. Researchers usually observe such traffic using *network telescopes* deployed on *darkspace* (unused address space). When darkspace observations began ten years ago, one-way traffic was minimal. Over the last five years, however, traffic levels have risen so that they are now high enough to require more subtle differentiation – raw packet and byte or even port counts make it hard to discern and distinguish new activities.

To make changes in composition of one-way traffic aggregates more detectable, we have developed `iatmon` (Inter-Arrival Time Monitor), a freely available measurement and analysis tool that allows one to separate one-way traffic into clearly-defined subsets. Initially we have implemented two subsetting schemes; *source types,* based on the schema proposed in [12]; and *inter-arrival-time (IAT) groups* that summarise source behaviour over time.

We use 14 types and 10 groups, giving us a matrix of 140 *type + group subsets.* Each subset constitutes only a fraction of the total traffic, so changes within the subsets are easily observable when changes in total traffic levels might not even be noticeable.

We report on our experience with this tool to observe changes in one-way traffic at the UCSD network telescope over the first half of 2011. Daily average plots of source numbers and their traffic volumes show clear long-term changes in several of our types and groups.

1   Introduction

Since about 2002, observations of unsolicited one-way Internet traffic have yielded visibility into a wide range of security-related events, including misconfigurations (e.g., mistyping an IP address), scanning of address space by hackers looking for vulnerable targets, backscatter from denial-of-service attacks using random spoofed source addresses, and the automated spread of malware such as worms or viruses. Researchers have generally observed such traffic using *network telescopes*, deployed on *darkspace* (unused address space). When unsolicited traffic observations began, one-way traffic was minimal. Because of increased botnet-related activities over the last five years, e.g., [11], one-way traffic at the UCSD network telescope has risen – for example Aben [1] observed the increase in sources scanning TCP port 445 from almost none to 220,000 per hour over the

N. Taft and F. Ricciato (Eds.): PAM 2012, LNCS 7192, pp. 179–188, 2012.

three months beginning on 21 November 2008. Now we see 6 GB/h of one-way traffic, i.e. high enough to require more subtle differentiation – raw packet and byte or even port counts make it hard to discern and distinguish new activities.

Seeking a better understanding of current and emerging one-way traffic behavior, we introduce and implement a methodology in a freely available measurement and analysis tool (iatmon) that provides an effective platform for separating one-way traffic into well-defined subsets, so that changes in a subset can be more easily recognised.[1] We implemented two subsetting schemes in iatmon, *source types* and *IAT groups*, described in section 3.3. This taxonomy facilitates analysis of not only the increasing unsolicited IPv4 traffic, but also pollution to IPv6 addresses, and comparison between the two. Tools such as iatmon can also enable consistent distributed monitoring of unused addresses across many different sites, effectively producing a wide-area view of unsolicited one-way traffic. The tool's utility is not limited to empty address space; one could equally deploy iatmon on partially populated address space, ignoring traffic to assigned hosts, or use it to monitor unsolicited traffic to all IP addresses on a stub network, since iatmon ignores bidirectional traffic.

We first review related work in darkspace traffic analysis, and then summarise research challenges and opportunities specific to darkspace measurement. In Section 3 we describe the data and our analysis methods. Section 4 presents results of our analyses. Section 5 summarises our contributions and future plans for one-way traffic analysis.

2   Related Work

Data from the UCSD network telescope has supported significant research on DOS attacks [9], Internet worms and their victims, e.g., Code-Red, Slammer, Witty, and the Nyxem email virus. Data sets curated from telescope observations of these events became a foundation for modeling the top speed of flash worms, the worst-case scenario economic damages from such a worm, the pathways of their spread, and potential means of defense.

In 2004, Pang *et al.*[10] analysed one-way traffic destined for five different empty prefixes (a /8, two /19's, two sets of 10 contiguous /24 subnets) announced from two sites. They found that, relative to legitimate traffic, traffic to darkspace "is complex in structure, highly automated, frequently malicious, potentially adversarial, and mutates at a rapid pace." TCP packets dominated in all of their traffic samples, 99% of which were TCP/SYNs indicating either scanning or backscatter.[2] Also in 2004, Cooke *et al.* found diversity in incoming traffic to ten unused address blocks [6] ranging in size from a /25 to a /8, announced from service provider networks, a large enterprise, and academic networks. They passively recorded incoming packets and actively responded to TCP SYN requests to obtain more data from the sources. They found traffic diversity along three dimensions: across protocols and applications; for a specific

---

[1] The iatmon tool is available at http://www.caida/tools/measurement/iatmon/.

[2] At UCSD from Jan–Jun 2012 only about 30% of the packets were TCP.

protocol/application using TCP port 135, and for a particular worm signature (Blaster).

In 2006 Barford *et al.* analysed the source address distribution of malicious 'Internet background' traffic. They evaluated traces from network telescopes running active responders on portions of two /16s and one /8 network, in addition to a large set of intrusion detection system logs provided by Dshield.org [2]. They found a bursty distribution of source addresses, many from a small set of tightly concentrated network locations, which varied across segments of darkspace but were consistent over time for each separate segment.

More recently, in 2010 Wustro *et al.* [14] analysed background traffic using one-week traces from four /8 darkspaces. Traces of one-way traffic destined to 35/8 from 2006 to 2010 showed an eight-fold rise in traffic rate over the five years, with daily variations during a week. The 2010 data rate (about 20 Mb/s) was similar to that at the UCSD network telescope. One-week traces from three of the four darkspaces suggest that the overall daily variations in traffic volume were similar across all sites. Their TTL distributions were also similar, suggesting that all the sites see similar spatial traffic distributions.

In 2011, Treurniet [12] proposed a traffic *activity classification schema* to monitors state changes in TCP, UDP and ICMP flows in order to help detect low-rate network scanning activities. She used state changes per sending host to classify that host as normal, DoS, backscatter, scanning, etc. She tested the approach on bidirectional trace data from outside the border of a /14 network with some responding servers in it, although fewer than 1% of observed flows were bidirectional communications with these servers. The rest of the observed traffic was malicious, mostly slow scans of various types.

3   Methodology

The UCSD network telescope [5,4] uses a /8 network prefix, most of which is dark. An upstream router filters out the legitimate traffic to the reachable IP addresses in this space, so we monitor only traffic destined to empty address space. Management of the UCSD network telescope requires continual navigation of the pervasive challenges in network traffic research methodology: collection and storage, efficient curation, and sharing large volumes of data. The large volume of data captured by the telescope incurs considerable expenses for data storage and limits the number of researchers who can realistically download data sets. The situation is worse during malicious activity outbreaks when the data volumes increase sharply, yet rapid analysis and response are necessary.

The UCSD network telescope remains a purely passive observer of unsolicited traffic. We do not rule out active response by the telescope in the future, but active responding requires resources and careful navigation of legal and ethical issues. We have found that much can be gleaned with non-intrusive methods and external knowledge of malware behavior. For example, we indirectly observed the rise of Conficker A and B because Conficker induced a conspicuous increase in the number of probe packets aimed at TCP port 445, using poorly randomized destination addresses [1].

Description	Type
TCP	TCP probe
	TCP vertical scan
	TCP horizontal scan
	TCP other
UDP	UDP probe
	UDP vertical scan
	UDP horizontal scan
	UDP other
Other	ICMP only
	Backscatter
	TCP and UDP
	μTorrent
	Conficker C
	Untyped

(a) Source Types

IAT distribution	Group
Long-lived	Stealth &3 s mode
	Stealth & Spikes
	Stealth other
3 s mode	Left-skew
	Even
	Right-skew
Other	Short-lived
	High-rate
	DoS
	Ungrouped

(b) IAT Groups

Fig. 1. Subsetting Schemes for One-way Traffic Sources

3.1 Data Set

The UCSD network telescope collects full-packet traces continuously. These traces are stored online for at least sixty days, allowing vetted researchers to analyse the data in various ways. (See CAIDA web page for access to data [3].) One of the goals of this research is to enable retention of efficient but rich summary statistics of historical raw data that is itself too expensive to archive indefinitely. [3]

We analysed each hourly trace from the UCSD network telescope for every hour from 3 Jan through 30 Jun 2011. During that time, 23% of the sources were TCP, contributing 30% of the packets and 69% of the volume (MB/h).

Note that since most traffic into darkspace represents failed attempts to initiate connections, about 99.9% of the TCP packets carry no payload. However, the number of UDP packets carrying payload has increased in recent years. As of January 2011, about 67% of the sources sent only UDP packets, accounting for about 55% of each hour's packets. In recent years the amount of UDP traffic has increased; in January 2011 the TCP traffic per average hour contributed only 66% of the bytes, 44% of the packets and 32% of the one-way sources – by June 2011, the hourly averages for TCP had changed to 70% of the bytes, but only 23% of the packets and 18% of the one-way sources.

3.2 Analysis Strategy

In 2002, when CAIDA began analyzing telescope data, one-way traffic volumes were low, so that rapid increases caused by viruses and fast-spreading worms were easy to discern. As of June 2011, we see 6 to 9 GB/h of one-way traffic, so that the early stages of a new rapidly spreading attack are much harder to

---

[3] Current storage pricing for researchers at SDSC are $390/TB-year, which at 6GB/hour results in over $20,000/year of storage costs, which multiply for each year of data to be stored, and increase as unsolicited traffic rates grow.

observe in the continuous swamp of background traffic. For example, we observe that each hour 76% of the sources send UDP packets, but these packets account for only 23% of the hourly byte volumes, so that the UDP sources are swamped (in terms of byte volumes) by TCP sources. One goal of our `iatmon` methods and tool is to separate the one-way traffic into various subsets so that changes within subsets are easier to detect.

3.3 `iatmon` Implementation

First, we consider the one-way traffic in terms of its *sources*. Specifically, we construct a *source table*, with entries that summarise the set of packets arriving from a source IP address. At the end of each hour's trace `iatmon` scans the source table, calling various classifying functions to separate the sources into clearly-defined subsets. We describe our initial implementation of these subsetting schemes below. `iatmon` has a Ruby outer block, which sets up `iatmon`'s configuration and writes its hourly summary file. However, most of the processing occurs in a C extension module that reads trace packets, maintains the source hash table, classifies sources using the various subsetting schemes, and passes results back to the outer block. For normal hours, `iatmon` running on an 8-core machine with 32 GiB of memory takes 7 to 15 minutes of elapsed time to process each hour's trace file, easily fast enough to keep up with new data from the telescope.

    `iatmon` handles its own storage allocation, requesting memory in 4 GB chunks as needed. Two such chunks are sufficient for most hour-long intervals of trace data, but for nine of the hours `iatmon` was unable to get enough memory to process the entire hour – even when using 28 GiB of real memory. We examined the first few thousand packets of each of those nine hours, and found that most of their sources sent just two TCP packets, from apparently random source addresses. To allow `iatmon` to handle traces when such DoS attack conditions occur, we discarded sources that only sent two packets and were then idle for at least 120 s. One of these nine traces had 122.5 *million* source addresses that we discarded (97% of the hour's sources), but most packets in the flood traces had the same TTL, suggesting a high-rate DoS attack using spoofed source addresses.

Source *Types*. One obvious approach to classifying one-way sources is to examine their use of IP addresses and ports. For example, a *probe* source sends all its packets to a single port on a single host. A *vertical scan* source sends packets to various ports on a single host. A *horizontal scan* source sends packets to the same port on many hosts. We used this approach in early development work on `iatmon`. Our current *source types* scheme is now based on Treurinet's [12] recent classification scheme, using the source types listed in Table 1(a).

    In 2008 we saw the rise of the Conficker worm/botnet. Conficker C may send both TCP and UDP packets as part of its p2p network establishment; SRI's algorithm [11] allows us to estimate which incoming packets are likely Conficker C p2p packets. We were curious as to whether BitTorrent has contributed to the rise in UDP one-way traffic observed in the last two years. The BitTorrent protocols are well-documented [8,13], allowing us to identify μTorrent sources from UDP packet payloads. Table 1(a) includes the two source types we added to represent these application-specific sources.

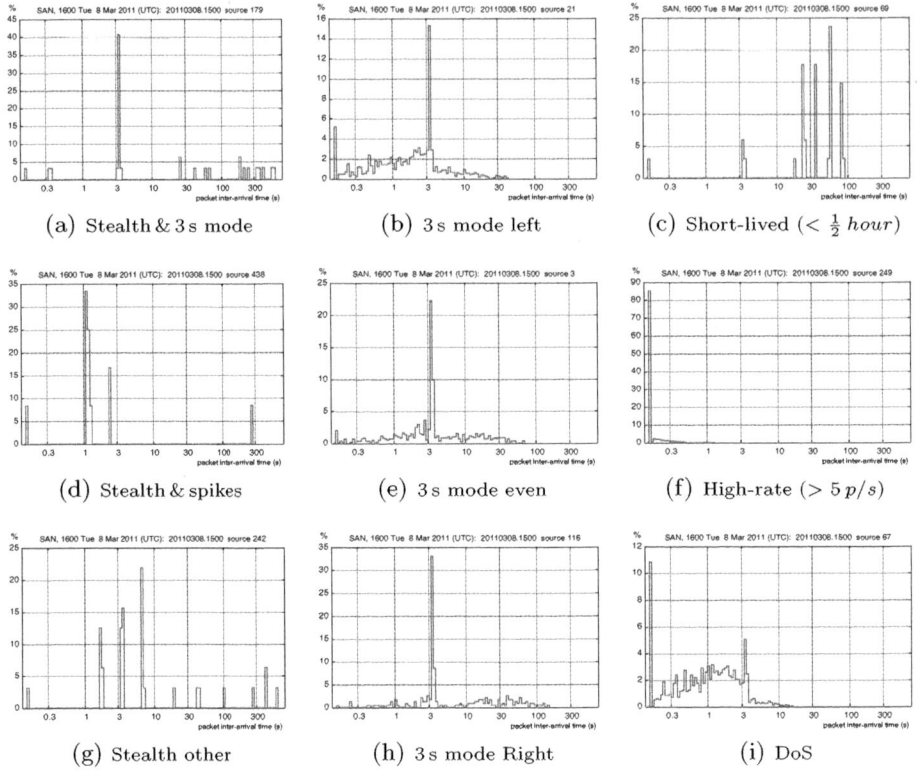

(a) Stealth & 3 s mode   (b) 3 s mode left   (c) Short-lived ($< \frac{1}{2}$ hour)

(d) Stealth & spikes   (e) 3 s mode even   (f) High-rate ($> 5\,p/s$)

(g) Stealth other   (h) 3 s mode Right   (i) DoS

Fig. 2. IAT groups: Packet Inter-Arrival Time percentage distributions for a typical hour, ending at 1600 on 8 Mar 2011. We determine each source's IAT group using a set of distribution metrics, such as % IATs $< 150\ ms$, mode %, skew, % $> 120\ s$; only 1% of the hour's sources remain unclassified.

Source *IAT Groups*. About 30% of the packets that reached the UCSD telescope in the first half of 2011 were TCP SYNs, carrying no payload. In order to further characterise the source behaviors, especially those from TCP sources, we investigated the inter-arrival time (IAT) distributions from sources active in a typical hour. To search for recognisable IAT patterns we plotted many sheets of 'postage-stamp size' IAT distribution plots, with each distribution's parameters shown on its plot. We examined these plots manually to find common patterns, then developed algorithms that captured these recognisable subsets of the sources, based on statistical properties of their IAT distributions. For example, many sources exhibit a strong inter-arrival time mode at 3 s, the standard time for TCP retries, aggregated with an underlying wide range of IATs. A Poisson process that sends TCP SYN packets, and resends each packet after 3 s intervals will produce this kind of distribution, with skew that depends on the process's average time between sending new packets.

Once we identified a clearly distinguishable IAT pattern, we developed an algorithm to capture it, and assigned it an *IAT group* label. After several cycles of that process, we settled on a scheme with nine different groups (listed in Table 1(b)) that meaningfully distinguished about 99% of the sources in each hour.

Figure 2 shows example distributions for each group. The centre column shows three groups that have a packet inter-arrival time mode at 3 s, the standard time for TCP retries. We also found that some UDP sources had IAT distributions suggesting an application with a 3 s retry time. These three group names end in *left, even* and *right* to show which side of their distribution's mode has more counts. The left-hand column shows *stealth* sources – those sending fewer than 120 packets, remaining active for more than 30 minutes, and having long ($>=$ 5 *minute*) quiet intervals. (IAT distributions are an effective way to detect stealth sources, in spite of their low average packet rates.) The right-hand column shows IAT distributions for three other groups: at the top, short-lived sources, active less than 30 minutes and sending less than 120 packets; in the middle, high-rate sources, sending packets almost back-to-back; and at the bottom, 'DoS' sources sending more than 10% of their of their packets in brief ($<=15$ *ms*) bursts.

4   Observations

4.1   Long-Term (Six-Month Plots)

Figure 3 shows daily average total counts and volumes per hour as stacked bars for source types and IAT groups observed at the UCSD network telescope from 3 Jan 11 to 30 Jun 11. Over those six months, typically between 0.5 and 2.0 million sources were seen on average during a typical 6-10 GB/hour of one-way traffic. The number of unique source IP addresses (in millions) declined from 1.08 in mid-January to 0.65 at the beginning of February, then rose again to 1.37 by mid-April, after which there was no obvious trend in total source counts or MB volumes.

For source types (Figure 3(a)), the number of *TCP horizontal scan* sources in the daily average hour showed a steady decline while *TCP probe, TCP vertical scan* and *untyped* source numbers remained at steady, much lower values. *UDP probe* and *unknown* source numbers increased gradually from about 1 February. Apart from the gradual long-term changes, Figure 3(a) also shows short-lived activity, for example the huge spike in *TCP probes* on 12 January, the increase in *TCP* and *UDP* during the first week of February, and the doubling of *UDP probes* in the first week of April.

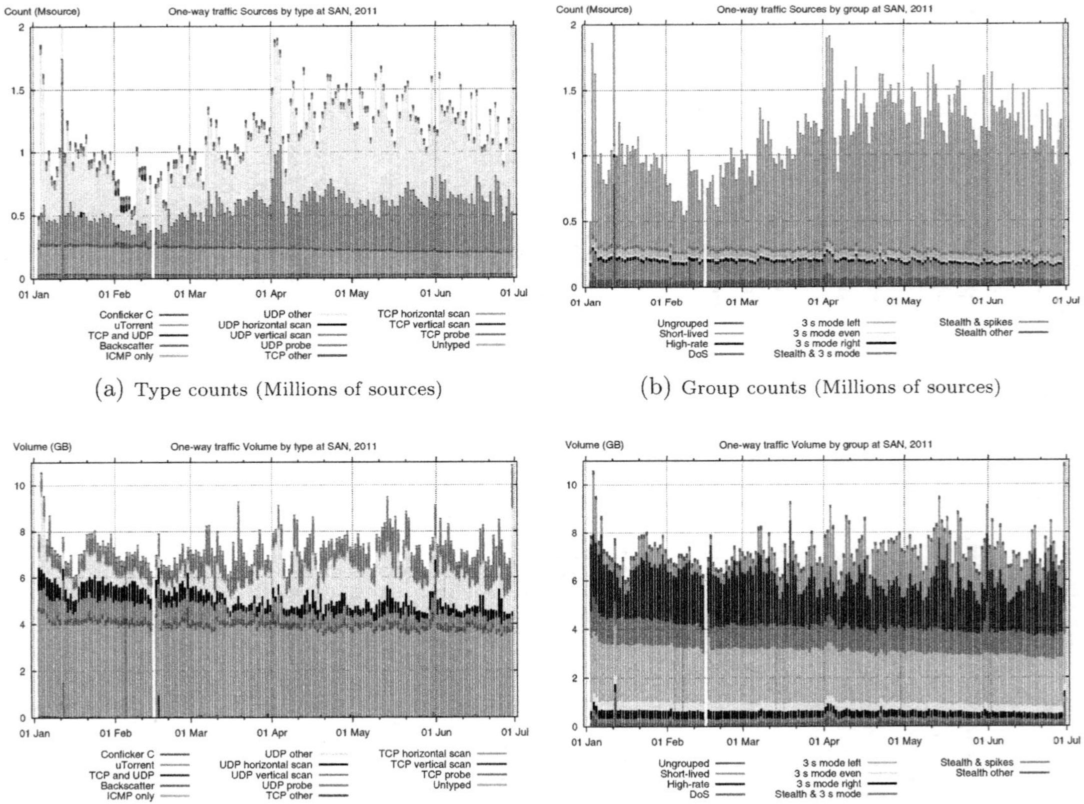

(a) Type counts (Millions of sources)

(b) Group counts (Millions of sources)

(c) Type volumes (GB)

(d) Group volumes (GB)

Fig. 3. Daily average total counts and volumes per hour for source types (left) and source groups (right); 3 Jan – 30 Jun 2011, UCSD Network Telescope

Figure 3(c) shows the daily average hour's traffic volume (in GB) for the source types. *TCP horizontal scan* traffic accounted for about half the total volume, around 4 GB/h. *UDP probe* traffic decreased to about 0.2 GB/h, which seems surprising since the number of *UDP probe* sources increased. Also, there was about 0.1 GB of *UDP horizontal scan* traffic each hour, even though the number of *UDP horizontal scan* sources was too small to be visible in Figure 3(c).

Considering source group activity, Figure 3(b) shows that short-lived sources dominate, accounting for about 3/4 of the sources observed. The number of *stealth 3s mode* sources (TCP and UDP) declined steadily from 100 M to 30 M sources during these six months, while the number of sources in the other groups remained steady. On 12 January we saw 78,000 *stealth other* sources, these correspond with the spike in *TCP probes* in Figure 3(a). Similarly, in the first week of April we saw a rise in *stealth other* sources, corresponding with a similar rise in *UDP probes*. Traffic volumes for the source groups are shown in Figure 3(d). Although the lower four bands on the plot correspond well with their group counts (Figure 3(b)), the next three groups – *3s mode left*, DoS and high-rate sources – account for up to 80% of the total traffic volume. Again, the *3s mode left* volumes declined from 2.5 to 1.8 GB/h over the six months, corresponding with our observation of the fall in *TCP horizontal scans*.

5   Conclusions and Future Work

Building on the demonstrated utility of the activity classification scheme in Treurniet [12], we have developed a taxonomy for one-way traffic sources using two independent classifying schemes: 14 source *types* and 10 *IAT groups*. These schemes separate the one-way traffic into 140 subsets, allowing us to determine which source subsets were active during any hour, and to track subset behaviour over weeks or months as the characteristics of one-way traffic evolve. Using these subsets, we found that:

– Long-term plots of *type* and *group* subsets indicate distinguishable changes in the proportions each *type* or *group* contributes to total traffic.

– For the first six months of 2011, although total daily average one-way traffic into the UCSD network telescope did not increase significantly, the composition of per-source traffic behavior has changed, with an increase in *TCP horizontal scan* and corresponding decrease in *stealth 3s mode* sources. Although we see many stealthy (long-lived low-rate) sources, most of the telescope traffic comes from short-lived ($< \frac{1}{2}$ hour) sources.

– We have used our `iatmon` tool to apply this taxonomy to hourly trace files, its implementation runs at least fast enough to be used on a live 1 Gb/s network. `iatmon` also includes tools to extract trace files for sources in 'interesting' *type* + *group* subsets that show interesting behaviour. Such 'source trace' files can then be examined in detail, for example to determine whether they represent traffic from known malware.

In the future, we plan to develop `iatmon` so that it can detect significant changes in source subset counts or volumes, experiment with the thresholds in our IAT group classification scheme, investigate other possible classification schemes (perhaps as 'plug-in modules' for iatmon), and most importantly, explore a cooperative global effort to compare unsolicited traffic across a wider diversity of address space. We are currently operating iatmon in real-time mode on the University of Auckland's production Internet gateway, a 1 Gb/s link carrying about 70,000 packet/s; we find that 3% of the total traffic inbound to the University each hour is one-way, consistent with another recent study of this link [7].

Acknowledgment. Thank-you to the anonymous reviewers, and to my colleagues at CAIDA for their helpful suggestions for improving this paper.

References

1. Aben, E.: Conficker as seen from UCSD Network Telescope (February 2009), http://www.caida.org/research/security/ms08-067/conficker.xml
2. Barford, P., Nowak, R., Willett, R., Yegneswaran, V.: Toward a Model for Source Address of Internet Background Radiation. In: Proc. Passive and Active Measurement Conference, PAM 2006, Adelaide, Australia (2006)
3. CAIDA. Ucsd network telescope data use policy and request form, http://www.caida.org/data/passive/telescope_dataset_request.xml
4. CAIDA. UCSD Network Telescope global attack traffic, http://www.caida.org/data/realtime/telescope/
5. CAIDA. UCSD Network Telescope Research, http://www.caida.org/data/passive/network_telescope.xml
6. Cooke, E., Bailey, M., Mao, Z., Watson, D., Jahanian, F., McPherson, D.: Toward understanding distributed blackhole placement. In: Proc. ACM Workshop on Rapid Malcode, WORM 2004, Washington DC, USA, pp. 54–64 (2004)
7. Lee, D., Brownlee, N.: Passive Measurement of One-way and Two-way Flow Lifetimes. In: ACM SIGCOMM Computer Communication Review (2007)
8. Loewenstern, A.: DHT protocol (2008), http://www.bittorrent.org/beps/bep_0003.html
9. Moore, D., Shannon, C., Brown, D., Voelker, G., Savage, S.: Inferring Internet Denial-of-Service Activity. ACM Transactions on Computer Systems (May 2006)
10. Pang, R., Yegneswaran, V., Barford, P., Paxson, V., Peterson, L.: Characteristics of Internet Background Radiation. In: Proc. of the 4th ACM SIGCOMM Conference on Internet Measurement, IMC 2004, Sicily, Italy, pp. 27–40 (2004)
11. Porras, P., Saidi, H., Yegneswaran, V.: Conficker C P2P Protocol and Implementation. In: SRI International Technical Report, September 21 (2009), http://mtc.sri.com/Conficker/P2P/
12. Treurniet, J.: A network activity classification schema and its application to scan detection. IEEE/ACM Transactions on Networking PP(99) (2011)
13. wiki.theory.org. Bittorrent protocol specification v1.0 (2006), http://wiki.theory.org/BitTorrentSpecification
14. Wustrow, E., Karir, M., Bailey, M., Jahanian, F., Huston, G.: Internet background radiation revisited. In: Proceedings of the 10th Annual Conference on Internet Measurement, IMC 2010. ACM (2010)

A Hands-on Look at Active Probing
Using the IP Prespecified Timestamp Option

Walter de Donato, Pietro Marchetta, and Antonio Pescapé

Department of Computer Engineering and Systems, University of Napoli Federico II
{walter.dedonato,pietro.marchetta,pescape}@unina.it

Abstract. In the last years, network measurements have shown a growing interest in active probing techniques. Recent works propose approaches based on the IP prespecified timestamp option and consider
its support to be enough for their purposes. On the other hand, other
works found that IP options are usually filtered, poorly implemented, or
not widely supported. In this paper, to shed light on this controversial
topic, we investigate the responsiveness obtained targeting more than
$1.7M$ IPs using several probes (ICMP, UDP, TCP, and SKIP), with
and without the IP prespecified timestamp option. Our results show
that: (i) the option has a significant impact on the responsiveness to the
probes; (ii) a not−negligible amount of targeted addresses return several
categories of non RFC−compliant replies; (iii) by considering only the
RFC−compliant replies which preserve the option, the probes ranking by
responsiveness considerably changes. Finally, we discuss the large−scale
applicability of two proposed techniques based on the IP prespecified
timestamp option.

Keywords: Internet measurements, Active probing, IP options.

1 Introduction

The Internet Protocol version 4 (IPv4), after more than three decades and several
minor updates, still represents the core of the Internet and many protocols and
services have been built on top of it. IPv4 has provision for optional header
fields in order to transport additional information. Particularly, the *Timestamp*
(TS) optional header (IP option type 68) is defined along with three variants:
(i) each router forwarding the packet, if enough space is available, should add a
timestamp; (ii) a (*IP, timestamp*) couple should be added; (iii) the sender requires
a timestamp for up to four "prespecified" IPs [1, 2]. We refer to them as TS_o,
TS_i, and TS_p respectively. Since recent works [3–5] reconsidered the utility of
TS_p, in this paper we focus our attention on such variant.

Works proposing applications based on TS_p consider its support to be enough
for their purposes [3,4]. On the other hand, previous works stated that IP options
are usually filtered, poorly implemented, or not widely supported [6, 7].

To the best of our knowledge, both claims have not been properly supported by
a large scale analysis comprising a set of destinations statistically significative.

N. Taft and F. Ricciato (Eds.): PAM 2012, LNCS 7192, pp. 189–199, 2012.

Moreover, previous analysis only considered TCP_{syn} and $ICMP_{request}^{echo}$ probes, thus not considering other possibilities to obtain a reply from a targeted destination.

In this paper, we present a detailed analysis of the TS_p support in Internet obtained by targeting more than $1.7M$ destinations from two vantage points (VPs). For the sake of completeness, we employ four different probes (ICMP, UDP, TCP and SKIP), with and without the TS_p option set. Such analysis allowed us to evaluate the impact of TS_p on the responsiveness to each probe and to investigate the RFC−compliance of different IP stack implementations.

The paper is organized as follows. While in Sec. 2 we discuss the most important related works, in Sec. 3 we briefly describe the background and the adopted methodology. Sec. 4 contains the results of our large−scale measurement campaign. In Sec. 5 we briefly discuss the impact of our findings on some TS_p-based applications. Finally, Sec. 6 ends the paper with conclusion remarks.

2   Related Work

Gunes et al. [8] conducted an experimental study of both historical and current responsiveness to probes concluding that the most effective is ICMP, followed by TCP and UDP. They also found a higher responsiveness of network devices to *indirect probes* (i.e. probes launched towards other destinations). Our work has a different goal: while the overall responsiveness is a well investigated topic, we aim at measuring the impact of the TS_p option on the responsiveness to several probes. Fonseca et al. [7], using Planetlab, estimated the *transit* filtering of packets crafted with and without TS and *Record Route* (RR) options by using a modified version of traceroute based on ICMP probes. They demonstrated, over a $7.5k$ IPs dataset, that transit filtering is mainly concentrated in a minority of edge ASes. In [6] Medina et al. covered the impact of TS and RR options on TCP by analyzing connections towards 500 web servers. Our work extends both analyses to $1.7M$ IPs and to probes other than ICMP and TCP, in order to estimate the overall utility in using TS_p probes, taking into account the effect of transit filtering by using two not−filtered VPs. Sherry et al. [3] proposed a novel alias resolution approach based on the TS_p option as well as a measurement study of its support. The latter made use of $ICMP_{request}^{echo}$ probes to target around $267.7k$ destinations. Our work extends such study targeting with several probes more than $1.7M$ destinations in order to globally estimate the impact and the support of the TS_p option as well as the RFC compliance. Our results and hypothesis experimentally justify part of the findings detailed in [3]. Finally, the TS_p option has been recently exploited in the reverse traceroute [4] and to infer router statistics [5]. We evaluate the applicability on large scale scenario of [3] and [4] in the light of the obtained results.

3   Background and Methodology

When using TS_p, the originating host composes the option data with a maximum of four $(IP, 0)$ records and sets the pointer field for pointing to the first record.

For instance, a forwarding router should stamp the pointed record only if it contains its own IP address. In such case, the pointer should be incremented to point to the next record. If the router cannot register timestamps due to lack of space, the overflow field should be incremented. The timestamp value should be inserted in a *standard* format, which represents the elapsed time in milliseconds since midnight UT. If such format is not respected the high order bit should be set to one, indicating the use of a *non−standard* value.

In order to estimate its impact on the responsiveness to the probes, a list of addresses is queried with a set of probes crafted with and without TS_p option. The list is extracted from a complete Archipelago [9] *cycle* and filtered to remove non−publicly routable addresses (e.g. 10.0.0.0/8, 172.16.0.0/12, 192.168.0.0/16, ...). We classify each IP from the list as *Pathending*, if it appears in the Archipelago dataset exclusively as a traceroute destination, and as *Router* otherwise. It is worth to notice that the *Router* set surely contains IP addresses belonging to network devices, while an unknown percentage of *Pathending* IPs consists of end hosts. Each address is then solicited with the following probes: *(a)* $ICMP_{request}^{echo}$; *(b)* UDP towards a presumably unused port (15616), to collect an $ICMP_{unreach}^{port}$ message; *(c)* TCP towards an unassigned well-known port (737), to solicit a TCP *reset* reply; *(d)* an IP packet carrying a SKIP message (an obsolete protocol), to solicit an $ICMP_{unreach}^{proto}$ message. We chose SKIP after a preliminary test demonstrated how unassigned protocol numbers obtain much less answers.

In line with [3], we use the TS_p option according to the (A|BBBB) format with A=B (A represents the destination address and BBBB the ordered list of prespecified IPs). In the following, we refer to the probes with TS_p option respectively as $ICMP_p$, UDP_p, TCP_p, and $SKIP_p$. When using $ICMP_p$ and TCP_p probes, the returned option (if present) is extracted from the IP layer of the reply packet, while, regarding UDP_p and $SKIP_p$, it is extracted from the original probe carried back by the ICMP error packet. A retransmission mechanism allows to deal with potential congestion events and rate limiting policies: before giving up each probe is sent four times with a timeout of two seconds. During a preliminary test, we found that some destinations not always stamp the option. We call such phenomenon *timestamp rate limiting*. In order to deal with it, we apply the retransmission mechanism also when the returned option records are empty.

4   Experimental Results

In this section, we present the results obtained with a measurement campaign conducted between the 16th and 20th of June 2011 from two VPs located in Napoli, Italy (NA) and Louvain−la−Neuve, Belgium (LLN)[1]. The collected dataset is freely available online[2]. In a preliminary campaign we also employed 10 Planetlab VPs, which we decided to discard because they do not support the SKIP protocol[3] and their access networks often filter probes with TS_p option.

---

[1] The authors would like to thank B. Donnet and P. Mérindol for their support.

[2] http://www.grid.unina.it/Traffic/Data/TSp_16-20_June_2011.tar.gz.

[3] Planetlab nodes currently support TCP, UDP, ICMP, GRE and PPTP protocols [10].

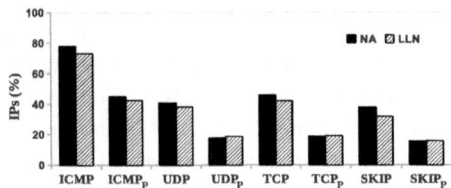

Fig. 1. Responsiveness to the probes per vantage point

After removing non−publicly routable addresses (1.4%), $1,776,095$ destinations were extracted from the Archipelago's cycle started on the 13th of June 2011. The obtained IPs resulted to be equally divided into *Pathending* (49.99%) and *Router* (50.01%).

All the results from the two VPs are very similar: for instance, as reported in Fig.1, the responsiveness to each probe is consistent between them. Therefore, given such consistency and for space constraints, in the following we discuss the results of the VP located in Napoli.

About 19% of the destinations were unresponsive to our probes, while a small portion (2.25%) returned non RFC−compliant replies (we call them *anomalies*). Hence, disregarding the anomalies, we first quantify the support of TS_p and its impact on the responsiveness to the probes. Then, we deeply investigate and characterize the isolated non RFC−compliant behaviors.

4.1 Support Analysis

Responsiveness. In Fig.2(a) the amount of destinations responsive to probes without option (P) is compared with the amount of them replying when TS_p is enabled by preserving the option (P_{opt}^{TS}) or regardless of this (P^{TS}).

In line with [8], the most effective probe without option is ICMP (78.1%) followed by TCP (46.1%), UDP (41.4%) and SKIP (34.7%). The insertion of TS_p heavily impacts the responsiveness to each probe (-33% ICMP, -24% UDP, -28% TCP, -19% SKIP), but preserves the ranking order. However, applications relying on TS_p generally require the reply to preserve the option and the ranking significantly changes when considering only such replies: $ICMP_p$ (40.7%), $SKIP_p$

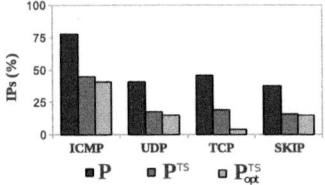

(a) impact of the TS_p option

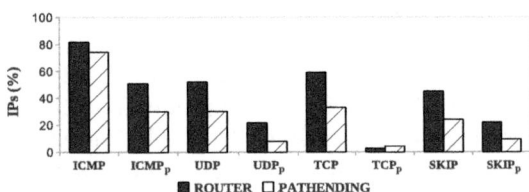

(b) breakdown on *Router* and *Pathending* IPs

Fig. 2. Responsiveness to the probes

Table 1. Responsiveness relation among different probes

		(a) without TS_p option (%)					(b) with TS_p option (%)		
	ICMP	UDP	TCP	SKIP		$ICMP_p$	UDP_p	TCP_p	$SKIP_p$
ICMP	**78.1**	40.6	44.9	32.6	$ICMP_p$	**40.7**	13.2	3.5	13.5
UDP	40.6	**41.4**	37.6	30.1	UDP_p	13.2	**15.0**	3.2	11.6
TCP	44.9	37.6	**46.1**	28.9	TCP_p	3.5	3.2	**3.6**	2.6
SKIP	32.6	30.1	28.9	**34.7**	$SKIP_p$	13.5	11.6	2.6	**15.8**

(15.8%), UDP_p (15%) and TCP_p (3.6%). It is worth to notice how most replies to TCP_p probes were received without option, while this effect is marginal for the other probes. Moreover, as shown in Fig.2(b), *Router* IPs resulted more responsive than *Pathending* ones for all the probes, with the only exception of TCP_p. In the rest of the paper, all the replies not preserving the TS_p option will not be taken into account.

Tab. 1(a) and 1(b) show the relation among different probes with respect to the responsiveness. Each element (i, j) represents the percentage of destinations responsive to both the probes on the ith row and j^{th} column. The main diagonal, therefore, points out the amount of destinations which responded to a specific probe. Without option, ICMP probes showed a significant marginal utility compared to the others. Anyway, even the other probes showed some marginal utility compared to ICMP: UDP (0.8%), TCP (1.2%) and SKIP (2.1%). When TS_p is enabled the scenario is similar: while only part of the IPs which replied to $ICMP_p$ also provided replies to the other probes, UDP_p and $SKIP_p$ collected answers respectively from $31k$ and $41k$ addresses which were unresponsive to $ICMP_p$.

Table 2. Timestamp rate limiting phenomenon

	D_0	$D_0 \cap D_1$	$D_0 \cap D_2$	$D_0 \cap D_3$	$D_0 \cap D_4$
$ICMP_p$	98,024	2,443	299	0	0
UDP_p	54,649	643	0	0	0
TCP_p	420	0	0	0	0
$SKIP_p$	56,213	646	0	0	0

Option Management. Henceforth we use the following notation: the term D_j represents the set of destinations which respond to the generic TS_p probe by stamping the prespecified address j times, while the D_j^{probe} notation refers to a specific probe. For instance, D_1^{icmp} is the set of destinations which, solicited with $ICMP_p$ probes, returned replies containing only one stamped record.

Regarding the *timestamp rate limiting* (see Sec. 3), Tab.2 reports for each probe the number of destinations classified both as D_0^{probe} and D_{1-4}^{probe}. This behavior mostly involved *Router* IPs probed with $ICMP_p$. To handle such phenomenon in the next analyses, we reassigned the involved destinations using the following criterion: an address belonging to both D_0^{probe} and D_j^{probe} is removed from D_0^{probe} to be exclusively part of D_j^{probe}. This process leads to the results reported in Tab.3(a), where the number of stamps per probe is pointed out as percentage of the responsive destinations.

Table 3. Deep analysis of the returned TS_p options

(a) breakdown of the replies on the probes(%)

	TOT	D$_0$	D$_1$	D$_2$	D$_3$	D$_4$
ICMP$_p$	723k	13.2	<u>26.4</u>	<u>54.9</u>	~0	5.5
UDP$_p$	267k	20.2	<u>74.5</u>	0.1	0	5.1
TCP$_p$	620k	0.7	~0	99.3	~0	~0
SKIP$_p$	281k	19.8	<u>80.1</u>	0.1	0	~0

(b) intersection between D_i^{icmp} and D_j^{udp}

		j=0	j=1	j=2	j=3	j=4
	TOT	54k	198.9k	246	-	13.7k
i=0	95.3k	**27.9k**	306	-	-	-
i=1	190.8k	12.1k	**32.8k**	112	-	-
i=2	397.5k	519	<u>147.8k</u>	92	-	-
i=3	168	6	2	19	-	-
i=4	39.6k	2	2	5	-	**13.2k**

Tab.3(a) suggests the rule followed by most devices to manage TS_p: *the option is stamped once every time the probe passes through the interface associated to the currently pointed prespecified address.* Since UDP$_p$ and SKIP$_p$ probes, unlike ICMP$_p$, return the option as affected by the forward path only, the similarity among $D_1^{icmp} \bigcup D_2^{icmp}$, D_1^{udp} and D_1^{skip} supports such hypotesis. Tab.3(b), in which the (i, j) element represents the size of $D_i^{icmp} \bigcap D_j^{udp}$, deeper investigates such scenario: the big intersection between D_2^{icmp} and D_1^{udp} (147.8k) confirms again our hypothesis. Hence, if a (D|DDDD) probe enters and leaves the destination node through the same interface D, the option is stamped twice, otherwise just once. As we will discuss in Sec. 5, such behavior may reduce the applicability of the technique proposed in [3].

We also investigated the small amount of destinations not respecting the previous rule. Analyzing D_3^{icmp}, we often observed records containing timestamps according to the $t_1 t_1 t_2$ pattern, with t_2 slightly higher than t_1. On the other side, regarding D_2^{udp} we found $t_1 t_1$ patterns, which suggests that the option is stamped twice when entering the node, but only once when leaving it. We deepened the analysis of D_4^{icmp} and D_4^{udp} by using IGMP probes with the MERLIN [11] platform. We only received replies from Juniper routers[4], while doing the same on D_1^{icmp} gave no replies. Moreover, we never observed Cisco routers stamping the option more than twice. Hence, we foresee novel fingerprinting and alias resolution techniques relying on how TS_p is managed.

4.2   RFC Compliance Analysis

Timestamp Format. According to the RFC 791, a standard timestamp should always be lower than $86.4 * 10^5$ ($24h * 3600s * 1000$), while a non−standard value should belong to the range $[2^{31}, 2^{32}]$. Hence, the range $]86.4 * 10^5, 2^{31}[$ consists of non RFC−compliant values. Among the 660k destinations stamping at least once, we found timestamp values according to the following distribution: 87.6% standard, 11.3% non−standard, 1.15% non RFC−compliant. We also found 449 destinations stamping different probes using different formats and 9 of them doing it inside the same answer.

---

[4] DVMRP [12] codes 3.x are commonly associated to Juniper, while 12.x to Cisco.

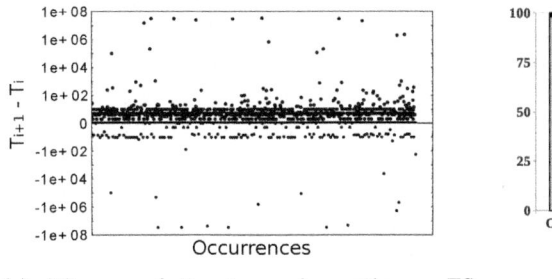 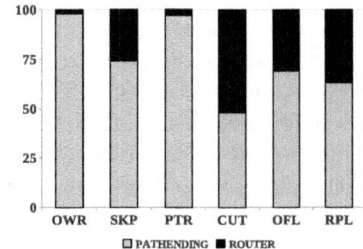

(a) difference of timestamps in contiguous TS_p records

(b) sources of the anomalies

Fig. 3. Non RFC−compliant behaviors

Focusing our attention on the standard values, we analyzed the difference between contiguous not null timestamps from the same reply. Fig.3(a) shows such values for $ICMP_p$ replies, where we identify three cases: *(i)* small positive and *(ii)* negative differences, *(iii)* both positive and negative huge differences. According to the rule described in Sec.4.1, the first case represents an estimation of the reply−generation delay on the destination node. Although limited by the milliseconds resolution, such estimation may represent a valid alternative to classic techniques based on round−trip time. The second case corresponds to transient anomalies which quickly disappeared. The third case represents a persistent behavior we observed on just 38 destinations, which seem to stamp the option by using two different clocks. Since such replies contain four timestamps following the $t_1 t_2 t_2 t_3$ pattern, where often $t_1 \approx t_3$, we speculate the presence of a middlebox along the path which is responsible of inserting t_1 and t_3.

Anomalies. Disregarding timestamp values, 40013 targeted destinations provided non RFC−compliant replies, which lead us to the following taxonomy:

- **OWR**: some prespecified IP addresses are overwritten;
- **SKP**: the destination stamps the option by skipping one or more records (e.g. the second IP is stamped, but not the first one);
- **PTR**: the pointer field is inconsistent with respect to the number of times-tamps;
- **CUT**: the original packet carried by the ICMP error message is truncated before the end of the option;
- **OFL**: the overflow field counts several *extra−stamps*, but the number of timestamps is less than four;
- **RPL**: the option data is replaced with part of the original packet header.

It is worth to notice that the CUT anomaly is different from a missing option. Indeed, the IHL field of the IP header carried back by the ICMP error message is 15 in the first case, pointing out the presence of the option, and 5 in the latter case. Regarding the PTR anomaly, the pointer value should belong to the set $\{5, 13, 21, 29, 37\}$, but we also found non−standard values: *253* and *9*.

Fig.3(b) shows that most anomalies, with the exception of CUT, were generated by destinations belonging to the *Pathending* set. Although such set may also contain IPs assigned to routers, the phenomenon seems reasonably related to end hosts having buggy TCP/IP stack implementations. As shown in Tab.4(a), which underlines the relationships among different anomalies, a destination can generate replies affected by more than one of them. The (i,j) element represents the amount of destinations (as percentage of 40013) affected by both the anomalies on the ith row and the jth column. OWR (73.3%) and PTR (74.8%) are the most common anomalies and appear simultaneously in most cases. As expected, since in the RPL anomaly part of the original packet is copied over the option data without modifying the pointer, such anomaly implies OWR and PTR ones. Moreover, all the IPs affected by the SKP anomaly are also source of the PTR anomaly. Finally, part of the addresses providing CUT replies to UDP_p and $SKIP_p$ probes also generated different anomalies when answering to $ICMP_p$ and TCP_p probes. Such behavior is more evident by looking at Tab. 4(b), which shows how a specific anomaly relates to the different probes: while CUT and RPL only affect UDP_p and $SKIP_p$, all the other anomalies mainly affect $ICMP_p$, which results to be the most affected probe.

Deepening OWR Anomaly. Regarding the OWR anomaly, we found prespecified IPs overwritten in different ways, which we discuss below.

The 85% of IPs generating OWR anomalies returned replies in which only the first IP address is overwritten. We further divide them in two cases: (a) 99.7% not stamping any address, (b) 0.3% stamping at least the first IP. The case a mostly involves *Pathending* destinations which failed to properly stamp the current option record by writing the timestamp in the location reserved to the address. Such hypothesis is confirmed by several findings: the returned option has always the pointer set to 13, meaning stamped once; by swapping the first prespecified IP with one not on the path towards the destination, the anomaly disappears: the first prespecified IP is not overwritten and the option is not stamped at all, as confirmed by the pointer value. The case b reveals the presence of network devices confusing TS_p with the TS_i option variant on the path to the destination, since the first TS_p record is filled with both the IP address and the timestamp of such device and the pointer is properly incremented. To better understand such behavior we targeted the same destinations by using TTL limited TS_p probes, in order to reach only the indicted device. As expected, the anomaly appeared a few hops before reaching the destination.

Table 4. Detailed analysis of anomalies

(a) relation among anomalies (%)

	OWR	SKP	PTR	CUT	OFL	RPL
OWR	**73.32**	0.03	63.60	0.02	0.02	0.96
SKP	0.03	**0.08**	0.08	-	0.04	-
PTR	63.60	0.08	**74.84**	0.02	0.04	0.96
CUT	0.02	-	0.02	**15.47**	-	0.01
OFL	0.02	0.04	0.04	-	**0.06**	-
RPL	0.96	-	0.96	0.01	-	**0.96**

(b) breakdown of anomalies on the probes

	TOT	$ICMP_p$	UDP_p	TCP_p	$SKIP_p$
OWR	29.3k	24.8k	293	3.8k	3.7k
SKP	32	28	4	2	3
PTR	29.9k	28.5k	725	3	4.5k
CUT	6.2k	—	5.6k	—	3.5k
OFL	26	26	—	6	—
RPL	383	—	249	1	287

Another 13% of IPs reset part of the prespecified addresses when replying to TCP_p probes. In order to identify the sources of such anomalies, we targeted such destinations using again the MERLIN platform. All the IGMP replies returned the following DVMRP codes: 37.90 and 21.95. Hence, we tried to detect a possible association between such codes and a specific brand/OS by targeting the same destinations with the *nmap* tool [13][5]. We found a highly probable association with Microsoft Windows versions: code 37.90 should correspond to version 2003, while 21.95 to version 2000.

The remaining 2% of destinations mixed the previously described behaviors.

Deepening RPL Anomaly. While RPL replies normally return already known information, for a specific destination we observed a peculiar behavior which may cause security concerns: probed several times with UDP_p, the option data appeared replaced each time in a different way. We identified such replacements as packet headers presumably stored in a dynamic buffer at the destination. In this way, we were able to collect remote MAC and IP addresses, mostly coming from ARP requests. Unfortunately, common OS fingerprinting techniques were not able to discover more information about such device.

5   Applicability of TS_p—Based Techniques

The results reported in Sec.4 allow a general discussion about the recently introduced techniques based on TS_p.

Reverse traceroute [4], when the RR option is unable to discover the next hop, takes advantage of TS_p in two different ways. In the first case, a candidate IP R – extracted from pre-collected topology information – is prespecified in $ICMP_p$ probes from S using the (D|DR) format, where D is the last discovered hop on the reverse path. In the second case, in order to avoid transit filtering, a spoofed $ICMP_p$ probe is sent, using the (D|R) format, from a selected VP to D acting as S. In both cases, if S receives a reply in which R is stamped, such address is part of the path from D to S. Based on our results, 40.7% of destinations answered to $ICMP_p$ preserving the option, but only 86.8% of them stamped the option. Thus, such approach works with about 35% of IPs from our dataset. Moreover, if R itself belongs to D_0^{icmp} (i.e. 13.2% of IPs), the spoofing approach is not effective.

The alias resolution technique proposed in [3] relies on TS_p as described in the following: for each pair (A, B) of candidate IPs, two $ICMP_p$ probes having (A|ABAB) and (B|BABA) format are sent respectively towards A and B. If both probes obtain replies stamped four times, A and B are alias. According to the rule defined in Sec.4.1, a D_2^{icmp} router stamps twice the (A|ABAB) probe only if the packet enters the node from interface A and exits from interface B and the same happens for the (B|BABA) probe by inverting the crossing order. This explains why in [3] they often obtain replies stamped twice for the first probe and without stamps for the second, which they partially recover exploiting topological constraints. However, they state to obtain much more success in identifying

---

[5] Since nmap OS fingerprinting consists in an aggressive probing process, we limited its use only to specific cases involving a reduced amount of IPs.

alias pairs for D_4^{icmp} addresses than for D_2^{icmp} ones. Our results confirm that the aliasing technique works well with D_4^{icmp} destinations (2.2%), and demonstrate that D_2^{icmp} IPs (22.3%) are not compliant with the technique, while D_1^{icmp} destinations (10.7%) support it[6]. Hence, from a single VP, the aliasing approach works on 12.9% of cases. Despite the relatively lower amount of collected replies, UDP_p and $SKIP_p$ may represent a valid alternative to implement a similar technique, since they are not affected by the reverse path.

6   Conclusion

Targeting more than 1.7M destinations with a set of probes crafted with and without the TS_p option, we draw the following conclusions: (i) the TS_p option has an important impact on the responsiveness to the probes (-33% ICMP, -24% UDP, -28% TCP, -19% SKIP); (ii) by considering just the replies preserving the option, as required by most applications, the probes ranking by responsiveness considerably changes (ICMP 40.7%, SKIP 15.8%, UDP 15%, TCP 3.6%); (iii) a limited amount of destinations not always stamp (*timestamp rate limiting*); (iv) the option is commonly stamped once every time the packet passes through the interface associated to the currently pointed prespecified IP; (v) around 2.25% of destinations showed non RFC$-$compliant behaviors classifiable in six non$-$disjoint categories, while about 7.6k IPs made use of timestamp values not allowed by the RFC. In the light of our findings, we evaluated the large$-$scale applicability of recent proposals based on the TS_p option, demonstrating that, from a single VP, the alias resolution technique [3] is effective just on 12.9% of destinations, while the reverse traceroute [4] can potentially work on 35% of IPs when the TS_p option is required.

In the future, we plan to (i) further investigate the TS_p option support per Autonomous System by exploiting more unfiltered VPs from the BISmark platform [14] and to propose novel measurement techniques based on it; (ii) exploit the TS_p option in active probing approaches for the monitoring of Internet Outages [15].

References

1. Su, Z.S.: Rfc 781: A specification of the internet protocol (ip) timestamp option (May 1981)
2. Postel, J.: Internet Protocol. RFC 791 (Standard) (September 1981)
3. Sherry, J., Katz-Bassett, E., Pimenova, M., Madhyastha, H.V., Anderson, T., Krishnamurthy, A.: Resolving ip aliases with prespecified timestamps. In: Proc. of IMC 2010, pp. 172–178. ACM, New York (2010)
4. Katz-Bassett, E., Madhyastha, H.V., Adhikari, V.K., Scott, C., Sherry, J., van Wesep, P., Anderson, T.E., Krishnamurthy, A.: Reverse traceroute. In: Proc. of NSDI 2010, pp. 219–234. USENIX (2010)

---

[6] Such percentage may significantly increase by using multiple VPs.

5. Ferguson, A.D., Fonseca, R.: Inferring router statistics with ip timestamps. In: Proc. of CoNEXT 2010 Student Workshop. ACM, New York (2010)
6. Medina, A., Allman, M., Floyd, S.: Measuring the evolution of transport protocols in the internet. SIGCOMM Comput. Commun. Rev. 35, 37–52 (2005)
7. Fonseca, R., Porter, G.M., Katz, R.H., Shenker, S., Stoica, I.: Ip options are not an option. Technical report (2005)
8. Gunes, M.H., Sarac, K.: Analyzing Router Responsiveness to Active Measurement Probes. In: Moon, S.B., Teixeira, R., Uhlig, S. (eds.) PAM 2009. LNCS, vol. 5448, pp. 23–32. Springer, Heidelberg (2009)
9. Claffy, K., Hyun, Y., Keys, K., Fomenkov, M., Krioukov, D.: Internet mapping: From art to science. In: Proc. of CATCH 2009, pp. 205–211. IEEE Computer Society, Washington, DC (2009)
10. Huang, M.: VNET: PlanetLab Virtualized Network Access. Technical Report PDN–05–029, PlanetLab Consortium (June 2005)
11. Marchetta, P., Mérindol, P., Donnet, B., Pescapé, A., Pansiot, J.J.: Topology discovery at the router level: a new hybrid tool targeting ISP networks. IEEE JSAC, Special Issue on Measurement of Internet Topologies 29(6) (October 2011)
12. Pusateri, T.: Distance vector multicast routing protocol version 3 (DVMRP). Internet Draft (Work in Progress) draft-ietf-idmr-dvmrp-v3-11, Internet Engineering Task Force (October 2003)
13. Lyon, G.F.: Nmap Network Scanning: The Official Nmap Project Guide to Network Discovery and Security Scanning. Insecure, USA (2009)
14. Sundaresan, S., de Donato, W., Feamster, N., Teixeira, R., Crawford, S., Pescapé, A.: Broadband Internet Performance: A View From the Gateway. In: Proc. of SIGCOMM 2011. ACM (2011)
15. Dainotti, A., Squarcella, C., Aben, E., Claffy, K.C., Chiesa, M., Russo, M., Pescapé, A.: Analysis of Country-wide Internet Outages Caused by Censorship. In: Proc. of IMC 2011. ACM, Berlin (2011)

Exposing a Nation-Centric View on the German Internet – A Change in Perspective on AS-Level

Matthias Wählisch[1], Thomas C. Schmidt[2],
Markus de Brün[3], and Thomas Häberlen[3]

[1] Freie Universität Berlin, Institut für Informatik, Berlin, Germany
[2] HAW Hamburg, Department Informatik, Hamburg, Germany
{waehlisch,t.schmidt}@ieee.org
[3] Federal Office for Information Security (BSI), Bonn, Germany
{markus.debruen,thomas.haeberlen}@bsi.bund.de

Abstract. The Internet has matured to a critical infrastructure in many countries. The national importance of routing motivates us to study the AS-level subgraph that is relevant for a country. In this paper, we report on a methodology and tool chain for identifying and classifying a 'national Internet', and evaluate detailed results for the example of Germany. Our contribution (a) identifies the ASes that are important for the country, (b) classifies these ASes into functional sectors, (c) constructs the AS routing graph of a country as well as subgraphs of specific sectors, and (d) analyzes structural dependencies between key players. Our methods indicate the importance of examining individual IP-blocks held by individual organizations, as this reveals 25% more stakeholders compared to only looking at prefixes. We quantify the centrality of ASes with respect to specific sectors and the robustness of communication communities. Our results show that members of sectoral groups tend to avoid direct peering, but inter-connect via a small set of common ISPs. Even though applied for Germany here, all methods are designed general enough to work for most countries, as well.

1   Introduction

The Internet was originally shaped to offer open transmission services on a global scale, but has now turned into a mission-critical infrastructure of local relevance for most countries and dedicated players. The coherence of the Internet is defined by peering relations at the Autonomous System (AS) level. Analyzing mutual impact, vulnerability and efficiency of the backbone requires the identification of ASes and corresponding transits between them.

Today, the global Internet is composed of more than 30,000 ASes with significantly more links, which challenge a clear picture on dependencies. Similar to traditional infrastructures, a country, its population as well as organizations share an obvious interest that the internal data exchange does not rely on weak third parties (cf., [1, 243 ff.]). In Internet terms, AS transits connecting key players of a country should be part of an apprehensible Internet ecosystem. However,

N. Taft and F. Ricciato (Eds.): PAM 2012, LNCS 7192, pp. 200–210, 2012.
© Springer-Verlag Berlin Heidelberg 2012

the Internet is a globally distributed network without boundaries, which makes the identification of nationally relevant subparts hard and leads to the following questions: Which Autonomous Systems are important for a reliable interconnection of the Internet infrastructure of a country? How do sectors of a country communicate? Rigorous insight into the country-wise nature of the Internet thus carries fundamental importance and it is somewhat surprising that only recently the inter-network structures of nations attracted attention [2,3].

This paper contributes with the following first steps to answer these questions: (1) A promising methodology to derive a country-centric view on the Internet structure. This is exemplarily verified for our home country Germany. The approach starts with IP-blocks. Compared to pure prefix-based techniques, we are able to identify approximately 25 % more members. (2) A novel, non-hierarchical AS taxonomy, as well as a heuristic sectoral classification technique. Both allows us to identify ASes with national relevance. By adding routing information, we are able to generate, visualize, and analyze the structure of communication flows between relevant public and business sectors. This has not been evaluated before. (3) The evaluation of the German inter-AS structure based on common and new graph metrics. This reveals for example that most eyeball providers peer dependent on the target AS, whereas the financial sector operates on static paths. (4) Finally, extracted and visualized data will be provided to the community for subsequent research and analysis.

The remainder of this paper is structured as follows: § 2 discusses the current state of Internet backbone analysis in the context of nation-state routing. Our methodology and corresponding toolchain, which allows for a nation-centric view on the Internet, is described and evaluated for Germany in § 3. § 4 analyses AS (sub-)graphs from Germany. Finally, § 5 concludes this paper.

2   Related Work

Research on the Internet AS structure continues to attract significant interest since more than one decade. This includes the analysis of structural properties of the inter-AS graph [4], the (mainly hierarchical) classification of ASes [5], and the inference of the relationship between them [6]. Active measurements within dedicated countries [7] reveal geographic reachability of ASes and thus follow a direction distinct from our work. Until now, there is only little work on a nation-state understanding of the Internet backbone routing, as well as on a horizontal classification of ASes that aims to identify key players of relevance for the Internet services of a country.

Dimitropoulos *et al.* [8] introduce a broader AS taxonomy (large/small ISPs, customer ASes, universities, IXPs, and network centers), but this does not include a detailed decomposition of customer ASes into dedicated sectors. The proposed inference algorithm analyzes the description value of the Internet Routing Registry [9] and follows a text classification technique. The authors focus on a complete mapping of ASes to classes. This differs from our perspective, as we do not intend to classify *all* ASes, but concentrate on *important* players of a country, viewed in further differentiated sectors. Cai *et al.* [10] introduce the interesting idea of an Internet AS ecosystem, which is based on a novel AS to organization map. The authors normalize contact records of the RIR WHOIS data to cluster AS numbers that belong to the same organization. Although this work could be applied to peering analysis and planning as well as threat analysis, our work is orthogonal as we classify ASes according to roles in a country.

The first paper that proposes a nation-state view on the Internet routing measures the impact of countries on the global data forwarding [2]. Karlin *et al.* start from IP prefixes, which they map to ASes. Routing paths are derived from an approximation of active traceroute measurements. We will show that IP prefixes are too coarse-grained to obtain an in-depth picture of a country and miss 25 % of German ASes. It is important to note that the base set of the national classification should be as complete as possible to judge on relevance.

Roberts and Larochelle [3] present a mapping project that visualizes and quantifies the relevance of ASes for countries. The AS to country mapping is based on the external service Team Cymru [11], which starts from IP prefixes. The authors introduce network maps of countries. Each map abstracts connections to the outside by a single Autonomous System that subsumes all foreign ASes. The relevance of an AS increases with the number of prefixes reachable via this AS. ASes with multiple upstream peers share routes equally among parents. This model oversimplifies common practice in Internet backbone routing. Normally, countries do not have a single entry point apart from China with the exclusive entry China Telecom. Furthermore, multilateral peering allows for path selection depending on the target AS. This diversity is not reflected and causes a weight distortion of AS importance.

To the best of our knowledge, current approaches do not provide sufficient mechanisms for identifying country-specific ASes, categorize ASes in business sectors, nor analyze importance of inter-AS communication between network domains for a country including international inter-connects. We will address these topics below.

3   Deriving Nation-Centric Subsets of the Internet

We want to identify all Autonomous Systems of the global Internet that host organisations from a specific country. Many organizations are normal ISP customers and do not own a prefix or AS. Thus we argue that the appropriate granularity must be IP blocks. An IP block is a subset of a prefix and will be assigned internally by the prefix owner to departments or customers. An organization and thus its hosting AS is coined to a country if the organization or its administrative contact person of an IP block is located therein. Consequently, we include also ASes in our view with primary base outside of the investigated country, as well as national organizations with IT infrastructure outsourced to foreign countries.

To demonstrate and validate our approach, we choose our home country Germany (*DE*). The introduced methodology, however, can be applied to other countries, as well. Its implementation is easily extendable and thus provides a good base for the community and subsequent work. In this section, we present the data sources, our inference and classification algorithm to derive a nation-state view, and the the automated construction of existing interconnects. These results enable us to analyse the composition of the nationally relevant part of the Internet in detail.

1. From Internet Members to ASes. Regional Internet Registries (RIR) maintain network and contact details of their region. IP addresses and AS information related to Germany are registered at the RIPE database (DB). We start by extracting all `inetnum` records, which represent IP-blocks, from the RIPE DB that carry the mandatory `country` attribute of either *DE* or *EU*. Additionally, we collect address data for the associated `admin-c` and `org` objects. Based on the latter, we created keyword lists of synonymic country codes (e.g., Germany, DE), local city names, and international dialing codes (e.g., 0049, +49) representative for Germany. Applying the keywords on the contact record allows us to further resolve *EU* IP-blocks to *DE* and to verify the *DE* classification of IP-blocks. The result is a list of all IP-blocks allocated by organizations in Germany.

Next, we determine the longest covering IP-prefix for each IP-block. Prefix lengths are subject to aggregation and thus depend on the point of observation. Using passively measured BGP data from distant route collectors would be too coarse grained and yield less specific prefixes. Assuming that RIRs provide the most detailed prefix mapping, it is reasonable to query the RIPE DB. The inter-AS route is specified in the `route` record, which is referred by the `inetnum` object.

Finally, we map the prefixes to origin Autonomous System Numbers (ASNs) by the `route` object. However, in this step using the RIPE DB alone would lead to several unresolved mappings. Therefore, we also consider data of Team Cymru [11] and the route collector RRC12 of the RIPE RIS [12]. The latter peers at the largest German Internet Exchange Point (DE-CIX) and thus provides localized data. We apply the different data sources in the following order to maximize the number of resolvable ASNs: (1) RIPE DB, (2) Team Cymru, and (3) RIS RRC12. In cases of Multiple Origin ASes, we keep all discovered ASNs. The resulting list contains the ASes that compose the nation-centric part of the Internet for the example of Germany.

Our fully automated tool chain was applied in Oct. 2010 and yielded 246,861 German IP-blocks. Thereof 240,237 are embedded in 6,278 IP-prefixes that belong to 1,471 ASes, ≈ 2 % could not be resolved to a prefix. To estimate errors of our IP-block-to-country mapping, we checked back with the well-known Max-Mind GeoLite Country service [13]. Deviations were found below 0.2% for both false positives and false negatives.

Our method of starting from IP-blocks rather than IP-prefixes identifies significantly more prefixes that carry relevance for the country Germany (cf., Table 1). When considering prefixes alone, only ≈ 84% can

Table 1. Number of identified prefixes

Approach	DE	EU	other
IP-Block	6,278	–	–
Prefix (RIPE DB)	5,243	–	1,035
Prefix (Team Cymru)	4,395	947	936

be identified as 'German' using RIPE-DB, while Team Cymru yields $\approx 70\%$ *DE* prefixes. Thus a significant fraction of prefixes that route traffic relevant for Germany is not directly associated to country or address values from the this country.

Providers from outside Germany are also selected by our scheme. The corresponding 301 ASes ($\approx 20\%$) are classified relevant for nation-state routing and internationally distributed as follows. More than a third (110) ASes originate from direct geographical neighbors, another third (107) from the remaining Europe, thereof 57 British, and 18 % (54) are North American ASes. These classifications are again based on RIR databases and Team Cymru with an estimated error of about 15 %.

2. Tier and Sector Classification of Autonomous Systems. Having categorized the nationality of the stakeholders, we add two further classifications to the selected ASes. First, we harvest the topological hierarchy (tier1, large/small ISP, and stub) from [14]. Additionally, we investigate the role of ASes within those public or business sectors that are operationally relevant for the country. As there is no AS classification available that describes the professional role of an organization in relation to the global BGP routing, we introduce a sectoral categorization. This extends the taxonomy of critical infrastructure published by the Federal Office for Information Security (BSI), Germany. We determine sectoral classification by applying an optimized and manually verified keyword spotting to names, descriptions, and address fields of the previously derived AS data. Our approach uses general terms such as "bank", but also specific company names (e.g., Siemens, Daimler) as keywords associated with classes to identify important ASes. Keywords are correlated to enhance the identification. Thereof we obtain an additional list of the 'relevant national ASes' including branch tags such as energy (cf., Table 3). It has been manually verified for a small sample.

99 % of the classified ASes belong to exactly one sector, five ASes are assigned to two sectors. Companies may attain multiple roles. For example, AS 31438 is a municipal utility responsible for waste water and DSL access in the City of Marburg. Overall 279 ASes have been selected as 'systemically relevant' with sectoral attribute attached.

We admit that this step includes manual pre-definition of keywords for sectors. However, mapping ASes to sectors is a fine-grained process, which requires specific information that cannot be derived completely automatically. Our taxonomy, methodology, and tools can be applied to other countries based on an updated keyword list. The creation of the list needs local knowledge.

3. Constructing Spanning AS Routing Graphs. Following the identification of all ASes relevant for the German Internet infrastructure and a classification of key players, we derive their interconnects. We limit the building of AS graphs to the construction of inter-AS paths without considering individual prefixes. This modeling step is meaningful for our purposes: Even though BGP policies and regional optimizations may lead to varying paths for differ-

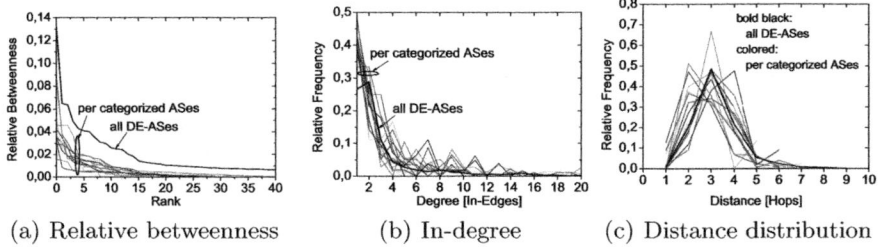

(a) Relative betweenness   (b) In-degree   (c) Distance distribution

Fig. 1. Properties of the Internet relevant for Germany and its categorized subgraphs

ent IP prefixes announced by the same origin AS, recent studies [15] show that
multiple prefixes are reachable via the same AS path for 75 % of origin ASes.
Additionally, we focus on a regionally bound network, which is densely meshed
by peering points. International redirections within service provider networks are
mainly outside the scope of our perspective. From this point of view, restricting
the routing on the AS level is a valid approximation.

We identify an AS routing graph for each sector, the bilateral exchange between two sectors, as well as the AS graph of all DE ASes based on the weighted
next hop matrix provided by the NECLab topology project [16]. This data is
calculated using the continuously updated measurements by the UCLA [14] and
reflects BGP policy decisions [15]. To exclude incomplete paths, we omit row
column values of -1 for distinct indices during matrix processing. Note, this occurs very rarely ($\ll 0.3\,\%$). Naturally, the set of ASes in the routing graphs has
been extended by intermediate ASes that we have not assigned before to the
nationally relevant part of the Internet. These transit nodes are required to link
nation-state subsets that would remain isolated otherwise.

4   Analysis of the AS-Structure

In this section, we investigate structural properties of the derived AS routing
graphs and measure the relevance of members in sectors and in the overall DE
AS graph. It is worth noting that we keep BGP policy modeling by a per path
analysis, each path derived from the *weighted* next hop matrix of the NEC
topology project. All measurements are relative to allow for comparing sectors
of different sizes. Unfortunately, the underlying next hop matrix does not provide
edges to connect the five ASes of the medical sector.

4.1   Node Centrality

Intermediate nodes between source and receiver attain a relevant role from
serving as transits. The number of shortest paths passing through a node m
is quantified by the betweenness $B(m)$. If the total number of shortest paths
between two nodes i and j is $B(i,j)$, and the number of these paths going

Table 2. Relative betweeness of the top ranked ASes for selected sectors

All DE		Large ISPs		Research	
Ranked AS	Betweenness	Ranked AS	Betweenness	Ranked AS	Betweenness
1. DTAG	0.131	1. DTAG	0.031	1. DFN	0.087
2. Level 3	0.065	2. Lambdanet	0.008	2. Verizon	0.037
3. Lambdanet	0.064	3. Telekom–AT	0.007	3. Manda	0.030
4. Colt	0.049	4. France Telecom	0.006	4. BELWUE	0.021

through node m is $B(i, m, j)$, then the betweenness of m is defined as the ratio: $B(m) = \sum_{i \neq m \neq j, i \neq j} \frac{B(i,m,j)}{B(i,j)}$. This measurement quantifies also the load at intermediate ASes. The betweenness is normalized by $(|V| - 1)(|V| - 2)$.

The *term shortest path* refers to the routing path that is actually taken. Our underlying BGP routing model reflects policies [15]. Using the NEC matrix, there exists exactly one effective path between two ASes. However, as discussed in Section 3, in our context of locally bound routing this is not a restriction. Independent of the nation-state view, BGP policies may lead to a violation of the triangle inequality. As the routing paths are based on a weighted graph, this property is preserved.

We calculate the betweenness of a node for the routing graphs under discussion. Figure 1(a) shows the relative betweenness, where ASes are ranked in decreasing order. Details for selected sectors are listed in Table 2. In 80% of the cases, this measurement exhibits sharp peaks at the transition from the top most important AS to the second one. This means that in the selected category a dedicated AS is part of a significant number of shortest paths and thus attains a major role in data forwarding. However, the decay from the top most ranked ASes is less steep in the overall German AS graph, showing a more evenly distributed relevance due to increased peering links. Looking at the actual rank orders reveals a relatively stable number of ASes among the top five in each category. For example, AS 3320 (Deutsche Telekom) has in 80% of the cases at least rank 5 and in 48% the highest betweenness.

4.2   Degree Distribution

The degree of a node denotes the number of its one-hop neighbors. Figure 1(b) shows the in-degree distribution. For visibility, we cut the tail at 20 edges. Overall, the relative frequency decays polynomially for all networks. Thus, there is a higher probability to maintain only a quite limited number of peering relations, but a non-vanishing likelihood for high peering numbers. The distribution of the full DE AS graph decays smoothly, while sectoral groups exhibit systematic peaks for selected node degrees between four and 13. Consequently, specific networks within the sectoral subgraphs are more densely connected than the full graph. These additional weights indicate regional star topologies in sectoral networks.

When comparing the topology within sectors to the complete DE network, we find more pronounced betweenness' and irregular peaks at increased node

Table 3. Absolute number of ASes per sector and DE graph as well as mean ($\langle X \rangle$) and standard deviation (σ_X) of the distance distributions for corresponding routing graphs

Sector (# ASes)	$\langle X \rangle$	σ_X	Sector (# ASes)	$\langle X \rangle$	σ_X
Transit providers (55)	2.41	0.92	Industry (28)	3.19	0.87
Trading (10)	2.69	0.87	Financial services (32)	3.21	0.89
Science & Culture (22)	2.77	1.12	Shipping & transportation (15)	3.22	0.8
Eyeball ISPs (23)	2.83	1.16	Public administr. & justice (14)	3.22	1.14
Peering points (8)	2.87	0.97	*DE All (1,471)*	3.23	1.04
Public services (4)	3.00	0.6	Energy (11)	3.34	0.79
Media & publishers (19)	3.08	0.94	Other public services (7)	3.40	0.73
Software and systems (31)	3.18	0.89	Medical services (5)	–	–

degrees. Jointly, these two structural metrics indicate that individual ASes provide enhanced connectivity within the specific communities as opposed to direct interconnects. A closer look on the corresponding AS graphs supports this observation. The majority of financial services, for example, tend to peer via Deutsche Telekom (AS 3320) and Colt (AS 8220), while no mutual peering is visible at all. Surprisingly, the governmental federation follows the same pattern. Governmental organizations are mainly interconnected by Deutsche Telekom and Versatel (AS 8881), but a small group uses Plusline (AS 12306) as upstream provider. The latter organizations require the external tier1 ISP AT&T to serve as inter-connect to the remainder of this sector.

4.3 Distances

The distance distribution of shortest paths measures the probability that two randomly selected nodes of a network are connected at distance k. This metric describes routing performance and usually follows a Gaussian law. This observation is also reflected in the analysis of the sectors and DE routing (cf., Fig. 1(c)) with average values between 2.4 and 3.4 (cf., Table 3). Routing distances, thus, largely depend on the sector under investigation. Naturally, connections between ISPs are shorter as compared to other branches. Surprisingly, ASes of the trading sector are significantly short, as well. In this group, the majority of members are connected via the same ISPs. Deutsche Telekom (AS 3320) and Vodanet (AS 3209) play a dominant role for transit. Even though there is no bilateral peering within the sector, many traders (e.g., Ebay AS 6907) maintain extensive peering relations. Paths that consist of only one transit hop are easily established. In general, our results show a similar behaviour compared to the global AS topology [17]. Even in the relatively small sectors, interconnects are not significantly denser and path lengths are not generally reduced. Most of the members from the same sector seem eager to stay at distance to each other.

4.4 Context Dependent Peer Selection

To analyze the peering behaviour in more detail, we answer the following question: How likely does a member of a sectoral group chooses its upstream peer

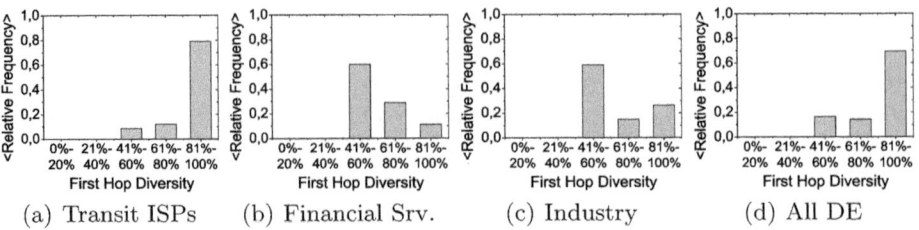

Fig. 2. Relative upstream diversity for selected sectors

dependent on the sector it communicates with? For each member of a sector, we count the number of different upstream peers relatively to the overall number of paths towards members of distinct sectors. We quantify the relative frequency of corresponding diversity classes over all members of a sector. For ASes that peer with many ISPs, it indicates high probability for high first hop neighbor diversity.

The calculated upstream peer diversity is very heterogeneous and may appear as a characteristic feature of the sectors. Figure 2 presents the measurements for selected sectors. Members of the financial services, for example, exhibit constant paths in about 50 % of the cases with enhanced probability (cf., Fig. 2(b)). In contrast to this, 80 % of the transit providers select above 80 % of the time neighbors dependent on the target. In general, target specific peering is dominant, as 8 of 10 ASes choose their one-hop neighbor with respect to the destination.

Combining the results with our previous findings indicates that multilateral peering has dominant routing effects on the Internet subpart relevant for Germany. For sectors, however, this higher amount of interconnections does neither result in more densely meshed inter-AS links nor in shorter paths.

5   Conclusions and Outlook

A clear understanding of the inter-AS structure at the country-level is needed to cope with the interdependencies and intrinsic vulnerability of the Internet. In this paper, we presented a methodology to identify and classify the relevant ASes of a country. This led to a fine-granular view onto meaningful subsets of Internet stakeholders and a detailed analysis. To the best of our knowledge, this is the first inspection of a country and its key players at the Internet routing substructure. The evaluation was exemplified for our home country Germany (DE), and created a list of relevant DE ASes including administrative data and sectoral classification, which will be publicly available.

We associated Autonomous Systems with a country whenever they host IP address space for an organization from there. Our approach outperformed prefix-based techniques by identifying 25 % more ASes. In particular, we were able to spot parts of the public sector hosted by international providers. Our analysis further revealed that members of the same public or business sector tend to not peer with each other, but interconnect via some few national and also international

ASes. Deutsche Telekom, Level 3, Lambdanet, Colt, and Versatel were found to be the most important transit ASes for intra-DE communication. Multilateral peering was seen to have dominant routing effects on the German Internet, but the degree of variable upstream selection strongly depends on the sector.

Our future work will extend the current results in both directions, structural analysis and further countries, including their interdependencies. We expect structural properties on a fine-grained basis. In addition, we will extend our analysis towards IPv6. Regarding integration, we will employ current aggregation techniques for ASes belonging to the same organization to derive a condensed national Internet AS ecosystem. Finally, we will also concentrate on the application of our work to existing monitoring systems (e.g., [18]), which may help to reduce complexity due to selected observation points.

Acknowledgements. We would like to thank Lixia Zhang, Jennifer Rexford, Rolf Winter, and the DENOG community for enlightening discussions on the intrinsic topic of Internet backbone routing, as well as Steve Uhlig for advices on a previous version of this paper. Sebastian Meiling and Andreas Krohn have importantly contributed to the creation and verification of the toolchain. This is gratefully acknowledged.

References

1. Slane, D.M., Bartholomew, C., et al.: 2010 Report to Congress, U.S.–China Economic and Security Review Commission, Annual Report (November 2010)
2. Karlin, J., Forrest, S., Rexford, J.: Nation-State Routing: Censorship, Wiretapping, and BGP. arXiv.org/CoRR, Tech. Rep. abs/0903.3218 (March 2009)
3. Roberts, H., Larochelle, D.: Mapping Local Internet Control. Berkman Center, Harvard University, Tech. Rep. (2010)
4. Faloutsos, M., Faloutsos, P., Faloutsos, C.: On Power-Law Relationships of the Internet Topology. In: Proc. of ACM SIGCOMM 1999, pp. 251–262. ACM (1999)
5. Govindan, R., Reddy, A.: An Analysis of Internet Inter-Domain Topology and Route Stability. In: Proc. of the IEEE INFOCOM 1997, pp. 850–857. ComSoc (1997)
6. Gao, L.: On Inferring Autonomous System Relationships in the Internet. IEEE/ACM Trans. Netw. 9(6), 733–745 (2001)
7. Zhou, S., Zhang, G.-Q., Zhang, G.-Q.: Chinese Internet AS-Level Topology. IET Communications 1(2), 209–214 (2007)
8. Dimitropoulos, X., Krioukov, D., Riley, G., Claffy, K.: Revealing the Autonomous System Taxonomy: The Machine Learning Approach. In: Allman, M., Roughan, M. (eds.) Proc. of the PAM Conf. 2006, pp. 91–100 (2006)
9. Internet Routing Registry (2010), http://www.irr.net
10. Cai, X., Heidemann, J., Krishnamurthy, B., Willinger, W.: Towards an AS-to-Organization Map. In: Proc. of the 10th ACM IMC, pp. 199–205. ACM (2010)
11. Team Cymru, http://www.cymru.com/
12. RIPE Routing Information Service (RIS), http://www.ripe.net/projects/ris/rawdata.html
13. MaxMind – GeoLite Country, http://www.maxmind.com

14. Zhang, B., Liu, R., Massey, D., Zhang, L.: Collecting the Internet AS-level Topology. ACM SIGCOMM CCR 35(1), 53–61 (2005)
15. Winter, R.: Modeling the Internet Routing Topology – In Less than 24h. In: Proc. of the 2009 ACM/IEEE/SCS 23rd PADS 2009, pp. 72–79. ComSoc (2009)
16. Internet AS-level topology construction & analysis, http://topology.neclab.eu/
17. Mahadevan, P., Krioukov, D., Fomenkov, M., Huffaker, B., Dimitropoulos, X., Claffy, K.C., Vahdat, A.: The Internet AS-Level Topology: Three Data Sources and One Definitive Metric. ACM SIGCOMM CCR 36(1), 17–26 (2006)
18. Chi, Y.-J., Oliveira, R., Zhang, L.: Cyclops: The AS-level Connectivity Observatory. SIGCOMM CCR 38(5), 5–16 (2008)

Behavior of DNS' Top Talkers, a `.com`/`.net` View

Eric Osterweil[1], Danny McPherson[1], Steve DiBenedetto[2],
Christos Papadopoulos[2], and Dan Massey[2]

[1] Verisign Labs
[2] Colorado State University

Abstract. This paper provides the first systematic study of DNS data taken from one of the 13 servers for the `.com`/`.net` registry. DNS' generic Top Level Domains (gTLDs) such `.com` and `.net` serve resolvers from throughout the Internet and respond to billions of DNS queries every day. This study uses gTLD data to characterize the DNS resolver population and profile DNS query types. The results show a small and relatively stable set of resolvers (i.e. the *top-talkers*) constitute 90% of the overall traffic. The results provide a basis for understanding for this critical Internet service, insights on typical resolver behaviors and the use of IPv6 in DNS, and provides a foundation for further study of DNS behavior.

1 Introduction

The Domain Name System (DNS) [9] is one of the Internet's core protocols and is essential to looking up Internet resources. The DNS translates names to IP addresses, identifies the SMTP servers for email addresses, and provides a wide range of other mappings. Virtually every Internet application depends on some form of DNS data, and this makes it critical Internet infrastructure.

In addition, the DNS is also quite flexible and extensible. It has been extended to include security extensions[4] and the IETF has multiple working groups investigating new uses [1,2]. Researchers are investigating both DNS behaviors and the potential impact of design changes[11,3,7,5]. Characterizing the use of the DNS at the top level can be quite useful for anyone trying to understand the global DNS or add new extensions to this critical service. However, there are still many aspects of the DNS that have yet to be investigated. These missing pieces are not simply corner cases. To the contrary, top level DNS domains such as `.com` and `.net` are some of the largest and most widely used DNS zones, but relatively little is known about their characteristics and the characteristics of their client resolvers. In fact, due to the caching behavior of DNS, large TLD zones see more traffic diversity than even the root zone. Thus, observations from the largest TLDs (`.com` and `.net`) offer the greatest aggregate view of global DNS traffic. We discuss this further in Section 2. There are no profiles of the resolvers contacting these TLDs and no profiles to provide even basic information such as the types, names, and frequencies of queries.

In this paper we present the first study of all resolver query traffic seen by `g.gtld-servers.net` (G GTLD), a unicast instance of one of the 13 sites serving

N. Taft and F. Ricciato (Eds.): PAM 2012, LNCS 7192, pp. 211–220, 2012.

the two largest TLDs in the Internet today: .com and .net. Our study uses data collected from the second quarter of 2011. To address confidentiality restrictions, we do not list specific dates in the graphs. By observing queries at the G GTLD server, one obtains a view of resolvers from throughout the Internet and observes clients ranging from the caching recursive resolvers of large ISPs to smaller *stub* client DNS tools running on end systems. The data volume to this single instance of the 13 .com/.net name server set was in excess of 900 million queries and roughly 900 thousand unique sources *per day*. These numbers represent typical daily traffic counts and do not include any large attack traffic. To the best of our knowledge, this is the largest study of resolver traffic and query patterns to date. We use this query traffic to create empirical profiles of all resolvers seen.

2   Background

The domain names in DNS form a tree-like hierarchical name space in which each node is called a *domain*. At the top of the tree, the root domain delegates authority to *Top Level Domains* (TLDs) like .com, .net, .org, and .edu. The .edu domain then delegates authority to create the colostate.edu domain, .com delegates authority to create verisigninc.com domain, and so forth. The repository of information that makes up the domain database is divided up into logical name spaces called *zones*, which each belongs to a single administrative authority and are each served by a set of *authoritative name servers*. The multiple servers for each zone provide redundancy and fault tolerance.

Clients that query for DNS information are called *resolvers*. Typically, an end system (desktop, laptop, smartphone, etc.) is called a *stub resolver* and only implements a very small portion of the DNS resolution process. These stubs are typically configured with the address of one or more local caching resolvers, to which they send all of their queries. The local caching resolver is configured with the IP addresses of the DNS root servers and if no other information is cached, the caching resolver starts by send a query to the root server. For example, to find the IP address for www.verisigninc.com, a caching resolver will first query a root server and the root server will refer the caching resolver to the .com servers. The caching resolver will then query one of the .com servers (for the entire domain name, www.verisigninc.com) who will refer the caching resolver to the verisigninc.com servers. Finally, the caching resolver will query one of the verisigninc.com servers who return the desired address for www.verisigninc.com (in the form of *Resource Records*, RRs).

Throughout this process, it is important to note a resolver may have the authoritative servers for popular TLDs in cache. The caching resolver learns of the .com servers upon its first query to ⟨anything⟩.com and should cache this information for two days (the TTL value specified in the RR). Thus in our example above, the caching resolver almost certainly does not start the query for www.verisigninc.com at the root servers. Instead, the caching resolver has cached the authoritative servers for .com and begins by querying one of these servers. This means that client resolvers will forward the first query for a Second Level Domain (SLD) to the Top Level Domain. Thus, traffic to .com will show a view of all active sub domains of .com. By contrast, none of these queries are sent to the root, because recursive resolvers will have already cached .com (a more specific match). This is why the largest TLDs (.com and .net) see much more traffic that even the root zone.

3   Profiling Resolvers

For the second quarter of 2011, we examined all DNS query traffic sent to g.gtld-servers.net (G GTLD); one of the authoritative name servers sites for .com and .net. This site is unicast from a prefix that is announced from California, in the USA. During this study we recorded pcap files from a SPAN port. Query types include A, AAAA, MX and all other DNS RR types that were actually seen. Query names were fully qualified DNS domain names such as www.somezone.com.

As one might expect, the G TLD server receives queries from millions of sources including institutional DNS resolvers, mail servers, polling systems, botnets, laptop users typing commands like dig, and so forth. In order better understand both DNS operations and the nature of query sources, we examined a set of DNS-specific features to help us quantifiably profile the resolvers observed in our study. Based on the scope of the .com and .net TLDs, we believe that these results provide the largest, most diverse, and perhaps the most detailed profile of global resolver behavior to date.

3.1   What We Can Observe

Due to the fact that our data is taken from a very large TLD registry, we generally do not expect to see end systems such as web browsers or smart phones in our study. This is because these stub resolvers typically send their queries to a local caching resolver. This local caching resolver will either service the request from its cache (if it can), or forward the request to the TLD (and then serve future requests for that name from its cache). Mapping between end system addresses and caching resolver addresses is of interest to services such as content distribution networks, and remains an open and active area of research[8]. However, our study does not make effort to map caching resolvers back to stubs.

While we will not see *every* caching resolver in the Internet, we do expect to see a large portion of the full list of caching resolvers that send traffic to .com or .net. In Section 2 we explained that resolvers query TLDs while looking for referrals. However, even though our data is only taken from one of the 13 sites that comprise these TLDs, we still claim that over time we will observe queries from almost all caching resolvers. This is because of a behavior we call *polling and pinning*.

There are several main variants of DNS resolvers that are commonly deployed today: ISC's BIND, NLnet Labs' unbound, PowerDNS, and Microsoft's DNS. Each of these servers attempts to provide its users with the fastest possible resolution. One way they do this is to measure (or *poll*) the Round Trip Time (RTT) to each authoritative name server for each DNS zone they query. Generally, they each have an algorithm to choose (or *pin* themselves to) a specific name server for each zone that appears to be responding the fastest. Furthermore, the polling process is generally ongoing so that the resolvers can adapt to changing network conditions and in some types of servers, the polling volume and frequency is amortized on existing query traffic. As a result, we expect that over time, every resolver that uses this approach will send at least polling queries to our monitored G GTLD site, and sometimes polling will result in a resolver changing its selection and re-pinning itself to a new server.

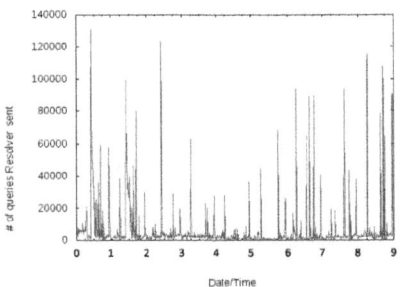 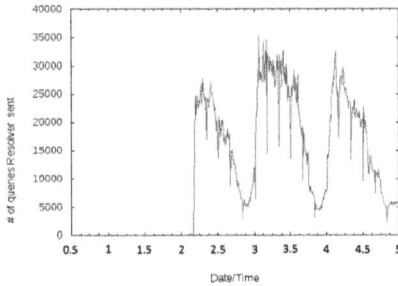

(a) This resolver periodically sends bursts as it pins/unpins itself to the G server.

(b) This resolver polls briefly and then 2 days later pins itself to G with a diurnal pattern.

Fig. 1. Pinning and polling behavior of two resolvers

For example, Figure 1(a) shows the polling behavior of one resolver over the course of five days. Figure 1(b) shows a resolver that had been seen polling at a very low rate and volume for two days before re-pinning itself from another server instance to G GTLD. We can see that server selection does occur, but the approach for selecting an authoritative server is implementation dependent and even varies between versions of the same implementation[6]. Some implementations may simply select a preferred server and pin themselves to the server without polling the zone's other authoritative servers. A complete discussion of server selection is beyond the scope of this paper, but more information can be found in [12,10].

3.2   Who Talks to the G GTLD Server?

Figures 2(a) and 2(b) provide a high level overview of the sources sending queries to the G GTLD server. Figure 2(a) is a Hilbert graph showing the location of all sources that contacted the G GTLD server during one example ten minute

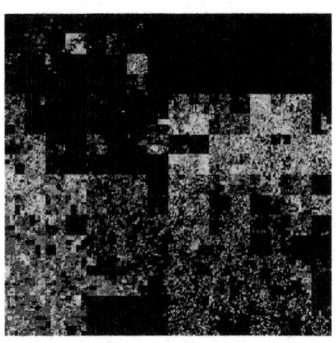

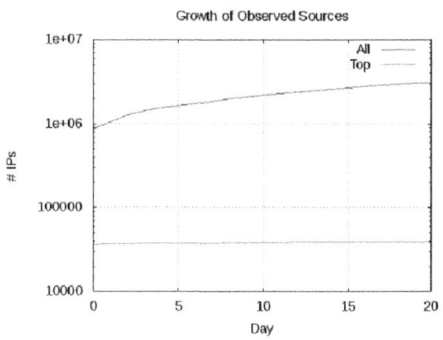

(a) Location of Sources Querying G   (b) Cumulative Number of Sources Sending Queries

Fig. 2. Who is querying g.gtld-servers.net

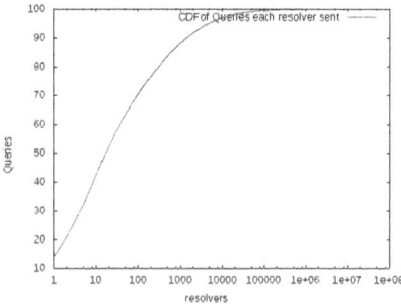

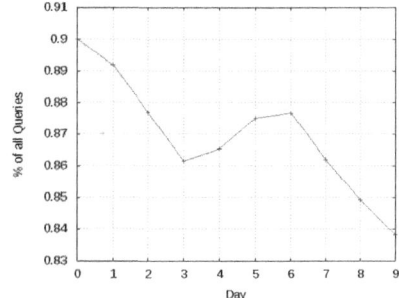

(a) Resolver Query Rates: A relatively small number of resolvers account for 90% of all Queries

(b) A static top-talkers list (rather than rolling) accounts for less of the overall traffic after 10 days (note the the y-offset from 0)

Fig. 3. Query rates and top-talkers

period. This Hilbert graph divides the Internet IPv4 address space into /16 address blocks. The color indicates the volume of coming from that address block. The large empty spaces correspond to unallocated or inactive address. For example, the upper right corner of the graph corresponds to the multicast address space; which should not be used as the source in any DNS queries. The main point of the figure is that, even in a relatively short ten minute span, the G GTLD server does indeed serve the global Internet. This figure is very similar during other periods.

The top curve in Figure 2(b) shows the cumulative number of source addresses over a 20 day period. We can see that initially there is a brief super-linear learning phase. This is a cold-cache artifact of our measurements, and shows that some query sources have longer inter-query periods, and take longer to appear in our measurements. By contrast, active caching resolvers from campus networks, organizations, and ISPs are frequently querying the .com and .net zones and quickly appear in our data set. Caching resolvers that serve smaller user bases send less frequent queries and likely make up the population of resolvers that take longer to appear. Inactivity due to time of day and caching resolver polling behavior (discussed above) can also delay the time it takes for the G GTLD server to observe the first query from a caching resolver.

Following the initial learning phase, the figure shows there is a constant growth of unique IP sources. Even 20 days into the study, the G GTLD server continues to discover new resolvers at a rapid pace (note the log scale). There are many legitimate explanations for resolvers growth such as a network administrator configuring a new resolver, a user may use the dig command to send a query directly to G GTLD server, a DNS monitoring tool may query G GTLD server. There are also illegitimate behaviors in this growth such as bots directed to send attack traffic and attacks using spoofed addresses. As one may expect, a large portion of the "slow to appear" legitimate sources send a very small amount of traffic; many as little as a single query. In contrast, resolvers that send a high volume of queries during some period are classified as *top-talkers* and we examine this group in more detail.

3.3   Query Volume and Top-Talkers

While the set of all resolvers numbers in the millions and continues to grow in our study, Figure 3(a) shows 90% of the overall traffic is generated by just under 40,000 resolvers. This indicates that the large-scale behavior seen at the .com/.net TLDs is dictated by a relatively small number of query sources. We call these resolvers *top-talkers*. The lower flat line in Figure 2(b) shows the cumulative number of *top-talkers* and indicates that top-talkers are discovered quickly. The set of *top-talkers* is also dynamic, as the behaviors of resolvers change over time. There are long term structural changes where new resolvers are added, old resolvers are retired, users migrate, and new services are provisioned. In addition, there are observable shorter term patterns as load changes due to the time of day, the day of the week, and even due to routing changes. To account for the long term structural changes and shorter term patterns, we developed a rolling list of *top-talkers* where at any given moment the list is based on the previous seven days of data.

In order to see the dynamism in this list, we first compared two top-talkers list from different months. At the beginning of one month, the top-talker list included 39,304 source IP addresses. At the beginning of the following month, the top-talker list included 39,936 sources. 30,071 of the sources were common to both lists. Next, a separate examination (seen in Figure 3(b)) found that the accuracy of a top-talkers list degraded daily if it was *not* continually updated. By definition, the top-talker list initially accounts for 90% of all queries seen on day 0. As seen in Figure 3(b), if we keep the list fixed, the top-talker list accounts for only 84% of all queries seen on day 10.

3.4   Query Type Profiling

Figure 4(b) shows the distribution of query types over our study period. The figure shows queries for IPv4 addresses (type A) clearly dominate. IPv6 addresses (AAAA) are the second most popular type requested and requested more frequently than mail server (MX) records. Other types including DNSSEC record types[4], service location (SRV) record types, and even obsolete A6[1] records are all observed in Figure 4(a), but we can see that they constitute only small portion of the the query traffic. Note the type distribution is roughly the same for top-talkers and the entire set of query sources.

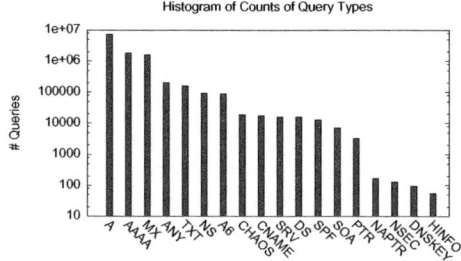 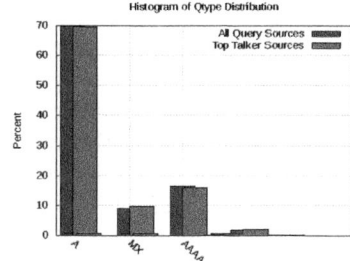

(a) Full qtype distribution of all qtypes seen (note log-scale).

(b) Qtype distribution for all sources and top-talkers.

Fig. 4. Qtype histograms

To help digest the query type behaviors of resolvers, we developed a profiling scheme, seen in Figure 5(a). This figure shows the profile types and also shows how both resolvers and total queries distribute across the profiles during one study day (though the distribution on other days is similar). The top node in the tree shows that we observed 975,391,055 queries from 958,558 distinct addresses.

In the figure, the line thickness of the node's border is proportional to the percent of resolvers that fall into the node. The top node includes all resolvers and has the thickest line. The leaf node second from the left still accounts for a substantial percentage of all resolvers and has a proportional thickness. Very few resolvers fall into the rightmost leaf node and it is proportionally less thick.

Our profile begins by considering whether the resolver sent any A record queries, the most popular type observed in our study. 94.07% of all resolvers observed on this day sent at least one query for A records. These 901,762 resolvers next split into two nearly equal groups. 55.63% of these resolvers also sent queries for AAAA records and 44.37% never requested an AAAA record.

Profiling resolver behaviors can help one detect unexpected behaviors or attacks, better simulate resolvers, and analyze DNS behaviors. For example, this distribution has implications for issues such as tracking the IPv6 deployment

---

[1] A6 was an alternate IPv6 address format and moved to experimental status in 2002, see http://www.ietf.org/mail-archive/web/dnsop/current/msg05437.html

progress. It is encouraging that over half of resolvers that request IPv4 addresses also request IPv6. However, this DNS query behavior does not directly translate to IPv6 usage. For example, many operating systems and versions of web browsers, automatically request both IPv4 and IPv6 addresses. Thus, these systems may request both IPv4 and IPv6 addresses in parallel, thus causing the local resolver resend both. Corresponding behavior is observed in the data; a query for the IPv4 address of `www.somezone.com` is followed in close succession by a query, from the same source, asking for the IPv6 address of the same name. Interestingly, there were 40,211 resolvers whose DNS queries were for IPv6 `AAAA`s only. These 40,211 resolvers sent a combined 122,998 queries and yet never request a single IPv4 address. Again, note this is the behavior observed from the TLD and does not definitively show these resolvers are IPv6 only.

Completing our query type profile, the bottom row of the tree considers whether a resolver sends queries for `MX` records. The leftmost leaf node in Figure 5(a) are resolvers that send `A`, `AAAA`, and `MX` queries. For example, one type of resolver that fits in this group is the resolver for a small or medium company. The company caching resolver supports users who request both `A` and `AAAA` as well as the company mail server that requests `MX` records. Note there are also many other examples of resolvers that can fit this profile. Another resolver that fits this group may be a mail server that does its own DNS resolution; the `MX` records are requested by the mail server and `A`/`AAAA` queries are for those servers.

Finally, it has been said that virtually all types of behavior that can occur in the Internet will occur at some point. The rightmost leaf node would support this statement. We observe DNS resolvers that do not request any `A`, `AAAA`, or `MX` records but *do* query for other types of records. On this day, there were 10,658 such resolvers. Examples of the resolvers here include various DNS monitoring tools that may solely check for DNS name server (`NS`) records or DNSSEC records or other specialized features. The data in Figure 5(a) includes all resolvers, even resolvers that sent only one query during the day. This one query may happen to be polling and may happen to request say `TXT` record. In fact, the low volume talkers could potentially skew the numbers in any one of the nodes.

Figure 5(b) shows the profile (on the same day) for only the top-talkers. The restriction to top-talkers still covers 90% of the traffic, but reduces the total number of resolvers from over 900,000 to under 40,000. Note the top-talkers are more likely to request `AAAA` records in addition to `A`. Of all top-talkers, over 80% of the resolvers who request IPv4 records also request IPv6 records. This can be partly explained by polling by resolvers. Consider a resolver who has selected a server other than G as its preferred `.com`/`.net` server. Further suppose during the day that this resolver sends one poll query to G GTLD server. The poll query is chosen from the existing queries sent by the caching resolver and the most popular query type is `A`. If the one poll query is sent during the the day is an `A` query, to G it will appear the caching resolver is only requesting `A` records. Similarly, if this one query happens to be an `AAAA` query, to the G GTLD server it will appear the caching resolver is only requesting `AAAA` records. Top talkers send large numbers of queries and their profiles are more likely to be an accurate reflection of the resolver type distribution.

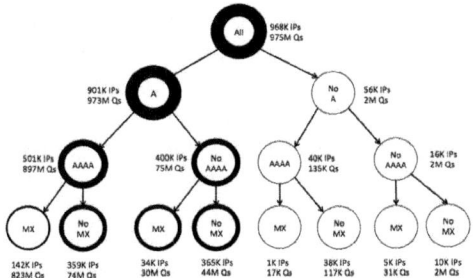

(a) Resolver Query Type Profiles - Includes All Resolvers

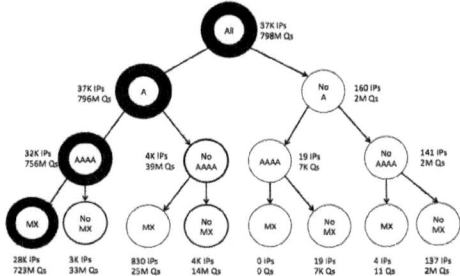

(b) Resolver Query Type Profiles - Includes Only Top-Talkers

Fig. 5. Resolver taxonomy

This classification scheme proves to be useful. In the case of A6 queries, this technique can be used to identify specific types of resolvers.

4   Conclusions and Future Work

In this paper we present what we believe to be the first analysis of DNS query traffic at one of the .com/.net TLD server sites. Our analysis includes characterization of the IP addresses of the DNS resolver population, the distribution of query volume including the top-talkers, and query type profiling.

The motivation for our analysis is to define and understand important features of normal resolvers. However, this immediately begs the questions: how does one define a "normal" resolver (vs. the numerous other sources of DNS traffic), and how important is this distinction? Analysis of query types provides insights on issues ranging from identifying typical resolver behaviors to the use of IPv6 in DNS. What we found is that resolvers display an interesting *pinning and polling* behavior pattern, the query type distribution highlights just three types as the main targets of traffic, and that the prominence of A6 queries demonstrates the old Internet adage that, "nothing ever really dies in the Internet."

Our results indicate that of all of the hundreds of millions of queries seen at this one instance of the .com/.net name servers, the bulk of them come from a relatively small and dynamic group. Under 40,000 resolvers account for the 90% of the traffic and this set of *top talkers* evolves daily. Based on these measurements we conclude that when measuring large-scale DNS behaviors, the top-talkers dominate the observed behavior and serve as a useful low-pass filter when trying to characterize typical traffic patterns. For example, many clients were seen to have issued a single query during our measurement period. Indeed, including the non-top-talkers in analysis of (say) average query rates of caching resolvers skews the results. The top-talkers allow our results to focus on typical, well-maintained, and active resolvers when determining the global behaviors.

The dynamism in the list of top-talkers presents several interesting open questions: how does the top-talker list cutoff of 90% compare with other values (such as 80%, 95%, 99%, etc.), can the sources that migrate out of the top-talkers list for G GTLD be seen to pin to another instance, and is there a stable global set of top-talkers? This is future work that we have already begun to investigate.

References

1. DNS-based Authentication of Named Entites (DANE),
   https://datatracker.ietf.org/wg/dane/charter/
2. Electronic Numbering (ENUM), http://tools.ietf.org/wg/enum/
3. Ager, B., Mühlbauer, W., Smaragdakis, G., Uhlig, S.: Comparing DNS Resolvers in the Wild. In: Proceedings of ACM IMC 2010, Melbourne, Australia (November 2010)
4. Arends, R., Austein, R., Larson, M., Massey, D., Rose, S.: Protocol Modifications for the DNS Security Extensions. RFC 4035 (March 2005)
5. Brownlee, N., Nemeth, E.: Dns measurements at a root server. In: Proceedings of IEEE Global Telecommunications Conference, Globecom 2001 (2001)
6. Internet Software Consortium. ISC BIND Features,
   http://www.isc.org/software/bind/new-features/11.6/
7. Jung, J., Sit, E., Balakrishnan, H., Morris, R.: DNS Performance and the Effectiveness of Caching. In: Internet Measurement Workshop (2001)
8. Mao, Z.M., Cranor, C.D., Douglis, F., Rabinovich, M., Spatscheck, O., Wang, J.: A precise and efficient evaluation of the proximity between web clients and their local dns servers. In: USENIX Annual Technical Conference (2002)
9. Mockapetris, P., Dunlap, K.J.: Development of the domain name system. In: SIGCOMM 1988 (1988)
10. NLnet Labs. unbound DNS resolver, http://www.unbound.net/documentation/
11. Osterweil, E., Ryan, M., Massey, D., Zhang, L.: Quantifying the operational status of the dnssec deployment. In: IMC 2008 (2008)
12. Wang, X., Wang, Z., Lee, X.: Analyzing bind dns server selection algorithm. International Journal of Innovative Computing, Information and Control (2010)

The BIZ Top-Level Domain: Ten Years Later

Tristan Halvorson[1], Janos Szurdi[2], Gregor Maier[3], Mark Felegyhazi[2],
Christian Kreibich[3], Nicholas Weaver[3], Kirill Levchenko[1], and Vern Paxson[3]

[1] UC San Diego
[2] CrySyS Lab., Budapest University of Technology and Economics
[3] International Computer Science Institute

Abstract. On May 15, 2001 ICANN announced the introduction of the biz and
info generic top-level domains (gTLDs)—the first new gTLDs since the incep-
tion of the Domain Name System—aiming to "increase consumer choice and
create opportunities for entities that have been shut out under the current name
structure." The biz gTLD, in particular, was to become an alternative to the popular com top-level domain.

In this paper we examine the current usage of the biz gTLD in order to determine whether it has evolved into the role intended by ICANN, and whether
concerns expressed in the early discussions of this expansion have been justified.
In particular, using DNS zone files, DNS probing, and Web crawler data, we attempt to answer the question of whether biz has become a viable alternative to
com, giving trademark holders who find themselves unable to register a com name
an attractive alternative; or whether it has merely induced defensive registrations
by existing trademark holders who already had equivalent com domains.

1 Introduction

The Domain Name System (DNS) serves as the main means of giving names to entities
on the Internet. Now over 25 years old, its original goal was to provide a way to consistently map host names to IP addresses. Since then, DNS has grown to identify the
Internet presence of brands, companies, products, political campaigns, and individuals.

Compared to other means of navigating the Internet, DNS has a very rigid lookup
structure: a user must know the name precisely and completely in order to perform a
lookup. While search engines provide a more flexible navigation mechanism, we still
perceive the need for a direct mechanism like the domain system: one that remains
free of third-party mediation, succinct enough to allow expression in print, and easy for
users to act on.

In part for historic reasons, DNS is arranged hierarchically: names associate with a
suffix, usually a top-level domain (TLD). The original DNS design included generic
TLDs (gTLDs) (com, edu, etc.) following administrative considerations, matching the
classes of organizations with Internet hosts to name. The growth of the Web created
the need to name not individual hosts but broader entities. Of the original gTLDs, com
proved the most open and best suited choice, becoming the de facto TLD for Web
addresses.

To the average user, com became synonymous with the Web, its iconic status earning
it a place in the Oxford English Dictionary in 1994. As a consequence of its popularity, the com landscape quickly became crowded. To ease the pressure on com, ICANN

N. Taft and F. Ricciato (Eds.): PAM 2012, LNCS 7192, pp. 221–230, 2012.

moved to create more gTLDs, introducing `biz` and `info` in 2001. The success of this endeavor hinged on how users would perceive TLDs: whether users accepted the notion of TLDs as simply reflecting different potential homes for various Internet entities, or whether they viewed "dot com" as the sole TLD where they would expect to find prominent Web enterprises. Would users find it confusing to encounter the same subdomain in different TLDs?

A decade has passed since, and ICANN now promotes a new, more open system for introducing new TLDs which could dramatically change the Domain Name System. To answer some of these questions, and to re-evaluate some early predictions, this paper takes stock of the `biz` gTLD, which largely promoted as an alternative to `com`. We find that approximately 20% of domains in both `biz` and `com` are *parked*, contrary to original intention to avoid domain speculation in `biz`. Furthermore, between 10% and 25% of `biz` registrations appear only to exist to defend against name infringement.

The rest of this paper proceeds as follows. Section 2 gives a background on the `biz` TLD with a survey of related work. Section 3 describes our data collection methodology, followed by our analysis in Section 4, and a brief discussion of our findings in Section 5. Section 6 concludes the paper.

2   Background

In June 1998, the US Department of Commerce called for the creation of a new not-for-profit organization to assume responsibility for the technical coordination functions performed by the IANA. Later that year, the Internet Corporation for Assigned Names and Numbers (ICANN) was formed to fulfill that role. ICANN obtained "the authority to manage and perform a specific set of functions related to coordination of the domain name system, including the authority necessary to ... oversee policy for determining the circumstances under which new TLDs are added to the root system" [8]. In 1999 ICANN formed the Domain Name Supporting Organization (DNSO), an advisory body within ICANN, to handle matters concerning the Domain Name System [6], chartering, within the DNSO, Working Group C to study the issues surrounding the formation of new generic top-level domains (gTLDs). The Working Group's task was to gauge the need for new gTLDs, and, if deemed required, to determine what should be their nature and deployment policy [3]. In March 2000 Working Group C released its final report, addressing these questions [10]. The ICANN board adopted its recommendations in July 2000 [5].

2.1   The Working Group C Report

The Working Group C report [10] addressed two important questions: whether to create new gTLDs, and, if so, how to introduce them. On the need for new gTLDs, the report argued: "Expanding the number of TLDs will increase consumer choice, and create opportunities for entities that have been shut out under the current name structure." Moreover, the report observes:

> Existing second-level domain names under the .com TLD routinely change hands for enormously inflated prices. These are legitimate trades of ordinary, untrademarked words;

their high prices reflect the artificial scarcity of common names in existing gTLDs, and
the premium on .com names in particular.

...

If the name space is expanded, companies will be able to get easy-to-remember domain
names more easily, and the entry barriers to successful participation in electronic commerce will be lowered. *Addition of new TLDs will allow different companies to have the
same second-level domain name in different TLDs* (emphasis added).

Arguing against the consensus position of the report, some members of the Working
Group suggested that "an increase in the number of top-level domains could confuse
consumers," and that expanding the domain space "will likely increase trademark owners' policing costs and the costs of defensive registrations." Members expressed concerns about *"trademark holders simply duplicating their existing domains"* (emphasis
added).

On the nature of the initial rollout, the report weighed two opposing approaches: au-
thorizing "hundreds of new TLDs over the course of the next few years" and introducing
new TLDs "slowly and in a controlled manner, and only after effective trademark protection mechanisms had been implemented and shown to be effective." In arguing for
the introduction of many new TLDs, some members argued that "a small number of new
gTLDs with no commitment to add more ... *would encourage pre-emptive and speculative registrations based on the possibility of continued artificial scarcity"* (emphasis
added). The report ultimately proposed "deploying six to ten new TLDs."

2.2   Recent Studies

In its recent move to open TLD registration to the general public, ICANN commis-
sioned several reports analyzing the economic consequences of their new initiative.
Among other concerns, the reports address the danger that new gTLDs will compel
trademark holders to defensively register their marks in each new TLD. The 2009 Carlton report [2] dismisses this as a problem, arguing that "many registrations that 'redirect
traffic' to other sites serve productive purposes of attracting and retaining Internet traffic, not merely to prevent cybersquatting." Furthermore, the report argues: "While some
of the registrations for domain names under the new gTLDs may have been made for
defensive purposes, the limited number of registrations for new gTLDs indicates that
the vast majority of .com registrants did not find a compelling reason to undertake defensive registrations in the new gTLDs." The 2010 Katz, Rosston, Sullivan report [7]
looked back at past TLD introductions: "A broad look at the evidence to date suggests
that other gTLDs provide little competition for .com as those gTLDs have neither attracted a large number of domains nor shown any signs of catching up with .com."[1]

Most closely related to our work is the 2002 survey of biz registrations by Zittrain
and Edelman [11]. They found that 90.5% of names registered in biz also occur in com
(consistent with our finding). To assess whether biz and com registrants overlapped, the
survey authors examined Whois records, comparing records based on registrant postal
code, email address, and name server second-level domains. They found that 35.4% of
biz-com pairs matched in at least one attribute, 25.8% in two, and 12.9% in all three.

---

[1] The report also notes that "the prospects of cyber-squatting within new gTLDs could force
parties to undertake defensive registrations."

3   Data and Methodology

This paper aims to answer two basic questions: how do owners of biz domains use their domains, and, if in active use, whether the biz domain forms the *primary* domain of the registrant or whether it merely *defends* one registered under another gTLD. To start, we obtained the biz and com zone files, dated June 27, 2011, to coincide with the 10-year anniversary of the biz TLD's addition to the authoritative root server. We use three sets of domain names: all 2.1 million biz domains, their 2 million (94%) com namesakes, and a random sample of 2 million com domains. We rely on four sources of data to classify domains: zone files, active DNS queries, Whois registration records, and Web content.

3.1   Zone Files

A zone file contains the DNS records used by a name server, typically in BIND format. We obtained the zone files for the biz and com gTLDs from their respective registries. We used the zone files to get the list of biz and com domains and determine which domains were registered in both gTLDs. We also gathered their name server information for the DNS crawler.

3.2   Whois

We retrieved the whois registration information for each biz–com pair in our data set. Since whois records consist of free-form text, we use a customized version of phpwhois[2] to parse the whois records and extract the domain registrant (owner) information. Many registrars have limits on the number of whois queries they will answer. Additionally, phpwhois could not parse all whois entries. Due to these limitations, we could only extract registrant information from 65% of our biz–com pairs.

In order to assess whether the biz domain and its com namesake share the same owner, we compare the registrant information returned by phpwhois. We first exclude domains that use whois privacy mechanisms (e.g., the Domains by Proxy service). We compute the Levenshtein distance between both domains for each of: the registrant's name, e-mail address, phone, and fax number. We mark each of these fields as missing if they are absent or less than 5 characters long in either domain. We mark a field as a match if present and the Levenshtein distance between biz and com does not exceed 2 (requiring an exact match does not significantly alter our results). We also mark registrant names as a match if the name from one domain forms a substring of the other domain.

We consider two whois records a strong match if at least two of the four categories match and at most one category is missing. We consider them a weak match if any of the four categories match. We use both types of matches, but differentiate between them in our analysis.

We note that for a significant number of com domains, the whois record we retrieved only contained the registrant name but no further fields. We therefore cannot have a strong match for any of these domains.

---

[2] http://sourceforge.net/projects/phpwhois/

3.3 DNS Probing

We queried the DNS records for a list of all `biz` domains and their `com` counterparts, as well as the randomly selected set of `com` domains. For each name, we queried (starting at the root) to find the authoritative name servers for the `biz` and `com` versions of the domain. We performed the crawling with a custom Python library on September 12th and 13th, 2011.

3.4 Web Crawl

We collected the content of the web pages belonging to the registered domain in our data sets. First, we downloaded the pages for the domains in the `biz` zone file, e.g., `foo.biz`. Then, we crawled the corresponding `com` domain `foo.com` to check the registration purpose for the biz domain. When downloading the web pages, we recorded the HTTP status codes for success, redirection, errors and other standardized events. We also recorded unknown errors. Note that at times we could not retrieve the Web pages, either because the domains' owners want to serve no Web content, or due to the time interval (several months) between the zone file creation and our active Web crawling.

3.5 Content Classification

To identify parked domains, we built a simple classifier that searches for a set of regular expressions in the downloaded content. We created highly specific patterns to match templates for the largest known parking sites. We relied on unique features of the page, such as JavaScript libraries or image servers used by the parked pages.

4 Analysis

Recall that we set out to evaluate a number of predictions made about the effects of introducing a new gTLD: whether it would lead to "trademark holders simply duplicating their existing domains" or "will allow different companies to have the same second-level domain name in different TLDs"; whether it "would encourage pre-emptive and speculative registrations based on the possibility of continued artificial scarcity" [10]. To answer these questions, we first group `biz` domains into three functional categories:

Primary. *Primary* domains identify a company, product, service, or organization, either publicly or internally. In other words, the registrant *actually uses* primary domains. For example, NeuStar, Inc. and UC San Diego use `neustar.biz` and `ucsd.edu`, respectively, as the primary domain names by which they identify themselves on the Internet.

Defensive. A registrant uses a domain registration only to *defend* a name while not actively employing the domain to identify itself, its service, or network resources. Examples of defensive registrations are `google.biz` and `gooogle.com`, both of which redirect to `google.com`.

Parked. Registrants *park* domains with the purpose of reselling them or generating advertising revenue from accidental user visits to the site.

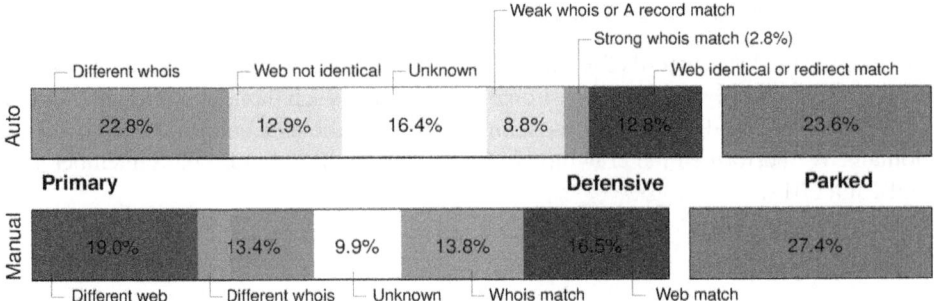

Fig. 1. Disposition of `biz` domain names with respect to their `com` namesakes based on our automatic classification (top) and manual classification of a sample of 485 domains (bottom). Excludes 6.2% of `biz` domains without a corresponding `com` namesake. Darker bands indicate higher confidence.

Defensive registrations prevent another party from misrepresenting itself as the registrant or from simply capturing traffic (intended for the registrant) for advertising purposes. A defensively registered domain is one not used by the registrant to name and identify products, services, or network infrastructure.[3]

Although it is nearly impossible to divine the registrant's intention with absolute certainty, certain network-visible characteristics of a domain serve as indicators of primary or defensive use. In particular, we consider domain ownership, Web content, and hosting infrastructure sharing as indicators of primary or secondary use. Our results are summarized in Figure 1.

4.1   Parked Domains

A parked domain is not actively used by the registrant, and does not represent a name or brand used by the registrant. Registrants typically hold parked domains with the intention of selling them at a profit or monetizing accidental Web traffic through advertising. Parked domains are easily identified by prominent advertising on the domain's site that one may purchase the domain and usually includes additional advertising.

We rely on the Web content hosted at the domain as our primary indicator of a parked domain. Table 1 shows the proportion of parked sites in the `biz` and `com` gTLDs. Figure 1 shows the number of parked `biz` domains (23.6%) having a `com` namesake.

4.2   Identical Web Content

Owners of defensively registered domains frequently reroute all Web traffic to the intended (primary) domain, usually via HTTP redirection [4]. Because the browser

---

[3] The difference between a defensive registration and either cybersquatting or typosquatting (registering misspellings of popular brands) lies in the identity of the registrant: when the registrant also owns the intended brand name or trademark, the registration is defensive; when the registrant is a third party with no legitimate claim to the name, the registration constitutes cybersquatting or typosquatting.

Table 1. The Web behavior of domains in the biz and com gTLDs. The biz column shows statistics for the 2.1 million domains in the biz TLD, the com column for a random sample of 2 million com domains.

Category	biz	com
No server	23.5%	17.4%
HTTP Error	3.4%	3.3%
Parked	22.8%	19.4%
Redirect	18.5%	17.3%
On-site	5.1%	8.5%
Namesake	4.1%	0.4%
Other site	9.1%	8.7%
Content served	31.7%	39.9%
Same as com	3.0%	—
Distinct	27.7%	—

Table 2. Comparison of registrants of biz domains and their com namesakes using Whois records, showing absolute and relative number of biz–com name pairs in each category. Rightmost column shows value relative to total number of biz–com name pairs (93.8% of biz names)

Category	Abs	Rel
Unknown	693,393	35.1%
Privacy guard	281,417	14.2%
biz only	97,802	5.0%
com only	82,161	4.2%
both	101,454	5.1%
Match	424,683	21.5%
Weak	308,337	15.6%
Strong	116,346	5.9%
No match	573,388	29.1%

actively follows HTTP redirects, this method has the advantage of changing the user-visible address bar to reflect the new address (the target of the redirect). The user thus sees the *correct* address, consistent with the branding of the site.

Table 1 includes statistics about this mechanism: 18.5% of biz and 17.3% of com domains host a Web server that redirects the user. However, 4.1% of biz sites redirect to a site hosted at the same domain name in a different TLD, compared to 0.4% for com. We also see defensive registrations where both the biz and com Web servers redirect a user to the same third domain. In our set of domains in both biz and com, 6.1% have identical redirects.

Despite the effectiveness of HTTP redirects and their advantage of "correcting" the user, site operators also may simply maintain identical Web sites under both domains. To detect this condition, we compared the content of each biz site to that of its com namesake. Upon examination, we found that 3.0% of non-parked sites did indeed serve the same content. We only classify pages as identical if the source matches exactly, meaning a match almost certainly indicates a defensive registration, but a mismatch only weakly indicates a primary one.

As shown in the dark red portion of Figure 1, 12.8% of biz–com domains have identical web content or redirects, a strong indicator of a defensive registration. 12.9% of biz–com domains have different web content and no stronger classifiers, and so are weakly classified as primary registrations.

4.3   Common Registrant

The identity of the registrant provides another classification feature. One registrant owning both a biz domain as well as its com namesake likely suggests defensive registration. To identify such cases, we extracted registrant information from publicly available Whois records, as described in Section 3.2.

We could retrieve and successfully parse both Whois records for 65% of all biz–com pairs.[4] Of these 65%, 10.1% of biz domains and 9.3% of com domains showed some manner of "privacy protection" mechanism, blocking the registrant information from appearing in the Whois record and leaving 50.6% of all biz–com pairs that could potentially match.

We grouped these pairs into three categories based on the degree to which we believed we identified the same registrants: weak matches, strong matches, and no match. Using the methodology described in Section 3.2, we determine 5.9% of pairs a strong match, another 15.6% a weak match, and 29.1% unlikely to be the same registrant. (Put another way, we found at least some degree of a match for around 40% of the pairs we could assess.)

As shown in Figure 1, we consider whois data to be more reliable than common hosting or different web content, since either of those may be incidental. We consider it to be less reliable than HTTP redirects and identical web content, since those are strong indicators of a defensive registration. After using stronger indicators, we classify 11.6% of biz domains as defensive based on whois and A record data (see Section 4.4) and 22.8% as likely primary.

4.4   Shared Infrastructure

We also used DNS crawling to observe infrastructure sharing between a biz domain and its com counterpart. In particular, we used CNAMEs and common A records as evidence of defensive registrations.

We identify a CNAME match in two different cases: first, when domains in both biz and com have CNAMEs pointing to the same domain; second, when the domain in biz has a CNAME pointing to its com namesake, or vice versa. Of the 2 million domains in both biz and com, 32,431 (1.6%) show common CNAMEs, which demonstrates a clear relationship between the two domains. We include these in the "redirect match" category in Figure 1.

We see many more domains with common A records. Our crawler observed common A records in 439,890 domains (22%) between biz and their com counterparts. We see three plausible explanations for such sharing: first, defensive registrations; second, coincidental common hosting, with unrelated owners of the biz and com employing common hosting infrastructure; third and finally, parking the biz and com domains in the same domain parking infrastructure. Since we classify parked domains first and only distinguish between primary and defensive registrations after considering all parked domains, we can ignore the third case.

While common A records do suggest a defensive registration, we cannot reliably distinguish true sharing and common hosting. Because of this, we consider common A records weak evidence of a defensive registration.

---

[4] The delegated nature of the com Whois system means that these 65% necessarily constitute a biased sample, because being able to retrieve and parse a given Whois record depends on the registrar, specifically on their query rate limitations and record formatting.

5   Discussion

Our analysis finds 22.8% of biz domains *parked* with a known parking service. We can with certainty classify another 12.8% of biz domains as *defensive* registrations, leaving two thirds undetermined. At least 27.7% of these served some kind of content (excluding cases where this content proved identical to the com namesake). In addition, of the pairs for which we could assess non-private registrant information, we found at least a degree of match between the biz and com registration in 40% of the instances (§ 4.3), indicating a substantial level of registrations likely made defensively.

To get at the fundamental value (to registrants) of the biz TLD, we can approach the question from the other direction: how many biz domains do registrants use actively? We assessed the popularity of biz domains in the Alexa [1] Web site rankings, as well as the popularity of biz domains in the Open Directory Project [9]. We show the results in Table 3, along with other common TLDs.

Table 3. TLD frequency in the Alexa listings and the Open Directory Project. In the Alexa 1,000,000, biz ranks (in frequency of occurrence) between com.cn and ir, while in the ODP, it falls between cat and za. Only one biz domain, livedoor.biz (a blogging site), resides in the Alexa 500.

TLD	Alexa 1M	Alexa 500	ODP
com	55.3%	64.6%	41.7%
net	6.26%	4.60%	3.74%
org	4.01%	2.80%	9.00%
ru	3.75%	2.40%	1.46%
de	3.70%	1.40%	9.33%
info	1.82%	0%	0.480%
biz	0.396%	0.200%	0.188%

The biz TLD occurs 140 times less frequently than com in the Alexa 1 million, 323 times less frequently in the Alexa 500 (based on 1 occurrence), and 218 times less frequently in the Open Directory Project. Note that the com zone is about 46 times larger than biz. Although not a formal assessment of usage, these statistics suggest a disproportionally lower popularity of biz compared to com.

6   Conclusion

In this paper we examined the current state of the biz TLD on its ten-year anniversary. We found that in many respects, most notably in the prevalence of domain speculation (parking), biz resembles com. And while one could conclude that it has failed to rival com, biz did extract defensive registrations from existing domain owners. Although registering these domains costs no more than $10 each, this cost is dwarfed by the additional costs of defending trademarks (via resolution procedures and litigation) in a new TLD.

On the eve of a bold new initiative by ICANN to open TLD registration to the general public, biz provides a valuable lesson in the costs and benefits associated with expanding the DNS name space. In particular, we anticipate a level of defensive registrations that, in aggregate, will reflect significant imposed expenditures.

Acknowledgements. This work was supported in part by the National Science Foundation under grants CNS-0905631 and CNS-1111672; by the Office of Naval Research under MURI Grant No. N000140911081; and a fellowship within the postdoctoral program of the German Academic Exchange Service (DAAD). This work is connected also to the scientific program of the "Development of quality-oriented and harmonized R+D+I strategy and functional model at BME" project. This project is supported by the New Széchenyi Plan (Project ID: TÁMOP-4.2.1/B-09/1/KMR-2010-0002). Opinions expressed in this material are those of the authors and do not necessarily reflect the views of the sponsors.

References

1. Alexa: Alexa top 500 global sites (June 2011), http://www.alexa.com/topsites
2. Carlton, D.: Report of Dennis Carlton regarding ICANN's proposed mechanism for introducing new gTLDs (June 2009),
   http://www.icann.org/en/topics/new-gtlds/
   carlton-re-proposed-mechanism-05jun09-en.pdf
3. Domain Name Supporting Organization: Working Group C – creation of new gTLD (June 1999), http://www.dnso.org/dnso/notes/19990625.NCwgc.html
4. Fielding, R.T., Gettys, J., Mogul, J.C., Nielsen, H.F., Masinter, L., Leach, P.J., Berners-Lee, T.: Hypertext Transfer Protocol — HTTP/1.1. RFC 2616, The Internet Society (June 1999)
5. Internet Assigned Numbers Authority: Iana report on establishment of the .biz and .info top-level domains (June 2001),
   http://www.iana.org/reports/2001/biz-info-report-25jun01.html
6. Internet Corporation for Assigned Names and Numbers: Domain Name Supporting Organization formation concepts (March 1999),
   http://www.icann.org/en/meetings/singapore/dnso-formation.htm
7. Katz, M.L., Rosston, G.L., Sullivan, T.: An economic framework for the analysis of the expansion of generic top-level domain names (June 2010),
   http://www.icann.org/en/topics/new-gtlds/
   economic-analysis-of-new-gtlds-16jun10-en.pdf
8. National Telecommunications and Information Administration: Statement of policy on the management of internet names and addresses (June 1998),
   http://www.ntia.doc.gov/federal-register-notice/1998/
   statement-policy-management-internet-names-and-addresses
9. ODP – Open Directory Project (September 2011), http://www.dmoz.org
10. Weinberg, J.: Report (part one) of Working Group C of the Domain Name Supporting Organization Internet Corporation for Assigned Names and Numbers,
    http://www.dnso.org/dnso/notes/20000321.NCwgc-report.html
11. Zittrain, J., Edelman, B.: Survey of usage of the .BIZ TLD (June 2002),
    http://cyber.law.harvard.edu/tlds/001/

Xunlei: Peer-Assisted Download Acceleration on a Massive Scale

Prithula Dhungel[1], Keith W. Ross[1], Moritz Steiner[2],
Ye Tian[3], and Xiaojun Hei[4]

[1] Polytechnic Institute of NYU, Brooklyn, NY, USA
[2] Bell Labs, Alcatel-Lucent, Holmdel, NJ, USA
[3] University of Science and Technology of China, Hefei, China
[4] Huazhong University of Science and Technology, Hubei, China

Abstract. We take a close look at Xunlei, an enormously popular download acceleration application in China. Xunlei forms a complex ecosystem, with Xunlei peers extensively interacting with independent HTTP and FTP servers, cyberlockers (such as megaupload and hotfile), the BitTorrent and eDonkey file-sharing systems, as well as with other Xunlei peers. After performing a protocol analysis on Xunlei, we develop a comprehensive measurement infrastructure, enabling us to gain new insights into the scale of content, swarm sizes, and several unique characteristics of the system mechanisms in Xunlei.

1 Introduction

In this paper, we take a close look at Xunlei, an enormously popular download acceleration application in China. Xunlei is largely confined to China and has received relatively little attention in the research community to date. It is an interesting application for many reasons. First, it employs several interesting innovations, many of which we will explore in this measurement study. Second, it forms a complex ecosystem, extensively interacting with independent servers, cyberlockers (such as megaupload and hotfile), and two major peer-to-peer (P2P) file sharing systems. Third, as demonstrated in our study, it is deployed on a massive scale. To the best of our knowledge, only a few preliminary studies of Xunlei have been carried out to date, focusing on the protocols used for transferring data among peers [4,5].

When installing the *Xunlei client*, a plug-in is also installed into Internet Explorer. With this plug-in installed, when a user downloads a file from within the browser, the Xunlei client takes over the download. Xunlei can be used to download various types of files including video files, pdf files, executables, and even email attachments. The Xunlei client supports multiple protocols for file download, including HTTP, FTP, RTSP, and MMS. The Xunlei client also serves as a BitTorrent (BT) and eDonkey client. It was reported recently that Xunlei has recently become the most popular BitTorrent client [2].

Xunlei further provides peer-assisted and server-assisted download acceleration. Whenever the Xunlei client is instructed to download a file from an HTTP

N. Taft and F. Ricciato (Eds.): PAM 2012, LNCS 7192, pp. 231–241, 2012.
© Springer-Verlag Berlin Heidelberg 2012

server, from an FTP server, from the BT system, or from the eDonkey system, the Xunlei client contacts Xunlei's centralized tracker, which provides the client a list of other Xunlei peers that share this file. The client can then download portions of the file from other Xunlei peers while also downloading portions from the original source. Xunlei clients communicate with the tracker and communicate with each other using proprietary Xunlei protocols. Moreover, in addition to providing a list of Xunlei peers that have the file, the tracker also provides servers (HTTP, FTP) that have the file. To the best of our knowledge, Xunlei is the only widely-deployed download manager that provides both *peer and server* assistance when downloading files.

To assist users in locating files, Xunlei provides a search engine, *gougou.com*, which indexe a subset of the content indexed by the Xunlei tracker system. For each Gougou indexed file, there is a pointer to a download link (e.g., to an HTTP server, an FTP server, or a BT infohash) for initiating download with the Xunlei client. Recently, the Xunlei network also started a VoD service, known as *Xunlei Kankan*, which serves thousands of movies and TV shows. To view Kankan videos, a user needs to install the proprietary *Kankan client*. As with Xunlei file downloads, Kankan video distribution is peer-assisted. An extended version of this paper is available as a technical report [3]. Our contributions in this paper include:

1. Xunlei uses encrypted proprietary protocols for communication between Xunlei clients, between Xunlei client and Xuneli tracker, and between Xunlei client and Xunlei's proprietary distributed hash table (DHT). We performed a protocol analysis, uncovering Xunlei protocol message formats, and formats for Xunlei peer IDs.
2. Based on our understanding of the Xunlei protocols, we developed a measurement infrastructure for the Xunlei ecosystem. Our measurement platform consists of a Xunlei DHT crawler, a Xunlei tracker crawler, and several website crawlers.
3. Given that the Xunlei tracker tracks content emanating from many different sources and protocols, we investigated the scale of content being tracked. We compared the amount of content being tracked by Xunlei with the amount of content being tracked by the (currently) most popular BT tracker. We found swarm sizes in Xunlei and BT to be of comparable size.
4. We performed an analysis of whether content flows from BT to HTTP and FTP servers via Xunlei. We found that such flows are common for popular BT content, and often the files are deposited into cyberlocker sites. We observed that Xunlei is also providing peer-assisted download acceleration for large email attachments hosted in mail servers.
5. By crawling the Xunlei trackers, we determined the swarm sizes for the VoD movies available from Kankan. We found Kankan swarm sizes to be much larger than the largest swarms in BitTorrent.

2   New Insights into Xunlei

Xunlei uses a proprietary, closed source, protocol. In order to develop measurement tools for the Xunlei ecosystem, we carried out a laborious analysis of the

Xunlei protocols, including determining the syntax and semantics of many of the protocol messages, as well as the formats for Xunlei peer IDs. This was a particularly challenging task since most of the fields in the Xunlei packets are encrypted. In this process, we discovered that Xunlei clients also join two separate DHTs: its own proprietary DHT and also the Mainline BitTorrent DHT. As part of our packet analysis, we were also able to understand how the Xunlei DHT operates and many of the DHT message formats. To this end, we have also understood the details of the encryption/decryption algorithms used.Xunlei uses AES in ECB mode for encrypting messages exchanged between its entities. The 64-bit key for each message is pre-pended to the message itself. To understand the details of the Xunlei protocol, we used Wireshark to passively monitor the traffic flowing in and out of a Xunlei client in our university network, and then later studied this data.

The Xunlei tracker plays a central role in the Xunlei ecosystem. It not only tracks a huge number of files, but also tracks files originating from many different sources, including cyberlockers, FTP servers, mail servers. We have found that whenever a Xunlei peer downloads a file (or a portion thereof) from some source, it notifies the tracker. In this manner, when another Xunlei client wants to download the file, the tracker can provide all known sources, including peers and servers.

We have observed that each peer in Xunlei uses different identifiers for itself when joining different networks. For example, it uses a 16-byte identifier when joining the KAD network, a 20-byte identifier in the Xunlei DHT, a 20-byte identifier for BitTorrent, and a 16-byte unique identifier when registering itself with the Xunlei central trackers when downloading files. We refer to this last type of identifier as the *Xunlei ID* for the peer. Its first 12 bytes correspond to the hexadecimal equivalent of the MAC address of the machine the client is running on. Therefore, each Xunlei client can be uniquely identified by its Xunlei ID over extended periods of time.

Different types of sources use different types of identifiers for the same file: Servers use URLs, BT uses a 20-byte infohash of the file, and eDonkey uses the 16-byte eDonkey hash extracted from the ed2k link. In order for the tracker to provide cross-protocol sources for a particular request, the Xunlei client constructs an internal hash for each file it has been downloaded, and then sends this hash to a tracker, along with the identifiers of the sources from which it downloaded the file. The tracker most likely has a hash table, with the internal hash being the key, and a list of all sources that are known to have the file, with the identifier type being source specific. These sources can include HTTP, FTP, RTSP, and MMS URLs, a BT infohash, an eDonkey hash, and the Xunlei IDs of the peers holding the file.

One can view Xunlei as an effort to consolidate the many different ways of exchanging content on the Internet. The user does not need to be concerned about whether the content is hosted by cyberlockers, available on some P2P file-sharing network, or on traditional web servers. The underlying infrastructure is abstracted and made compatible on a chunk level.

2.1 Multi-protocol Support

As an example of Xunlei's cross-protocol operation, consider a file that is present in an HTTP server and also within BT. Suppose initially the tracker is not aware of this file. When a Xunlei client downloads the file from BT, it calculates the internal hash of the file and informs the tracker of the mapping between the BT infohash and the internal hash. When another Xunlei client downloads the same file directly from the server, it calculates the (same) internal hash for the file and informs the tracker of the mapping between the HTTP URL and the internal hash.

In this manner, the Xunlei tracker knows that the BT infohash and the HTTP URL correspond to the same file. Thereafter, if a Xunlei client initiates a download with the BT infohash, the Xunlei tracker can provide it with the HTTP server link and the Xunlei peers that have copies of the file. We performed several simple tests for verification. *For example, when using Xunlei to download a particular BT file, only 4% of the file came from BT, the remainder of the file came from an HTTP server (74%) and from Xunlei peers using the Xunlei protocol (22%).*

2.2 Bandwidth Leeching

Since the Xunlei tracker provides the Xunlei client with a list of servers currently hosting a file, when a user initiates download for a file from gougou.com (or any other location), the Xunlei client can often download much of the content in the file from a non-Xunlei server, which typically use advertising to generate revenue. Xunlei thus negatively impacts their profits, since users are downloading from them without eyeballing their websites. This phenomenon is referred to as *bandwidth leeching*. Xunlei allows, however, such servers to receive compensation by joining the *Xunlei Union*. We also note that Xunlei provides bandwidth assistance to non-Xunlei servers and sources. For example, when a Xunlei client initiates a download directly from an HTTP server (for example, a cyberlocker such as megaupload), if other Xunlei peers have already downloaded the file (or are currently downloading it), then those peers can assist the server. As we will discuss in the body of the paper, even the downloading of e-mail attaches can benefit from Xunlei's bandwidth assistance.

As mentioned earlier, the Xunlei client acts as a BT client during BT downloads. However, unlike other BT clients, it does not allow a user to create a .torrent file. The user instead would have to use a traditional BT client to do that. However, once the .torrent file (and then the file corresponding to the .torrent) is downloaded using a Xunlei client, the file gets tracked by the Xunlei tracker and hence enters the Xunlei domain. After this, when a Xunlei client begins to download the BT file, it receives peer-assistance from Xunlei peers (which may no longer be active in the swarm but nevertheless have a copy of the file).

2.3   Tracker and Client Protocol

By monitoring and analyzing the traffic at a local Xunlei client, we were able to identify the details of messages exchanged by the client with the Xunlei trackers when requesting the resource list for any given file. We now discuss some of the more important observations we made about the protocol.

When downloading a file using a resource link (e.g., made available by gougou.com), the Xunlei client sends a message with the link to the central tracker, which in turn returns two 20-byte hash values and a single 8-byte code corresponding to the file. These hash values and the code are then used to request the peer and server resource lists for the file. The two hash values and the code for a file can also be obtained from the trackers by sending the unique 20-byte identifier for the file. For files indexed in gougou.com, the identifier is also available in its gougou page.

For BitTorrent files, the Xunlei client uses the infohash of the file as the 20-byte identifier in the message sent to the tracker. For eDonkey files, the 20 byte identifier is obtained from the 16 byte hash extracted from the ed2k link along with the file size. When the Xunlei client sends to the tracker an identifier that is *not* currently being tracked by Xunlei, the tracker does not return the two hash values and the code. Through out the paper, we consider a file as being "tracked" by Xunlei if the trackers return the two hash values and the code for the file. This is the technique that we use in Section 3.1 to evaluate the fraction of BitTorrent and eDonkey files tracked by Xunlei.

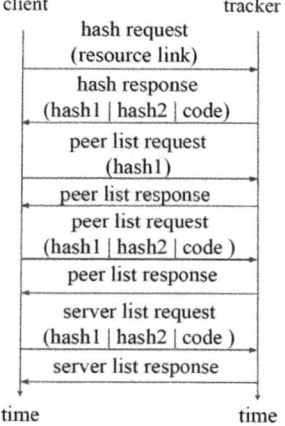

Country	Peers	Population	Ratio
Mainland China	5,261,157	1,330.1	3,955
Taiwan	57,852	23.0	2,512
Hong Kong	20,222	7.1	2,852
Malaysia	7,340	26.2	280
Korea	7,043	48.7	144
Singapore	4,865	4.7	1,034
Japan	4,326	126.8	34
United States	4,237	310.2	13
Macau	2,995	0.6	5,273
Italy	1,802	58.1	31
United Kingdom	1,497	62.3	24
Canada	1,150	33.8	34
Australia	813	21.2	38
Venezuela	616	27.2	22
France	470	64.8	7

Fig. 1. Message exchange between Xunlei client and trackers when requesting resource list

Fig. 2. Country Level Distribution of Peers

3   Measuring the Scale of Xunlei

We used the results from protocol analysis to develop a measurement infrastructure for the Xunlei network. As shown in Figure 3, our measurement platform consists of three major components: a Xunlei DHT crawler, a Xunlei tracker crawler, and several website crawlers.

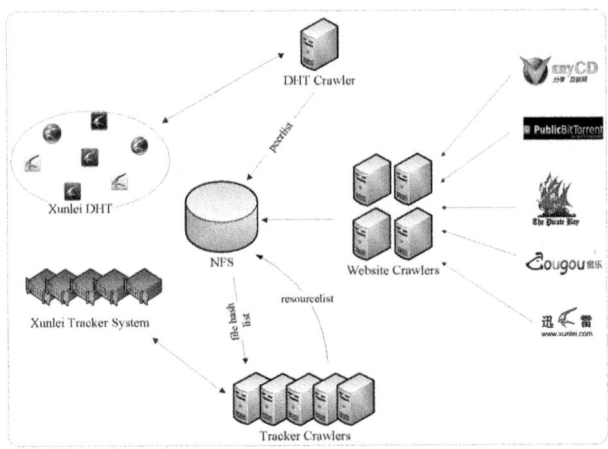

Fig. 3. Measurement Platform

Our *Xunlei DHT Crawler* recursively crawls the routing tables of currently online Xunlei peers to enumerate the list of Xunlei peers in the DHT. For a given 20-byte hash, the crawler works by contacting a Xunlei peer, and asking that peer for the list of peers in its routing table that are close to the hash. After receiving new peers, the crawler again contacts these peers to get more new peers and so on. Given an identifier for a particular file (URL, BT or eDonkey identifier), the *Xunlei Tracker Crawler* continuously contacts the Xunlei central tracker infrastructure to get the list of Xunlei peers that have the file. The tracker crawler also obtains a list of HTTP and FTP servers hosting the file.

We developed 4 different website crawlers and web page parsers customized for each website. The *Gougou Crawler* crawls the movie database in the gougou website. For each indexed movie, it extracts the download link from its movie information page and passes the links to the Tracker Crawler for gathering peer lists and server lists. The *PirateBay Crawler* monitors the Pirate Bay website for the latest TV shows uploaded to the website; immediately after a TV show is uploaded, it extracts the corresponding BT infohash for the TV show, and passes it to the Tracker Crawler to gather the Xunlei peers and HTTP/FTP servers.

The *Public BitTorrent Crawler* downloads the list of BT infohashes being tracked by the public BT tracker site publicbt.com - the largest BT tracker during the time of our experiments. Finally, the *Verycd Crawler* extracts the ed2k links for the eDonkey files indexed by the popular Chinese eDonkey website verycd.com.

3.1   Scale of Content Indexed

Given that the Xunlei tracker is tracking content originating from many different sources and protocols, it is of interest to estimate the scale of the tracker, that is, the number of files being tracked by Xunlei. In particular, how does the scale of the China-centric Xunlei tracker compare with the 2.9 million files (see below) tracked by the largest BT tracker, which targets a culturally diverse user base?

One approach to getting a handle on the Xunlei content scale is to determine the fraction of the content in BT and in eDonkey that is being tracked by Xunlei. To this end, for BT we used the Public BitTorrent Crawler to get the list of $2,920,045$ BT infohashes being tracked by the public BT tracker. For eDonkey, we used the Verycd Crawler to extract the hashes being indexed in the verycd.com website. We extracted $384,612$ different file pages indexed by verycd.com, corresponding to a total of $1,064,525$ different ed2k hashes (each file can have multiple parts, each of which has a distinct hash value). These BT and eDonkey hashes were then passed to the Tracker Crawler that determines which of these are being tracked by Xunlei trackers. *We found that 90.3% of the files indexed by verycd.com and 47.4% of the files indexed by Public BitTorrent are being tracked by Xunlei. Thus, the scale of Xunlei's tracking is at least on the order of BT, perhaps significantly larger (see below).*

Another approach to getting a handle on the Xunlei content scale is to crawl gougou.com and determine the number of files indexed there. Using our Gougou Crawler, we found that gougou indexes $1,092,114$ distinct files in the movie category. There is also over one million distinct files in the other Xunlei categories. So the Xunlei tracker is tracking over 2 million files. But does the Xunlei tracker track files that are not indexed by Gougou? Perhaps the files in Gougou only represent the tip of the iceberg? To this end, we observed that approximately 110,000 Gougou movie files have sources in BT. On the other hand, of the 2.9 million files indexed by Public BitTorrent tracker, roughly 600,000 are movie files. Of these 600,000 movie files indexed by Public BitTorrent tracker, roughly 280,000 are indexed by the Xunlei tracker (see the 47.4% overlap result above). Therefore, the number of BT movie files the Xunlei tracker is tracking at least 2.5 times more than indexed by the Gougou. Hence, the Xunlei tracker is indeed tracking significantly more content than indexed in Gougou.

3.2   Xunlei Swarm Scales

The gougou.com website provides a list of all versions of the top 100 movies in Xunlei. Using our Gougou Crawler, we extracted the download links for each of these movie versions and passed them to the *TrackerCrawler* component. Figure 4(b) shows the swarm size distribution of the top 75 movies in Xunlei. For a comparison, we also plot the total swarm sizes for top 75 movies in Pirate Bay. For calculating the total swarm size for each movie title in Pirate Bay, we used carefully (manually) chosen strings as inputs to the Pirate Bay movie search engine and obtained the list of versions for each of the top 75 movie titles and added up the swarm sizes for all the versions. *Although the largest movie swarm* *in Xunlei is smaller than that for Pirate Bay, we see that the swarm sizes start to converge to similar values after the 60th most popular movie.* We also crawled the trackers for lists of peers watching movies and TV show episodes served by Kankan. Figure 4(a) shows the snapshot of distribution of swarm sizes for all 1, 591 movies available for VoD. (We performed a number of tracker crawls from Dec 2010 to Jan 2011. In Figures 4(b), 4(a), we plot the results for crawls that are close representatives of other crawls.) *Kankan movie swarms are as large as 69, 573, much larger than the largest movie swarms in BT.* By crawling Kankan TV shows for a week, we collected 7, 358, 040 unique users. Recall that Kankan peer IDs can be used to uniquely identify different peers. *Extrapolating this value indicates that there should be well over 20 million unique users in a month for Kankan TV shows.* Also, it appears that the VoD component of the Xunlei network is more popular than the file downloading component. Nevertheless, Kankan swarms being larger than the BT swarms and over 7 million unique users in a week for just the TV show category certainly indicate a huge user base, probably at least as huge as the user base of BT.

When returning the list of Xunlei peers currently watching a queried Kankan movie, the Xunlei trackers return private IP addresses for peers coming from behind NATs. Out of the total 7, 358, 040 unique Kankan IDs collected, 44% of these peer IDs had private IP addresses. Assuming the Xunlei/Kankan users form a random sample of the Internet users in China, we can conclude that approximately 44% of Internet users are behind NATs.

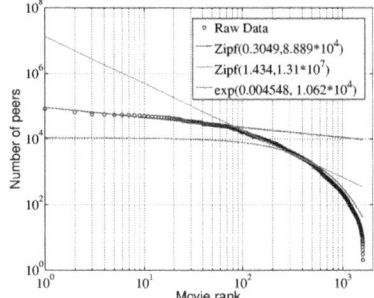 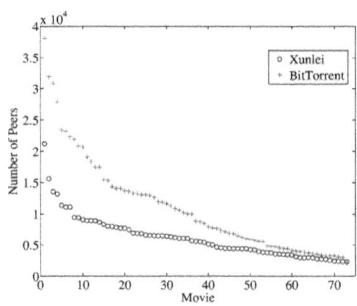

(a) Snapshot of Swarm Size Distribution for Kankan Movies

(b) Swarm Sizes of top 75 Xunlei and Bit-Torrent Movies

Fig. 4. Xunlei Swarm Scales

3.3   Geographic Distribution

We now examine the geographical distribution of Xunlei peers. We ran our DHT crawler for 72 hours and collected 5, 381, 746 peers with distinct <peer ID, IP, port>. Those peers are from 140 countries, 3, 935 cities and 2, 052 ISPs.

Table 2 lists the top 15 countries with the most number of Xunlei peers. To no surprise, almost 98% of peers come from Mainland China. The population values are given in millions, and the last column shows the ratio of number of peers to the total population multiplied by 10^6. Xunlei client being available only in Chinese language, this table provides some insight into relative Chinese populations in different countries. For example, Italy has a smaller population than UK and France, but yet has many more Xunlei users. This is consistent with recent reports of large Chinese immigration to Italy [1].

3.4   Content Flow from BitTorrent to Servers via Xunlei

Having observed a large fraction of BT content being tracked by Xunlei, we now investigate the flow of data from BT to Xunlei. To this end, we used our PirateBay Crawler to continually monitor the upload pages for two of the most active uploaders in Pirate Bay. As soon as a new TV show gets uploaded by either uploader, the BT infohash for the file is passed to our Xunlei Tracker Crawler, which then continuously crawls the Xunlei trackers to obtain the list of Xunlei peers and HTTP/FTP server resources every 5 minutes for several days.

None of 219 torrents we monitored were registered in the Xunlei tracker during the first crawl. However, 217 out of 219 were indexed by Xunlei trackers within 12 hours of the upload of the torrent to Pirate Bay, with 85% being indexed by Xunlei within less than 1 hour. We also observed that for 177 of the monitored torrents (80%), the Xunlei trackers returned at least one HTTP/FTP server within 6 days of appearance of the torrent in Pirate Bay. This means that the files corresponding to these torrents must have been uploaded to the servers. *In summary, for 177 of 219 popular torrents, the torrent first appeared in Pirate Bay, then in the Xunlei tracker without reference to a server, and finally in the Xunlei tracker with reference to one or more servers.* The following sequence of events can result in such a flow of data : 1) A Xunlei user obtains the .torrent file from Pirate Bay and then downloads the corresponding file using the Xunlei client. As a result of which, Xunlei trackers start tracking this particular file. 2) The same user (or some other Xunlei user who also performed the actions in step (1)) uploads the file to an HTTP/FTP server (e.g., to a cyberlocker, which often provides incentives to uploaders). This user advertises the link of the file in the server via an out-of-band channel, for example, a chat forum. 3) Another user finds the server link, and uses its Xunlei client to download the file. As a result, the server link is now listed as one of the resources for the file in Xunlei trackers.

4Into what kinds of servers were these 177 files uploaded? The three domains serving the most files were megaupload.com, hotfile.com, and fileserve.com, serving 103, 96, and 61 files respectively. All three of these domains are cyberlockers. Although Xunlei can leech bandwidth from these (and other) cyberlockers, a user who directly visits a cyberlocker and uses Xunlei to download a file will quite possibly download parts from other sources, including other Xunlei peers. In this regard, Xunlei provides peer assistance to the cyberlockers.

4   The Gougou Content Index

We now analyze Xunlei from the perspective of content indexing site gougou.com. Using our Gougou Crawler, for each of $21,469$ movies indexed by Gougou, we downloaded the corresponding Gougou page and extracted the meta data. Because each movie typically has many versions, we obtained meta data for $1,092,114$ distinct files. Of these $21,469$ movies, 34% came from Hollywood, 20% from China, 18% from Japan, 13% from Hong Kong, and the remaining 15% spread over several other countries.

We extracted the types of sources from each page of movies indexed by Gougou. HTTP (41%) and FTP (34%) sources clearly dominate the other types (MMS, RTSP, BT, ed2k, etc.) of sources available. BT takes the 3rd rank with about 10% of sources. For the HTTP and FTP sources, $24,513$ and $11,642$ different server IPs were found, respectively. The top HTTP server is sharing $23,727$ files from three domains, and the top FTP server is serving $5,029$ files under 73 different domains. A considerable fraction (12%) of FTP servers come from Chinese universities. A single FTP server located in a university in China is sharing as many as $2,701$ files. Unlike Xunlei peers, a large fraction of sources originate from outside China, in particular 10% from the US.

5   Conclusion

We studied Xunlei, a download acceleration application that is enormously popular in China. We uncover the details of several unique technical features in Xunlei. By developing a comprehensive measurement infrastructure, we observed that the scale of content indexed by Xunlei is comparable, or perhaps, larger than the scale of content indexed by the most popular BitTorrent trackers. Similarly, we observed Xunlei/Kankan movie swarm scales to be comparable to that of BitTorrent. We found that HTTP and FTP sources make up the largest fraction of file sources indexed in Xunlei. Xunlei users benefit from increased content availability and increased download speeds. We also observed that Xunlei is currently providing bandwidth assistance to various cyberlockers and email distributions.

Acknowledgements. This work is partially supported by the NSFC under Grant No. 60972014, the fundamental research funds for the central universities under Grant No. HUST:2011QN015 and the technology support plan of China under Grant No. 2011BAK08B01. This work is also partially supported by NSF grant 0917767.

References

1. Chinese Remake the Made in Italy Fashion Label,
   http://www.nytimes.com/2010/09/13/world/europe/13prato.html
2. Thunder Blasts uTorrent's Market Share Away,
   http://torrentfreak.com/
   thunder-blasts-utorrents-market-share-away-091204/

3. Dhungel, P., Ross, K.W., Steiner, M., Hei, X., Tian, Y.: Measurement Study of Xunlei: Extended Version. Technical report, Polytechinc Institute of NYU (2011), http://cis.poly.edu/~prithula/papers/XunleiTR.pdf
4. Zhang, M., John, W., Chen, C.: A Measurement-Based Study of Xunlei. In: Student Workshop, PAM (2009)
5. Zhang, M., John, W., Chen, C.: Architecture and Download Behavior of Xunlei: A Measurement-Based Study. In: International Conference on Education Technology and Computer (2010)

Pitfalls in HTTP Traffic Measurements and Analysis

Fabian Schneider[1,2,*], Bernhard Ager[2], Gregor Maier[2,3],
Anja Feldmann[2], and Steve Uhlig[4]

[1] NEC Laboratories Europe, Heidelberg, Germany
[2] TU Berlin / Telekom Innovation Laboratories, Berlin, Germany
[3] International Computer Science Institute, Berkeley, CA, USA
[4] Queen Mary, University of London, London, UK

Abstract. Being responsible for more than half of the total traffic volume in the
Internet, HTTP is a popular subject for traffic analysis. From our experiences
with HTTP traffic analysis we identified a number of pitfalls which can render a
carefully executed study flawed. Often these pitfalls can be avoided easily. Based
on passive traffic measurements of 20.000 European residential broadband customers, we quantify the potential error of three issues: Non-consideration of persistent or pipelined HTTP requests, mismatches between the Content-Type header
field and the actual content, and mismatches between the Content-Length header
and the actual transmitted volume. We find that 60 % (30 %) of all HTTP requests (bytes) are persistent (i. e., not the first in a TCP connection) and 4 % are
pipelined. Moreover, we observe a Content-Type mismatch for 35 % of the total
HTTP volume. In terms of Content-Length accuracy our data shows a factor of at
least 3.2 more bytes reported in the HTTP header than actually transferred.

1 Introduction

HTTP has become the preferred protocol for many Internet services. Internet users exchange most of their content via HTTP. They download videos from YouTube, share
photos and status updates via Facebook and Twitter, send and read emails with Gmail
or Yahoo, or get the latest news and shop online. Thus analyzing HTTP traffic has been
the focus of many recent studies [1–6, 9, 10]. Often these studies are based on passive
packet-level traffic measurements. These measurements often imply huge amounts of
data to be analyzed, sometimes requiring simplifications to scale the analysis. Some of
these simplifications will lead to potential biases in the results or even render a study
flawed, as we show in this paper.

In prior analysis of large HTTP traces [1, 6, 9, 10], we encountered such inconsistencies and identified and solved the problem. In this paper we quantify the potential
errors of those issues. We study the prevalence of pipelined and persistent HTTP connections, and the accuracy of the Content-Length and Content-Type HTTP header fields.
Our results are drawn from anonymized HTTP traffic from roughly 20,000 European
residential DSL customers (Section 2). Our contributions are the following:

- **Persistence and pipelining:** By not considering pipelined and persistent HTTP
  connections, e. g., by only considering the first request in a HTTP connection, the

---

* Work done at UPMC Sorbonne Universités, LIP6, Paris, France.

N. Taft and F. Ricciato (Eds.): PAM 2012, LNCS 7192, pp. 242–251, 2012.
© Springer-Verlag Berlin Heidelberg 2012

Table 1. Overview of anonymized HTTP data sets

Name	Start date	Duration	HTTP volume	Name	Start date	Duration	HTTP volume
SEP08	18 Sep 2008	24 h	≈ 2.5 TB	MAR10	04 Mar 2010	24 h	≈ 3.3 TB
APR09	01 Apr 2009	24 h	≈ 2.5 TB	JUN10	23 Jun 2010	24 h	≈ 3.2 TB
AUG09	21 Aug 2009	48 h	≈ 5.9 TB	HTTP14d	09 Sep 2009	14 d	≈ 42 TB
				HTTP12d	07 May 2010	12 d	≈ 38 TB

number of HTTP requests is highly underestimated. Indeed, each connection contains more than 2 requests on average. We find (Section 3) that 60 % of all HTTP requests are persistent, i.e., they are not the first in a TCP connection. These persistent requests are responsible for 30 % of the HTTP volume, and will be missed if not taken into account in the analysis. Contrary to our expectations, we find that the most influential aspect on the use of persistent or pipelined requests is the contacted web service, not the user's browser.

– **HTTP content type:** HTTP servers can specify the mime-type of the transferred object in the Content-Type header. However, there is no guarantee that this information is correct. Indeed, we find (Section 4) that for 35 % of the HTTP volume, the Content-Type header is different from what is found by libmagic.

– **HTTP content size:** The Content-Length field in HTTP headers can state incorrect values for canceled transfers or erroneous Web servers. In our dataset we record at least 3.2 times more bytes reported in Content-Length headers than is actually transferred (Section 5).

2 Data and Methodology

In this section we present our data sets before describing our methodology. We conclude this section by introducing the user population with respect to Browser and OS usage.

Anonymized HTTP Data. Our study is based on multiple sets of anonymized packet-level observations of residential DSL connections collected at a large European ISP over the course of more than 2 years. Data anonymization and analysis is performed immediately on the secured measurement infrastructure. We use Bro [8] with a customized HTTP analysis script. The monitor operates at the broadband access router connecting customers to the ISP's backbone and observes the traffic of more than 20,000 DSL lines. The monitor uses Endace monitoring cards. While we typically do not experience any packet loss, there are several multi-second periods with no packets (less than 5 minutes overall per trace) due to OS/file-system interactions. We summarize the characteristics, including start time, duration and size, of the traces in Table 1. HTTP14d and HTTP12d do not include request headers. Please refer to Maier et al. [6] for detailed characteristics of this user population (e.g. DSL session lenght, application usage or network performance).

Persistence and Pipelining. We investigate the prevalence of persistence and pipelining in HTTP connections. We define the first request/response of a connection as *initial*, and mark all follow-up requests/replies as *persistent*. Hence, *persistent connections* are connections with more than one request.[1] This allows us to derive the following metrics: *(i)* The fraction of connections that are persistent, *(ii)* the fraction of requests that are persistent, and *(iii)* the fraction of bytes transported in persistent request/response pairs.

Next, if a request is issued before the response of an earlier request in the same connection is finished, we mark this request as *pipelined*. Moreover, if pipelined requests are sent in the *same IP packet*[2], we mark them as such. Similarly to the persistent requests, we derive the same fractions as metrics for the pipelined/same packet marking method. Because HTTP14d and HTTP12d do not include request timestamps, we cannot use those to determine pipelined/same packet requests.

Note that we never mark the first request of a connection as persistent nor do we mark the first request of a pipeline (or same-packet) as such. The reasoning behind this is that we want to focus on the differences to a one request per connection model (HTTP/1.0). Also note that each request marked as pipelined will always be marked as persistent as well, and thereby the set of pipelined requests is a subset of persistent requests. Similarly, the set of same-packet requests is a subset of pipelined requests.

We also investigate whether different operating systems or browsers influence our results. Therefore, we annotate our data sets accordingly and perform our analysis for each subset. We extract browser type and operating system information from HTTP user-agent strings using an open source parser [3].

Content Type.   Another potential error can be made by relying on the Content-Type header to identify the mime type of transferred files. To assess this error, we extract the Content-Type header and analyze the initial portion of the HTTP body with libmagic. We then compare the type reported by HTTP headers and libmagic and analyze cases in which they disagree.

Content Length and Download Volume.   HTTP servers can set a Content-Length header in the response indicating the size of the body. For persistent HTTP connections, the existence of either a Content-Length or a Content-Encoding header is mandatory. When measuring the volume downloaded via HTTP, one can choose to *(i)* measure the bytes transported on the wire, or *(ii)* use the Content-Length header of the HTTP response. The second option may introduce errors, caused by user interaction (e. g., interrupted downloads), software errors, or the lack of Content-Length headers. While canceling a download leads to larger values reported than actually downloaded, the lack of Content-Length headers will typically cause to ignore the request and therefore underestimate the volume. We define the estimation error as the ratio of the size announced by the Content-Length header and the actually downloaded volume. If an HTTP response does not include a Content-Length header, we define the ratio as 1.

---

[1] Bro terminates connections at control packets (SYN, FIN/RST) or an inactivity timeout.

[2] Packet capture is often configured with a snap-length so that the first lines of the HTTP header are captured. Often, such traces would include persistent requests but not second (pipelined) ones in the same packet.

[3] http://user-agent-string.info/download/UASparser

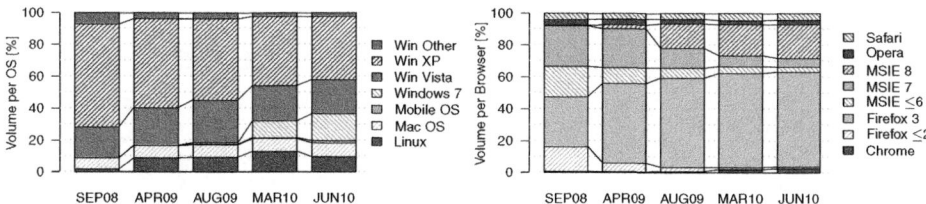

Fig. 1. Operating system popularity   **Fig. 2.** Browser popularity

Browser and OS Popularity. In order to better understand the data sets and the monitored user population we present the popularity and distribution of operating systems and browser families. In Figure 1 we plot the traffic volume per operating system and in Figure 2 the traffic volume per browsers family. We only include popular, regular browsers (Internet Explorer, Firefox, Safari, Opera), and exclude other user-agents (e. g., software updates, media players).

In terms, of operating system popularity we see that Windows clearly dominates, with more than 80 % traffic volume. With time users are switching from older Windows versions to newer ones. Mac OS consistently accounts for 8 % while Linux increases its contribution from 2 % to 13 % in 2010.

When we look into browser popularity, we see that the majority of bytes are requested by Firefox users. Microsoft's Internet Explorer (MSIE) is the close second. As for OSes we see the adaption of new browser versions by users (e.g., Firefox 2 → Firefox 3), which significantly changes the contribution by browser *version*. In the overall share of browser families, Firefox gains 13 % and Google's Chrome rises to 2.5 %. While Opera and Safari remain at 3 % and 4 %, Internet Explorer declines.

3   Persistent and Pipelined Requests

3.1   Persistent Requests

We first determine the amount of persistent requests. In Figure 3 we plot the complementary cumulative distribution function (CCDF) of the number of requests per connection for JUN10, HTTP12d, and HTTP14d. We observe that 30 % of the connections (y-axis at $3 \cdot 10^{-1}$ in log-scale) have two or more requests. One connection in one thousand has more than 100 requests. We even observe connections with several tens of thousands of requests. The CCDFs for the other traces look similar. On average, each connection has 2.2 to 2.4 requests. This is consistent with Callahan et al. [2].

It also indicates a potentially high error for analyses that only consider the first request in a connection. The TimeMachine [7] suggests that "the most interesting information is in the beginning of a connection" and showed significant recording and analysis savings when only considering the first few bytes (the "cutoff") of a connection. If this cutoff is too low, successive persistent requests will be skipped from the analysis.

In Figures 4 and 5 we present the results of our three metrics—connections with (Conns) marked request, number (Reqs), and volume (Bytes) of marked requests—for the persistent, pipelined, and same packet requests for all 24h traces. Recall that

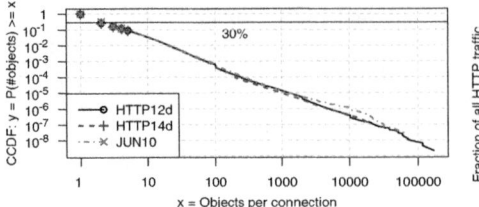
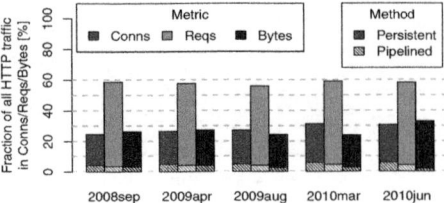

Fig. 3. CCDF of requests per connection for HTTP12d, HTTP14d, and JUN10

Fig. 4. Persistent requests/bytes/connections

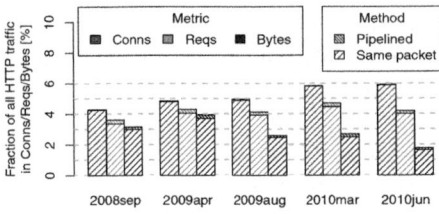
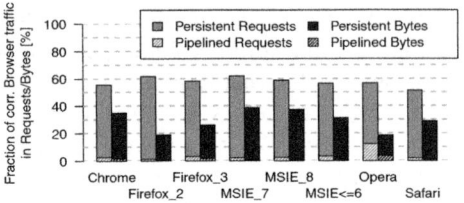

Fig. 5. Pipelined requests/bytes/connections

Fig. 6. Results per browser family for JUN10

pipelined is a subset of persistent and same packet is a subset of pipelined. Thus, the bars are not stacked, but overlay each other. Note the different scale on the y-axis. Again, we find the 30 % from Figure 3 for the combination of the persistent method with the Conns metric for JUN10.

Looking at persistent requests (solid bars in Figure 4), we do not observe significant changes over time/traces. The fraction of connections with persistent requests increases slightly from 25 % to 30 %. While the fraction of persistent requests is fairly constant around 60 %, the volume transferred in persistent requests is around 25 % with the exception of JUN10 where it is over 30 %.

Summary. When only considering the first request in a HTTP connection, one would miss around two thirds of the request, and one third of the volume transferred.

3.2   Pipelined Requests

Pipelined requests (shaded bars in Figures 4 and 5) exhibit considerably lower values for all metrics. While the fraction of connections with pipelined requests increases from 4 % to 6 % from SEP08 to JUN10, the contribution in terms of volume of pipelined requests decreases from 4 % to below 2 %.

If a HTTP traffic analysis does look at multiple request in HTTP connections, but only includes those that are at the beginning of a packet, it would miss around 4 % of the requests and up to 4 % of the volume. Similarly, if the analysis assumes only one request per packet and just greps for the last string that matches a certain header field in the packet, 4 % of the requests would be affected.

3.3 Impact of Browser

Common wisdom[4] suggests that pipelining is disabled by default in the most popular browsers. Our traces on the other hand show a non-negligible amount of pipelined requests. We therefore drill down into the data and analyze it across browser families, operating systems, and content-types. In addition we select a number of—in our dataset—popular and high-volume web services for comparison.

We expect that browsers have a significant impact on the number of persistent and pipelined requests. While the server needs to support HTTP/1.1 for persistent and pipelined request, the browser ultimately has to issue the request. Callahan et al. [2] observed a drastic change in the number of requests per connection and attributes the change to a different default browser version in the environment they monitor.

In Figure 6, we show per browser results for the persistent and pipelined request marking methods for JUN10, as in Figure 4. We observe that the variance among the different browser categories is limited. Microsoft's Internet Explorer (MSIE), has around 10 % more persistent bytes than Firefox. Together, they account for 70 % of the volume and 80 % of the requests. Opera does stand out with an unusually high fraction of pipelined requests, which is expected as it is the only browser that has HTTP pipelining enabled by default. Yet, it comprises only about 2.5 % of the total requests and volume. We do find similar results for the per OS analysis. Linux and MacOS X have lower fractions of persistent bytes than Windows, although the fraction of requests is similar.

3.4 Impact of Web Service

We now select the 30 most requested and/or highest volume second level domains from our dataset and calculate our metrics as for the browser categories. We then group together domains from *(i)* the same web service (e. g., facebook.com and fbcdn.com) and *(ii)* similar types of pages when the results are similar: "OSN" consists of three locally popular online social networks (Jappy, Mein/StudiVZ, and Schueller.cc) with similar results and "Adult" consists of three video portals offering adult content. The fraction of persistent and pipelined requests and bytes of the resulting 18 web services are shown in Figure 7 for JUN10.

The plot shows more variations across web services compared to across browsers versions in Figure 6. Web services have a stronger influence on persistence and pipelining. The fraction of persistent requests ranges from 11 % (Uploaded.to) up to 88 % (WindowsUpdate), and the fraction of bytes in persistent requests even ranges from <1 % (MegaVideo and MegaUpload) to 95 % (again WindowsUpdate). In terms of pipelined requests we see maxima at 33 % for Microsoft and 11 % for RapidShare for requests and volume, respectively. These fractions are significantly higher than those we observe for Opera, which achieved the highest fraction so far. We do not observe a strong relation between the type of web service and persistence/pipelining. Consider for example the One-Click Hosters MegaUpload, RapidShare, and Uploaded.to. While MegaUpload has more than 70 % of persistent requests, the other two have barely more the 10 %. Moreover, all request that are persistent are also pipelined for RapidShare,

---

[4] Wikipedia (version 11 August 2011): http://en.wikipedia.org/wiki/Pipelined_HTTP.

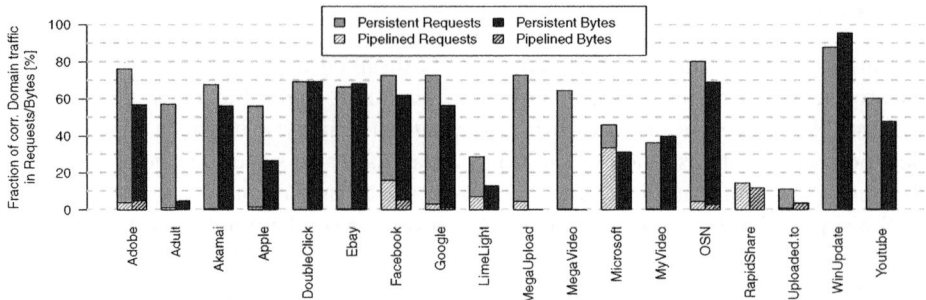

Fig. 7. Percentage of persistent/pipelined request/bytes for selected web services for JUN10

yet the other two have almost no pipelined requests at all. The two CDNs (Akamai and LimeLight) also exhibit largely different fractions for persistent requests and volume.

The effects of different web services also translates into differences when examining the results by Content-Type. Similarly to YouTube, MegaVideo, and MyVideo, flash-video (`video/flv`) has less than 1 % pipelined requests and bytes. On the other hand, `application/rar` has the largest amounts of both pipelined requests and bytes, being mostly delivered by RapidShare.

The limited impact of browsers on persistence and pipelining can be explained by two trends in web content delivery. First, distributed content delivery infrastructures can prevent persistent requests. Second, more and more web services rely on service-supplied code to be executed in the browsers, such as AJAX-based clients [9], which issue the HTTP requests instead of the browser. For example, in all traces except JUN10 the fraction of persistent bytes for YouTube never exceeded 4 % and but is at 47 % for JUN10. A likely explanation for this change is prolonged server restructuring after Google's acquisition of YouTube in 2006: Over all the traces we observe the `googlevideo.com` domain emerge and vanish again. Evidence for the second explanation can be seen from the high fraction (15 %) of pipelined request in Facebook, which heavily uses AJAX, as it is unlikely that all these requests are issued only from Opera browsers.

4   Content Type

We next turn our focus to HTTP's Content-Type header. In Figure 8 we plot the fraction of HTTP bytes for which the Content-Type header and an analysis by libmagic disagree. We normalize the mime type strings by removing leading x- but otherwise perform a string comparison between the header and libmagic's results. We find that up to 36 % of HTTP volume exhibits mismatches. The most common case with up to 27 % is when the Content-Type header uses a generic type (e.g., application/octet-stream or text/plain[5]) but libmagic yields a known type. We label this class of mismatches Gen::NonGen. The opposite case (NonGen::Gen, in which the Content-Type specifies a type but libmagic fails to detect one is the second most common one. We observe that 4.6–6.6 % of HTTP

---

[5] We only count text/plain as generic if the Content-Type header specifies text/plain and libmagic yields a non-text type.

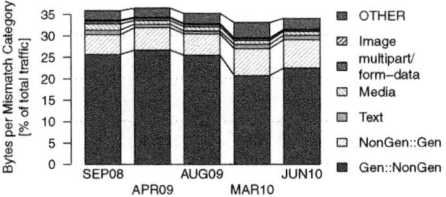 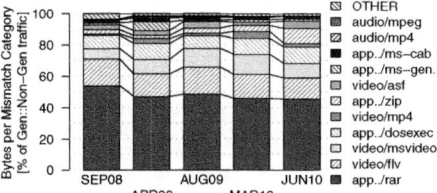

Fig. 8. Mismatches between Content-Type and libmagic as fraction of HTTP volume

Fig. 9. Generic Content-Type but specific libmagic type: breakdown by libmagic class

bytes fall into this class. While some of the types are not supported by libmagic, e. g., Google safe browsing chunks, others include audio or video formats that should be supported by libmagic. It is hard to exactly assess whether libmagic or the Content-Type header are "correct" in such cases. In the Text, Media, and Image classes the Content-Type header agreed on the general category of the type (e.g., image) but disagreed on the actual file format (JPEG vs. PNG). While libmagic should be accurate for image data, other media (audio, video) is harder to assess, given that there is a plethora of different container-types and codecs often with similar names.

When we investigate the largest class, Gen::NonGen, in more detail, we find that (in terms of bytes) RAR-archives are responsible for around 50 % of these mismatches, see Figure 9. In addition, we find that 50–74 % of all bytes with Content-Type header of text/plain are used as a generic type, i.e., libmagic indicates a non-text type (not plotted). In such cases, one would incorrectly infer a significantly higher fraction of text/plain than is actually the case.

We note that we excluded cases of mismatches for which the Content-Type header specified Javascript or CSS and libmagic yielded another text type (e.g., C-code). Such types are inherently hard for libmagic to classify correctly since the syntax of these languages is similar to C. Up to 4.1 % of bytes fall into this category.

An analysis relying on the Content-Type header alone would thus be unable to classify up to 27 % of HTTP bytes, since the Content-Type header is generic and the analysis would also over estimate the amount of text/plain content due to the frequent use of this type as a generic type. Up to an additional 10 % of HTTP bytes further show other disagreements. While it might be possible to roughly classify some of these (e.g., as video content), a more detailed breakdown (e.g., what kind of video) appears challenging.

5 Content Length

The Content-Length header is commonly used to analyze the size of HTTP transfers [4]. Unfortunately, this can lead to errors if the header size does not accurately reflect the downloaded volume, e. g., due to software bugs or interrupted downloads. In this section, we quantify the extent of the overall error and characterize its variance over time. We choose the HTTP14d and HTTP12d traces for this analysis to show the time-dependent behavior.

We find that the Content-Length headers over-estimate the actually downloaded volume by a factor of 3.65 for HTTP14d and a factor of 127 for HTTP12d. A closer

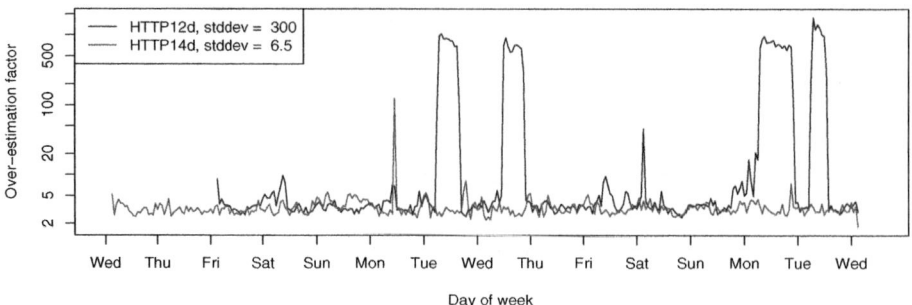

Fig. 10. Over-estimation factor of the Content-Length header (60 min bins, logarithmic y-axis)

examination of HTTP12d shows that a single user downloading two large files from a single host with a badly (mis-)configured download manager is the culprit. This download manager opened over 400,000 connections for each of these files to parallelize the download and requested large, overlapping byte ranges. However, the download manager aborts each download after receiving enough data to cover the whole file. Overall, the requested download volume from Content-Length headers sums up to over 4 PB, an over-estimation by a factor of more than 60,000. After removing these two files from the data set the over-estimation factor for HTTP12d drops to 3.82. We observe a similar case in HTTP14d, though to a far lesser extent and involving only a single file. After removing the corresponding file, the over-estimation factor reduces from 3.65 to 3.28 for HTTP14d.

This highlights how much the over-estimation factor depends on events of limited duration. This leads us to further investigate this volatility over time. Figure 10 plots the over-estimation factor for 60 minute bins. We align our traces by day of week. In general, the over-estimation factor is between 2.2 (2.4 for HTTP12d) and 5 for each 60 minute bin. However, we observe spikes exceeding these baselines by several orders of magnitude. Furthermore, we see the mis-configured download manager in HTTP12d that causes the over-estimation factor to rise to 500 to 2000 for several hours.

We note that based on these 60 minute time bins, the standard deviation for both traces exceeds the average by far. Moreover, there is no apparent weekly or daily pattern. Accurate HTTP object size measurement therefore requires to parse the whole HTTP stream.

6   Conclusion

In this paper we identify and investigate three potential pitfalls in HTTP traffic analysis. We study the accuracy of information in Content-Length and Content-Type headers, as well as the amount of persistent and pipelined traffic.

Our results indicate a significant over-estimation, at least 3.2 times, when relying on the HTTP Content-Length header for volume inference. For accurate volume accounting, complete processing of the data after the HTTP response header is required to detect transfer abortions, erroneous HTTP servers, and misconfigured download managers. The mismatch between Content-Type header and libmagic content types amounts to 35 % of the HTTP volume. Relying on the Content-Type header for content classification can lead to a significant amount of unclassified content due to a generic Content-Type, and to a lesser degree in misclassification of the content. Finally, only analyzing the first packet of a connection discards 60 % of the total HTTP requests and 30 % of the HTTP volume. Simplifying the analysis by capturing just enough bytes per packet to include HTTP headers leads to another risk: We find 4 % of the requests to be pipelined and transmitted together with the previous request in a single packet.

As future work, we plan to further analyze the use of pipelining and persistence by different web services and applications, especially with respect to application design and content delivery.

Acknowledgements. This work was partly supported by a fellowship within the post-doctoral program of the German Academic Exchange Service (DAAD).

References

1. Ager, B., Schneider, F., Kim, J., Feldmann, A.: Revisiting cacheability in times of user generated content. In: Proc. of IEEE Global Internet Symposium (2010)
2. Callahan, T., Allman, M., Paxson, V.: A Longitudinal View of HTTP Traffic. In: Krishnamurthy, A., Plattner, B. (eds.) PAM 2010. LNCS, vol. 6032, pp. 222–231. Springer, Heidelberg (2010)
3. Doverspike, R., Gerber, A.: Traffic Types and Growth in Backbone Networks. Tech. rep. In: Proc. of OFC/NFOEC (invited paper) (March 2011)
4. Erman, J., Gerber, A., Hajiaghayi, M.T., Pei, D., Spatscheck, O.: Network-aware forward caching. In: Proc. International World Wide Web Conference, WWW (2009)
5. Labovitz, C., Iekel-Johnson, S., McPherson, D., Oberheide, J., Jahanian, F.: Internet inter-domain traffic. In: Proc. ACM SIGCOMM Conference (2010)
6. Maier, G., Feldmann, A., Paxson, V., Allman, M.: On dominant characteristics of residential broadband internet traffic. In: Proc. Internet Measurement Conf., IMC (2009)
7. Maier, G., Sommer, R., Dreger, H., Feldmann, A., Paxson, V., Schneider, F.: Enriching network security analysis with time travel. In: Proc. ACM SIGCOMM Conference (2008)
8. Paxson, V.: Bro: A system for detecting network intruders in real-time. Computer Networks Journal 31, 23–24, 2435–2463 (1999), Bro homepage: http://www.bro-ids.org
9. Schneider, F., Agarwal, S., Alpcan, T., Feldmann, A.: The New Web: Characterizing AJAX Traffic. In: Claypool, M., Uhlig, S. (eds.) PAM 2008. LNCS, vol. 4979, pp. 31–40. Springer, Heidelberg (2008)
10. Schneider, F., Feldmann, A., Krishnamurthy, B., Willinger, W.: Understanding online social network usage from a network perspective. In: Proc. Internet Measurement Conf., IMC (2009)

A Longitudinal Characterization of Local and Global BitTorrent Workload Dynamics

Niklas Carlsson[1], György Dán[2], Anirban Mahanti[3], and Martin Arlitt[4,5]

[1] Linköping University, Sweden
[2] KTH Royal Institute of Technology, Sweden
[3] NICTA, Australia
[4] HP Labs, USA
[5] University of Calgary, Canada

Abstract. Workload characterization is important for understanding how systems and services are used in practice and to help identify design improvements. To better understand the longitudinal workload dynamics of chunk-based content delivery systems, this paper analyzes the BitTorrent usage as observed from two different vantage points. Using two simultaneously collected 48-week long traces, we analyze the differences in download characteristics and popularity dynamics observed locally at a university campus versus at a global scale. We find that campus users typically download larger files and are early adopters of new content, in the sense that they typically download files well before the time at which the global popularity of the files peak. The noticeable exception is music files, which the campus users are late to download. We also find that there typically is high churn in the set of files that are popular each week, both locally and globally, and that the most popular files peak significantly later than their release date. These findings provide insights that may improve the efficiency of content sharing locally, and thus increase the scalability of the global system.

1 Introduction

Today, the Internet is heavily used for content delivery. To reduce the content delivery cost, many scalable delivery techniques have been proposed. These include both server-based and peer-to-peer based designs. One promising approach is to split large files into smaller chunks, and allow clients to download these chunks in parallel from servers and/or other clients (i.e., their peers). While this chunk-based approach has proven highly effective, an open problem is how to best manage large-scale content replication systems. For example, a content distributor may want to allocate and manage resources to best match the current workload characteristics. One of the main reasons that this problem remains is due to the adage that "You cannot manage what you do not measure." In particular, the large scale of many of these content delivery systems have made the task of measuring and understanding the relationships between the workloads observed in different parts of the network very challenging.

As a first step towards understanding these distributed workload dynamics, this paper analyzes BitTorrent usage as observed both locally and globally. BitTorrent is the original and most successful chunk-based protocol. While the use

N. Taft and F. Ricciato (Eds.): PAM 2012, LNCS 7192, pp. 252–262, 2012.

of BitTorrent for sharing copyrighted material has resulted in the shutdown of some large trackers and file hosting sites, the protocol is still responsible for a sizable fraction of Internet traffic.

In this study, we measure BitTorrent content popularity from two different vantage points over a 48-week period. First, we used passive measurements to capture all non-encrypted peer-to-tracker communication to/from a large university campus. Second, we simultaneously used active measurements to perform weekly "scrapes" of 721 unique BitTorrent trackers to extract a list of the files each maintained information on (i.e., tracked). Overall, the two datasets provide the longitudinal popularity patterns for more than 50 thousand and 10 million torrents, respectively. Our analysis is the first longitudinal multi-torrent analysis, and the first to capture the differences in the download characteristics and popularity dynamics of a large set of files observed both locally and globally. What makes this comparison particularly interesting is that there is a significant overlap in the files observed in the two datasets; 93.1% of the files downloaded on campus were observed in the globally collected tracker-based dataset. This overlap is a testament to the scope of our extensive global measurements.

Some of our key findings include: the campus users typically download larger files, particularly movies and TV shows; they typically download files well before the time at which the global popularity of the files peaks, with the exception of music files, which the campus users are late to adopt and show little interest for. These findings provide insights into what content in chunk-based systems should be "cached" locally. This would not only improve the experience for users on campus, but potentially increase the scalability of the global system as well.

While we find that there typically is high churn in the set of files that are popular each week, both locally and globally, we observe that most of the popular files in fact peak well after their initial use. This is in contrast to the behavior predicted by flash crowd models, which typically suggest that the popularity peaks close to the release of a torrent [10,19]. Our results indicate that BitTorrent experiences the effects of the "rich-get-richer" phenomenon [1], which suggests that the future popularity of a file is proportional to the current popularity (to date) and files with many downloads in the past therefore will receive relatively more downloads in the future. This is particularly encouraging for chunk-based systems, which rely on peers to upload chunks that they already have downloaded, and often perform worse under flash crowds.

2   Related Work

Many measurement studies have looked at the characteristics of P2P content popularity. A significant number of works focused on the characteristics of content popularity over a fixed time interval, e.g., the number of downloads or the concurrent number of peers in swarms. Some of these works performed the measurements locally at ISPs or university campuses using deep packet inspection [9,17]. Other works used global measurements to characterize the popularity of contents over a time interval, e.g., through monitoring search requests [12,11], or by performing tracker scrapes [7,20,19]. Most of these studies show that the popularity of contents shows Zipf-like characteristics.

A different set of studies considered the performance dynamics of individual swarms over time. These works were either based on measurements of global content popularity [2,13,14], or on measurements of local content popularity [10,16]. Such studies (e.g., [10,16]) indicate that typical swarms stop growing very soon after their introduction, while a recent study by Zhang et al. [19] suggests that most swarms continue to grow after their major flash crowd ends.

Content popularity has been considered in many other contexts too. The majority of these works have considered the file popularity distribution over a time interval and for a specific system. For example, Zipf-like file popularity was found to apply to Web objects [4], to user generated content [6,5,8] and to on-demand streaming media [18]. Other studies have looked at the temporal evolution of popularity based on a single system, e.g., for the case of social media [15,3].

In contrast to the above, our work is the first to capture and to compare the temporal popularity dynamics as observed locally (through passive measurements) and globally (through active measurements) for a content distribution system. Furthermore, to the best of our knowledge both datasets analyzed here are among the most comprehensive measurement datasets of torrent popularity.

3   Methodology

3.1   BitTorrent Overview

To facilitate scalable and efficient file sharing, BitTorrent splits content (files) into many small chunks. Each chunk may be downloaded from other peers downloading the same content. Volunteer trackers maintain state information about all peers that currently have chunks of a specific file. A peer that wants to download a file can learn about the peers sharing that content by contacting such a tracker. Upon request, the tracker provides the peer with a subset of the known peers. In exchange, the peer has to provide the tracker with information about its download progress. Additionally, the peers must inform the tracker about changes in their status (i.e., when they join or leave).

Peers typically learn about trackers by downloading a `.torrent` file from a regular Web server, or from a torrent search engine. Users may download these `.torrent` files from many sites, and many trackers may be involved in helping the local peers. The message format and information communicated to the trackers is protocol specific. In this paper, we leverage the protocol specifications to capture the information communicated to the trackers in the peer-to-tracker communication.

3.2   University Campus Measurements

Our first dataset is a trace of all non-encrypted peer-to-tracker communication at the University of Calgary. This university has approximately 35,000 faculty, staff and students. The data were collected between Sept. 15, 2008 and

Table 1. Summary of datasets

Property	University (tracker communication)	Global (tracker scrapes)	Mininova (screen scrapes)
Trackers	2,371	721	1,690
Torrents	56,963	11.2M	911,687
Downloads	1.73M	37.0B	–
HTTP requests	249M	–	–
Start date	Sep. 15, 2008	Sep. 15, 2008	Sept. 2008
End date	Aug. 17, 2009	Aug. 17, 2009	Aug. 2009
Frequency	All requests	Weekly scrapes	Twice

Aug. 17, 2009. The measurements were collected using a Bro[1] script that extracts the application-layer information about all HTTP transactions across the University's Internet link in real time.

For the purpose of this paper, we focus on one specific type of HTTP transaction. In particular, we look at all peer-to-tracker HTTP requests. These transactions can easily be identified, as the URIs of these requests contain the strings "peerID", "info_hash", etc. The URI also contains other useful information, such as the amount of content downloaded and uploaded thus far to/from the peer. As a download typically consists of a sequence of these requests, we can track the file sharing progress as reported (to the different trackers). We do not analyze the data that the peers downloaded, or otherwise try to assess the indirect impact the content itself may have on the observed file popularities and system dynamics.

Our anonymized traces do not allow us to identify individual users across downloads, but we could identify that most of the downloads were associated with recent versions of the Vuze (52.78%) and μTorrent (23.7%) clients. Other common clients where Tranmission (10.6%), the mainline client (5.7%) and Bit-Comet (4.2%). A more fine grained classification augmented with information about which clients had implemented various extension protocols, suggested that up to 97.5% of the downloads may have been done by a peer that implemented the peer-exchange protocol (PEX) and the DHT functionality. While these functionalities may reduce the peers' incentive for peer-to-tracker communication, these standard clients are expected to follow the BitTorrent standards and periodically communicate with the trackers.

3.3 Global Tracker-Based Measurements

Our second dataset is tracker-based, and provides a global view of content popularity. This dataset is obtained using two kinds of measurements. First, we performed "screen scrapes" (i.e., systematically extracted information from Web pages that would normally be viewed on a screen) of the torrent search engine www.mininova.org, the most popular torrent search engine according to

---

[1] http://www.bro-ids.org/

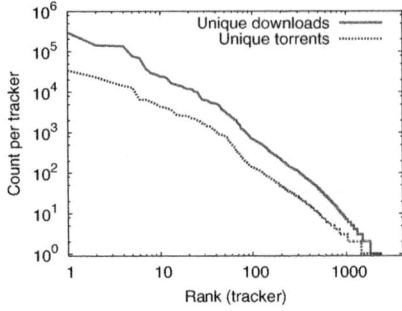

Fig. 1. Tracker load and content per tracker, as observed from the University

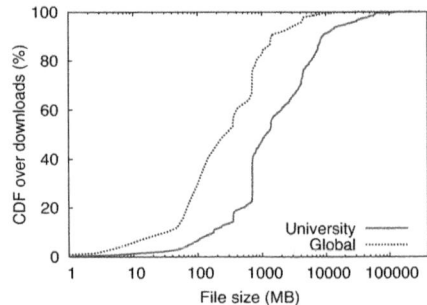

Fig. 2. File size distributions for university and global dataset

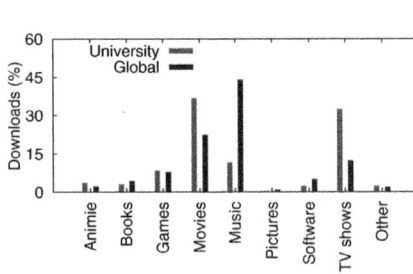

Fig. 3. Breakdown of downloads per category (based on Mininova classification)

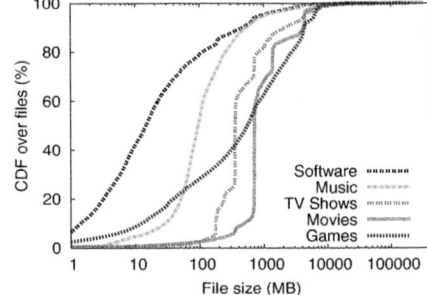

Fig. 4. File size distributions category breakdown using Mininova dataset

www.alexa.com at the time of the measurements (Alexa rank of 75, August 1, 2008). From the initial screen scrape we obtained 1,690 tracker addresses. Second, we scraped all the 1,690 trackers for peer and download information of all the torrents they maintain. This allowed us to efficiently obtain the number of leechers, seeds, and completed downloads as seen by each tracker. We performed the tracker-scrapes weekly from Sept. 15, 2008, to Aug. 17, 2009, the same 48-week period as the University measurements. All scrapes were performed at 8pm GMT. We removed redundant tracker information for trackers that share information about the same swarms of peers, and identified 721 independent trackers.

3.4   Overlap between Datasets

During our 48-week measurement period, the University users used BitTorrent to download 56, 963 unique files, while the 721 unique trackers maintained state information about 11.2M unique torrents. Using the mininova screen scrapes, we obtained file size and category information for 911, 687 distinct files. Table 1 summarizes our datasets.

While the local peers contacted 2, 371 different trackers (about 3 times as many as the monitored trackers), a total of 45, 404 files (93.1% of all files observed lo-

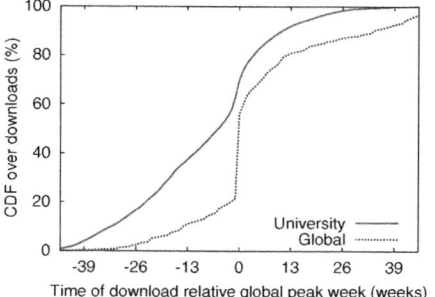
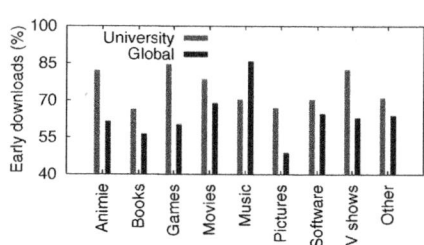

Fig. 5. Time of downloads relative to the global peak week of that file

Fig. 6. Downloads at or before global peak week for different file categories

cally) are observed in both the local and the global datasets. This large overlap is due to the extensive global dataset and the high skew in tracker usage. This is illustrated in Figure 1, which shows the number of files and downloads associated with each tracker. The lines in this figure clearly have Zipf-like characteristics, suggesting that a few of the trackers are responsible for much of the load generated by the University. However, there is also a long tail of trackers that are responsible for a significant fraction of the total load (although each of these trackers is not responsible for much of the load). Finally, two screen scrapes (one at the beginning and one at the end of the measurement period) provide the file size statistics and category information for 16, 119 (33.1%) of these files.

4   Content Download Characteristics

We first take a closer look at the differences in the downloaded content. Figure 2 shows the cumulative distribution function (CDF) of the file sizes observed in the two datasets. While the majority of downloads in both datasets are for files between 100 MB and 10 GB, there is a very large difference in the file size distributions. Overall, the files downloaded in the University network are much bigger. (Note that x-axis is in log scale.) This difference suggests that globally, many users have lower access bandwidths than the relatively high access bandwidths of the local university users. As a result, the global users may be more reluctant to download larger files.

Figure 3 shows the number of downloads per category in each dataset. The categories used here are those defined by Mininova. Figure 3 shows that the university users download a much larger fraction of movies and TV shows (i.e., video) than the global users, which download a lot more music (these tend to be much smaller files). This further explains the large difference in file sizes observed locally and globally. To set these results in context, Figure 4 shows the file size distributions for the five most downloaded file categories in our datasets. While the distributions differ significantly between categories, all of the categories have highly variable files sizes.

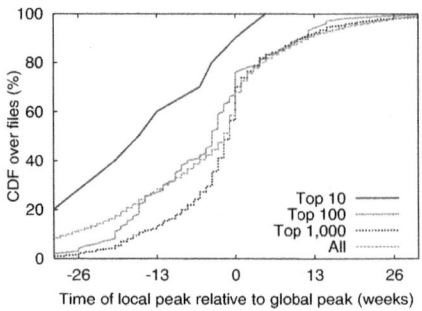
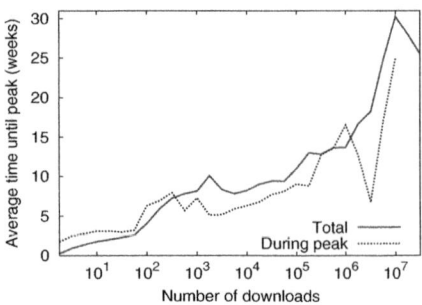

Fig. 7. Time of the local peak week relative to the global peak week

Fig. 8. Average time until peak for files of different popularity

5 Download Popularity Dynamics

We next compare the download dynamics of the two datasets. Figure 5 shows the cumulative distribution function of when the downloads take place relative to the time that each (individual) file's popularity peaked globally. We calculate the peak popularity of each file as the mid-point of the week that had the most downloads. In the case of ties, we pick the earlier week. Approximately 40% of the downloads in the global dataset happen during the peak week, 20% before the peak week, and 40% after the peak week. Furthermore, there is a substantial tail of downloads both before and after the peak week.

Figure 5 also shows the results for the university dataset. There is a substantial difference in when the downloads take place on campus. For example, more than 70% of the downloads in the university dataset take place before the global peak week. In fact, roughly 40% of the downloads takes place at least 10 weeks before the global peak week. This is particularly interesting as it may suggest that users at well-connected universities can be used for predicting content that will become increasingly popular.

To assess the generality of this observation, Figure 6 breaks down the percentage of downloads that took place on or before the week that the global popularity peaked for each distinct file in a particular category. The fraction of early downloads is much higher in the university dataset for almost all categories, particularly for anime, games, and TV shows. For music files, on the other hand, the University users seem to be late to follow current trends. We hypothesize that the combination of high speed Internet access and tech-savvy users alters the user behavior, thereby changing the workload. We note user groups that are early adopters of a content type provide good content-sharing opportunities for that content, and that peer storage could be prioritized based on the content types for which the peer have been found to be an early downloader.

We next consider the difference in the actual peak week, as observed at the university and globally. Figure 7 shows the CDF of the relative difference in weeks. In addition to the CDF for all files, we also show three lines for the set of videos that are among the 10, 100, and 1,000 most popular files, as observed

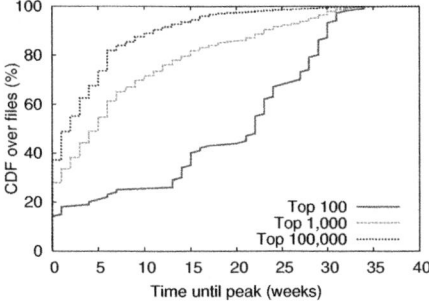
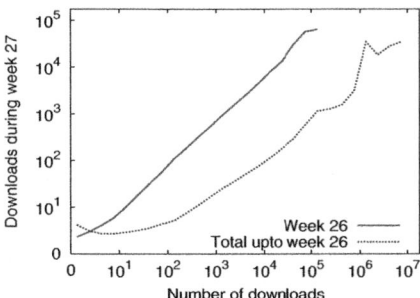

Fig. 9. Time until global peak   **Fig. 10.** Rich get richer analysis

globally. These results confirm our earlier observation that the university users are early downloaders; however, they also show that the differences in peak times are biggest for the files that are the most popular (e.g., in the top 10 curve). This suggests that well-connected university users may be particularly early to download content that will become highly popular. The significant number of early local peaks for the "all curve", suggests that there is also a substantial tail of niche content that the University users are early to download. Thus, there may be lessons to be learned about future (global) popularity, by observing content consumption trends on (well-connected) university networks.

While previous studies have observed early flash crowd behavior immediately after the release of content [10], the fact that we observe big differences in the peaks of popular content suggests that the global peak of popular content often happens well after the release of the content. Figure 8 shows the average time (in weeks) until the global peak for content of different popularity, as a function of the number of downloads during the files' peak week and over the full measurement period, respectively. Here, we applied logarithmic binning, with four bins per scale-factor 10. This figure supports our hypothesis that popular content in fact often peaks well after its release (or in this case, conservatively, after we first discover it having been released). While local results are omitted for brevity, this observation is consistent both locally and globally.

Figure 9 shows the CDF of the time until peak for the most popular files in the global dataset. We note that the most popular files (top 100) peak well after we first discover them; e.g., more than 60% of these files peak at least 20 weeks after we first observe downloads. As suggested by the previous figure, for less popular files there are more files that peak early. However, also for these files there is a substantial amount of files that peak several weeks after first observed.

The fact that most of the popular files peak rather late suggests that the popularity dynamics of these files are not determined by any initial flash crowd behavior when the file is released [10], but that popular files instead often build popularity over time. Preferential attachment and rich-get-richer models have been applied to various domains, and suggest that files that have gained many downloads typically gain even more downloads due to the fact that they are popular. To validate if the global popularity in fact follows this characteristic,

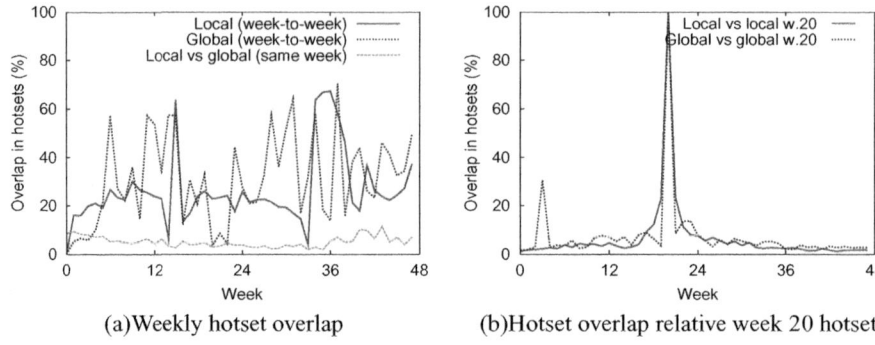

(a)Weekly hotset overlap   (b)Hotset overlap relative week 20 hotset

Fig. 11. Hotset churn analysis

Figure 10 shows the number of downloads in week 27 of a video's lifetime, as a function of the number of downloads in week 26, and as a function of the total number of downloads up to and including week 26. This corresponds to the views at the half-year mark of the video's lifetime. Again, we used logarithmic binning (with four bins per scale factor 10). We note that the previous week's downloads (in week 26) on average is a very good predictor of the number of downloads during the following week. In fact, the slope is very close to one. Also, the total number of downloads (up until the current week) shows strong correlation; however, the direct relationship is much weaker.

In general, ignoring the age of the videos, the Pearson's correlation coefficient between consecutive weeks (after log transformation) is on average 0.35 and 0.68 (with standard deviations of 0.12 and 0.15) for the university and global datasets, respectively.

To summarize, our results suggest that rich-get-richer models may help describe the BitTorrent popularity, and that a (popular) file's popularity often peaks long after it is released. This observation is in contrast to previously proposed flash crowd models that include a decreasing number of downloads per time unit following the initial flash crowd, but is similar to recent observations by Zhang et al. [19]. This suggests that search mechanisms are not as effective as they could be. The adoption of other technologies (e.g., RSS feeds, online social networks) may also reduce the delay between when content is released and when its popularity peaks.

6   Hotset Churn

We next assess the weekly churn in content popularity. For this analysis we focus on the "hotset", the set of most downloaded files in a given week. Figure 11(a) shows the overlap in the hotset observed in consecutive weeks at the university or global dataset, and the fraction of files in the university hotset that simultaneously are in the global hotset. While there are high variations, we note that there typically is high churn in the hotset, with on average only 20-40% weekly overlap. The overlap between the hotsets of the two datasets for any given week is even lower, with less than a 10% overlap.

Among the files that at some point are in the hotset, we found that 33.4% (19.2%) of the files at the university (globally) enter the hotset multiple times. While the majority of files (84.8% and 93.7%) only remain in the hotset for a single week, 1.6% (0.7%) of the files remained in the hotset for at least five weeks. We note that the smaller percentage of long-term popular files in the global dataset is likely due to a higher overall churn (as indicated by more one-timers and one-week cases). As a fraction of the number of files in the hotset, however, the datasets appear much more similar. These observations are illustrated by Figure 11(b), which shows a given week's overlap with the hotset of week 20. In a few weeks the hotset is almost entirely replaced, both datasets contain files that remain in the hotset for a longer period, and some number of files (in both datasets) appears to move in and out of the hotset multiple times.

7 Conclusions

Using two simultaneously collected datasets, capturing the download character-istics and the content popularity dynamics observed both at a university campus and by a large set of global BitTorrent trackers, this paper analyzed the differ-ences in workload dynamics observed locally versus at a global scale. We find that users on a well-connected university network download larger files and are early adopters of new content; they download files well before the time at which the global popularity of the files peaks. These characteristics suggest design mod-ifications to content replication systems such as BitTorrent, to localize the effects of "rich" users, and improve the scalability of the global system. Exploring these alternative designs is left for future work.

References

1. Barabasi, A., Albert, R.: Emergence of scaling in random networks. Sci-ence 286(5439), 509–512 (1999)
2. Bharambe, A.R., Herley, C., Padmanabhan, V.N.: Analyzing and Improving a Bit-Torrent Network's Performance Mechanisms. In: Proc. IEEE INFOCOM (April 2006)
3. Borghol, Y., Mitra, S., Ardon, S., Carlsson, N., Eager, D., Mahanti, A.: Character-izing and modeling popularity of user-generated videos. In: Proc. IFIP PERFOR-MANCE, Amsterdam, Netherlands (October 2011)
4. Breslau, L., Cao, P., Fan, L., Phillips, G., Shenker, S.: Web Caching and Zipf-like Distributions: Evidence and Implications. In: Proc. IEEE INFOCOM (March 1999)
5. Cha, M., Kwak, H., Rodriguez, P., Ahn, Y., Moon, S.: I Tube, You Tube, Everybody Tubes: Analyzing the World's Largest User Generated Content Video System. In: Proc. ACM IMC (2007)
6. Cheng, X., Dale, C., Lui, J.: Understanding the characteristics of internet short video sharing: Youtube as a case study. In: Proc. IWQoS (2008)
7. Dán, G., Carlsson, N.: Power-law revisited: A large scale measurement study of P2P content popularity. In: Proc. International Workshop on Peer-to-Peer Systems (IPTPS) (April 2010)

8. Gill, P., Arlitt, M., Li, Z., Mahanti, A.: YouTube Traffic Characterization: A View from the Edge. In: Proc. ACM IMC (2007)
9. Gummadi, K., Dunn, R., Saroiu, S., Gribble, S., Levy, H., Zahorjan, J.: Measurement, modeling, and analysis of a peer-to-peer file-sharing workload. In: Proc. SOSP (2003)
10. Guo, L., Chen, S., Xiao, Z., Tan, E., Ding, X., Zhang, X.: Measurement, Analysis, and Modeling of BitTorrent-like Systems. In: Proc. ACM IMC (October 2005)
11. Hefeeda, M., Saleh, O.: Traffic modeling and proportional partial caching for peer-to-peer systems. IEEE/ACM Trans. on Networking 16(6), 1447–1460 (2008)
12. Klemm, A., Lindemann, C., Vernon, M.K., Waldhorst, O.P.: Characterizing the query behavior in peer-to-peer file sharing systems. In: Proc. ACM IMC (2004)
13. Legout, A., Urvoy-Keller, G., Michiardi, P.: Rarest First and Choke Algorithms Are Enough. In: Proc. ACM IMC (October 2006)
14. Menasche, D., Rocha, A., Li, B., Towsley, D., Venkataramani, A.: Content Availability in Swarming Systems: Models, Measurements and Bundling Implications. In: ACM CoNEXT (December 2009)
15. Mitra, S., Agrawal, M., Yadav, A., Carlsson, N., Eager, D., Mahanti, A.: Characterizing web-based video sharing workloads. ACM Tran. on the Web (2), 8:1–8:27 (2011)
16. Pouwelse, J.A., Garbacki, P., Epema, D.H.J., Sips, H.J.: The Bittorrent P2P File-Sharing System: Measurements and Analysis. In: van Renesse, R. (ed.) IPTPS 2005. LNCS, vol. 3640, pp. 205–216. Springer, Heidelberg (2005)
17. Wierzbicki, A., Leibowitz, N., Ripeanu, M., Woźniak, R.: Cache replacement policies for P2P file sharing protocols. Euro. Trans. on Telecomms. 15, 559–569 (2004)
18. Yu, H., Zheng, D., Zhao, B., Zheng, W.: Understanding User Behavior in Large-Scale Video-on-Demand Systems. SIGOPS Oper. Syst. Rev. 40(4), 333–344 (2006)
19. Zhang, B., Iosup, A., Pouwelse, J.A., Epema, D.: Identifying, analyzing, and modeling flashcrowds in bittorrent. In: Proc. IEEE Peer-to-Peer Computing, Kyoto, Japan (August/September 2011)
20. Zhang, C., Dhungel, P., Wu, D., Ross, K.W.: Unraveling the bittorrent ecosystem. IEEE Transactions on Parallel and Distributed Systems 22, 1164–1177 (2011)

Author Index